Deaf Studies *Today!*

Waypoints

CONFERENCE PROCEEDINGS

UTAH VALLEY UNIVERSITY • OREM, UTAH
APRIL 9–12, 2014

Edited by Bryan K. Eldredge,
Doug Stringham, and Ben Jarashow

The biennial Deaf Studies *Today!* conference brings together the best and brightest minds in the interdisciplinary field of Deaf studies. Over three days, scholars from around the country (and beyond) present the latest research and thinking in the field in an environment conducive to the open exchange of ideas. Open to everyone interested in Deaf studies, including scholars, educators, students, Deaf people, and parents of deaf children, Deaf Studies *Today!* also aims to provide networking opportunities and promote Deaf-World interests.

Deaf Studies *Today!* includes presentations and workshops that cover a broad range of topics related to Deaf people, their language, culture, and associated issues. Presentations are based on original work and present current research/thinking relevant to the field of Deaf Studies, including but not limited to perspectives from anthropology, history, linguistics, interpretation and translation, education, psychology, sociology, public administration, political science, social work, philosophy, ethics, art, literature, American Sign Language instruction, and any number of other allied disciplines.

Proceedings of Deaf Studies *Today!* are published by the American Sign Language and Deaf Studies Program at Utah Valley University. Opinions expressed by the authors of these papers are their own and do not necessarily reflect those of the editors or of Utah Valley University. Authors are responsible for the accuracy of the references cited. While we have altered some terminology for consistency, use of the words '*Deaf*' or '*deaf*' in each paper also follows the authors' original manuscripts. American Sign Language-representative glosses are represented by small caps (e.g. DEAF, not 'deaf'). Deaf Studies *Today!* takes no responsibility for copyright infringements made by or in behalf of presenters or authors, and presenters agree to indemnify the publishers of Deaf Studies *Today!* against any illegal use of original artwork or creation.

The conference exists only because of the thousands of hours of work put forward by many different people. Most of those hours are volunteered by students and faculty at Utah Valley University. This work is dedicated to them.

Editors:
Bryan Eldredge, PH.D.
Co-Chair, Deaf Studies *Today!*
Program Coordinator, ASL and Deaf Studies
Utah Valley University

Doug Stringham, MS
Adjunct Instructor, ASL and Deaf Studies
Utah Valley University

Benjamin O. Jarashow, ABD
Instructor, Department of Communication Sciences & Disorders
University of South Florida

ISBN 978-0- 9762906-5-0. ©2018 Deaf Studies *Today!* American Sign Language and Deaf Studies Program, Utah Valley University, Orem, Utah. All rights reserved; no part of this publication may be reproduced, stored in a retrieval system, or transmitted in any form or by any means, electronic, mechanical, photocopying, recording, or otherwise, without prior written permission of the publisher. Printed in the USA on acid-free paper.

Table of Contents

1   Deaf Accused: The Deaf Defendant in the Criminal Justice System
AMBER FARRELLY

15   Research and Development of Inverted-type Pedagogy in American Sign Language Courses
RONALD B. FENICLE; JODY H. CRIPPS, PH.D.; SHERYL B. COOPER, PH.D.; AND AIMEE SEVER

27   Communication and Longevity in Deaf/Hearing Marriages
MICHAEL BALLARD

53   Teaching the Cinematic Parallels of Visual Languages: A Proposed Approach to Educating Second Language Learners in American Sign Language
SHAY TAYLOR AND BRIDGET KLEIN

63   What is the Motivation for Deaf Children to Learn English as Their Second Language?
DANIEL GOUGH, ED.D., AND DAMARA GOFF PARIS, ED.D.

77   A Milestone in Deaf Studies: The Berlin Digital Memorial Board for Deaf Jewish Life Destroyed Under the Nazi Regime
MARK ZAUROV

81   American Sign Language: From Deaf Community to General Society
RUSSELL S. ROSEN, PH.D.

97   Watering the Roots of Self-Driven Motivation A Positive Self-theory and Life-long Resiliency in Deaf and Hard-of-hearing Children
TODD LAMARR, LISALEE EGBERT, JODEE CRACE, CARRIE DAVENPORT, AND TAMI HOSSLER

103   "A Language of Action": James Smedley Brown and the First American Dictionary of Sign Language
DOUG STRINGHAM

131   Directionality of Movement in American Sign Language
KERI BROOKS

137   Using Contextual Cues in Deciphering Fingerspelling: Introducing the Historical Sign Language Database
TED SUPALLA, PH.D.

149	Writing Signed Languages: FOR-FOR? FORM? DON GRUSHKIN, PH.D.
179	Signed Music: An Emerging Inter-performative Art JODY H. CRIPPS, PH.D.; ELY ROSENBLUM; AND ANITA SMALL
187	Destination Unknown: The Specialized Field of Designated Interpreting ANNETTE MINER
203	Machine Translation: English to ASL Gloss, TRUE-BIZ? MARY BONHAM
223	ASL Cinema: An Exploration of a Genre BRIDGET KLEIN
231	What Successful Deaf Readers Can Tell Us About Deaf Studies AARON KELSTONE, ED.D.
239	Deaf Education in the United States and Morocco KRISTINA DOMANEY, JENNY SIPIORA, AND JOHN PIRONE
259	Sign Language: An Advertising Tool? REBECCA CLARK
269	Tracing Deafhood: Exploring the Origins and Spread of Deaf Cultural Identity, Part III JORDAN EICKMAN, PH.D.
307	Writing a Visual Language: A Method for Writing Signed Languages MARY SHAWVER
323	A Preliminary Report on Initialized Signs Accepted and Used in the Deaf Community DAISY CARTWRIGHT
341	Misjudged: The Tragic Case of Stephen Brodie AMBER FARRELLY

About Deaf Studies at Utah Valley University

In addition to being the home of Deaf Studies *Today*!, Utah Valley University (UVU) is home to a robust program in ASL & Deaf Studies.

Courses
Deaf Studies *Today*! is the creation of the American Sign Language and Deaf Studies Program at UVU in Orem, Utah. The UVU American Sign Language and Deaf Studies program is part of the Department of Languages. From its birth as a single beginning-level ASL class offered in the evening during the mid-1990s, the program has expanded to offer over fifty courses serving over 800 students each semester.

The program's course offerings range from beginning ASL courses to advanced classes in Deaf culture and history, Deaf literature, ASL grammar and linguistics, interpreting, Deaf-World discourse and much more.

Degrees
UVU offers five degree choices in Deaf Studies:

- Deaf Studies Major (B.A.)
  Emphasis 1: General Deaf Studies
  Emphasis 2: Interpreting
- ASL & Deaf Studies Education Major (B.A. — secondary education)
- A minor in Deaf Studies
- An ASL emphasis in Integrated Studies (B.A.)

Of course, many students majoring in other fields take ASL courses to fulfill the language requirements for B.A. degrees.

Information
More information about the UVU ASL & Deaf Studies Program is available at www.uvu.edu/asl.

About the 2014 Conference

The sixth Deaf Studies *Today!* Conference was held at Utah Valley University, Orem, Utah, April 9–12, 2014. Highlighting the conference were keynote addresses by distinguished scholars.

Sponsors
Deaf Studies *Today!* expresses gratitude to Utah Valley University, The Office of the Academic Vice President, The College of Humanities, Arts, and Social Sciences, Interdisciplinary Studies, The Department of Languages and Conferences and Workshops who made this conference and these proceedings possible through their generous support.

Volunteers
Deaf Studies *Today!* would simply not exist were it not for the hundreds of hours of work volunteered by the students of Utah Valley University. They inspire us, and we give them our heartfelt thanks.

Deaf Accused:
The Deaf Defendant in the Criminal Justice System

AMBER FARRELLY

"[They are] shuttled into prisons, branded as criminals and felons, and then when they're released, they're relegated to a permanent second-class status, stripped of the very rights supposedly won in the civil rights movement — like the right to vote, the right to serve on juries, the right to be free of legal discrimination and employment, and access to education and public benefits. Many of the old forms of discrimination that we supposedly left behind during the Jim Crow era are suddenly legal again, once you've been branded a felon." — Michelle Alexander, speaking to the issue of young black males in the criminal justice system.

NO ONE EVER PLANS TO BE ARRESTED OR TO FIND THEMSELVES IN THE criminal justice system. When an individual is arrested and accused of a crime, it can be an extremely difficult and confusing time. For the deaf individual caught in the criminal justice system, the experience can be overwhelming. The system is fraught with intricacies and terminology that are only minimally familiar to the hearing population. For the deaf or hard of hearing, there are a multitude of complex issues that are required not only for effective communication, but also to ensure due process.

All too often, the due process rights of deaf and hard of hearing are unintentionally violated with little or no recourse after-the-fact. This is an in-depth look at the deaf individual in the criminal justice system, focusing on criminal law and procedure; the structure of the criminal court system and the roles of all parties involved — including the interpreter, legalese and vocabulary; and a basic construct of the process, charges, and consequences of the criminal justice system. This paper presents a defense perspective, based on my clientele. It will illustrate how the rights of the accused are important and often unknowingly violated.

KNOWN PROBLEMS IN THE CRIMINAL JUSTICE SYSTEM: RACE, ETHNICITY, EDUCATION, AND ECONOMICS

Extensive studies have shown that there are grave racial and ethnic disparities in the U.S. criminal justice system. Just as race and minority status have played a major part in the underrepresentation of people in the criminal justice system, so too have education, poverty, and unemployment. Aggravating these disparities are the continued barriers to economic opportunity and education (Rosich, 2007).

Similarly situated in the criminal justice system are deaf defendants. The issues of race and ethnicity, education, and poverty also affect deaf defendants; however, the situation is compounded by additional factors that specifically affect deaf individuals.

Not only are there racial and ethnic minorities represented in the deaf population, but the population itself is a minority. There are a great number of deaf defendants that are indigent, unemployed, or whose only earnings are from some type of governmental assistance. Deaf defendants caught in the criminal justice system more often than not have significantly lower reading ability than do similarly situation hearing individuals.

An extensive study was produced by Katrina Miller in the deaf prison population in the state of Texas (Miller, 2004). In her study, she found that

> "a significant number of deaf defendants with linguistic incompetence have been prosecuted and incarcerated without any recognition of their condition....For the fifty deaf inmates in this study (51.5%) who demonstrated functional illiteracy (reading below third-grade level) the use of legal terminology clearly would present a barrier to due process during legal proceedings, where time allotments for lengthy interpretations are limited" (Miller, 2004; cf. Davis 1993; Miller & Vernon, 2002; Wilson by Branch v. North Carolina, 1996).

Further, 18.5% of deaf inmates "did not have an adequately developed first language with which they could communicate competently" (Miller, 2004).

Most often, the defense attorney is unaware of the concept of linguistic incompetency so the issue is rarely raised during the course of representation. More often than not, "courts fail to recognize the significance of their linguistic incompetence." Further, since most cases are resolved by way of plea bargain, the issue of linguistic incompetence or due process violation is never preserved or raised on appeal.

DISPROPORTIONALITY AND DISPARITY OF DEAF DEFENDANTS

There is an innate disproportionality and disparity among the deaf population in the criminal justice system. Several studies have been done that show the disproportionality among minorities in the criminal justice system, yet few have focused on the deaf minority. My experiences and deaf clientele were used as the basis for this paper. In the approximately 179 deaf clients I have represented, I have discovered certain facets in representing them that I find imperative to effective representation.

In assessing language among deaf clients, I have discovered the following language information to be useful not only in how I communicate with them, but also useful in identifying appropriate interpreters for communication access: (1) Deaf-of-deaf, ASL-based, (2) Deaf of hearing, ASL-based, (3) English-based Deaf, (4) PSE-based Deaf, (5) Minimal Language Skills Deaf, (6) Deaf with multilingual influences, e.g. Spanish, and (7) Deaf with additional cognitive or mental disabilities. Additional disabilities include deafblind, cognitive impairments, mental illness such as bipolar, schizophrenia, significant emotional issues, and Primitive Personality Disorder. Those who had minimal language skills, multilingual influences, or who had additional cognitive or mental disabilities required the use of a certified deaf interpreter (CDI). Those deaf defendants who were ASL based, more often than not required a native ASL interpreter for effective communication (Table 1).

Category	Number	Percent
Deaf cases	244	
Deaf clients	179	
Defendants requiring CDIs	23	12.8
Defendants utilizing other means of communication	8	4.4
Defendants with cognitive or mental issues	24	13.4

Table 1. Breakdown of author's cases involving actual Deaf clients

"Disproportionality occurs when groups are represented unequally relative to their numbers in the general population. Disparity occurs when two offenders who are similarly situated are treated unequally" (Whisner, 2011). This occurs in several ways.

Within the deaf population, there are "variations in the educational backgrounds and language proficiencies of deaf defendants, those who communicate adequately in American Sign Language (ASL), English-based sign systems, and/or indigenous or foreign sign languages [who] do not always demonstrate adjudicative competence in legal situations" (Miller, 2004).

Those who are proficient in ASL and English-based sign systems are more likely to understand the proceedings than those who are not competent in ASL or English-based sign system and have little or no comprehension of the English language.

For those who use indigenous or foreign sign language, have minimal language skills (MLS), are highly visually oriented, or have other language barriers, a certified deaf interpreter (CDI) is required. A CDI is "an individual who is deaf or hard of hearing and has been certified by the Registry of Interpreters for the deaf (or other certifying entity) as an interpreter" (RID, 1997). A CDI is utilized when the communication level of the deaf individual cannot be adequately accessed by hearing interpreters (RID, 1997). When not utilized, communication and understanding of the process is ineffectual.

HEARING VS. DEAF

Deaf defendants are disproportionately represented in the criminal justice system as compared to hearing defendants. One reason for this is the lack of effective communication. In most cases the attorney and the defendant speak the same language and can communicate in the same tongue. In those situations where the defendant speaks a language other than English, it is typical that the defendant seeks out or is appointed an attorney that speaks that same language. In those occasions where a hearing defendant speaks a language that is foreign to the local attorney bar, an interpreter is appointed by the court to ensure that attorney and client may effective communicate. Often times in the situation of the deaf defendant, the assumption by both the court and the attorney is that the deaf defendant is proficient in English and therefore written communication between attorney and client is acceptable.

Second, the hearing defendant almost always has at least some knowledge of the U.S. criminal justice system, whether this be from previous experience, exposure in some other form, or "common knowledge." The deaf defendant typically has no specialized knowledge about the criminal justice system. Without any access, contact, or specific education, there is little to no knowledge about the criminal justice system. This includes common phrases and terminology such as "prosecutor," "plea," "adjudication," etc.

Third, the hearing defendant almost always has the language and education to adequately read and understand the forms used in court as well as the legalese that are spoken by the court and the attorneys involved. Hearing defendants can typically understand, through some form of superfluous knowledge or through context, the meaning of legalese presented to them. Deaf defendants more often than not do not possess a strong enough grasp of the English language to understand Latin, Greek, and French-based legalese when presented with those terms. "The functional illiteracy evidence in this deaf inmate population dramatically reduces the likelihood that most would understand complex legal terminology if they were not familiar with the American criminal justice system" (Miller, 2004). "One important aspect of being literate in our society is possessing the knowledge and skills to process information found in documents" (Kirsch & Mosenthal, 1990). Further, there is typically no sign for legal words, so the interpreter simply fingerspells the word. The deaf defendant is left with numerous legal words that are essentially meaningless to them. Still, significant accommodations must be made for those who communicate primarily in ASL to put them on par with their hearing counterparts.

Due process is directly related to linguistic competency. Those who are "highly visually oriented, low functioning, semilingual, language disordered, or have minimal language skill (MLS) or Primitive Personality Disorder (PPD) all experience major barriers to due process" (Miller & Vernon, 2002; cf. Vernon & Coley, 1978; Vernon & Miller, 2001; Vernon & Raifman, 1997). This disparity emphasizes the inherent unfairness in regards to the deaf defendant and the serious concerns regarding due process.

DUE PROCESS

When one combines those factors with MLS, the effect/disproportionality is compounded, and due process is seriously put into question. "Up to 50% of deaf state prison inmates may not have received due process throughout their arrest and adjudication. Despite their adjudicative and/or linguistic incompetence, these individuals were convicted in many cases, possibly violating their constitutional rights and their rights under the American with Disabilities Act" (Miller, 2004). The study of deaf inmates in Texas prisons undertaken by Miller (2004) found that between "twenty to fifty percent may not have received due process throughout their arrests, trials, and other legal proceedings, even with the provision of qualified sign language interpreters."

The Fifth and Fourteenth Amendments of the United States Constitution provide for due process and equal protection under the law. In particular, the Fourteenth Amendment states, "No person shall be deprived of life, liberty, or property, without due process of law; nor deny to any person within its jurisdiction the equal protection of the laws."

When we consider due process as it relates to deaf defendants,

> "*due process* refers to the court ensuring that a defendant understand the charges against him or her, is able to assist in the development of a defense, can decide which plea to enter, is aware of the implications of his or her

position as a defendant, and has an understanding of the roles of the defense, prosecution, and judge" (Miller, 2004).

Based upon the disproportionality and disparity within the criminal justice system, the deaf population is at serious risk of their due process rights being violated in nearly every situation.

MIRANDA

Prior to ever entering the courtroom, the deaf defendant will have experienced an arraignment after their arrest or questioning by law enforcement. In both situations, it is mandatory that the person be advised of their rights (Texas Code, Article 14.06). In order to properly advise a deaf person of their rights, it is usually necessary to have the Miranda warnings administered by a qualified interpreter.

When looking at a deaf defendant's due process rights, the Miranda warning is significant: the first question becomes, did the suspect understand Miranda? In my experience, many deaf know that certain rights exist, however they do not know what they are. Some deaf defendants can tell me that their "rights" start with the letter "M," however few are able to articulate the word "Miranda." Without any basis of knowledge about the criminal justice system, it is impossible to understand the implications of their rights.

Coupled with understanding Miranda warnings, is the question of whether the warnings were interpreted properly? "The interpretation of the Miranda warning, as well as many other legal texts and technical jargon, is arguably the most difficult of all interpreting situations to work in" (Sheprow, 1999). Many interpreters lack the legal vocabulary and education necessary to adequately interpret the Miranda warnings. Few states require that the interpreter be certified or have additional legal certification to interpret Miranda warnings (LaVigne & Vernon, 2003). However, certification itself does not resolve the problem of inadequate interpretation of Miranda warnings. "Despite...certification, an individual interpreter may not have the skills, intuition, judgment, or knowledge needed to interpret for a particular deaf person in a particular case" (State v. Hindsley, 2000).

Finally, can a defendant intelligently and knowingly waive their rights? In Texas, the Code of Criminal Procedure states that "no evidence obtained in violation of the law shall be admitted" (Texas Code, Article 38.23), no written or oral statement made by the accused as a result of custodial interrogation unless the accused, prior to making the statement, is warned of their rights (Texas Code, Article 38.22), and no statement of an accused may be used in evidence if it was not freely and voluntarily given without compulsion or persuasion (Texas Code, Article 38.21).

In the state of Texas, interpreters for deaf persons are separated in the Code of Criminal Procedure (CCP) from spoken language interpreters. The court is required to "appoint a qualified interpreter to interpret the proceedings in any language that the deaf person can understand, including but not limited to sign language" (Texas Code, Article 38.31(a)). The Texas CCP states that a

> "'qualified interpreter' means an interpreter for the deaf who holds a current legal certificate issued by the National Registry of Interpreters for the deaf or a current court interpreter certificate issued by the Board for Evaluation of Interpreters at the Department of Assistive or Rehabilitative Services" (Texas Code, Article 38.31(g)(2)).

Further, a statement made by a deaf accused, is not admissible unless the warning is interpreted to the deaf person by an interpreter who is qualified (Texas Code, Article 38.32(3)(d)). This is significant in providing some protections for deaf persons in the Texas criminal justice system, but does not cure all harm.

LaVigne & Vernon (2003) performed an extensive study for the University of Wisconsin, noting that

> "the mere presence of an interpreter during the reading of Miranda warnings will not be sufficient to allow a court to make a finding that a defendant's knowingly, intelligently, and voluntarily waived his Miranda rights. In order to meet that standard, the warnings must be interpreted accurately and into a language that conveys the substance of the warnings to the particular suspect, even if that requires special accommodations. An interpretation that falls short will be grounds for suppression" (cf. State v. Hindsley, 2000 WI App 130, § 23–24, 28–29, 237 Wis. 2d 358, 372–75, 614 N.W.2d 48, 55–57.)

LINGUISTICALLY INCOMPETENT

Most competency issues in the criminal justice system revolve around mental competency. However, deaf defendants who lack the education and/or language basis to comprehend and understand the proceedings against them are considered *linguistically incompetent.*

In order to be competent to stand trial, the defendant must be able to present sufficient ability to consult with his attorney with a reasonable degree of rational understanding, to understand the nature of the charges against him, and to understand the proceedings in his case: "A defendant is presumed competent to stand trial and shall be found competent to stand trial unless proved incompetent by a preponderance of the evidence" (Texas Code, Article 46B.003(b)).

Factors considered in examining a defendant for mental competency may also be used in determining whether the deaf defendant is linguistically competent. The examination must consider ((Texas Code, Article 46B.024)
1) the capacity of the defendant during criminal proceedings to:
   a. rationally understand the charges against the defendant and the potential consequences of the pending criminal proceedings;
   b. disclose to counsel pertinent facts, events, and states of mind;
   c. engage in a reasoned choice of legal strategies and options;
   d. understand the adversarial nature of criminal proceedings;
   e. exhibit appropriate courtroom behavior; and
   f. testify.

Based on the educational and linguistic factors in the disproportionally and disparity of deaf defendants, there are many times when the deaf defendant is linguistically incompetent.

> "Deaf inmates with reading scores below the federal standard for literacy (grade level 2.9) were the group most likely to demonstrate linguistic incompetence to stand trial, meaning that they probably lacked the ability to understand the charges against them and/or were unable to participate in their own defenses" (Miller, 2004)

When the deaf defendant also presents with additional mental disabilities or illness, the probability that he is incompetent greatly increases. When a defendant is considered incompetent, he cannot stand trial or enter a plea since it is neither freely nor voluntarily given.

COUNSEL

The Sixth Amendment provides for the right to counsel. However, deaf are underrepresented in their right to counsel. There are few criminal attorneys that are deaf or who are fluent signers or qualified interpreters. Because there are so few criminal attorneys who sign, few deaf clients have the opportunity to communicate on an equal basis as do hearing defendants. This limitation to communication is bound to have a direct effect on the representation of the defendant. Compounding the problem is that, often, attorneys who represent deaf clients, either do not use or underutilize interpreters further limiting access to communication with the client.

JURIES

Even within areas with a large deaf population, deaf *venire* men are seldom empanelled and are rarely selected to serve on the jury. Many times, the deaf *venire* man is selected and fills out the jury questionnaire. The court is unaware that the *venire* man is deaf until arrival at the courthouse to serve. At that time, no interpreter has been scheduled to accommodate the deaf *venire* man. The deaf *venire* man is then excused with an opportunity to be in another panel or excused from serving altogether. In most cases, even with an interpreter, many hearing people believe that deaf people lack

> "the language skills and ability to evaluate credibility that are essential to a juror's function and required by the Sixth Amendment to guarantee a criminal defendant a fair jury at her trial" (Lee, 1989)

The deaf *venire* man goes through *voir dire* and is then struck either for cause or peremptorily struck from the panel. Therefore, in most instances involving a deaf defendant, there is no deaf juror to hear his case, calling into question by the deaf defendant the notion of a jury of his "peers."

MISREPRESENTATION

A more concerning issue in the representation of deaf defendants in the criminal justice system is the misrepresentation of deaf. Misrepresentation means insufficient or inadequate representation. Most often inadequate representation of deaf defendants is unintentional, but gross examples of this verge into ineffective assistance of counsel.

A large percentage of deaf defendants are considered indigent under the law and are provided court-appointed attorneys to represent them.

> "Research has addressed whether minority defendants are disadvantaged at the pretrial stage of the criminal justice system because: (1) Public defender or other programs established by states to provide counsel for indigent defendants do not provide the same quality of legal assistance as do retained counsel for defendants who can afford to pay; (2) The bail system creates conditions that increase the chances for detention of poor defendants" (Rosich, 2007)

In these instances, deaf defendants are relegated to misrepresentation.

Most often, misrepresentation occurs unintentionally because the attorney is unfamiliar with deafness. This includes a lack of education on deaf language (typically ASL) and deaf culture. Most hearing attorneys are unaware that ASL and English are two separate and distinct languages. Hearing attorneys and law enforcement often believe that writing back and forth is a sufficient and adequate form of communication. Further, most hearing attorneys are unaware of deaf culture and its nuances. Culture is important in representing deaf clients in understanding the facts of the case, how to address and communicate with the deaf client, and in defending them adequately.

BIAS OF KNOWLEDGE

Another form of misrepresentation is bias. There is an inherent bias in the criminal justice system regarding deaf defendants. This bias is the *bias of knowledge*. Hearing attorneys and those involved in the criminal justice system believe that deaf individuals are equally situated as hearing defendants. They are unaware of the lack of exposure and education in regards to the criminal justice system among the deaf population. Often times when this is discovered, the response to the deaf person is incredulity and cynicism. The reaction is seen by the deaf person as judgment and criticism. A common reaction from the deaf person is to try to hide their lack of knowledge so they do not appear ignorant.

The bias of knowledge encompasses the system and the vocabulary. Legal terms such as "prosecutor," "arraignment," "magistrate," "warrant," "indictment," and the concept of trial are often lost on the typical deaf individual. The bias of knowledge expects that the deaf person shares the same literary and cultural experiences as do hearing individuals, and, as such, the same basis of knowledge. These include literary experiences, such as the reading in school of classic novels like *To Kill a Mockingbird*, and cultural experiences of television and movie preferences that expose the viewer to legal terms, shows such as "Law & Order," "CSI," and the like. Because not all deaf students are educated in public schools, they may not have access to literary works or may not possess the reading levels required to read them or to follow along with close captioning of legal television programs or movies.

Most attorneys in the criminal justice system are unaware of the linguistic abilities of deaf defendants. According to the studies of Dr. Jean Andrews, professor of Deaf Studies at Lamar University, the average reading level of deaf adults is between the third and fourth grade, with 30% reading below a 2.8 grade level (Andrews, 2010)

The attorney and the court are unaware that in many situations, the deaf defendant is linguistically incompetent. One significant risk is that those that are linguistically incompetent may confess to crimes they did not commit (Andrews, 2010; cf. La Vigne & Vernon, 2003).

Additionally, there is a mentality within the system that the attorney knows what is best for the defendant, so little effort is put into examining the deaf defendant. Compounded is the attitude of the path of least resistance. The attorney often assumes the responsibility of making the decision as to the outcome of the case for the deaf defendant. Even in the instances where the offer is good, or the case is dismissed, the easiest thing is to make the decision for the client with little to no explanation. Rarely is this questioned by the defendant since the attorney is deemed as holding power over the defendant.

In a majority of settings, the cost factor of an interpreter is forefront in the mind of the court. The attorney is often pressured to not request an interpreter because of the expense. The court often pressures the attorney to not ask for an interpreter until one is absolutely needed, e.g., something is going to happen with the case (more often than not, plea). When the primary concern is one of money, representation inevitably suffers as well as due process.

On the occasion that an attorney is provided with an interpreter, there is a perception among hearing attorneys that "an interpreter is enough." As LaVigne & Vernon (2003) point out, however, that this is simply not true. Just as the absence of an interpreter hinders communication and understanding, so too does an unqualified or ineffective interpreter. Inadequate interpretation between the defense attorney and in the proceedings seriously affects due process of the deaf defendants. Most ineffective interpretations are due to the lack of training and knowledge of the interpreter. Coupled with ineffective interpretation is the underutilization of CDIs. For the attorney who utilizes CDIs throughout the adjudication process and where the defendant is thus able to sufficiently comprehend the charges against him and is able to communicate effectively with his attorney, due process may occur. In those instances where there is a lack of language and education, and other factors are present, a CDI may not bridge the gap sufficiently so that substantial comprehension and communication under the law may take place. In those instances, the deaf defendant may be considered linguistically incompetent. Attorneys not aware of these barriers may effectually misrepresent their clients, violating their due process rights.

When attorneys are uneducated as to interpreter issues — including the quality of the interpretation itself, certification requirements for interpreters, and the role of the interpreter — the deaf defendant is misrepresented.

Additionally, the lack of cultural mediation by both the interpreter and the attorney plays an important role in determining whether full communication, and due process under the law, exist. Language and cultural barriers may adversely affect the ability for due process and effective representation.

The Sixth Amendment ensures that the criminal defendant has the right to have assistance from counsel. Since Powell v. Alabama, it has been accepted that a defendant has the right to the assistance of counsel whose performance does not fall below a minimum level of effectiveness; however, the courts have been struggling to give meaning to the term "effectiveness of counsel" (Foust, 1979). Ineffective assistance of counsel is a legal standard determined by the U.S. Supreme Court as a violation of a defendant's Constitutional right to due process. In Strickland v. Washington (1984), the Court held that an attorney's assistance is ineffective if it "so undermined the functioning of the adversary process that the trial cannot be relied upon as having produced a just result." For those who do not provide any communication access outside themselves, or deprive their clients of access to an interpreter, their representation is egregiously ineffective.

On occasion, there are attorneys who have some exposure to deafness. However, with this exposure comes the precarious possibility that even they may be ineffective in their representation of deaf clients. This may be due to an elementary understanding of the deeply nuanced language and culture and diversity inherent in the deaf population.

For those attorneys who know basic conversational sign language, their eagerness to represent deaf clients may overshadow their judgment on when to request the assistance of a qualified ASL interpreter. Those signers in their representation may actually do more harm than good. Because there is some knowledge on the part of the hearing attorney, they may neglect the other facets required when counseling deaf defendants. Culture, language and education proficiency, and the inherent power perceived by the deaf person toward the hearing attorney cannot be separated from language when representing a deaf person. The attorney who can fingerspell, or is conversationally proficient in ASL often misrepresents the deaf defendant by assuming the role of interpreter and lawyer at the same time. Providing subpar language access is ineffective communication and representation.

SOLUTION

Numerous studies on racial inequality correlate and prove the disparity among the minority population in the criminal justice system. However, there are few studies on the ineffective representation of deaf individuals in the criminal justice system. The reason for this is not that society does not care; but, rather, is based on a lack of knowledge. There is an abundance of unintentional ignorance within the criminal justice system regarding deaf people, be they defendants, witnesses, jurors, or victims.

The solution is education. There must be more education within the court system — education of attorneys, judges, court staff, and interpreters — and within the deaf community.

Statutes must be enacted to protect the rights of deaf defendants. The court system needs to recognize the deaf defendant not just as an English-speaking subgroup, but as a unique minority that not only communicates in another language but also is a protected class under the Americans with Disabilities Act (ADA). Priority of the due process rights of deaf individuals must be forefront in the court's mind. The cost concern of interpreters needs to be abandoned when considering access and the rights of deaf individuals.

Attorneys need to be educated not only on the laws that are in place to protect the deaf defendant, but also on the nuances of deaf culture, on ASL, the qualifications and roles of ASL interpreters, and the linguistic issues often involved in representing deaf defendants.

Interpreters need to be educated on their role in the courtroom and their responsibility to not only provide effective communication, but also to be a cultural mediator. Interpreters need to be fluent in language as well as culture and resource identification. They must be empowered so that they effectuate their role and prevent ineffective representation when recognized.

Finally, deaf individuals must be educated about their rights under the Constitution, the assertion of those rights, and to be empowered when faced with ineffectiveness in communication, interpretation, and representation.

CONCLUSION

Known problems exist in the criminal justice system in regards to race and ethnicity, poverty, and lack of education. These problems afflict not only minorities, but deaf defendants as well. In addition, deaf defendants face a reality of disproportionality and disparity of representation as well. The lack of communication, knowledge of the criminal justice system, language and education put the deaf defendant in severe danger of having their Constitutional right of due process violated. Deaf defendants also face underrepresentation and misrepresentation. The bias of knowledge is prevalent in the court system. Attorneys mistakenly assume that effective communication and representation may be solved by the addition of an interpreter. However, when the interpretation is ineffective due to inadequate skills or linguistic barriers, the lack of a CDI, and/or the lack of cultural mediation, misrepresentation borders on ineffective assistance of counsel.

Education to the courts, judges, court staff, attorneys, interpreters, and the deaf population are necessary to begin to ensure effective and adequate representation of deaf individuals involved in the criminal justice system.

REFERENCES

Andrews, J. F. (2010, October 22). "Reading and Language Abilities and Deaf Adults: Issues and Concerns." EPALL Conference, El Paso, Texas, p. 9.

Foust, B. (1979). "Ineffective Assistance of Counsel." National Criminal Justice Reference Source, 1979. http://www.ncjrs.gov/App/publications/abstract.aspx?ID=80246

LaVigne, M. & Vernon, M. (2003). "An Interpreter isn't Enough: Deafness, Language, and Due Process." *Wisconsin Law Review*, 844, p, 843, University of Wisconsin Legal Studies Research Paper. Available at SSRN: http://ssrn.com/abstract=1744291

Lee, R. (1989, January)."Equal Protection and a Deaf Person's Right to Serve as a Juror." Widenor University School of Law, p. 81 (citing Eckstein v. Kirby, 452F. Supp.1235, 1242-43 (E.D. Ark. 1978).

Miller, K. R. (2004) "Linguistic Diversity in a Deaf Prison Population: Implications for Due Process." University of Arkansas Rehabilitation Research and Training Center for Persons who are Deaf or Hard of Hearing. *Journal of Deaf Studies and Deaf Education*, 9(1), Oxford University Press.

Registry of Interpreters for the Deaf Professional Standards Committee (1997). "Use of a Certified Deaf Interpreter (Standard practice paper)."

Rosich, K. J. (2007). "Race, Ethnicity, and the Criminal Justice System." American Sociological Association, Washington, D.C., p. 8. (Available at http://asanet.org.).

Sheprow, G. J. (1999, 10 December) "Interpreting for the Miranda Warnings." American Sign Language Interpreting Resources. http://asl_interpreting.tripod.com/situational_studies/gjs1.htm.

State v. Hindsley (2000). WI App 130, §§ 4, 24, 237 Wis. 2d at 362, 373, 614 N.W.2d at 50, 55.

Strickland v. Washington (1984).

Texas Code of Criminal Procedure, http://www.statutes.legis.state.tx.us/?link=CR.

Whisner, M. (2011, January 31)."Race in the Criminal Justice System." Gallagher Law Library University of Washington School of Law.

Research and Development of Inverted-type Pedagogy in American Sign Language Courses

RONALD B. FENICLE; JODY H. CRIPPS, PH.D.;
SHERYL B. COOPER, PH.D.; AND AIMEE SEVER

AMERICAN SIGN LANGUAGE (ASL) IS A VISUAL-GESTURAL LANGUAGE used in the Deaf community in the United States and parts of Canada. William Stokoe identified ASL as a legitimate human language using established linguistic principles during the 1960s (Maher, 1996). In more recent years, ASL has become one of the most popular languages taught in high schools, colleges, and universities nationwide (Cooper, 1997; Cooper, Reisman, & Watson, 2008; Quinto-Pozos, 2011; Rosen, 2008). Unlike other foreign language classes, lectures in ASL require the use of visual (or tactile) perception. This phenomenon requires a modality shift from spoken to signed, which requires a new type of learning for hearing students, using visual and motor skills in order to learn the language.

Towson University's Deaf Studies program provides ASL classes from beginning (ASL I) to advanced levels (ASL V). It is important to acknowledge that the field of Deaf Studies typically includes the study of signed language, history, literature, community, and culture of deaf people through the considerations of sociological, anthropological, and ethnographic perspectives (Marschark & Humphries, 2010). One goal of a Deaf Studies program is to develop students' competence in ASL and knowledge of the Deaf community, enhancing continuing education and employment opportunities in a variety of fields. The purpose of providing a high level of competence in ASL is to enable students to obtain better career opportunities in a variety of disciplines working with deaf people (e.g., teaching, counseling, social work, rehabilitation, and research) and to enable graduates to provide the best quality services to the Deaf community. These careers require the ability to combine knowledge of the experiences of deaf people, the cultural aspects of the Deaf community, and the use of ASL (Cooper & Cripps, in press; Cooper, Cripps, & Reisman, 2013; Cooper, Emanuel, & Cripps, 2012; Cripps & Cooper, 2012).

As part of the Deaf Studies program, a nationally standardized ASL assessment called the *American Sign Language Proficiency Interview* (ASLPI) is used as an external assessment to rate individuals' signing abilities (see http://www.gallaudet.edu/asldes/aslpi.html for further details of this assessment) without faculty biases. Based on a scale of 0–5, Deaf Studies students are required to pass the ASLPI with a level of > 2+ as a prerequisite for the off-campus capstone internship experience. This screening requirement is to validate a sufficient level of linguistic competence for Deaf Studies students who will interact with Deaf people at their internship sites and later workplaces. It can be challenging for Deaf Studies students to achieve the ASL skill level necessary to gain entrance into the internship program and future careers.

This paper will begin by discussing a new approach to teaching called *inverted-type pedagogy* that may enhance Deaf Studies students' conversational signing skills in higher-level ASL classes. It includes a rationale for implementing the inverted-type pedagogy in ASL V classes, and a comparison between traditional and inverted ASL V pedagogies. Lastly, instructor's reflection as part of action research is included and the outcomes of the inverted-type instruction in this preliminary study reveal some implications for the Deaf Studies program and the field of ASL pedagogy.

ISSUES IN ASL CURRICULA IN DEAF STUDIES

This Deaf Studies program adopted a nationally standardized ASL curriculum called *Signing Naturally*, which is commonly used on post-secondary campuses across the country. ASL V is the highest-level language course in this Deaf Studies program and utilizes the *Signing Naturally Level 3* textbook (Mikos, Smith, & Lentz, 2001). This curriculum provides substantial signed vocabulary, phrases, sentences, and personal anecdotes from deaf individuals. Since its implementation in Fall 2008, Deaf Studies faculty members have noticed pedagogical weaknesses in the curriculum that could be resolved with revision and supplemental materials.

In the current format, students taking ASL V obtain insufficient conversational opportunities. Students in the ASL V class often express frustration with limited time focused on conversational skills due to the time required for introducing signed vocabulary and grammar in the classroom. Also, there is limited time for the instructor to provide feedback on students' vocabulary and grammar production in the classroom, which may create inadequate preparation for passing ASLPI with the level of 2+, or for later employment in the Deaf community.

Another challenge for the traditional pedagogical format is the inability for students to take notes during a voice-off class. While using visual perception to receive information from the instructor or other students conversing in ASL, students are unable to take notes, which would require looking down and missing crucial information. It is unlikely that the students have ample opportunities to have information repeated or re-demonstrated. This may lead to missed information and incorrect assumptions about signed words and grammar.

CONSIDERATIONS REGARDING INVERTED-TYPE PEDAGOGY

Evidence from the challenges above indicates that the ASL V curriculum presentation needs to be revised to help students achieve the course's learning outcomes. The current method of curriculum delivery lacks conversational opportunities, which is inadequate for higher-level ASL courses. The lecture-style model reduces students' opportunities to learn and refine signing skills via meaningful real-time feedback from the instructor in the classroom. Hands-on activities beyond the level of the games and dialogues provided in the curriculum are necessary to ensure and enrich students' language exposure and practice through conversation.

An innovative new pedagogical design called an *inverted classroom* (also known as a *flipped classroom*) provides extensive hands-on learning experiences. Lage, Platt, and Treglia (2000) explain that in an inverted classroom "...[learning] events that have traditionally taken place inside the classroom now take place outside the classroom and vice versa" (p. 32). Using this format, students view classroom lectures through multimedia technology outside of class as homework, while doing activities that were formerly perceived as homework in the classroom. Disciplines such as economics, engineering, and mathematics adopted this pedagogical model and have demonstrated positive outcomes from students and instructors in quantitative and/or qualitative studies (Cannod, Burge, & Helmick, 2007; Lage et al., 2000; Strayer, 2012).

Inverted-type pedagogy in foreign language courses was implemented at the University of Alabama (Cipria, 2006; Witkowsky, 2008), the University of North Carolina-Chapel Hill (Henshaw, 2008), and the University of North Carolina-Charlotte (Pyke, 2010). In particular, Pyke (2010) used this technique to address the issues of inadequate class time to engage students in activities that require speaking Spanish, because a significant amount of class time was used to present grammatical information, discuss assignments and other class management issues.

Nationwide, there is scant research on ASL pedagogy for L2 learners, so research on the effectiveness of using the inverted classroom model will be beneficial in several ways. Researchers (e.g., Henshaw, 2008) found that the inverted redesigned pedagogy provided more engaging approaches to learning grammar and other rote concepts, and the instructors were able to better monitor student progress. Students had more options for customizing their own learning experiences, were able to work at their own pace using the online materials, and were able to devote additional time to those concepts they found challenging. The opportunity to utilize small group activities in class encouraged informal interaction and a more social and pleasant atmosphere. Greater consistency across course sections was ensured through the standardization of pre-recorded multi-media course materials. Witkowsky (2008) interviewed professors who noted that they were able to keep track of students' progress by checking to see if they were logging into their assignments and keeping pace with the class.

In the field of second language acquisition, implementation of conversational skills in second language (L2) classrooms has been on the rise since the mid-1980s. Researchers found that L2 students improve targeted language comprehension and production better when they experience conversation with their teachers and peers in the classroom (Gass & Varnois, 1994; Mackey, 1995; Pica, Young, & Doughty, 1987). Celce-Murcia, Dörnyei, and Thurrell (1995) pointed out that in order to have conversational competence in L2, one must be able to perform openings, re-openings, closings, and pre-closings. These dialogue techniques include establishing and changing topics, interrupting and collaborating, holding and yielding the floor, and recognizing and producing adjacency pairs.

In the classroom, role-playing and group discussions are the pedagogical techniques used to assist L2 learners with their learning opportunities (Kormos, 1999; Long & Porter, 1985; McNamara, 1997). Van Lier (1989) cautioned that oral language proficiency tests do not actually measure the L2 learners' conversational competence due to the interviewer's control of the conversation. For this reason, some scholars proposed assessing L2 students' conversational competence through role-playing instead, as it provides equal conversational ground for both parties (e.g., Kormos, 1999; McNamara, 1997). Inverted-type pedagogy uses a variety of activities such as role-playing and interviews to develop many dialogue features found in conversations. These conversational features provide Deaf Studies students with hands-on experiences and assessments using various conversational characteristics in ASL that are not always used in the traditional classroom format.

Additionally, these types of activities help students prepare to score higher on the ASLPI.

The pedagogical technique of "active learning" as a part of this ASL V course is emphasized because the primary goal is to promote students' experience in learning and using the language in a conversational setting. This course shifts students from passive to more active learning by emphasizing interactive activities in the classroom. The hands-on activities include dialogue features such as whole class discussion, one-to-one and group conversations, dialogues, debate, presentations, and interviews. Through these activities, students (in pairs or groups) learn to correct their signed words and grammatical errors. The instructor is able to provide feedback while observing in-class exercises. This course has an in-class structure to prevent students from becoming uncomfortable with the "loose" class formation (e.g., Stayer, 2012).

For each lesson, the instructor begins with a ten-minute review of ASL vocabulary and grammar, focusing on one topic, to monitor students' production and comprehension based on their learning outside the classroom. If there is difficulty with the first ten-minute review, the instructor will then clarify or expand this part to ensure that every student comprehends and receives what they need before moving on with next part of the lesson. The second part of the lesson focuses on topic-centered communication (dialogues, debates, interviews, etc.), where students will experience real-life conversational features with immediate feedback from their peers and the instructor. In the last part of the lesson, the instructor leads a five-minute wrap-up to review the topics of the day.

The "supplemental model" of the inverted-type pedagogy was adopted as well. The materials from the Signing Naturally Level 3 curriculum were used along with additional external resources (e.g., ASL storytelling videos). The course includes intensive, out-of-class, interactive, on-line lessons and resources delivered through technology. Classroom lessons consisting of video with PowerPoint presentation are posted into special on-line software called Mediasite (http://www.sonicfoundry.com/mediasite). One significant advantage to this type of technology is access to class lectures on-line 24 hours a day, seven days a week, so that students can view and review the lessons at times that fit into their schedules. The external web-based ASL resources are beneficial to all students, especially to those individuals who need additional assistance, repetitions, and/or time.

The computer-based learning resources as described above also feature a variety of signers on the videos in order to provide exposure to different signing styles and regional or cultural variations. This promotes the concept of Universal Design for Learning, a practice that supports the need for flexible approaches to teaching and learning to meet the needs of different kinds of learners (e.g., Rose & Meyer, 2006).

The goal is for students to view two twenty-minute lessons each week (total of 13–15 weeks) to cover the course materials from the *Signing Naturally* curriculum, including Units 20–24. These units cover topics such as rules, accidents, finances, major decisions and health conditions. An additional unit, developed by the faculty at this university, was designed to focus on contemporary issues and/or current events.

COMPARISON BETWEEN TRADITIONAL AND INVERTED PEDAGOGIES IN THE ASL CLASSROOM

Both the traditional and inverted-type ASL V classes use the same curriculum. It is worthwhile to examine the pedagogical approaches to understand more about their similarities and differences. The main difference between these approaches is in and out-of-classroom lectures. In the inverted classroom, the students have more time to practice conversational skills in class while the students in the traditional classroom are likely to spend classroom time "listening" to the instructor's lectures.

Traditional ASL Pedagogy

Traditional teaching tends to utilize a teacher-oriented approach. In the traditional approach, students are expected to attend the class, then learn the subject at hand as taught by the instructor. Oral presentation from instructors is an educational technique commonly used in the traditional classroom. Hands-on activities (i.e., group discussions, language-related games, and dialogues in pairs) used in the classroom are seen as secondary to instructor's lecture. Feedback and comments to the students from the instructor are done through homework assignments. This kind of traditional teaching has been around for decades (see Mascolo, 2009 and Skourtou & Kourtis-Kazoullis, 2003 for further definition of traditional-style pedagogy).

In traditional ASL pedagogy, students attend to the instructor's lecture and ask questions when necessary. Per the *Signing Naturally* curriculum, each class session ranges from one to two hours. The traditional class in this study included a fifty-minute class three times per week. The instructor also used computer-based visual technology (e.g., Keynote, Smartboard, and Powerpoints) to assist with teaching vocabulary, grammar, and discourse rules.

Since there is no conventional written form of ASL, the technique of ASL gloss is used to provide an intermediary written form of ASL. ASL gloss is a hybrid writing system that is comprised of capitalized English words and ASL's morpho-syntactic structure along with additional conventions

(Supalla & Cripps, 2011). ASL gloss can be seen in published ASL textbooks and it is used to guide instructors and/or students to be able to teach and learn the sentence structure of ASL (Baker-Shenk & Cokely, 1980; Humphries & Padden, 2004; Madsen, 1982; Mikos, Smith, & Lentz, 2001; Smith, Lentz, & Mikos, 2008; Zinza, 2006).

An example of ASL gloss sentence along with its comparable English equivalent sentence used in unit 22, discussing the topic of money, is demonstrated here as:

ASL Gloss	English Translation
fs-JIM POS=3 AUNT RICH.	Jim's aunt is rich.
AUNT IX=3 DIE, IX=3 _____ $50,000.	When his aunt died, he _____ $50,000.

In the first glossed sentence, a proper name such as Jim is fingerspelled and POS=3 represents the third-person possessive pronoun. In the second glossed sentence, the underline represents the grammatical markers in ASL where individuals are to raise their eyebrows expressing the conditional sentence indicating when something happens. Also, IX=3 represents the third-person pronoun. This gives the readers an idea of what ASL sentence structure looks like on paper.

After showing this sentence to the class, the instructor began with asking students the question, "Which signing vocabulary fits with this type of sentence?" Students are supposed to answer the blank part of the sentence with a list of signed vocabulary that was introduced during the previous classes. Students then suggest possible signed vocabulary and the instructor then points out the correct sign. After receiving the correct sign, the instructor demonstrates the complete sentence. To expand this sample, the instructor then introduces more signed vocabulary and phrases with similar structures. This assists students in becoming familiar with this type of sentence structure. Hands-on activity such as groups of students discussing on the topic of money follows.

Inverted-type Pedagogy

Unlike the traditional class, students in the inverted class are required to watch their instructor's lectures on-line, outside of the classroom before they attend their class. They are encouraged to take notes while watching the on-line lectures, and they can watch and re-watch portions of the video as needed. During the first ten minutes of the class, they are able to ask their instructor for clarification about the lectures and discuss the signs and phrases in ASL covered in the video. In addition to a general review, the purpose of this activity is to allow students to utilize vocabulary signs, from on-line lectures by the instructor, during the conversations in the classroom.

The inverted lesson opens with the same fill-in-the-blank activity as the traditional class. However, students then work collaboratively in small groups to discuss the assigned phrases. During the student-to-student discussion, the instructor travels around the room and provides feedback or explains how to use signed words correctly to the groups. When the groups finish their discussions, each group takes a turn to explain their phrases to the other groups. Next, students create new sentences with assigned words from the curriculum. The instructor then randomly asks the students to read and explain scenarios to the class, and students correct and provide feedback to each other.

Five minutes prior to end of the class, the instructor explains the upcoming assignment that includes on-line lectures and distributes copies of articles relating to the content area to the students. Students are expected to read the article as homework and be prepared to discuss the content for the next class period. Students are encouraged to participate in the on-line discussion forum as part of their homework, including posting questions that other students and the instructor can answer or clarify outside of class.

INSTRUCTOR'S REFLECTIONS

When implementing a new pedagogy, it is helpful to identify critical reflections from the instructor. These reflections can help with analysis of the success of the new technique, and guide the faculty to any needed changes for future success. The instructor of the inverted ASL V class was an active part of the research process (see "action research;" Mills, 2000) to determine if the inverted-type pedagogy is effective. The instructor taught using the inverted pedagogy for two semesters, and his reflections from these semesters are carefully analyzed as the faculty considers further research work. The instructor expressed that the inverted method provided students with benefits, and was a positive experience for both students and faculty. Some of the benefits from this class format include the opportunities to 1) participate in advanced dialogues, 2) engage in extensive practice with signed vocabulary, and 3) work with peers independently. Other challenges and obstacles that this instructor faced include 1) students not viewing on-line lectures, 2) student frustration with watching lengthy videos, and 3) problems with technology and communication with technology staff.

The instructor conceded that some issues or problems exist with the inverted pedagogy; however, most of these can be fixed or avoided. For example, several students did not view the on-line lectures, yet expected to learn from other students during class time. To remedy this, the instructor required students to post their responses and/or comments related to these instructional videos in an electronic discussion forum. Providing "pop quizzes" during class to check if they viewed the on-line lectures is another way to alleviate this problem. The instructor could also check the electronic access log to see which students logged in, and for how long, and contact those students who fell behind to remind them.

During the semester, the instructor noticed that several students were overwhelmed with the length of the homework videos. The instructor realized that students might benefit from videos with shorter lengths, divided into two or three parts instead of videos lasting more than 20-30 minutes. To support student learning, the instructor allowed the students a few days to view an on-line lecture before discussing topics relating to the lecture and participating in related activities.

The most challenging issues the instructor encountered were the process of developing the technology for the inverted classroom, and providing optimal access to students. By depending on experts from the university's technology staff, the instructor was not able to modify or troubleshoot issues with videos and PowerPoint Slides. Only the university's technology support staff had access to "unlock" videos according to a schedule developed by the instructor, and only the technology services staff had access to fix and update on-line lectures. Unfortunately, the technology support staff is only available during office hours. When videos were unavailable, or students were unable to access them due to technical issues, students notified the instructor about these problems and the instructor reported the technical problems to the technology services staff. It usually took some time to get problems fixed, and sometimes the students had no access to on-line lectures during the entire weekend. The instructor suggests that the technology services staff should designate one instructor to be trained and have full access to the on-line system, or the university should provide technology support services twenty-four hours a day, seven days a week.

CONCLUSION AND FURTHER RESEARCH

Reflections from the instructor provided much insight for future research direction. The suggestions gleaned from the instructor enabled the faculty to work out some of the initial kinks during preliminary semesters, and to move forward with collecting data on the inverted pedagogy during the coming semesters. The authors of this article, under the direction of primary investigator Cripps, plan to gather data comparing the traditional and inverted pedagogy using several different instruments. Measures to be compared include student grades, ASLPI scores, and class environment issues using a variety of previously validated scales. Next steps also include gathering input from students regarding their perceptions and suggestions for the inverted classroom format.

In response to van Lier's (1989) concern that oral language proficiency tests do not actually measure the L2 learners' conversational competence due to the interviewer's control of the conversation, the authors agree that the ASLPI score should not be the sole measure of a student's conversational ASL skills. Grades in all classes throughout the Deaf Studies program, and experiences in the community (e.g., service-learning and internships; see Cooper & Cripps, in press, Cripps & Cooper, 2012 and Cooper, Emanuel, & Cripps, 2012) should also be part of the whole picture of a student's conversational skills. However, the authors believe there is relevance to the ASLPI score as an external, unbiased rating of a student's communication skill. There appear to be many benefits to implementation of the inverted classroom for ASL classes. The authors noted benefits in addition to those identified by Henshaw, such as the opportunity for instructors to modify lesson plans and provide feedback based on students' needs in their learning process. Specifically, the inverted pedagogy allows supplemental opportunities for students to receive instructor's feedback through ASL in the classroom through direct conversation and informal social interaction, and increased opportunity for note-taking at the student's preferred pace.

This preliminary experience using inverted pedagogy with ASL instruction provided a model with positive results. Clearly, more research is needed to compare the language learning outcomes of students in traditional versus inverted classrooms, and to validate the benefits noticed during the trial semesters. Research and development focused on inverted pedagogy for ASL classes could revolutionize ASL instruction across the country.

REFERENCES

Baker-Shenk, C. L., & Cokeley, D. (1980). *American Sign Language: A teacher's resource text on curriculum, methods, and evaluation*. Silver Spring, MD: T. J. Publishers.

Cannod, G. C., Burge, J. E., & Helmick, M. T. (2007). Using the inverted classroom to teach software engineering. *Technical Report: MU-SEAS-CSA-2007-001*. Oxford, OH: Miami University School of Engineering & Applied Science.

Celce-Murcia, M., Dörnyei, Z., & Thurrell, S. (1995). Communicative competence: A pedagogy motivated model with content specifications. *Issues in Applied Linguistics*, 6(2), 5–35.

Cipria, A. (2006). *The roadmap to redesign (R2R): Introductory Spanish I & II*. Saratoga Springs, NY: The National Center for Academic Transformation.

Cooper, S. B. (1997). The academic status of sign language programs in institutions of higher education in the United States. Unpublished doctoral dissertation, Gallaudet University, Washington, DC.

Cooper, S. B. & Cripps, J. H. (in press). Service-Learning: Deaf Studies in the community. In O. Delano-Oriaran, M. W. Parks, & S. Fondrie (Eds.), *Service-Learning and civic engagement*. Thousand Oaks, CA: SAGE Publications.

Cooper, S. B., Emanuel, D. C., & Cripps, J. H. (2012). Deaf studies alumni perceptions of the academic program and off-campus internship. *American Annals of the Deaf*, 157(4), 373–390.

Cooper, S. B., Reisman, J. I., & Watson, D. (2008). The status of sign language instruction in institutions of higher education: 1994–2004. *American Annals of the Deaf*, 153(1), 78–88.

Cripps, J. H. & Cooper, S. B. (2012). Service-Learning in Deaf Studies: Integrating academia and the deaf community. *Journal of the American Deafness and Rehabilitation Association*, 46(1), 354–368.

Gass, S. M. & Varnois, E. M. (1994). Input, interaction, and second language production. *Studies in Second Language Acquisition*, 16(3), 283–302.

Henshaw, B. (2008). *Colleagues committed to redesign (C2R): Introductory Spanish*. Saratoga Springs, NY: The National Center for Academic Transformation.

Humphries, T. L. & Padden, C. A. (2004). *Learning American Sign Language: Levels I & II — Beginning & intermediate, 2nd edition*. Upper Saddle River, NJ: Pearson Education, Inc.

Kormos, J. (1999). Simulating conversations in oral-proficiency assessment: A conversation analysis of role plays and non-scripted interviews in language exams. *Language Testing*, 16(2), 163–188.

Lage, M. J., Platt, G. J., & Treglia, M. (2000). Inverting the classroom: A gateway to creating an inclusive learning environment. *The Journal of Economic Education*, 31(1), 30–43.

Long, M. H. & Porter, P. A. (1985). Group work, interlanguage talk, and second language acquisition. *TESOL Quarterly*, 19(2), 207–228.

Mackey, A. (1995). Stepping up the pace: Input, interaction, and interlanguage development: An empirical study of questions in ESL. Unpublished doctoral dissertation, University of Sydney, Sydney, New South Wales, Australia.

Madsen, W. J. (1982). *Intermediate conversational sign language, 2nd edition*. Washington, D.C.: Gallaudet University Press.

Maher, J. (1996). *Seeing in signs: The works of William Stokoe*. Washington, DC: Gallaudet University Press.

Marschark, M. & Humphries, T. (2010). Deaf studies by any other name? *Journal of Deaf Studies and Deaf Education*, 15(1), 1–2.

Mascolo, M. F. (2009). Beyond student-centered and teacher-centered pedagogy: Teaching and learning as guided participation. *Pedagogy and the Human Sciences*, 1(1), 3–27.

McNamara, T. F. (1997). 'Interaction' in second language performance assessment: Whose performance? *Applied Linguistics*, 18(4), 446–466.

Mikos, K., Smith, C., & Lentz, E. M. (2001). *Signing naturally: Teacher's curriculum guide — Level 3*. San Diego, CA: DawnSignPress.

Mills, G. E. (2000). *Action research: A guide for the teacher researcher*. Upper Saddle River, NJ: Prentice-Hall.

Pica, T., Young, R., & Doughty, C. (1987). The impact of interaction on comprehension. *TESOL Quarterly*, 21(4), 737–758.

Pyke, G. (2010). *Colleagues committed to redesign (C2R): Elementary Spanish I*. Saratoga Springs, NY: The National Center for Academic Transformation.

Quinto-Pozos, D. (2011). Teaching American Sign Language to hearing adult learners. *Annual Review of Applied Linguistics*, 31, 137–158.

Rose, D. H. & Meyer, A. (Eds.) (2006). *A practical reader in universal design for learning*. Cambridge, MA: Harvard Education Press.

Rosen, R. (2008). American Sign Language as a foreign language in US high schools: State of the art. *Modern Language Journal*, 92(1), 10–38.

Skourtou, E. & Kourtis-Kazoullis, V. (2003). The step from traditional pedagogy to transformative. *International Journal of the Humanities*, 1, 1329–1337.

Smith, C., Lentz, E. M., & Mikos, K. (2008). *Signing naturally: Teacher's curriculum guide, units 1-6*. San Diego, CA: DawnSignPress.

Strayer, J. F. (2012). How learning in an inverted classroom influences cooperation, innovation and task orientation. *Learning Environment Research*, 15, 171–193.

Supalla, S. J. & Cripps, J. H. (2011). Toward universal design in reading instruction. *Bilingual Basics*, 12(2), 1–13.

van Lier, L. (1989). Reeling, writhing, drawling, stretching, and fainting in coils: Oral proficiency interviews as conversation. *TESOL Quarterly*, 23(3), 489–508.

Witkowsky, K. (2008). Increasing learning and reducing costs through technology: The University of Alabama story. *Change: The Magazine of Higher Learning*, 40(2) 32–39.

Zinza, J. E. (2006). *Master ASL!: Fingerspelling, numbers, and glossing*. Burtonsville, MD: Sign Media, Inc.

Communication and Longevity in Deaf/Hearing Marriages

MICHAEL BALLARD

GUY MEETS GIRL; GIRL MEETS GUY. THEY FLIRT. GUY ASKS GIRL FOR text messaging number. Girl says she does not text message very often. Guy explains he cannot hear on the phone and communicates via text message. Girl understands; they trade numbers. They date. They get engaged. They marry. The marriage causes conflict with each other and with family members. They struggle. Guy is Deaf. Girl is hearing. Husband and wife are in love. Husband and wife are worlds apart. Husband and wife are conflicted.

Should Guy and Girl give heed to social stigmas such as 'Deaf/hearing marriages are doomed to end in divorce;' Deaf people marry hearing people because of the "invaluable interpreter role" (Powell & Buschmann, 1978); Cultural and language barriers make Deaf/hearing marriages miserable.

"Marriage with a hearing person is frowned upon. Deaf marry Deaf approximately nine times out of ten" (Lane, et al, 1996, p. 71). The relationship between the aforementioned husband and wife is not uncommon. It has been suggested, or even accepted knowledge that 90% of all [Deaf/hearing] marriages end in divorce (Solomon, 1994). Endogamous marriage is prevalent among Deaf individuals, between 85% to 95% (Lane et al., 1996; Erting, 1978; Fay, 1896; Woodward, 1989). Should deaf individuals reject their own culture and marry a hearing person, rendering themselves traitors to their own community? The same question is asked of hearing people. What harm is there then, marrying for love?

STATEMENT OF THE PROBLEM

Communication is the glue, the nail, and the key to every relationship, regardless of cultural backgrounds. To better understand the dynamics of Deaf/hearing marriage, my research question is "What communicative practices do spouses use to contribute to the longevity of Deaf/hearing marriages?"

This article examines how couples use communication foundations to effectively communicate their differences across cultures. The first step to effective communication is recognizing Deaf culture as its own culture, as opposed to a subgroup within the larger, Hearing society and forced to follow the current societal norms displayed by the hearing majority. Moore and Levitan (1993) explain Deaf culture in this manner:

> One possible definition of U.S. Deaf culture is: a social, communal, and creative force of, by, and for Deaf people based on American Sign Language (ASL). It encompasses communication, social protocol, art, entertainment, recreation (e.g., sports, travel, and Deaf clubs), and (to a point) worship. It's also an attitude, as such, can be a weapon of prejudice — "You're not one of us; you don't belong." (Moore & Levitan, 1993, p. 217)

Although Deaf culture encompasses many aspects, this article will only focus on the *communal* communication aspects between Deaf/hearing couples. Without strong communication skills, partners in a Deaf/hearing marriage may not accurately relay differences and thus be unable to recognize, understand, and respect cross-cultural differences, nor be able to resolve differences and have longer, more successful marriages. There is little empirical research that is beneficial to understanding communication in Deaf/hearing marriages. Academics may liken understanding Deaf/hearing marriages to understanding other intercultural marriage, however, every marriage is unique. This research focuses on Deaf/hearing couples that are currently dating, courting, and married and to help provide comfort to those who are scared by the general unempirical consensus that 90% of all Deaf/hearing marriages fail. This research will also help identify tools couples can employ for the benefit of their current relationships (intercultural or otherwise).

This article is centered on the idea that couples in Deaf/hearing marriages endure cultural and language (communication) issues daily, and the idea that they have to work through these challenges constantly to have a long, successful marriage.

ORGANIZATION

This article is organized into four parts. The current section focuses on the importance of this study and provides insight to how this study will benefit the Deaf community and those who wish to enter into a Deaf/hearing marriage. The next section describes the theoretical foundations and philosophical framing of the study and briefly reviews the existing literature addressing the conflicts between Deaf culture and hearing society at large. (A more complete literature review can be found at dissexpress.umi.com (UMI 1558608). The following section describes the scope and methodology of this study as well as the ethical considerations of this research. The final section reveals analysis and findings and discusses the results of the study. This section also addresses the limitations of the study, makes recommendations for further and future studies on the subject, as well as provides the conclusion of this research. The full thesis also includes an appendix section in which provides the Letter of Informed Consent, lists the survey questions asked, and provides empirical data received from the study.

PHILOSOPHICAL AND ETHICAL ASSUMPTIONS

The pursuit of educating deaf individuals has always been a battle. Socrates seems to be the first person that has spoken out in support of sign language; he asked Hermogenes: "Suppose that we had no voice or tongue, and wanted to indicate objects to one another, should we not, like the deaf and dumb, make signs with hands, head and the rest of the body?" Hermogenes responded, "How could it be otherwise?" (Nomeland & Nomeland, 2012, p. 7). This argues that deaf individuals existed in history and they were accepted by society.

However, society's acceptance of deaf people is conflicted in Aristotlean logic: "[Men] that are deaf are also speechless; that is they can make vocal sounds but cannot speak" (Nomeland & Nomeland, 2012, p. 7). Because they cannot speak, "[Those] who are born deaf all become senseless and incapable of reason" (Nomeland & Nomeland, 2012, p. 7). For the next two thousand years, Aristotle was accused of oppressing because he believed intelligence was acquired via spoken word (Nomeland & Nomeland, 2012, p. 7).

The philosophical war rages on, although much more subtly. How a deaf person communicates today is paramount to his or her survival. Today, a deaf person may use their voice to communicate with those around them. They may sign. They may use a combination of both.

However, because deaf people are still perceived as different, they are shunned by the society at large. They have looked to each other for help, and have formed a community and a culture of their own. When Deaf people marry hearing people, communication (whether signed or voiced) will almost always be an issue that needs constant pruning. Because we now recognize Deaf culture as its own entity, we also recognize cultural conflicts may arise. Lane (1993) is hearing and discusses issues Deaf individuals have with the hearing culture:

> They accuse us hearing people of having a low opinion of them and revealing it in our actions and our words. We rudely leave them out of conversation. We change our manner of speaking and exaggerate it when we learn someone is deaf, making lipreading [and other activities] more difficult. We expect Deaf people to perform on *our* terms and never we on *theirs*. (Lane, 1993, p. 12, italics added)

With this understanding, communication philosophy tends to privilege speech over sign language. Communication philosophy needs to include consideration of the many ways our societies communicate.

THEORETICAL BASIS

The theoretical basis for this article is founded in Burgoon's (1988) Expectancy Violations Theory and Philipsen's (1997) Speech Codes Theory. A description for each respective theory is explained in this section.

Expectancy Violations Theory

Burgoon (1988) uses the term expectancy as a model that "posits that people hold expectations about the nonverbal behaviors of others. Violations of these expectations are posited to trigger change" in relationships (Burgoon & Hale, 1988, p. 59). The Expectancy Violations Theory (EVT) consists of three parts: (1) context, (2) relationship, and (3) communicator characteristics. *Context* refers to cultural norms, *relationship* factors include "similarity, familiarity, liking, and relative status" (Griffin, p. 89) and *communicator* characteristics refer to demographic facts and personal features such as physical appearance, personality and communicative style (Griffin, p. 89).

Burgoon's EVT is one possible explanation of longevity in Deaf/hearing marriages. Applying EVT means that Deaf/hearing spouses expect others to assimilate to their native cultural norms, adhere to cultural relationship standards, and are willing to accept cultural differences in their relationship. It would be nearly impossible for two individuals to enter into matrimony without communicating and understanding something about their future spouse's cultural norms.

When a hearing spouse talks on his/her cell phone, while at a predominately Deaf social gathering or event without group permission, this hearing spouse would be considered acting inappropriately by the members of the Deaf culture. When the hearing spouse first obtains permission before making a phone call, s/he recognizes that there are different cultural norms and values: s/he is respecting the members of the Deaf community and the people in the Deaf community are more willing to welcome the hearing spouse as part of their own.

EVT steers us to look at acceptable communicative behavioral rules within a culture or group of people. For example, when there is a Deaf speaker or performer on stage, or a Deaf person making a joke while hanging out among friends, it is polite to do a "hand-wave" as a symbol of approval akin to when hearing people clap hands. When people venture outside their culture, it is expected that they follow the cultural rules of which culture they are visiting. Moore and Levitan (1993) encourage that when "we wish to honor people of a different culture, we do it by expressing our esteem for them in their own language — or, at least, in terms they can understand" (p. 309). Hearing people can show their support for deaf people as humans by the waving of the hands. Deaf people tend to take clapping as offensive it violates expectations. To a Deaf person, seeing a sea of waving hands is as glorious as a hearing person hears shouting and clapping.

My wife is hearing. There are unwritten cultural rules that apply to hearing cultures that do not typically apply in Deaf culture. One such rule is when Deaf couples come over unannounced and prolong their "welcome." This act is taboo to the hearing community. Generally, hearing people make attempts to forewarn the person they wish to visit, see if s/he is home, and stay an acceptable length of time, usually less than a half-hour. However, a visit should not exceed more than an hour. It is the opposite in Deaf culture. Stays are often two or three hours long. My wife does not want to entertain someone for three hours when there is laundry and dishes to be done, or kids that need putting to sleep. While my wife is often respectful and tolerant to the Deaf culture, I need to be respectful of the hearing culture and politely say good-bye after the business of the visit is completed. This is just one example illustrating EVT and how my wife and I work through cultural differences.

To hypothesize this theory, couples that exhibit and apply EVT are more apt to communicate more effectively and resolve cultural differences.

Speech Codes Theory
Philipsen's (1997) Speech Codes Theory (SCT) revolves around interpersonal relationships founded in two or more cultures. "A speech code, then, is defined here as a system of socially constructed symbols and meanings, premises, and rules, pertaining to communicative conduct" (Philipsen, 1997, p. 126). When there are different cultures, there is bound to be succinctly different speech codes and speech norms. Philipsen at first ascribed to this theory as the ethnography of communication (Griffin, 2009, p. 415); do the spouses each understand the speech codes enough to respect one another?

In any given situation, Deaf cultural norms and hearing cultural norms can and do contradict on what types of communication and responses are required. Sometimes the speech codes will overlap, and other times the speech codes are points of contention.

Liu & Chang (2011) posit that SCT not only constructs "rules about how to use language to communicate, but also rules about how to interpret language use. That is to say, the meanings attached to a communicative act depend on the speech code that is used" (p. 3). Part of what makes language a language is having a culture, a group of people to employ language. The culture will construct cultural norms via language to express what is culturally acceptable and unacceptable. SCT suggests that misunderstandings are bound to happen when two different speech codes dictate the same communicative event. SCT hypothesizes that couples who understand each other's cultural norms and practices have more longevity in their marriage, thus supporting a more successful marriage.

One example of different speech codes in Deaf culture as compared with hearing culture is the use of replying "You're welcome" after one says "Thank you." "Some English speakers [have] said that ASL signers don't say, 'you're welcome' enough" (Hoza, 2007, p. 209). This is a perception that hearing people have because as members of the larger, mainstreamed society, they expect people to conform to their manners. However, this is not the case (and may point to the need for more training in cross-cultural interpreting for ASL interpreters). While there is a sign for "You're welcome," it is not commonly used as a response to "Thank you." More commonly, the response would be "Fine-fine," "No problem," the "OK" or "thumbs up" sign. Also a head nod acknowledging the "Thank you" suffices as "You're welcome" in ASL. ASL interpreters may be seeing these signs correctly, but incorrectly voicing, or not voicing, them at face-value rather than cross-culturally and saying the proper "You're welcome."

More pertinent to interpersonal communication, however, is the fact that Deaf individuals are generally more straightforward in their conversations than hearing people. Such straight talk is considered rude in hearing culture, but perfectly acceptable in the Deaf-world. Mindess (2006) writes that this straight talk may be the toughest part of Deaf culture for hearing people to accept, saying:

> I have heard several skilled interpreters say, regarding this behavior, "That's not culture, that's just rude!" What kind of remark can provoke such "insensitive" criticism? Probably being greeted by a Deaf person with a remark about one's appearance such as, "Boy, you've put on a lot of weight!" or "Oh, you dyed your hair, it's not a good color. It looked better before," or "Wow! You are getting bald so fast!" Deaf people maintain that such com-

ments demonstrate closeness, connection, loyalty, sincerity, and friendship. (Mindess, 2006, p. 87)

Such direct commentary made by the Deaf individual usually occurs right after the trading of initial greetings. Deaf people feel insulted if with whom they are communicating choose to disregard or acknowledge change in physical appearances (Mindess, 2006, p. 88). This is explained in two reasons: first, Deaf people value the sharing of information more than they value considerations; and two, Deaf people consider others in their social circles as if they were family and feel they can share comments to and with each other as if they were in an intimate relationship (Mindess, p. 88). Another factor in this straight talk conflict is that ASL is a visual language (not auditory) and Deaf people live in a visual world (Mindess, p. 88).

These speech codes demonstrate that there is a clear and succinct difference between cultures that need to be more closely examined within the Deaf/hearing context. More important, are partners in Deaf/hearing marriages willing to understand the speech codes of their spouses? "Learning a particular way of speaking is part of one's acquisition of a language and becoming a full member of a language community. That is to say, people learn to express themselves in socially appropriate ways" (Hoza, 2003, p. 203). To fully learn a language, one must acknowledge the inner meanings and meta-communication of certain speech codes; in this case, Deaf/hearing couples learning and understanding their spouse's language.

One example in showing how EVT and SCT explain communication in Deaf/hearing marriages is the differences in the meaning of time. Time in Deaf culture is half-jokingly referred to as "Deaf Standard Time." Deaf Standard Time dictates when Deaf people arrive at, begin, and leave a social gathering. Hearing people mean "good-bye" when they say they are leaving the group. Deaf people alter the definition of "good-bye" to mean that it is *almost* time to leave. After mentioning that they will soon leave, leavetaking can last upwards to a half-an-hour or more (Mindess, 2006, 52–53). This type of interaction identifies that two different speech codes, Deaf culture and hearing culture, are dictating the same communicative event.

THE DEAF/HEARING MARRIAGE LITERATURE

The late Gordon B. Hinckley (1991) said, "Stormy weather occasionally hits every household. Connected inevitably with the whole [marriage] process is much of pain — physical, mental, and emotional." Every marriage is tested, repeatedly. Deaf/hearing marriages are no different.

To start off, opposition for Deaf/Deaf marriage is centuries old. For unknown reasons or "reasons that are not understood, an estimate that ninety percent of [Deaf/hearing] marriages dissolve has persisted in the [Deaf] Studies literature with little empirical support since the late 1800s" (McIntosh, 1995, p. 1). The study of Deaf/hearing marriages began as a response to Alexander Graham Bell's (1883) paper presented to the National Academy of Science at New Haven. Bell argued that Deaf/Deaf marriages "are not the exception, but the rule" (p. 4). Bell insisted that deafness is a hindrance to progress. He negatively and sarcastically mocked sign language:

> "The deaf-mutes *think* in the gesture language, and English is apt to remain a foreign tongue. They can communicate with hearing persons by writing, but they often write in broken English, as a foreigner would speak. They think in gestures, and often translate into written English with the idioms of the sign language. They are thus in a great measure cut off from our literature. This is another element in forcing them into each other's society." (Bell, 1883, p. 42)

Bell (1883) proposed options for limiting and reducing deaf populations, and the deaf offspring of Deaf/Deaf marriages. He proposed that "a law forbidding congenitally deaf persons from [marrying] would go a long way towards checking the evil" (p. 45). Bell proposed preventive measures for the promises of "lessening the evil" (p. 46) guided by the principle that "determine the causes that promote [marriages] among the deaf and dumb; and remove them" (p. 46).

Bell then suggested that deaf children be segregated from each other, for the purpose that they learn English: "We commence our efforts on behalf of the deaf-mute by changing his social environment" (p. 46). Bell's idea was that if deaf children were unaware of a population outside of their environment, then they would not marry each other and produce "evil" offspring.

Lane, et al.'s (1996) research seems to take this movement one step further, acknowledging the legal ability to sterilize deaf individuals, claiming that "there have been movements in the United States and in Germany, for example, to sterilize Deaf people by law and to encourage Deaf people in voluntary sterilization" (p. 381). As such, this observation may contribute to the myth that there is a 90% divorce rate in Deaf/hearing marriages.

Many scholars, and the Deaf community in general, assume that Deaf/hearing marriages are not stable, hence the generally assumed 90% percent divorce rate. In the conclusion of a study on the viability of Deaf/hearing marriages versus Deaf/Deaf marriages, argued in opposition to Bell, Fay (1898) countered that "marriages in which both of the partners are deaf are more likely to result happily than those in which one of the partners is deaf and the other is hearing" (p. 121). In Fay's study of 4,471 marriages, 72.5% (3,242) of deaf individuals married other deaf individuals, as compared to 20% (894) of marriages that were Deaf/hearing combinations (p. 123). (The remaining 7.5% (336) did not report whether or not they were married to either deaf or hearing spouses.)Of note, however, is Fay's response to Bell's assertion that Deaf/hearing marriages will curtail "evil" deaf offspring. Fay found that only 9.7% of Deaf/Deaf couples produced deaf offspring, compared to 9.2% of Deaf/hearing couples (Fay, pp. 125–126). Bell's argument is thusly rendered moot. However, studying deaf offspring brought forth the study of Deaf/hearing divorces.

Fay (1898) found in his study that of the 894 Deaf/hearing marriages, 54 total couples (6.5%) reported they were either separated or divorced. In contrast, of the 3,242 Deaf/Deaf marriages, only 84 (2.6%) reported they were separated or divorced (p. 120). Fay reasoned that Deaf/Deaf marriages were more successful because "the strong bond of mutual fellowship growing out of their similar condition [deafness], the ease and freedom with which they communicate [sign language] with each other, and the identity of their social relations" (p. 135). Other studies also support this statistic:

> "Marriage is an area where deaf people have resisted assimilation and remained separate from hearing society; they tend to marry one another. As indicated in the 1972 statistics…84.6% of deaf people marry another deaf or hard of hearing person" (Overstreet, 1999, p. 21).

Hinckley's (1991) comments, "Stormy weather occasionally hits every household" holds true when deaf individuals choose to marry someone who is hearing, and vice versa. "The opposition to Deaf/hearing marriages has been a more recent controversy" (Kingsbury, 2011, p. 24). McIntosh (1995) states that

> "[relationships] break up or dissolve for a variety of reasons and the same is true for [Deaf/hearing] relationships. But the added nuances such as different cultural backgrounds and different languages, including modality of languages may make [Deaf/hearing] more susceptible to failing" (p. 3).

Fast forward from Bell and Fay to Powell and Buschmann's (1978) assertion that culturally hearing spouses dominate the relationship. According to Powell & Buschmann, this "is assumed to be true by many because of the invaluable interpreter role that the hearing person plays. The hearing person is sometimes seen as the 'giver of new life' to a deaf person in a mixed marriage. For this reason, it is taken for granted that the hearing person is the leader in the relationship" (p. 18). "Many Deaf people desire to be in control of their own lives and do not want interpreters to make decisions for them" (Mindess, 2006, p. 173).

Powell and Buschmann (1978) surveyed thirteen Deaf/hearing couples as well as five single individuals in an attempt to discover the pros and cons of Deaf/hearing marriages from both spouses. They also state that the "marriage between a deaf person and a hearing person is not popularly mentioned as a 'mixed marriage' because the general hearing public is not exposed to deafness" (p. 17). Powell and Buschmann observed that most deaf people do not want to marry hearing people, that it is "not an attractive choice" (p. 19). We can hypothesize that this "unattractive" choice is heavily rooted in cultural differences and lack of communication between partners. McIntosh (1995) explains:

> Deaf/hearing marriages produce strong feelings in both ... communities. Some members of the [Deaf] community think [Deaf] individuals should marry within their culture — that is, marry other deaf people. Some hearing individuals envision deaf people as defective and have the attitude of: "Who would want to marry a handicapped person?" (p. 4)

Kingsbury (2011) provides insight to why there are fewer Deaf/hearing marriages than Deaf/Deaf marriages:

> For the Deaf/hearing couple, the Deaf partner may be concerned about peer judgment for breaking group norms and may be labeled [hearing-minded] by his or her peers. The hearing partner may be concerned about defending being Deaf as culture rather than disability to family and friends and may be labeled a Deaf-wanna-be by Deaf or by hearing people involved in the Deaf community. (Kingsbury, 2011, p. 17)

Mindess (2006) asserts that because the Deaf world is so small, the idea of friendship is ever-so-important because the "way we deal with difficulties that arise in our friendships also has cross-cultural overtones. Since friendships are expected [in Deaf culture] to be lifelong, a problem between friends can become a lifelong one" (Mindess, 2006, p. 74). Scholarly studies on Deaf/hearing marriage, admittedly, are still in their infancy.

RATIONALE

Deaf/hearing marriage in this study is considered to be intercultural because the marriage consists of two different and distinct cultures and languages: Deaf culture and hearing culture; American Sign Language and English. A further challenge for couples in Deaf/hearing marriages, and other intercultural marriages, is that couples do not give much "thought into what they expect from such a relationship and how their expectations and assumptions may differ from their partners" (Williams, 2010, p. 192). While cultural differences may have brought couples together in the beginning of their budding relationships, often overlooked is how differences are communicated long-term. Williams (2010) suggested:

It is important to [recognize] that cross-border [and Deaf/hearing] marriages do have a high rate of breakdown, which is hardly surprising given the pressure placed upon them through the social scrutiny they are subject to as well as because of problems that are intrinsic to each individual relationship." (p. 200)

Lane, et al. (1996) state that 90% of all Deaf marriages are deaf people marrying other deaf people (p. 71). Sustaining a marriage is difficult enough endogamously, even during the best of times. Sustaining exogamous marriages is that much harder. This study is extremely important in helping us understand how successful Deaf/hearing couples maintain their marriages via love and understanding each other's culture to the best of their abilities. This study is also important in understanding how Deaf/hearing dyads communicate across cultures.

RESEARCH QUESTIONS

What communicative practices do spouses use to contribute to the longevity of Deaf/hearing marriages? This research question is critical to an understanding of Deaf/hearing marriages because communication has not been examined in depth within Deaf Studies scholarship. In this section, the scope and methodology of this research will be explained and the ethical considerations of this research will be discussed.

Scope of the Study
Data collection for this study began with a sample survey of the targeted population (Rubin, et al., 2010, p. 201). The scope of the sample survey should be regarded as a stratified sample because it allows the researcher to "compare certain subgroups in a population" (p. 201). The two subgroups (subjects) beings studied are Deaf and hearing individuals in a Deaf/hearing marriage. Cluster sampling is also recognized because the researcher finds it "impractical and impossible to compile a list of everyone" in the Deaf/hearing marriage population (p. 202). The study will be made public via Facebook, email, and word of mouth. The researcher will then contact each interested participant and invite him or her via email to take the survey. The researcher will not cut off the data at n = 50. The more participants, the more inclusive the data collected.

METHODOLOGY

Research began with the literature review related to Deaf/hearing marriage found in the previous section. The researcher searched EBSCOhost and

WorldCat searching for any journal articles relating to Deaf/hearing marriage, as well as journal articles relating to intercultural communication. The researcher also searched ProQuest theses and dissertations to discover papers written on Deaf/hearing marriages. Archival/documentary research was conducted from the libraries at Utah Valley University and Brigham Young University (Ballard, 2014). The archival/documentary research included books written on Deaf culture and how Deaf culture relates to the hearing world, history, Deaf identity and intercultural relationships.

Additionally, an original mixed-method survey was collected via fluidsurveys.com, a web-based survey company. Survey participants were composed of both deaf and hearing individuals who are in Deaf/hearing marriages. In addition to individuals in a Deaf/hearing marriage, a control group of Deaf/Deaf dyads was surveyed for comparison. (Survey questions are listed in the full thesis under Appendixes B through E.)

Survey questions were administered in both written English and via a video recording of the researcher asking survey questions in American Sign Language to ensure access for all research participants. Research questions are rooted in EVT and SCT; however, no questions asked directly refer to each respective theory. The purpose of this method was to cross-examine the data collected with the theories used for this study. The researcher hopes to through interpretive social science discover which communicative practices are successful in increasing the longevity of Deaf/hearing marriages, and to discover in what ways miscommunication and misunderstandings occur.

Interpretive social science can be traced to the German philosopher and sociologist Max Weber (1864–1920), who believed that social science should study social action with the purpose of learning the personal reasons or motives that shapes a person's internal feelings and guide decisions to act (Neuman, 2011, p. 101). Neuman argues that "interpretive social science concerns how people interact and get along with each other" (p. 101). The researcher interprets the association between communication and longevity in Deaf/hearing marriages. What is the association between two distinct cultures (Deaf and hearing) that occur "together in a patterned way or appear to act together" (Neuman, 2011, p. 75)?

DATA ANALYSIS

The survey used for the study included both multiple-choice and open-ended questions. This was a mixed-method survey that used only two qualitative response questions. The rest of the questions were examined quantitatively. The researcher used an "objective approach" to examine how communication prompts "cause-and-effect relationships" between Deaf/hearing spouses (Griffin, 2009, p. 14). After distributing and receiving survey questionnaires, the researcher conducted a content analysis which cross-examined each participant's responses for common themes that surface. Data for multiple-choice questions is dissected into percentages based on subjects' responses. Additionally, a background questionnaire was conducted to provide demographic results.

VALIDITY AND RELIABILITY

The researcher here focused on *representative reliability*, the "reliability across subpopulations…It addresses the question: Does the indicator deliver the same answer when applied to different groups?" (p. 208). The different groups compared here are recently-married and longer-married Deaf/hearing couples. These subgroups were also compared with the control group of Deaf/Deaf married couples.

ETHICAL CONSIDERATION

Ethical considerations for this study begin and end with the researcher. The researcher respects the rights and privacy of each of the participants in the study and adheres to the rule of thumb: do no harm. The 'do no harm' rule states that if "you would not be willing to be a participant in your research project, you probably shouldn't be asking others to participate in that project" (Rubin et al, 2010, p. 204). The Deaf community is a close-knit community. It is imperative that the participant's exclude identifying markers in this anonymous survey. If participant's includes names of themselves or their spouses, it is not included in the results.

Each subject/participant in the study was required to sign an Informed Letter of Consent (Appendix A). Without this agreement, the researcher would not accept responses and include responses in the data collected.

Questions in the survey were not meant to cause unnecessary harm or irreversible injury to any participant in the study. The study is also not meant to degrade or humiliate an individual or couple who is struggling in their current Deaf/hearing marriage.

RESULTS OF THE STUDY, DISCUSSION, AND CONCLUSION

Part A: Expectancy Violation Theory-based Questions
In this section, participants were asked questions rooted in Expectancy Violations Theory specific to how they resolved cultural conflicts.

Survey participants were first asked to rate how frequently cultural disagreements arose in their marriages both currently as well as early in their marriages. The goal of this question was to compare how frequently cultural differences arose in Deaf/hearing marriages as opposed to Deaf/Deaf marriages. The assumption was that early in a marriage cultural disagreements would occur more frequently than at present as a couple learned to resolve those conflicts.

Response	Deaf/hearing Couples (percentage/count)	Deaf/Deaf Couples (percentage/count)
Daily	6.8% (3)	5.6% (1)
Weekly or monthly	36.4% (16)	38.9% (7)
Every 3-4 months or yearly	56.8% (25)	55.6% (10)

Table 1. Results of the question "How often do you and your spouse currently need to resolve conflicts related to cultural differences?"

Interestingly, both Deaf/hearing couples and Deaf/Deaf couples reported that currently they needed to resolve cultural conflicts at nearly identical rates (see Table 1).

In both groups, around 55% couples reported the need to currently resolve cultural conflicts every few months to once a year. Only about 6% of couples in both groups reported daily conflict. Thus *both* Deaf/hearing and Deaf/Deaf couples experience some conflicts but at fairly low rates overall.

Survey participants were then asked to assess the frequency of cultural conflicts early in their marriage. The purpose of this question was to assess if the frequency of conflicts decreased over time. Surprisingly, Deaf/Deaf couples reported they struggled more frequently at the beginning of their marriages than Deaf/hearing couples (See Table 2.)

Response	Deaf/hearing Couples (percentage/count)	Deaf/Deaf Couples (percentage/count)
Daily	15.9% (7)	33.3% (6)
Weekly or monthly	56.8% (25)	38.9% (7)
Every 3-4 months or yearly	27.3% (12)	27.8 (5)

Table 2. Results of the question "How often did you and your spouse need to resolve conflicts early in your marriage?"

As predicted, early in marriage conflicts did occur more frequently for both sets of couples. Of Deaf/hearing couples, 16% reported daily conflicts.

One interesting result was that Deaf/Deaf couples reported double the rate of daily conflict (33%) as Deaf/hearing couples. These findings suggest that the widely held belief that Deaf/hearing marriage is more difficult may be false. Additionally, further research may be required to better understand why Deaf/Deaf couples struggle with frequent cultural conflicts early in their marriages.

The next two questions in this section were meant to gauge how couples responded to cultural violations. Responses indicated how well violations or possible violations were communicated between spouses.

Response	Deaf/hearing Couples (percentage/count)	Deaf/Deaf Couples (percentage/count)
Both of us stay home	20.5% (9)	5.6% (1)
Go alone while your spouse stays home	18.2% (8)	38.9% (7)
Both go to the event even though your spouse does not feel comfortable	20.5% (9)	5.6% (1)
Help your spouse understand cultural norms so your spouse feels more comfortable and both go to the event	40.9% (18)	50% (9)

Table 3. Results of the question "What do you do when your spouse does not want to go to an event or social gathering where most people will be from your culture?"

The first question asked "What do you do when your spouse does not want to attend an event or social gathering where most people will be from you culture?" Considerable variation between the Deaf/hearing group and the Deaf/Deaf group was observed (see Table 3).

Of the Deaf/hearing participants, 40.9% responded they would help their spouse better understand cultural norms that may arise so they feel more comfortable attending such events. However, of the Deaf/Deaf couples, 50% stated they would help their spouse feel comfortable with various social rules (10% higher than the Deaf/hearing couples). This response would represent an excellent communication and resolution of possible cultural violations. This data suggests that couples are willing to communicate their differences and cultural expectations, but that this conflict is a difficult one with lots of variation in responses.

The second question asked "What do you do when your spouse does not follow [a] specific desirable cultural rule or norm at a social gathering or event?" The majority in both the Deaf/hearing couples (78.6%) and the Deaf/

Deaf couples (88.2%) stated that these cultural issues were to be ignored at the moment, but discussed and resolved in private. This data suggests that couples in both groups understand that etiquette is expected in communicating the corrections of cultural violations. Additionally, only 4.8% of Deaf/hearing couples and 5.9% of Deaf/Deaf couples reported they would simply ignore the issue suggesting that couples understand the importance of resolving violations of cultural norms rather than just letting them persist.

The final section of this portion of the survey allowed participants to provide specific examples regarding how they resolved cultural conflicts their marriage. It is important to note that couples in Deaf/hearing marriages reported more specific examples than those in Deaf/Deaf marriages.

However, within both groups, many responses observed how compromise was necessary for both parties. From a hearing female:

> "There are some areas where we have had to learn to agree to disagree or compromise. For example, I don't do well with deaf [culture's] late nights and long visits. My spouse knows this is particularly hard for me and we try to wrap things up sooner than he would if I wasn't there, but still later than a typical hearing culture event."

Another respondent echoed this sentiment, stating, "Deaf social tends to stay much longer and chat, I love to be part of it, but [sometimes] it goes a little too long."

Also, many responses discussed the need to discuss issues at hand and find an acceptable solution. One hearing female commented that showing up at social events with a deaf person was socially unacceptable if there was no serious commitment. She remarked:

> "At first, we argued greatly about how this would appear to others (we both had very different opinions on this matter which created quite a conflict in that beginning stage of our relationship!). What was effective in resolving the issue(s) was both being willing to discuss the issue(s). As with any relationship, if both parties are willing to try and see it from the other's perspective then the issue lends itself to a quicker resolve. It does require both, however. It is nice to mention at this point in our relationship that these kinds of cultural issues and conflicts do not arise nearly as often as they had at the beginning of our relationship."

Another respondent argued that forgiveness is required:

> "Usually it starts by recognizing that it is the cultural differences that are causing the conflict. Then [it is] a matter of applying the understanding to the situation, maybe adding more explanation. We are both pretty laid-back and forgiving. [Usually] the cultural conflicts cause more a temporary frustration than a real conflict and given a little time to resolve themselves."

Part B: Speech Codes Theory-based Questions

In this section, survey participants were asked questions rooted in Speech Codes Theory specific to understanding or misunderstanding language usage. Demographic information was collected to assess what languages couples used and how frequently both English and ASL were used in their homes. Interestingly, twenty-nine of thirty-nine (69.2%) respondents in Deaf/hearing dyads stated the hearing spouse is comfortable expressing and understanding complex messages and were fluent in ASL. Additionally, thirty-seven of thirty-nine respondents (94.8%) reported the deaf spouse either is comfortable expressing and understanding complex messages (and is fluent) in ASL or is a native ASL user. While the hearing spouse may be comfortable with ASL, the opposite is not true with the deaf spouse and English. Twelve of thirty-eight (31.5%) respondents reported that the deaf spouse has basic reading and writing skills, but is not comfortable expressing and understanding complex messages in English. Seventeen reported that the deaf spouse is a native English speaker (user).

As for method of communication used in the home, fourteen of thirty-nine (35.8%) respondents reported that ASL is used the majority of the time, but English is used on occasion when hearing friends or family is present. Eleven of thirty-nine (28.2%) reported that ASL and English are used approximately half the time each. Surprisingly to the researcher, only six of thirty-nine (15.3%) respondents reported ASL is used exclusively in the home. Clearly, for all the Deaf/hearing couples surveyed, language barriers do exist and the majority of couples use both languages in their homes.

For comparison, of the Deaf/Deaf spouses, ten of seventeen (58.8%) reported that ASL is used exclusively in the home while four of seventeen (23.5%) reported that ASL and English are used approximately half of the time. Zero Deaf/Deaf couples reported that English is used exclusively to communicate. In contrast to their Deaf/hearing counterparts, Deaf/Deaf couples would theoretically have less language barriers as they communicate in the same language (ASL) more frequently than they are mixing languages in their homes.

As in Part A, questions in this section progressed from first assessing the frequency, then looking at responses to specific examples, and finally asking for open ended responses. The first two questions looked at how frequently language misunderstandings were addressed as well as how well spouses were able to clarify the intended meaning. The first question asked "When you don't understand a word, sign, or phrase your spouse uses, how often do you ask for clarification?" (See Table 4.)

Response	Deaf/hearing Couples (percentage/count)	Deaf/Deaf Couples (percentage/count)
Rarely	12.5% (5)	21.1% (4)
Sometimes	12.5% (5)	15.8% (3)
Most of the time or Always	75% (30)	63.2% (12)

Table 4. Results of the question "When you don't understand a word, sign, or phrase your spouse uses, how often do you ask for clarification?"

In both groups, the majority of couples asked for clarification when they do not understand each other either most of the time or always (75% of Deaf/hearing and 63% of Deaf/Deaf). This data suggests that couples understand the importance of taking a few moments to explain a misunderstanding. On the other end of the spectrum, 12.5% of Deaf/hearing couples reported only rarely asking for clarification. Nearly double in percentage of Deaf/Deaf couples (21.1%) said they rarely ask for clarification. This may be due to the assumption of Deaf/Deaf couples that because they use the same language as their spouse they do not need to ask for clarification. However, for both sets of couples, not seeking clarification of language may be leading to misunderstanding and fueling marriage conflict.

The next question asked (see Table 5) "When you ask your spouse to explain a word, sign, or phrase you do not understand, how often is he/she able to do so in a way you understand?" The goal of this question was to discover if each partner in the dyad can understand fully the message their spouse is attempting to convey. In this question, it is expected that because Deaf/Deaf couples presumably use the same language, they will struggle with understanding less than their Deaf/hearing counterparts.

Response	Deaf/hearing Couples (percentage/count)	Deaf/Deaf Couples (percentage/count)
Never or Rarely	4.9% (2)	15.8% (3)
Sometimes	14.6% (6)	5.3% (1)
Most of the time or Always	80.5% (33)	78.9% (15)

Table 5. Results of the question "When you ask your spouse to explain a word, sign, or phrase you do not understand, how often is he/she able to do so in a way you understand?"

Surprisingly, Deaf/hearing couples were equal to their Deaf/Deaf counterparts in the ability to explain words, signs, or phrases their spouse did not understand. Also for both couples, the vast majority could express their meaning most of the time to always (80.5% of the Deaf/hearing couples and 78.9% of Deaf/Deaf couples). This data suggests that while language barriers do exist, particularly for the Deaf/hearing couple, most couples are able to adequately negate misunderstandings with clear explanations. In fact, only 4.9% of Deaf/hearing couples reported they could never or rarely provide a clear explanation. It can be safely assumed that, despite their language differences, Deaf/hearing couples can and do effectively communicate with one another as well as Deaf/Deaf couples.

The final question was an application of these skills to a situation. It asked "When language misunderstandings occur between you and your spouse, how often are you able to recognize a language barrier, not your spouse, was the source of the problem." The purpose of this question was to learn whether couples recognize language misunderstandings, rather than their spouse, as the source of conflict (see Table 6).

Response	Deaf/hearing Couples (percentage/count)	Deaf/Deaf Couples (percentage/count)
Never or Rarely	10% (4)	52.9% (9)
Sometimes	27.5% (11)	29.4% (5)
Most of the Time or Always	62.5% (25)	17.6% (3)

Table 6. Results of the question "When language misunderstandings occur, how often are you able to recognize a language barrier, not your spouse, was the source of the problem?"

The data shows that 52.9% of Deaf/Deaf couples "fail" to realize that language is a barrier in their marriage. One participant in a Deaf/Deaf marriage stated that language problems is "not an issue because we came from the same culture." Another concurred, "This is never an issue for us since we use the same language to communicate all the time." This two respondents seem to be in the minority. A third respondent explained the discord in communication between Deaf/Deaf spouses, saying, "We never had a language misunderstanding. I want to bring up a point. Identity is [a] huge factor in cultures which often ties with [the] language they use."

This provides a stark contrast and refutes an assumption that Deaf/Deaf couples actually communicate better than Deaf/hearing couples. To compare, 57.5% of Deaf/hearing couples indicated that they recognize language issues as a barrier in their marriage most of the time or always. This large difference in responses suggests that Deaf/hearing couples may be more aware of the potential for conflict due to language misunderstandings. Thus when problems arise they may look first for misunderstandings rather than immediately placing blame on the spouse.

An example of this would be this Deaf respondent's comments:

> "Sometimes there are play on words or idioms that I am not sure [of]. I ask my wife what [it means]. Sometimes she does not want to take the time to

explain it to me but she [does] anyways. It just takes longer [to elaborate] the meaning of it to me but it never [affects] our marriage."

Another respondent noticed language issues impacted how the couple communicated. She wrote a prime example of Philipsen's (1997) SCT:

> "We kept using the word 'maybe' with each other, not realizing it has a different inclination in each culture. Hearing maybe is more like 'no,' Deaf maybe is more like a 'yes.' We have stopped using it so much and it has helped with perceived expectations."

More language difficulties appeared to be physical in nature rather than actually understanding the language. Three respondents reported that language struggles happen when a spouse is trying to sign with one or no hands while holding a baby or other items at the same time.

Part C

Part C summarizes the demographics of the participants in the study, such as age of participants in the study, how long couples have been married, and if couples have seriously considered divorcing one another (see Table 7). Further questions were asked with regards to religious influences on individual marriages.

Response	Deaf/hearing Couples (percentage/count)	Deaf/Deaf Couples (percentage/count)
Average length of time married	6.26 years	12.12 years
Have considered divorce	25.6% (6 respondents)	25% (4 respondents)

Table 7. Results of the question regarding average length of time married, and percentage that had considered divorce

The data show that Deaf/Deaf marriages have lasted an average of 12.12 years so far while Deaf/hearing marriages have lasted 6.26 years. However, it is important to note that as a whole, the Deaf/hearing respondents were much younger with the majority in their early 20s and 30s than the Deaf/Deaf respondents with the majority in their 30s and 40s (details of this data may be viewed in Apendix F). As they are younger overall, the Deaf/hearing couples have not had the potential to be married for as long as their Deaf/Deaf counterparts. Were the data to be adjusted for the age difference, it would presumably show a much smaller difference in average years married.

Additionally when asked if they had ever seriously considered separation or divorce, both groups had 25% of couples responded that they had, suggesting that the rates of marriage strain are similar for Deaf/hearing couples and Deaf/Deaf couples.

One surprising fact about the majority (94.9% of Deaf/hearing couples and 88.2% of Deaf/Deaf couples) of those who participated in the survey stated that they share the same religion and religion is a large influence on their marriage. This information merits further study about where Deaf/hearing people tend to meet, socialize and how religion impacts the marriage. Does sharing the same religion help Deaf/hearing dyads communicate their relational and spiritual goals better? Further data regarding religion in marriage can be found in the appendix.

DISCUSSION

What communicative practices do spouses use to contribute to the longevity of Deaf/hearing marriages?

The theories discussed in this research (Expectancy Violations Theory and Speech Codes Theory) were chosen for the ability to explain cultural and language conflicts in interpersonal relationships. Burgoon (1988) uses expectancy as a model that "posits that people hold expectations about the nonverbal behaviors of others. Violations of these expectations are posited to trigger change" in relationships (Burgoon & Hale, 1988, p. 59). Philipsen's (1997) Speech Codes Theory revolves around interpersonal relationships and language founded in two or more cultures. "A speech code, then, is defined here as a system of socially constructed symbols and meanings, premises, and rules, pertaining to communicative conduct" (Philipsen, 1997, p. 126).

As a conclusion, EVT supports — and the research suggests — that both Deaf/hearing couples and Deaf/Deaf couples experience similar amount of cultural conflicts and work equally in their efforts to resolve issues. For both groups, EVT explains that violated expectations need to be communicated and addressed, or violations will have a negative impact on their marriage.

Also as a conclusion, SCT explains that variations in language both among Deaf/hearing couples and Deaf/Deaf couples can lead to conflicts. However, Deaf/hearing couples appear to be more aware of this potential for conflict as they ask for clarification more frequently and recognize language, rather than the spouse, as the source of conflict. Disregarding language is a warning sign to couples who are struggling, and need to resolve language confusions before it becomes an issue.

Both EVT and SCT explain how Deaf/Deaf couples struggle communicating effectively. Deaf individuals come from all walks of life, especially educationally and linguistically. Some Deaf people attended residential institutions where the exposure to Deaf culture (which includes the acquisition of ASL) is as important, if not more, as education. Other deaf people (like myself) attend oral schools, or are mainstreamed in a public setting and learn ASL later in life. These scenarios influence culture and language in Deaf/Deaf marriages. Because Deaf/Deaf dyads appear to share the same culture and language, it is easy to overlook and lack recognition of underlying cultural expectations and separate speech codes.

With regards to marriage, every marriage is tested, repeatedly. However different our backgrounds, whether deaf or hearing, educated or uneducated, signed or spoken, accepted or rejected, male or female, all of these factors play into how well we communicate in marriage. Bell (1883) suggested that deaf individuals are to be separated from one another for the prevention of passing down through heritage both a physical deafness via birth and cultural Deafhood via communities of people. He viewed this as a negative attribute to society. Fay (1898) argued that Deaf/Deaf marriages were more successful because of the communication factors including similar cultural backgrounds leading to greater overall happiness in marriage. However, data suggests that both Deaf/Deaf and Deaf/hearing couples rely heavily on cultural aspects (including language) of each respective spouse contributing to a longer lasting marriage.

The data also renders the idea that 90% of all Deaf/hearing marriages end in divorce inconclusive and opens the doors for the statistic to be refuted. Only 25.6% of the Deaf/hearing marriage respondents seriously entertained the thought of divorce, a far cry from the widely-held belief that 90% divorce. Of the 25.6%, only 3 individuals stated they were separated from their spouse, but are currently back together. This statistic shows that if Deaf/hearing couples are able to communicate their culture and show understanding of their spouse's language, they will have already planted seeds of nourishment for a lengthy and more successful marriage.

SUMMARIES AND CONCLUSION

The most important take-away from this research is knowing that communicative effort is required of both spouses in both Deaf/hearing marriages and Deaf/Deaf marriages to nurture longevity and overall happiness. It is required of both parties to effectively communicate their cultural and language differences. One respondent wrote of negative challenges in his Deaf/hearing marriage, "I have made the choice not to remember the conflict and prefer to remember and enjoy the good times." If couples are able to effectively communicate cultural norms and rules, in a way their spouse understands, then that alone will go a long way toward a happy, more than satisfied, and lengthy marriage.

EVT and SCT theory illuminate the central problems in marriage communication. These problems consist of cultural and language barriers that couples may or may not be in tune with, thus not fully able to resolve conflicts. The theories shed light on how couples exhibit a general need to comprehend one another more fully.

LIMITATIONS OF THE STUDY

There are weaknesses in this study. Several answers to the written questions could not be included in the study because the answers were subjective (either because the respondents did not answer the question in written English that is standard in the hearing community, or the researcher did not sign the question well enough in the ASL version of the question). The researcher was left to judge if a written response matched what the question that was asked.

Another weakness of the study is there was no definite average age of respondents in either Deaf/hearing or Deaf/Deaf study groups. Asking for specific ages rather than having participants select an age range would provide more clarity. This suggestion should be included in further research on marriage in the Deaf community. Along with the subjective age-range, the study provided a small sample size. Additionally, the question regarding the role of religion is unique. This sampling discovered that close to 90% of the couples stated they shared the same religion. Can and would this percentage be reduplicated if the study were to be re-administered by another researcher?

RECOMMENDATIONS FOR FURTHER STUDY

Further research may include studying the exact causes for Deaf/hearing couple divorce. Is it because they could not navigate cultural and language misunderstandings, thereby could not communicate culture, or understand language? Should further research include studying more subgroups such as hearing-hearing marriages and/or interpreter-hearing (non-signing) marriages? Further research on these suggestions is indeed needed because marriage in the deaf community is seldom researched and seldom understood.

Another area of future research needed is to highlight the communication gaps in Deaf/Deaf dyads. Why does the data suggest cultural and language conflict when the written responses say they do not experience conflicts in marriage?

Lastly, but not least, this research focused on dyads currently married. Further research should include individuals who have been in Deaf/hearing marriages and are now divorced, or married endogamously. This will provide insight to why the marriage ended. Was it cultural, language, or a combination of both?

CONCLUSIONS

Researching marriage in the Deaf community is admittedly in early stages; additionally, this data opens the door for many research avenues to be explored. The call now is to continue exploring marital relationships of all kinds within the Deaf-world. Expectancy Violations Theory explains that when Deaf/hearing couples recognize and avoid violating non-verbal cultural norms and rules, there will be less tension placed on the relationship. Speech Codes Theory explains that when Deaf/hearing couples understand the distinct nuances of each spouse's language, it is easier to communicate.

Data indeed suggests that Deaf/hearing couples reportedly communicate better than Deaf/Deaf couples. This statement is not placing Deaf/hearing couples on a pedestal, or to make claim that Deaf/hearing marriages are better than Deaf/Deaf marriages. This claim is only stating that Deaf/hearing couples seem to be quicker in recognizing that there are culture and language conflicts in their marriage, thus they are able to more quickly resolve any tension that may build. Most importantly, it is vital to choose your love, and love your choice, regardless of the personal storms that will inevitably arise in your marriage.

REFERENCES

Abberley, P. (1987). The concept of oppression and the development of a social theory of disability. *Disability, handicap & society*, 2(1). London, UK: Carfax Publishing Company. 5–19.

Allen, B.J. (2011). *Difference matters: Communicating social identity (2nd ed.)*. Long Grove, IL: Waveland Press.

Baker-Shenk, C. L., & Cokely, D. (1980). *American sign language: A teacher's resource text on grammar and culture*. Silver Spring, MD: T.J. Publishers.

Bell, A.G. (1883, November). *Memoir upon the formation of a deaf variety of the human race*. Paper presented at the National Academy of Sciences, New Haven, Conn.

Burgoon, J.K., & Hale, J.L. (1988). Nonverbal expectancy violations: Model elaboration and application to immediacy behaviors. *Communication Monographs*, 55(1), 58–79. New York: Taylor & Francis.

Erting, C. (1978). Language policy & deaf ethnicity in the United States. *Sign Language Studies*, 19(1). University Park, IL: TJ Publishers. 139–152.

Fay, E.A. (1898). *Marriages of the deaf in America*. Washington, D.C.: Gibson Bros., Printers and Bookbinders.

Gallaudet University. (n.d.). The history behind dpn. Retrieved from, https://www.gallaudet.edu/dpn_home/issues/history_behind_dpn.html

Griffin, E. A. (2009). *A first look at communication theory (7th ed.)*. Boston: McGraw-Hill Higher Education.

Harris, J. (1995). *The cultural meaning of deafness*. Brookfield, VT: Avebury.

Hinckley, G. B. (1991, May). What God hath joined together. Ensign, 21(5), 74.

Hoza, J. (2007). *It's not what you sign, it's how you sign it*. Washington, D.C.: Gallaudet University Press.

Kingsbury, D.S. (2011). Marital quality and stability in Deaf/Deaf and Deaf/hearing couples. (unpublished thesis) St. Paul, MN: Bethel University.

Lane, H. (1984). *When the mind hears*. New York: Vintage Books.

Lane, H. (1993) Foreword. In M.S. Moore & L. Levitan *For hearing people only*. Rochester, NY: Deaf Life Press.

Lane, H., Hoffmeister, R., & Bahan, B. (1996). *A journey into the deaf-world*. San Diego, CA: DawnSignPress.

Lang, H. (2002). Do deaf people have a disability? *Sign Language Studies*, 2(4). University Park, IL: TJ Publishers. 356–379.

Liu, J., & Chang, Y. (2011). *Native message in nonnative form: Self mention as distinct speech codes in english language use in intercultural communication*. Conference papers: International communication association.

McIntosh, R.A. (1995). Self-disclosure in Deaf/hearing, deaf-deaf, and hearing-hearing married couples: A look at frequency, value, and contexts in relation to marital satisfaction (Doctoral dissertation). Retrieved from ProQuest, UMI Dissertation Publishing (9534883).

Mindess, A. (2006). *Reading between the signs* (2nd ed.). Boston: Intercultural Press.

Moore, M.S., & Levitan, L. (1993). *For hearing people only (2nd ed.)*. Rochester, NY: Deaf Life Press.

Morgan-Jones, R.A. (2001). H*earing differently: The impact of hearing impairment on family life*. Philadelphia, PA: Whurr Publishers.

Mosier, A.G. (1999). Marital quality in Deaf/Deaf and Deaf/hearing marriages. (unpublished thesis) Logan, UT: Utah State University.

Neuman, W.L. (2011). *Social research methods: Qualitative and quantitative approaches (7th ed.)*. NJ: Pearson Education.

Nomeland, M.M., & Nomeland, R.E. (2012). *The deaf community in America*. Jefferson, NC: McFarland & Company, Inc. Publishers.

Overstreet, S.V. (1999). Deaf-centered or hearing-centered: understanding deaf identity (unpublished dissertation) Provo, UT: Brigham Young University.

Padden, C., & Humphries, T. (1988). *Deaf in America: Voices from a culture*. Cambridge, MA: Harvard University Press.

Philipsen, G., & Albrecht, T.L. (1997) *Developing communication theories*. Albany, NY: State University of New York Press.

Powell, J.L., B.J. (1978). Mixed marriage ... it's not as simple as deaf and hearing. T*he deaf American*, 28(7). Washington, D.C., pp. 17–19.

Preston, P. (1998). *Mother father deaf: Living between sound and silence*. Cambridge, MA: Harvard University Press.

Rexroat, N. (1997). The colonization of the deaf community. *Social work perspectives* (Spring 1997). p. 19.

Rubin, R.B., Rubin, A.M., Haridakis, P.M., & Piele, L.J. (2010). *Communication research (7th Ed.)*. Boston, MA: Wadsworth.

Scoggins, B.B. (2010, April). NAD letter to Meriam-Webster [Letter to the editor]. NAD urges dictionaries to recognize "audism." Silver Spring, MD: National Association of the Deaf.

Solomon, A. (1994, August 28). Defiantly deaf. *The New York Times*.

Williams, L. (2010). *Global marriage*. New York, NY: Palgrave MacMillan.

Woodward, J. (1972). Implications for sociolinguistic research among the deaf. *Sign Language Studies*, 1(1). University Park, IL: TJ Publishers. 1–7.

Woodward, J. (1989). How are you gonna get to heaven if you can't talk with Jesus? The educational establishment vs. the deaf community. In S. Wilcox Editor, *American deaf culture* (pp. 163–172). Burtonsville, MD: Linstok Press.

Teaching the Cinematic Parallels of Visual Languages:

A Proposed Approach to Educating Second Language Learners in American Sign Language

SHAY TAYLOR AND BRIDGET KLEIN

THE LITERATURE AND RESEARCH ON SECOND LANGUAGE (L2) LEARNING is vast. The research on second learning in a second modality (M2L2, specifically, from spoken to signed language) is in comparison, very small. In the United States, the study of signed language acquisition is still young. The field is barely adolescent compared to research related to spoken language acquisition. Many of the conventions of sign language teaching and assumptions about sign language learning still rest within the framework of spoken language norms. Spoken language teaching methods have thus far provided the basis for teaching all second languages in schools across the country, both secondary and post-secondary.

With nearly twenty years of teaching ASL between the authors, we believe that for too long we have been using spoken language models and materials to teach ASL, while wondering why we get less than fluent results in a large percent of students. We propose that not only should we reevaluate the content and philosophies that have guided sign language teaching thus far, but we should build a new teaching model, that includes content and philosophy more connected to teaching a visual language. Specifically we recommend a cinematic approach to teaching ASL. The same spiraling skill development approach used to train photographers and videographers can be used in M2L2 classrooms to "train" signers to produce mechanically fluent and conceptually articulate ASL expressions.

Both ASL and videography depend on highly visual modalities. As such, it seems more than logical that parallels in use of space, movement, and visual depictions would exist between both. These particular features are at the heart of ASL, yet students are often weak in their use of space, role shifting, and classifiers. This proposed approach encourages visualization and use of cinematic theory to help students improve weak areas encourage students to be able to think in visualization with ASL.

THE BASIS

The goal of this paper is to consider whether alignment with the canonical models of spoken language instruction has truly benefited ASL second-language learners in the conceptual visualization needed for ASL fluency. If language is language is language, Spanish class for English speakers and ASL class for English speakers could successfully and effectively be taught the same way, producing the same levels of fluency and comprehension, yet we do not see this result in ASL classrooms.

THE CURRENT STATE OF ASL L2 LEARNERS

Ruth Ann Schornstein sees what many ASL teachers see and what few ASL students recognize: M2L2 learners often do not show the expected ability to produce expected language output as they advance through class levels:

> ...I relied on published texts and prepared curriculums. When I used traditional methods of teaching, my students were not realizing the level of success that I had hoped for. It was disheartening to see that their communication skills were still somewhat basic. There are actually many fine resources on the market. However, when I tried to follow certain very popular books and series, I found that my students were using them as "vocabulary books" and still following English word order. When I showed a videotaped literature series, my students copied the signs they saw, but their communication skills were not improving. At that point I realized it was time to reevaluate not only the course content but also the fundamental teaching philosophies that I had been following (Schornstein, 2015).

Schornstein saw what many of us see: adult learners hit a proverbial "block" in relation to certain aspects of sign language production. We have identified three conceptual areas in which ASL/Interpreting students tend to struggle: overuse of English syntax and structure on the phrasal level; conceptual accuracy and appropriate use of depiction; and difficulty in producing linguistically variant expressions, or the "one word, one sign" phenomenon. Each of these challenges is a result of a lack of "visuality" — the degree to which communication employs visual techniques to be effective. In this proposal, a shift in the way we approach teaching to use a more visually-based pedagogy (like film and video) could lend itself not only to an increased efficacy in visual reception and fluency, but also aid the necessary mental shift of both students and teachers to embrace a more visual mindset when teaching and learning this visual language.

Current curriculum for ASL I students is often based on simple dialogue, starting with greetings and small talk, expression of feelings and commentary on family, friends and pets. There are likely to also be introductions to Deaf culture, including instructions for getting attention of a Deaf or hard-of-hearing person, the brief history and relevance of Deaf clubs and/or Deaf residential schools, and some history about Thomas Hopkins Gallaudet and the development of American Sign Language. Programs for ASL III and above focus on role shifting, eye gaze, and constructed space and dialogue with various levels of emphasis on depiction and nonmanual grammar. Based on current practices in community colleges and universities, students will have been learning ASL for a full year before being introduced to core concepts of visuality so inherent to sign language.

When an ASL program begins with minimal visual aspects of the language, students begin developing a concept of ASL that is also minimally visual. Students may begin to build a mental representation, or *schema* of ASL having fairly equivalent monosemantic connections to English words. In an ASL III classroom, personal experience dictates that the teacher may spend a great deal of time encouraging students *not to* think in terms of English syntax and structure, but to be more visual in sign production and to include more depiction, yet we do not explicitly teach students depiction until ASL III or later. They have already formed the habit of connecting signs with English words, and will now have a harder time struggling to disconnect from English. This is often the cause of the overuse of English syntax. Students have already built a schema of ASL that incorporates into their existing schema for spoken language, causing a lack of key features required for producing a manual language.

To illustrate the concept of schema-building, imagine that a monolingual student's concept of language is like a bathroom in a house. Encountering sign language for the first time presents a cognitive challenge: it's a new appliance that the learner must decide where to place. Generally speaking, at this point in the cognitive process, a student presented with new information has two choices: 1) build a new schema for this new information or 2) attach this information to an existing schema. This is the equivalent of deciding to build an entirely new home for your one new appliance, or to do a little remodeling to fit it into an existing room. The path of least resistance tells us to attach what we've just learned to what we already know. This means a little remodeling instead of new construction.

This new appliance of ASL has features similar to those in an already existing schema (room) of spoken language but the chrome finish of ASL doesn't quite fit with the décor of the bathroom. Yet this is how we believe ASL has been taught for so many years. We suggest instead of trying to 'install' ASL into the spoken language bathroom, why not make room elsewhere, like in the visual kitchen? Teachers should connect ASL's visual constructs and elements with those that students may already understand from their years or exposure to photographs, commercials, and movies.

Creating a place for ASL in the visual schema should start from day one of ASL class. Lack of visual schema building to facilitate full and appropriate use of visual based language actually hinders good expressiveness and understanding of depiction in ASL. When instructors use English to teach ASL, students often associate *one* ASL sign to *one* English word. This becomes problematic when students use the same sign to express conceptually different versions of the English word.

For example, there are three different meanings of 'across' following the meaning from the Oxford English Dictionary. The first meaning is *the movement over a place*, as in "The dog ran *across* the field." 'Across' can also be a position or orientation. For example, "Bob lives *across* the street from Sue." Another listed meaning for 'across' is measurement as in "The lilac bush will grow to be ten feet *across*." Here, the word 'across' has three different meanings depending on the sentence and context. So the sentence, "The tree is across the road" could have two different meanings: 'I see the tree over there' (on the other side of the road) or 'the tree fell down' (over the width of the road). In a signed conversation, the difference in meaning of ACROSS is inherent *based on the sign* (see Figures 1 and 2).

Figure 1. ACROSS ('on the other side')   Figure 2. ACROSS ('over the width of the road')

The *visual depiction* of a tree across the road would be the blending of hand and arm as TREE (Figure 3). The statement focuses on the tree on the ground, so the hand representing TREE would be down on the other arm, which is visually representing the road (Figure 4).

Teaching the Cinematic Parallels of Visual Languages

Figure 3. TREE

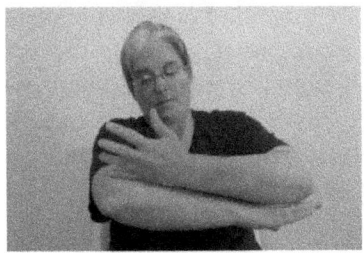

Figure 4. TREE-lying-down-across/on-road ("The tree is lying across the road.")

For the other sample sentence, "The tree is across the road," the signer needs to use conceptual accuracy to represent the specific meaning of 'across.' For this sentence, Figure 5 depicts the idea that the tree is located 'over there, and I see it.' The goal is to have visual clarity with ASL by using blending for the best understanding of the sentence and of the idea that the tree is across from the signer without relying on English comprehension. Maximizing the depiction in ASL leads to conceptual accuracy, clearer expression that is visual and uses space and blending. More visual depiction helps make sense of the message; leading to better reception of the intended message, which boosts confidence in language learners.

Figure 5. TREE, I SEE ("The tree is located over there [across the road] and I see it.")

In the visual language of ASL, a signer uses horizontal and vertical space to create a three-dimensional message, whereas spoken English does not. Thumann's research on depiction in ASL presentation found that ASL presenters used on average twenty depictions per minute. The second language student tended to gloss individual words rather than interpret the meaning within the context of the message (Thumann, 2010). Another issue discussed by Thumann (citing Gish, 1987) is that the M2L2 student often focuses on single words rather than on the context of the message. Gish encouraged students to focus on the larger context and understanding the meaning of the message rather than single words.

Another challenge that second language students have a hard time with is being able to modify depicting verbs. One common example is of a student thinking about a car and matching one classifier (CL:3) to the concept of "car." Cars however have different shapes and sizes, so the student needs the ability to modify the classifier to match the car's shape and size. Students with limited visualization have difficulty in linguistic conceptual variations of a car (Figure 6). This is an example of using visual schema to figure out how different kinds of depicting verbs could match with the visual characteristics of the object.

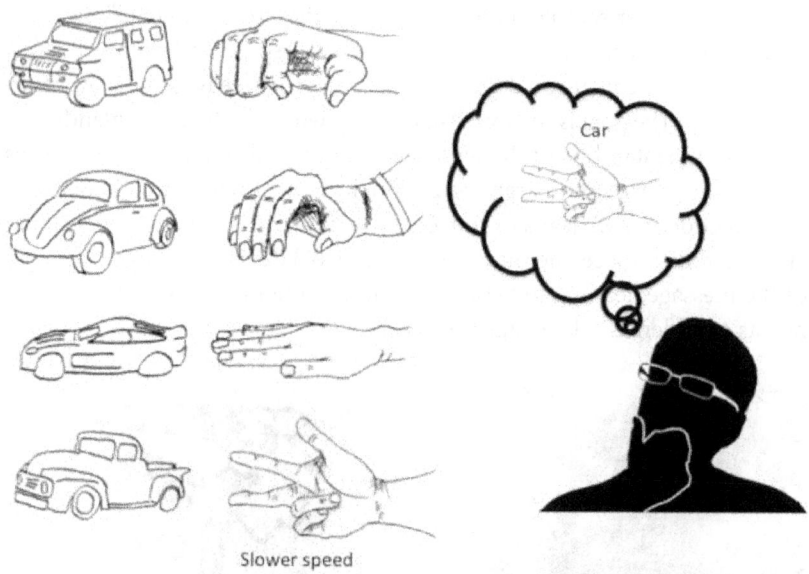

Figure 6. Various types of cars and difficulty in linguistic conceptual variation

When students do not learn how to recognize depiction, they miss critical information about who is doing what (Thumann, 2010, p. 17). Thumann referred to Taylor's work saying that students could be overlooking small and subtle aspects of a signer's communication, such as "direction of the signer's eye gaze, orientation of torso and head, characterization, pointing, change in style of signing, the body itself," all of which may change the meaning based on the referent (Thumann, 2010; Taylor, 2002). When students gloss ASL, they often miss visual aspects of the signs that would lead to missing important information (Thumann, 2010). So the idea of using video to create visualization would help students be able to recognize how to do depiction better.

THE PROPOSAL

Teaching ASL cinematics requires an understanding of both the basics of cinematic theory and video production as well as the cinematic features of ASL. It is beyond the scope of this paper to provide the foundation for production knowledge, but it is our intent to describe how the knowledge of video production can be a hugely beneficial tool for teaching ASL.

Beginning concepts: eliminating "HI MY NAME"

After a full semester of ASL I, most students have a significant list of vocabulary words, can effectively engage in sharing personal information, and can fingerspell with sufficient accuracy, but typically cannot demonstrate effective use of space in narrative, incorporate eye gaze or non-manuals only sporadically, if at all, and are likely to have difficulty encoding or decoding depiction in ASL production or reception. From our perspective, the core "production values" of ASL can and should be taught up front, and then built upon in each successive level of ASL, so that a student of ASL level I produces signs which incorporate, if only at a basic level, all the key elements of an ASL expression.

Students of videography learn that all videos are made up of a series of shots. A well composed shot is a skilled layering of attention to focus, lighting, depth, background, and framing, all coming together for a specific thematic (expressive) goal. The beginning videography student can create a shot that comprises these elements, even at the most basic level. If you ask a videography or photography teacher to teach how to compose the most basic shot, they would be remiss to *not* include these five elements. Even the intermediate and advanced film student is still learning about the core elements, but at a deeper, more advanced level, perhaps studying theory of, or the history behind one or more of these core elements.

To approach teaching ASL like we teach video, it is necessary to first identify the core requisite elements of fluent sign production and make them the building blocks to developing strong ASL skills. We propose that ASL, like video, has core elements inherent in every sign expression. Size, shape, movement, relationship, and reaction are the core aspects of a sign expression that could be taught from day one of a student's first ASL I course, and expanded throughout the levels.

If given a prompt expression GIRL BOY MEET, the ASL I student should be able to produce these signs, but also incorporate classifiers (size and shape) that depict the relative location (relationship) of each participant, the iconic action of meeting (movement) and can add information that may incorporate the reaction aspect. An ASL III or IV level student should be able to depict significantly more detail about this same situation, but at its base is still GIRL BOY MEET. Consider the ASL I rendering a standard definition video of the meeting, and the ASL III or IV level a High Definition (HD) version of the same scene. This is what ASL teaching could produce with the influence of video production.

Mapping video production concepts to ASL thinking and expression
Various film shots could also give ideas about constructed dialogue. For example, a wide shot can provide mapping of the location, while close up allows the viewers to see reactions and to capture the feelings of the person in the film. Applying this to ASL, students could learn how to setting up their signing space first by explaining the mapping of the space then explaining what happens within that space.

In film, another important aspect is point of view (POV), which hones in on first, second, and third person narrative. In writing, the first person point of view means using 'I' and 'me.' For example, a person might explain about his or her day from *his* or *her* POV. However, in film, first-person POV focuses on the camcorder as the eye. In writing, second-person POV is about the narrator ('you'). From the *reader's* POV, this often happens when given instructions on how to bake cookies. In film, second-person POV would be interacting with the camera. For example, in "Malcolm in the Middle," Malcolm talks directly to the camera. Third-person POV, in writing uses 'she,' 'he,' 'it,' and 'they.' For film, when the camcorder records the action taking place in the room, the camcorder does not become involved in the action, but functions neutrally like a wall.

Point of view applies to ASL in the form of surrogates, which means taking someone else's role in the signing space. Figures 7 and 8 demonstrate for the same message (SAY-NO-TO), but in second (YOU-SAY-NO-TO-ME) and third person (SHE-SAY-NO-TO-HE) point of view. An example in spoken/

written English might be "My mother told me 'no'" (second-person point of view), and "My mother told my father 'no'" (third-person point of view). More research is still needed on first person point of view in ASL.

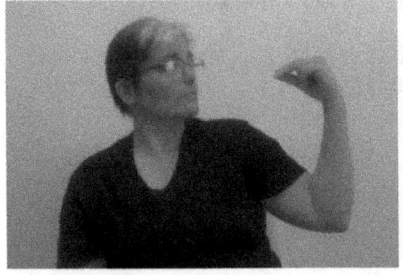

Figure 7. YOU-SAY-NO-TO-ME (second-person point of view)

Figure 8. SHE-SAY-NO-TO-HE (third-person point of view)

Visualization begins by considering a mental map. Pre-production follows, involving the development of a visual and personality of an actor, developing where the story happens, and then finally developing the visual aspects of the story. These things need to be thought through before starting to tell the story, a process much like preparing to make a movie.

By using the structures of film and video production, teachers of ASL have the chance to maximize the visual potential of ASL. We believe sign language teaching should take advantage of the parallels between ASL and video production, and aim to produce signers that can incorporate the cinematic features of American Sign Language at every level of learning.

REFERENCES

Across. (2014). http://www.oxforddictionaries.com.
Czubek, T. A. (2006). Blue Listerine, Parochialism, and ASL Literacy. *Journal of Deaf Studies and Deaf Education,* 11(3), 373–381.
Estaris, J. (2013) Cars. Illustrator Markers on paper. Washington, D.C..
Gish, S. (1987) I Understood All The Words, But I Missed The Point: A Goal-To-Detail/Detail-To-Goal Strategy For Text Analysis. In M. McIntire (Ed.) *New Dimensions In Interpreter Education: Curriculum And Instruction. Proceedings of the Sixth National Convention of the Conference of Interpreter Trainers.* Sliver Spring, Maryland: RID Publications, pp. 125–137.
Jkvetchy. (2013, September 28). Pedigree Dogs ad shot 1000 FPS using the Phantom Camera [Video file]. https://www.youtube.com/watch?v=mUCRZzhbHH0
Newsall. (2013, September 10). Owner Throws Treats To Dogs But One of Them Can't Seem To Catch [Video file]. https://www.youtube.com/watch?v=HpAkaZpbC5c
Openclipart. (2014, June 1). The collection of clip art imags are free content [Video file]. http://openclipart.org.

Schornstein, R. A. (2005). Teaching ASL in the University: One Teacher's Journey. *Sign Language Studies* 5(4), 398–414. Gallaudet University Press.

Taylor, M. (2002). *Interpretation Skills: American Sign Language to English*. Edmonton, Alberta: Interpreting Consolidated.

Thumann, M. A. (2010). Identifying depiction in American Sign Language presentations (Doctoral dissertation). Retrieved from Dissertations and Theses (ProQuest). (UMI Number: 3425466).

Valli, C., and Lucas, C., Mulrooney K. J., & Villanueva M. (2011). *Linguistics of American Sign Language*. Washington, DC: Gallaudet University Press.

What is the Motivation for Deaf Children to Learn English as Their Second Language?

DANIEL GOUGH, ED.D. AND
DAMARA GOFF PARIS, ED.D, CRC, NCC

RESEARCH INDICATES THAT DEAF INDIVIDUALS GENERALLY HAVE limited vocabulary acquisition (Andrews, 2012; Cannon & Guardino, 2012; Cannon, Fredrick, & Easterbrooks, 2010; Gough, 2014; Holt, 1994; Musselman, 1999; Paul, 1996). In addition, Deaf students' understanding of grammatical rules is often delayed as a result of their struggle to understand English structures (Bailes, Erting, Erting, & Thumann-Prezioso, 2009). Simms & Thumann (2007) stated that as a consequence of this struggle, Deaf students fail to achieve appropriate grade levels in literacy and that "The 'failure' of deaf education has been demonstrated through studies that have reported low levels of achievement in reading" (p. 303).

Motivation is one of the main factors of second language learning achievement (Dornyei, 1994). Motivation is recognized as a very common concept that encourages individuals to start or take action in a variety of situations. According to Koiso (2003), "Motivation is considered to be one of the main determining factors of success in developing a second or foreign language" (p. 96). Motivation will help students to find a reason to learn second language effectively.

Herzig (2009) noted that Deaf students became frustrated while struggling to learn English and as a result, their motivation declined. She further emphasized that and motivation was the essence of literacy, which in turn is essential for children. It is important that educators understand how Deaf students become motivated towards learning English as a second language in order to improve strategies for literacy programs within Deaf education. As a result, they will be able to use the proper incentives in encouraging Deaf students and their motivation levels for learning English as it will solidify their productive participation and engagement in education.

LITERATURE REVIEW

There appear to be few studies about Deaf children's motivation or attitude toward English as a second language, including a dissertation on the motivation of Deaf Latinos and second language acquisition (Herzig, 2009). According to Simms and Thumann (2007), "...research has shown that greater mastery of ASL in students is positively correlated with greater English proficiency" (p. 304). Their study showed a correlation between ASL and English; a student who is fluent in ASL will often achieve fluency in English. The same is also true for those who demonstrate a lack of proficiency in ASL; they often have limited fluency in English as well. It was alluded that motivation might be a factor in improving students' English and ASL skills (Simms & Thumann, 2007), and has been shown to be an important factor towards improving the English literacy skills of Deaf children (Tuner & Paris, 1995). Motivation plays an important role in the rate and success of second and foreign language learning in general, and in classroom language learning in particular (Dornyei & Ushioda, 2012; Gardner, 2006; Kaboody, 2013). Such motivation may have a major role in educational settings, as it promotes the success of second language acquisition, as it will contribute Deaf children's emerging bilingualism to have enhanced early learning.

Motivation in general plays a significant role in the learning process of any task. For Deaf children, learning English as a second language is an important issue that has not been well understood in Deaf education; it continues to evolve as Deaf education researchers try to find effective approaches. Even today, bilingualism is a popular approach in the Deaf education field (Humphries & Allen, 2008). While the desire to learn a second language is unique for each individual, motivation is recognized as playing a critical role in the acquisition of a second language (James, 2012). An individual needs to put in the effort to achieve a goal in order to satisfy the target community's communication needs.

For example, a person needs to put effort into learning Spanish that they can communicate with the Spanish-speaking community effectively. Studies show that the combination of effort and experience, along with a positive attitude, helps one achieve second language learning (James, 2012). Tremblay and Gardner (1995) stated, "An individual who expends effort at L2 learning without any desire to do so, or an individual who desires learning an L2 but makes no effort, can't be described as truly motivated" (p. 51).

Motivation is a factor in retaining information; an individual learning a second language needs motivation to successfully retain new information particularly a second language (Ryan & Dörnyei, 2013). L2 transmission motivation is a combination of effort, desire, and attitude that determines whether an individual will successfully apply L2 information from one context to another context (James, 2012). These three factors are essential for the successful transfer of information from one language to another.

Teachers might increase the motivation of literacy through critical explorations of texts. Deaf educators need to integrate ASL into Deaf students' reading courses as the primary language of instruction before they can start teaching students English because Deaf children have often not yet developed a primary language. Bailes, Erting, Erting, and Thumann-Prezioso (2009) expressed concern that deaf children are losing traction with language acquisition because they are not exposed to a fully accessible language. Many children who are Deaf find literacy challenging and leave formal education without having achieved a level of literacy that prepares them for the demands of a literate society (Harris & Marschark, 2011).

It is crucial to recognize the many factors affecting success, such as individual differences in children's cognitive abilities, their lived experiences at school and home, and their hearing levels, all important factors to language acquisition. Yet another critical factor is the type of educational settings that the Deaf children are in; increasing intrinsic motivation for literacy includes teachers using student's interest to encourage the development of long-term interest in literacy (Guthrie, Wigfield, Humenick, Perencevich, Taboada, & Barbosa, 2006).

When teachers in Deaf education have students who struggle with motivation, those students are likely to have difficulty in learning English as a second language (Harris & Marschark, 2011). A person with low motivation tends to experience negative external factors related to the learning environment such as the classroom and school (Dornyei, 2001). The most potent demotivating factors for all the age groups are related to the learning situations such as materials, the teacher(s), and teaching methods, which have a great impact on language acquisition and achievement (Nikolov, 1999).

Being an English-language learner (ELL) is already a challenging process for those learning to read. For students under pressure to acquire language and reading skills simultaneously, drumming up motivation to read in English can be a daily challenge (Peregoy & Boyle, 2000). Even when ELLs gain proficiency in the target language, it can still be difficult to find the motivation to continue reading in English for anything other than a grade or to complete an assignment (Robinson, 2010).

Gardner (1985), a researcher who studies motivation, stated that motivation is often referred to as the "combination of effort plus desire to achieve the goal of learning the language plus favorable attitudes toward learning the language" (p. 21). According to James (2012), motivation plays a critical role in learning a second language. Some individuals need to put in the effort to satisfy the target of the community's language while other individuals need to succeed at certain levels in order to satisfy personal or professional goals. Both educational and cultural variables should be considered when attempting to understand the process by which a second language is learned; the role of classroom dynamics and the learning environment are important in motivating students to improve their second language acquisition (SLA) in a formal context (Dornyei, & Ushioda 2009; Far, Rajab, & Etemadzadeh, 2012; Gardner, 1985, 2006; MacIntyre, Noels, & Moore 2010).

Students with English deficiencies often show improvement in their English skills through motivation (Gardner, 1985, 2006). Additionally, the aforementioned researchers encouraged the continuation of investigating the relationship between increased motivation and language achievement of individual students in the classroom (Gardner, 1985, 2006).

In documentation of the success of ASL/English bilingual techniques, Deaf education researchers have often underemphasized English instruction in favor of ASL instruction; traditional pedagogy in Deaf education has not focused on the role of motivation in the teaching of reading (Joong-O & Minjeong, 2011). For instance, classroom practices frequently overemphasize the use of ASL-only techniques for social discourse in Basic Interpersonal Communication Skills (BICS) and English-only techniques for written academic discourse in Cognitive Academic Language Proficiency (CALP) (Delana, Gentry, & Andrews, 2007). Yet many teachers underutilize ASL for academic discourse in CALP as well as written English for social discourse in BICS; this unbalanced model appears to hinder Deaf students' ability to learn ASL and English because they do not get the added experiences in English exposure and instruction within the context of ASL (Delana, Gentry, & Andrews, 2007).

In addition, many Deaf students do not seem to "own" both languages, and tend to view ASL as their primary language even though they may use both languages in their everyday lives and will continue to do so through adulthood (Grosjean, 2001). However, these students still need to learn English as a second language, an essential part of their life. According to Delana et al. (2007), "…39.5% of students are exposed to 'speech and sign' and 11.2% to 'sign only'; readers must guesstimate the amount of ASL usage among the remaining 50.7% of deaf students using some type of manual system" (p. 76).

THEORETICAL FRAMEWORK

The theories of motivational formation proposed by Robert Gardner (1985) were used in this study to assess the motivation of Deaf individuals who learned English as a second language. Gardner's two motivation theories are instrumental and integrative (Far, Rajab, & Etemadzadeh, 2012). Instrumental motivation refers to individuals who have a desire to please peers, family, and teachers. This includes an individual's experience with having a demanding teacher or difficult examinations and the influence of these factors towards motivation to learn the language.

Integrative motivation refers to individuals' favorable attitude towards the target language of the community. This includes an individual's wish to integrate and adapt to a new target culture through use of the language. The researcher used Gardner's theories to guide the study while assessing Deaf individuals' SLA motivation, and to determine whether instrumental or integrative motivation influenced these individuals to learn English as a second language.

PURPOSE OF THE STUDY

The purpose of this study was to explore Deaf participants' motivation in learning English as a second language. The intent of the study was to gather research that would potentially foster better understanding of second language motivation from a Deaf education perspective. The research questions for this study were: What motivates Deaf participants to learn English as a second language in academic and non-academic environments? What barriers are encountered regarding Deaf participants' motivation in learning English as a second language? How did Deaf participants overcome barriers learning English as a second language?

METHODOLOGY

A modified version of a subtest of the Attitude Motivation Test Battery (AMTB) was the instrument for conducting questionnaires to determine a range of low, medium and highly motivated ELLs. The AMTB was developed to assess the major affective components shown to be involved in second language learning (Gardner, 1985). The AMTB has been used in France, Canada, Belize, Finland, Philippines, and the United States with elementary to high school students. Major applications involved the correlations of sub-tests and test scores of language achievement and behavior intention to continue language study, attitudinal/motivational characteristics, and the relation of attitudes and motivation to classroom behavior. The modified test contained 20 questions customized to Deaf college students and their education backgrounds to find how they became Deaf and their primary and secondary languages.

Thirty-two participants were willing to be survey respondents. However, after reviewing the demographic responses given by the participants, it was determined that 10 did not meet the criteria for the study because they were not first-year college students or had other factors that precluded them. After the respondents participated in the questionnaire using pencil and paper formation, their data were gathered into three score-based categories: low, moderately and highly motivated. Participants who scored under 5.05 were considered low-motivated in learning English as a second language. Participants whose scores ranged from 5.06 to 5.24 were considered moderate in their English language motivation. Respondents whose scores were above 5.25 were perceived as highly motivated to learn English. There were ten participants in the low motivated category, five participants were moderately motivated, and seven who were highly motivated.

The second phase of the study employed a qualitative phenomenological approach through narrative inquiry, allowing participants to express the ways they experience things. The phenomenological approach focuses on participants' subjective perspectives while refraining from interpretative viewpoints (Creswell, 2007). In addition, the phenomenological approach focuses on a small population, so the data gained from interviews is as authentic as possible without the influence of the researcher. Neutrality in the data increases validity of the data (Wilder, Mackie, & Cooper, 1985).

Narrative inquiry is appealing to the teaching field, since it involves the participants' reflections on their lived experiences, their interest and how they are lived (Clandinin & Connelly, 2000).

DATA ANALYSIS

Through this analysis, seventeen themes were found to contribute to participants' motivation in learning English in all three categories. Out of these seventeen themes, seven were common across all nine participants. The remaining ten themes held commonalities within each motivation group, with four themes in the low motivation group, three themes in the moderate motivated group, and three in the high motivation group. The themes discussed in this article focus on seven themes across all nine participants.

All nine participants self-identified as Deaf, had ASL as their primary language, were first-year undergraduate students, and ranged in age from eighteen to the mid-twenties. Four were from California, Alaska, and Michigan, four participants were from Texas, and one was from Mexico, and had become an U.S. citizen when he moved to Texas. Of all nine, only one had attended a residential school for the Deaf for the entirety of his/her K-12 education. Five participants attended mainstream programs, and then transferred to a school for the Deaf later. One attended a mainstream program first then transferred to a residential school for the Deaf briefly before returning to the mainstreamed setting. Two of the nine participants attended mainstream programs only.

There were some commonalities among all of the three groups, creating seven themes. The first research question investigated what motivated Deaf participants to learn English as a second language in academic and non-academic environments. The responses to the first research question had three themes: The impact of teacher-student relationships, the influence of parents on motivation, and community interactions. Teachers were willing to sit down with participants to provide extra help in learning English. For example, one of the participant's teachers at California School for Deaf in Fremont (CSDF) encouraged him to learn English, and provided explanations, such as being able to communicate with his hearing parents, friends and other people. He also credited his English teacher, who developed visual aids for the participant.

This encouragement also emerged as a key factor in other participants' responses. According to Skinner and Belmont (1993), teachers should have a wide array of student-teacher interactions including guidance, modeling, enthusiasm, praise, positive reinforcement, and interest induction. Most of the participants mentioned that their family members were role models who gave great support. For example, one individual's mother tried to find a way to increase his English language experiences in the home in addition to school. She interpreted the spoken words of cartoons into ASL, ensuring that they were also closed-captioned.

The second research question investigated what barriers were encountered in Deaf participants' motivation in learning English as a second language. The responses had two emergent themes: a lack of accessibility creating hardships, and the impact of community interaction on self-confidence. Participants experienced hardships in the community and realized that if they wanted to prevent such hardships, they had to learn English. One participant stated,

> "Dentists and doctors motivated me to learn more vocabulary because they wrote down complicated, tough words and I could not comprehend what they were trying to say; I realized that I needed to learn more vocabulary to increase my English skills."

Other participants reported similar desires to learn English in order to minimize misunderstandings. Communities can promote positive reinforcement and interventions (Rutherford & Billig, 1995), such as inspiring the participants to learn English. An example is found in the experience one participant had when he tried to communicate with a mechanic about his car problem. After the mechanic was not able to understand his written English, the participant gave up and resorted to gestures, which worked. He reported that this made him feel inferior, but that he often tried to find solutions.

There often is a gap between what students bring to the community and what the community expects of them (Razfar & Simon, 2011; Spack, 1988). Lessons often were brief, restricting the participants' opportunity to retain new content when the interpreter was absent. Many considered this experience negative, but they tried to make the best out of it. For example, one participant stated:

> "When the ASL interpreter was sick, there was no substitute interpreter, and the teacher did not adjust [lectures] for me. The lessons just continued. I just sat and did nothing. I wanted to learn but I could not follow teacher's instructions."

Learning English is difficult for Deaf children because they often use other ASL as their primary language and therefore may not understand English structure or grammar (Foster, Long, & Snell, 1999). Participants cited communication struggles with people in the general, non-signing community, such as mechanics, dentists, doctors, and other service professionals.

The final research question investigated how Deaf participants overcame barriers to learning English as a second language. The responses to this question had two themes: 1) visual aids were imperative to increased learning, and 2) persistent community interaction fostered learning. One strategy participants adopted to overcome barriers was to ask teachers to repeat or clarify the lesson, or use visual aids such as charts or posters that had pictures with captions.

They understood that their English was not sufficient, so they created solutions. One participant thought he was proficient in English until an assignment he had difficulty with made him realize that his English skills needed work. The importance and usefulness of using visual learning aids in the classroom setting supports lesson text and learning tools for students (Dolati, & Richards, 2011).

One participant stated he benefitted from visual aids, which helped him understand words. Another participant credited ASL-fluent teachers who provided English support. She stated, "I requested visual aids from my teachers and they were willing to create aids, which really helped me a lot…"

Visual graphics aids contain important information for extended understanding (Wood, Stover, Pilonieta, & Taylor, 2012).

In the community, the participants were persistent in asking people to repeat themselves or to rephrase their comments. Many also said they resorted to gestures, but when that failed, they discontinued the conversations and asked to reschedule in order to bring in an ASL interpreter. English as a second language learners have high levels of persistence and use support resources or services (McElroy, 2007). This was indeed true for almost all the participants.

CONCLUSIONS

This study reviewed the lived experience of nine Deaf participants' motivation towards learning English as a second language. The range of educational backgrounds, communication modes, geographical locations, and the point at which they became Deaf were all distinct. This is representative of the diversity found in American Deaf communities. Deaf people are cultural people and have their own lived experiences influenced by a variety of community members (Humphries, 2013).

Through this analysis, common themes were connected to the theoretical framework based on Gardner's Integrative and Instrumental Motivation theories. As mentioned, integrative motivation is like intrinsic motivation; instrumental motivation is like extrinsic motivation (Gardner, 2006). Intrinsic motivation is when a person performs to experience pleasure or to satisfy one's curiosity; external motivation includes outside rewards that a person performs in order to receive, such as good grades, awards, or promotions (Ryan & Deci, 2000).

There were three major conclusions that arose from the findings. First, all groups demonstrated a clear desire to learn English as a second language. In particular, the moderate motivated group demonstrated expressed the most desire to learn second language. They were eager to learn English by reading books in their own time. They wanted to understand English better as they struggled with morphology and semantics; they demonstrated their persistency through verbalizations of their determination to better communicate with primary English users.

Second, providing support to ASL learners of English is supremely important; the impact of support increases motivation. This is where Gardner's theories of motivation seemed most evident. There existed a strong tendency among all participants towards integrative motivation, while instrumental motivation had a much weaker presence. All participants exhibited intrinsic motivation, such as being motivated by teachers, peers, parents, and the community. The characteristics of intrinsic motivation can be seen in a person being motivated to learn the target community's language. The research participants realized that they needed to learn English as a second language because it was the primary language of the community at large. The reasons were varied for each participant; for example, some participants felt motivated to learn English because they became employed and realized that English was the only way to communicate with coworkers. Yet another factor was experiencing communication barriers with doctors while struggling with medical jargon or even basic words. Some participants were motivated when their friends helped them or communicated with them using English.

Finally, participants demonstrated that their motivation was influenced by external factors and that it was important for them to feel connected to the community. In particular, that the community has a responsibility to empower the groups. As primary English users, reaching out, supporting and patiently demonstrating the correct usage of the language made the participants feel as though their efforts to fit in with the community at large were welcomed.

Understanding the participants' motivation helps professionals and researchers in the educational field design appropriate approaches or programs to work for individual students. Based on the interviews with nine Deaf and ASL users in various stages of motivation to learn English as a second language, there appears to be a strong relationship between Gardner's theories of intrinsic motivation and extrinsic motivation (Gardner, 2006).

Those who were highly motivated demonstrated that teachers who had a strong background in ASL, and invested extra time in teaching English through bilingual methods influenced their interest in English as a second language. In particular, parents who worked with their children in the homes to come up with innovative ways to increase English language literacy (especially parents who would sign stories or use captioning while "interpreting" cartoons) increased motivation in their children for English language learning.

It is vital that these external motivators work together to create a safe environment to nurture a child's desire to succeed in the second language acquisition of English. Teachers may want to set up a reward system that encourages Deaf children to complete clear, visual and obtainable language acquisition goals (Dornyei, 1994). It may start at the pre-kindergarten level so that it would strengthen school readiness of young emergent Deaf bilinguals. Also, this may include introducing students to the community made up largely of English language users at early age, and emphasize the importance of learning English so they can communicate with their family, friends, and the community. With the exposure to the community, increased visual aids, and parental involvement in the school may bring a Deaf child to be whole bilingual person.

REFERENCES

Andrews, J. F. (2012). Reading to deaf children who sign: A response to Williams (2012) and suggestions for future research. *American Annals of the Deaf*, 157(3), 307–319.

Applegate, A. J., & Applegate, M. (2010). A study of thoughtful literacy and the motivation to read. *Reading Teacher*, 64(4), 226–234.

Bailes, C., Erting, C. J., Erting, L. C., & Thumann-Prezioso, C. (2009). Language and literacy acquisition through parental mediation in American Sign Language. *Sign Language Studies*, 9(4), 417–456.

Cannon, J.E., & Guardino, C. (2012). Literacy strategies for deaf/hard-of-hearing English language learners (DHH ELLs): Where do we begin? *Deafness and Education International*, 1–22. doi: 10.1179/1557069X12Y.0000000006

Cannon, J.E., Fredrick, L.D., & Easterbrooks, S.R. (2010). Vocabulary acquisition through books in American Sign Language. *Communication Disorders Quarterly*, 31, 98–112. doi:10.1177/1525740109332832

Clandinin, D. J. (2007). *Handbook of narrative inquiry: Mapping a methodology*. Thousand Oaks, CA: Sage Publications, Inc.

Connelly, L. M. (2010). What is phenomenology? MedSurg Nursing. Retrieved from http://www.highbeam.com/doc/1G1-224932156.html

Creswell, J. W. (2007). *Qualitative inquiry and research design: Choosing among five approaches*. Thousand Oaks, CA: Sage Publications.

Delana, M., Gentry, M., & Andrews, J. (2007). The efficacy of ASL/English bilingual education: Considering public schools. *American Annals of the Deaf*, 152(1), 73–87.

Dolati, R., & Richards, C. (2011). Harnessing the use of visual learning aids in the English language classroom. *Arab World English Journal*, 2(1), 3–17.

Dörnyei, Z. (1990). Conceptualizing motivation in foreign language learning. *Language Learning*, 40(1), 45–78.

Dörnyei, Z. (1994). Motivation and motivating in the foreign language classroom. *Modern Language*, 78, 273–284.

Dörnyei, Z. (2001). *Teaching and researching motivation*. Harlow, England: Longman.

Dörnyei, Z., & Ushioda, E. (2009). *Motivation, language identity and the L2 self*. Bristol, UK: Multilingual Matters.

Dörnyei, Z., & Ushioda, E. (2012). Teaching and researching: Motivation. *Pearson Education Limited*, 16(2) 315–325.

Far, H., Rajab, A., & Etemadzadeh, A. (2012). Examining the relationship between L2 motivational self system and L2-learning among TESL students. *US-China Foreign Language*, 10(6), 1266–1270.

Foster, S., Long, G., & Snell, K. (1999). Inclusive instruction and learning for deaf students in postsecondary education. *Journal of Deaf Studies and Deaf Education*, 4(3), 225–235.

Gardner, R. C. (1985). *Social psychology and second language learning: The role of attitudes and motivation*. London, England: Edward Arnold.

Gardner, R. C. (2006). *The socio-educational model of second language acquisition: A research paradigm*. Amsterdam, The Netherlands: John Benjamins Publishing Company, 6237-260.

Gardner, R., & Lambert, W. (1972). *Attitudes and motivation in second language learning*. Rowley, MA: Newbury House Publishers.

Grosjean, F. (2001). The right of the deaf child to grow up bilingual. *Sign Language Studies*, 1(2), 110–14.

Harris, M., & Marschark, M. (2011). Literacy in the classroom and beyond. *Journal of Deaf Studies and Deaf Education*, 16(1), 1. https://doi.org/10.1093/deafed/enq047.

Herzig, M. P. (2009). Understanding the motivation of deaf adolescent Latino struggling readers. (Order No. 3365865, University of California, San Diego). ProQuest Dissertations and Theses, 141. Retrieved from http://search.proquest.com/docview/304853766?accountid=7043. (prod.academic_MSTAR_304853766)

Humphries, T. (2013). Schooling in American Sign Language: A paradigm shift from a deficit model to a bilingual model in deaf education. *Berkeley Review of Education*, 4 (1), 7–33.

Humphries, T., & Allen, B. M. (2008). Reorganizing teacher preparation in deaf education. *Sign Language Studies*, 8(2), 160–180.

James, M. (2012). An investigation of motivation to transfer second language learning. *Modern Language Journal*, 96(1), 51–69.

Joong-O Y., & Minjeong, K. (2011). The effects of captions on deaf students' content comprehension, cognitive load, and motivation in online learning. *American Annals of the Deaf*, 156(3), 283–289.

Kaboody, M. (2013). Second language motivation: The role of teachers in learners' motivation. *Journal of Academic and Applied Studies*, 3(4), 45–54.

Koiso, K (2003). The characteristics of motivation of Japanese adult English learners. *General Social Surveys[5] JGSS from JGSS-2003 Data*. Retrieved April 2, 2015 from http://jgss.daishodai.ac.jp/japanese/5research/monographs/jgssm5pdf/jgssm5_8.pdf

MacIntyre, P. D., Noels, K. A., & Moore, B. (2010). Perspectives on motivation in second language acquisition: Lessons from the Ryoanji Garden. In M. T. Prior, Y. Watanabe, & S. K. Lee (Eds.), *Selected proceedings of the 2008 second language research forum*. Somerville, MA: Cascadilla Press.

McElroy, E. V. (2007). The effects of the college student success course on the retention and academic performance of English as a second language students enrolled in developmental reading and English at Central Piedmont Community College. (Dissertation Abstracts International, 67–10.)

Nikolov, M. (1999). "Why do you learn English?" "Because the teacher is short." A study of Hungarian children's foreign language learning motivation. *Department of Language Teaching Research*, 3(1), 33.

Peregoy, S. F. & Boyle, O. F. (2000). English learners reading English: What we know, what we need to know. *Theory into Practice*, 39(4), 237–247.

Razfar, A., & Simon, J. (2011). Course-taking patterns of Latino ESL students: Mobility and mainstreaming in urban community colleges in the United States. *TESOL Quarterly*, 45(4), 595–627.

Robinson, J. (2010). English language learners' motivation to engage in reading. (Order No. 3421652, Washington State University, Pullman). ProQuest Dissertations and Theses, 141. Retrieved from http://search.proquest.com.libproxy.lamar.edu/dissertations/docview/756252303/fulltextPDF/13F33AFD44765FA8291/3?accountid=7043

Rutherford, B., & Billig, S. (1995). *Parent, family, and community involvement in the middle grades*. Urbana, IL: ERIC Clearinghouse on Elementary and Early Childhood Education.

Ryan, R. M., & Deci, E. L. (2000). Intrinsic and extrinsic motivations: Classic definitions and new directions. *Contemporary Educational Psychology*, 25(1), 54–67.

Ryan, S., & Dörnyei, Z. (2013). The long-term evolution of language motivation and the L2 self. Retrieved from http://www.zoltandornyei.co.uk/uploads/2013-ryan-dornyei-lang.pdf

Simms, L., & Thumann, H. (2007). In search of a new, linguistically and culturally sensitive paradigm in deaf education. *American Annals of the Deaf*, 152(3), 302–311.

Skinner, E. A., & Belmont, M. J. (1993). Motivation in the classroom: Reciprocal effects of teacher behavior and student engagement across the school year. *Journal of Educational Psychology*, 85(4), 571.

Spack, R. (1988). Initiating ESL students into the academic discourse community: How far should we go? *TESOL Quarterly*, 22(1), 29–51.

Tremblay, P. F., & Gardner, R. C. (1995). Expanding the motivation construct in language learning. *Modern Language Journal*, 79, 505–518.

Tuner, J., & Paris, S. G. (1995). How literacy tasks influence children's motivation for literacy. *Reading Teacher*, 48(8), 662.

Wilder, G., Mackie, D., & Cooper, J. (1985). Gender and computers: Two surveys of computer-related attitudes. *Sex Roles*, 13(3), 215–228.

Wood, K. D., Stover, K., Pilonieta, P., & Taylor, D. B. (2012). Don't skip the graphics! Focusing students' attention on the visual aids in digital and traditional texts. *Middle School Journal*, 43(4), 60–68.

A Milestone in Deaf Studies:
The Berlin Digital Memorial Board for Deaf Jewish Life Destroyed Under the Nazi Regime

MARK ZAUROV

FOR A LONG TIME, THE FATE OF DEAF JEWS UNDER THE NAZI REGIME has been absent from both mainstream culture and Holocaust Studies. Deaf-Jewish issues have historically been labeled as part of the Aktion T4 ("racial hygiene") program. Deaf Studies and Deaf history researchers, however, have interviewed survivors independent of this framework, establishing their biographies, and collecting related material (Zaurov, 2009; Ryan & Schuchman, 2002).

A memorial means recognition and respect by society. There are several memorials in Berlin for populations of murdered Sinti and Roma Jews, homosexuals, Jehovah's Witnesses, and mentally disabled and schizophrenic Jews. But what about *Deaf* Jews? Some may question why Deaf Jews should explicitly get their own memorial as there are already memorials for those in Aktion T4 programs.

Because of the lack of appropriate Deaf scholarship in this area (cf., Zaurov, 2012), Deaf survivors have historically been categorized with other disabled groups (e.g., Aktion T4), clearly a mislabeling. Other uninformed researchers of Deaf-Jewish survival have also misidentified Deaf labor and death camp survivors as 'hearing,' denying their language identity. It is these labels and removal of identity that are the essence of the "Deaf Holocaust" (Zaurov, 2009).

This is the basis for a potential memorial for Deaf European Jews. Unfortunately, at the Ort der Information in Berlin, there is currently no recognition of Deaf Jews as transnational or as a community (Zaurov, 2015). Though Deaf people joined the Hitler Youth and actually supported forced sterilization, this would not become law until 1933. The regime's Aktion T4 program ran from 1939 to 1941 and specifically used gas as a means of genocide. Aktion T4 did not require the use of sterilization against Deaf people and there is a need for a space or museum to exhibit this history, to better understand the difference between Deaf non-Jews and Jews and disabled people.

Following fifteen years of relentless lobbying, a memorial board was finally erected in Berlin, dedicated specifically to recognizing Deaf Jews as a minority. Although a full-fledged memorial has yet to be established, the board reminds mainstream culture and Holocaust scholars not only of the existence of the Deaf-Jewish minority but also of their unique heritage, their fate, and their place within the German historical landscape of diversity (Sonke, 1993; "Sehen statt Hören," October 30).

Without the interdisciplinary approach of Deaf Studies, Deaf persons would still be considered handicapped, void of identity or culture (Zaurov, 2015). Research gathered from the three respective disciplines of Deaf Studies, Deaf History, and Holocaust Studies has converged to help produce the state-of-the-art innovative Berlin memorial ("Sehen statt Hören," January 25). The elegant freestanding glass board bears, in German and English, information about Deaf-Jewish life that once flourished in the area of the memorial. A built-in solar-powered screen renders the same text in German Sign Language (DGS) and international signs, performed by a Deaf-Jewish professional sign language interpreter.

The author with the Deaf Jewish Life Digital Memorial Board in Berlin. Unfortunately, after just one year, the memorial board was removed because of technical and location issues. A new location has not yet been agreed upon as suggested alternatives were either too isolated from crowds or considered too expensive by the government. Photo: Mark Zaurov.

In the heart of Berlin, amidst the hustle and bustle of locals, tourists, businesspeople, students, and politicians, Deaf Jewish history and its contribution to society is alive and present.

REFERENCES

Ryan, D. F. & Schuchman, J. S. (2002). *Deaf People in Hitler's Europe*, Washington D.C.: Gallaudet University.
"Sehen statt Hören" (October 30, 2014). http://www.br.de/fernsehen/bayerisches-fernsehen/sendungen/sehen-statt-hoeren/sehen-statt-hoeren-machtergreifung-100.html.
"Sehen statt Hören" (January 25, 2014). http://www.br.de/fernsehen/bayerisches-fernsehen/sendungen/sehen-statt-hoeren/sehen-statt-hoeren-gedenktag-bloch-100.html.
Sonke, M. (1993). Die israelitische Taubstummen-Anstalt in Berlin-Weissensee. Von der Gründung 1873 bis zur Vernichtung 1942. In Bendt, V., et al., *Öffne deine Hand für die Stummen. Die Geschichte der Israelitischen Taubstummen-Anstalt Berlin Weissensee: 1873-1942 (pp. 43-76)*. Berlin: Transit.
Zaurov, M. (2003). *Gehörlose Juden — eine doppelte kulturelle Minderheit*. Frankfurt: Peter Lang.
Zaurov, M. (2009). Deaf Holokaust. In M. Zaurov & K-B. Günther (eds.), *Overcoming the Past, Determining its Consequences and Finding Solutions for the Present. A contribution for Deaf Studies and Sign Language Education. Proceedings of the 6th Deaf History International Conference July 31-August 04, 2006 at the Humbold University*, Berlin (pp. 173-197). Seedorf: Signum.
Zaurov, M. (2012): The Current Situation of Human Rights for Deaf People with Respect to the Deaf Holocaust. *International Graduate Students' conference on Holocaust and Genocide Studies Papers*, Paper 9. http://commons.clarku.edu/chgs_papers/9.
Zaurov, M. (2015). A postcolonial approach to Deaf Jews as a cultural minority. In B. Eldredge, D. Stringham & F. Fleischer (Eds.), *Deaf Studies Today! 2010: Beyond Talk* (pp. 273-283). Orem, UT: Utah Valley University.

American Sign Language: From Deaf Community to General Society

RUSSELL S. ROSEN, PH.D.

ONE OF THE AIMS OF SIGNING DEAF AND HARD OF HEARING (D/hh) people is to be able to access the larger society by having them accept and use their ideological, social, and material cultures not only with them but also with each other. For instance, signing D/hh people would like to access the general society by having hearing people communicate in American Sign Language (ASL) not only with them but also with each other.

There are several signing D/hh cultural products currently used by society at-large. Televisions with closed captioning capability, created for use by D/hh people to gain access to the spoken language on TVs, are placed in bars, gyms, and restaurants. The football huddle, created at Gallaudet University, was adapted and is used by youth, collegiate, and professional football teams. Several studies document uses of ASL and other sign languages by hearing people in courses where sign language is taught and used by hearing teachers with hearing learners (Cooper, Reisman, & Watson, 2008; Rosen, 2008), used among D/hh and hearing individuals (Sherley-Appel, & Bonvillian, forthcoming; Kusters, forthcoming), and Baby Signs, which is adapted and used by hearing teachers to teach hearing babies to aid in their development of cognitive skills before they develop their spoken language skills (Snoddon, forthcoming). These studies look at the variety of situations and contexts where sign language is used among signing D/hh and hearing individuals.

In order for society to adopt and use ideological, social, and material cultures of the signing D/hh community, including ASL, signing D/hh culture needs to be first developed within the signing D/hh community. The process whereby D/hh cultural products enter into society in general involves the creation of ideologies, social structures, and material products within the signing D/hh community, their adaptation and placement in general societal spaces, and their utilization by members of hearing society. Regarding ASL, for instance, the process begins with the initial incubation of ASL within the signing American D/hh community to meet the corporeal need of signing American D/hh people to communicate, toward its recognition and adaptation in the United States for use with signing D/hh people, and ends with its utilization as a language commodity by hearing people in general.

What is poorly documented and theorized in past studies is the historical process of the development, adaptation, and utilization of the signing D/hh community's ideological, social, and material cultures in general society. It is the purpose of this study to illustrate and theorize the movement of signing D/hh culture from the signing D/hh community to society at large, and specifcially, ASL as an example of a signing D/hh cultural product. More particularly, the study uses a theoretical framework to outline the development of ASL within the signing D/hh community, its recognition and adaptation in public general education high schools as a foreign language in the US, and its utilization as a language commodity by high school foreign language learners of ASL to communicate outside of the general education system. The motivations for this inquiry are recent studies on ASL as a foreign language in American high schools and a theoretical interest in the conditions for the assimilation of D/hh culture in general society.

Studies that I conducted on the history of ASL as a foreign language in American public high schools, and secondary learners' uses of ASL with each other outside of ASL classrooms (Rosen 2006, 2008, 2014), provided information regarding the process how ASL is adapted in education systems and the conditions under which ASL is used among hearing high school learners. This is an instance of a phenomenon whereby products that are created within the signing D/hh community become integrated into general society so that signing D/hh people can access markets and services by having the general public use ASL not only with them but also with each other. This generates a theoretical interest for this study: the analysis of the progression of signing D/hh cultural products from their initial development and progression towards acceptance and utilization by the general public may aid future Deaf Studies scholars in understanding the nature of the flow of cultural products in society and developers in their attempt to disseminate their ideas, products, and services to large audiences.

To frame the history of ASL from its development within the signing D/hh community to its utilization in society at large, this study turns to Cultural Studies. Cultural Studies looks at the conceptualization, production, dissemination, consumption, and shaping of culture by individuals, groups and institutions. This study focuses on theoretical models of subculture development and subculture geography in Cultural Studies.

A model of subculture development is drawn from Hebdige (1979), who, in his study of punk subcultures, described the process whereby their products and ideas are initially borrowed from the majority, modified by members of the subculture, and then readapted by members of majority. According to Hebdige, the dominant culture generates disenfranchised people and their subcultures. Individuals in subcultures are in a constant struggle for identity with mainstream culture. In doing so, they constantly resisted, renegotiated and twisted meanings, objects and identities with the dominant culture.

Within the "hearths" of subcultures, products that were originally created in the majority for mass populace undergo a bricolagic process whereby they are twisted, given their own meanings to reflect group values, situations, and experiences, and then used in subversive ways to generate subcultures. After bricolage comes homology; subcultures "sell," reproduce, and reallocate to its "followers" from general society the altered cultural products, including alternative values, lifestyles, and language forms. As this process takes place, dominant cultures try to make sense of subcultures though news reports in mainstream mass media and articles in scholarly literature. The dominant culture in turn tries to reintegrate the aberrant subculture, or at least place it within the dominant framework of meanings, by taking aspects of the subculture. According to Hebdige, when the dominant culture subscribes to subculture products, the subculture products undergo a "contagious diffusion" in general society and become commodities for mass utilization. Commodification is the end result of the process of subculture reintegration in the dominant culture.

A model of subculture geography is drawn from cultural-materialist geographical studies of subcultures in Soja (1989), Lefebvre (1991) and Fouberg et al. (2009). Cultural-materialist geographical studies are concerned with the process where subcultures occupy space in the general society and create, manufacture, and disseminate ideas and products for general public consumption (Fouberg, et al., 2009). According to Soja (1989) and Lefebvre (1991), cultural landscape, as the visible imprint of human activity on the landscape, is the material character of a culture and its complex of natural features and human structures and objects. Cultural geography informs that space that both shapes and is shaped by individuals' interactions and relationships with each other (Soja, 1989, Lefebvre, 1991, Fouberg, et al., 2009).

As members of a subculture arrive and occupy a place, they bring their own ideological, social, and material cultures and transform the landscape.

Social space experiences encourage occupancy and a reterriorialization for subculture groups. Different subcultures that occupy a landscape assign different meanings to objects in space which rescale the structure of activity and relationships (Fouberg, et al., 2009). In this way, places can be made, for instance, ethnicized, sexualized, genderized, and even disabilitized.

The progression of the development of a subculture's products to mass utilization in general society that was identified in cultural-materialist studies on subculture development and social geographical studies of subculture spaces suggest a multi-step process for the development and assimilation of ASL in general society. The first step is the development of ASL as a "hearth" of the signing D/hh community. Members of the signing D/hh community are "models" in which they use ASL and create an ASL identity in resistance to the dominant speaking and hearing culture. This attracts "followers" who are not originally from the signing D/hh community to join the community and use ASL as a part of their lifestyle. The second step occurs when signing D/hh members try to "sell" ASL to hearing members in society at large. To accompany the development and marketing its products, members of the signing D/hh community imprint ASL and D/hh culture in spaces and create social geographies where hearing members of the dominant culture can enjoy its offerings. This creates a "contagious diffusion" of products from the subculture to the dominant culture. The third step occurs when ASL is adapted by members of the dominant culture. They integrate ASL in the dominant speaking and hearing culture. This creates "contagious diffusion" of ASL from signing D/hh people to hearing people and becomes noted in the media with commentaries that identify the new D/hh subculture within a social and historical context. The final step occurs when there is mass utilization of ASL among hearing members in the general society. Once ASL becomes a language commodity for general use, it becomes part of mainstream culture.

This study draws information from research on the history of ASL as a foreign language in American public high schools (Rosen, 2006, 2008) and on the uses of ASL outside of high school foreign language classrooms (Rosen, 2014). Rosen (2006, 2008) outlined the history of D/hh learners in public schools, debates about the linguistic and foreign language status of ASL, governmental recognition of ASL as a language, and its inclusion in schools where learners take ASL for foreign language credit. Rosen (2014) identified certain interpersonal and social geographical conditions that enabled high school ASL student to use it, instead of their native languages such as English, with each other outside of foreign language classrooms.

AMERICAN SIGN LANGUAGE: FROM SIGNING D/HH COMMUNITY TO GENERAL SOCIETY

Examination of available evidence on the history of ASL as a foreign language in American high schools and its uses by students outside of classrooms reveals that ASL has transitioned from its development within the signing D/hh community to support from linguistic research that has validated ASL is a language, governmental legislation that recognizes ASL as a language of communication in education, its offerings as a foreign language in educational institutions and its adoption by non-Deaf people for their use with each other under certain interpersonal and social conditions.

CREATION AND USES OF ASL IN THE UNITED STATES: "HEARTH" AND THE BRICOLAGE PROCESS

As ASL linguists and Deaf Studies scholars know, modern ASL was originally developed in the "hearth" of signing D/hh people: the first schools for the deaf in the northeastern United States in the early nineteenth century. Contemporary ASL evolved out of a mixture of French Sign Language brought to the US by Laurent Clerc, and sign languages from indigenous, genetic-based families of signing D/hh villages in the northeast. ASL was used as the chief language for communication at these first schools. After leaving deaf schools, signing D/hh people forged a community and culture of their own; they created organizations, publications, arts, and literature, and used ASL as the language of communication at their community functions and in their artistic and literary works. The history, development, and utilization of ASL by signing D/hh people is well-documented in the scholarly literature.

ASL was not a product that was drawn from the dominant culture. Nonetheless, it is a language that is a bricolage of the dominant spoken English and contains linguistic principles and structures that are different from the principles and structures of English. The creation and perpetuity of ASL within the signing D/hh community is their form of resistance against the use of spoken English in the dominant American speaking and hearing culture. The signing D/hh community is viewed by scholars as one of the subcultures of the larger American society.

THE MAINSTREAMING OF "MODELS" OF ASL IN GENERAL EDUCATION

In order for ASL to transfer from the signing D/hh community to society at large, ASL "models" need to first enter public spaces in the general society. It was not until the latter part of the twentieth century that signing D/hh people attempted to introduce ASL into general society, particularly in the field of mainstream education. In order for ASL to be incorporated into hearing secondary schools, ASL needed to be offered as a foreign language. The introduction of ASL for foreign language credit in public secondary schools began with the presence of signing D/hh learners in classrooms as "models" of ASL (Rosen, 2006).

The Education for All Handicapped Children Act (EACHA) and its successor, the Individuals with Disabilities Education Act (IDEA) initiated the process of mainstreaming of ASL into general education. EACHA and IDEA privileged speech and hearing for learners with deafness. The two laws aimed for the integration of deaf students into the American general education system. Before the passage of these laws, most signing D/hh students were placed in special schools for the deaf which utilized a variety of signed language approaches, from Manually Coded English codes to ASL. These laws expressed a hope that the placement of signing D/hh learners into mainstreamed public education with hearing peers would enable them to acquire hearing and speaking communication skills and be mainstreamed effectively into the American hearing and speaking society.

Signing D/hh students, however, continue to experience difficulties in public classrooms. Signing D/hh children in the general education system did not become hearing and effective speakers; they manage communication barriers with their hearing student peers within and outside of school grounds, and the lack of opportunities for interaction with hearing teachers and peers in public schools (Foster, 1989; Gaustad & Kluwin, 1992; Stinson & Liu, 1999; Antia, Stinson, & Gaustad 2002; Charlson, Strong, & Gold, 1992; Kiger, 1997; Stinson & Kluwin, 1996; Stinson & Liu, 1999).

The communication challenges of signing D/hh learners, however, has received attention from advocates, researchers, and the D/hh community. They have battled over the definitions, evaluation, instructional program types, and placements of D/hh learners regarding communication needs and language preferences (Rosen, 2006).

THE "SELLING" OF ASL IN GENERAL EDUCATION

Since the nineteenth century, members of the signing D/hh community have established and "sold" ASL classes to the general public for profit. ASL classes are the spaces where there is contagious diffusion of ASL between signing D/hh people and the general public. Unfortunately, there is little to no information about the utilization of ASL among members of the general public who have taken private ASL classes. Whether such learners continue to use ASL after taking private ASL classes is an open question that needs further research. (Information *is* available, however, regarding hearing signers who acquired and used ASL after they took courses in public high schools (Rosen, 2006, 2008, 2014).

The attempt by signing D/hh people to assimilate ASL into hearing/speaking-dominant educational institutions has had contested beginnings. Research regarding ASL's linguistic structures is relatively young (Stokoe, 1960; Stokoe, Casterline, & Croneberg, 1965). By the 1970s and 1980s, however, ASL was declared an autonomous language, in spite of its distinct modality from spoken languages, since it carries several linguistic features that are similar to spoken languages by several linguists (Baker-Schenk & Cokely, 1980; Klima & Bellugi, 1979; Liddell, 1980; Padden, 1981; Valli & Lucas, 1992; Wilbur, 1979; Fischer & Siple, 1990; Fromkin, 1988; Neidle, et al., 2000; Sandler & Lillo-Martin, 2006).

However, the "discovery" of ASL as a language was followed by arguments, particularly among government officials and school administrators, regarding ASL as a legitimate language and determining whether it should be offered for "foreign" language credit in schools. There was initial resistance by administrators and educators at public educational institutions that were built on arguments that ASL is a manual representation of English and that signing D/hh people are not located in a separate country but are members of general American society. For supporters of ASL as a foreign language, the evidence of ASL linguistics and Deaf community and cultural studies in scholarly and literary works, coupled with the post-colonialist notions of "foreign" in languages and communities, have for the large part put the arguments into disbelief.

Signing D/hh community scholars and advocates were empowered by researcher's recognition of ASL's legitimacy as well as arguments in support of ASL as a foreign language and sought its adoption in state education departments and secondary schools. Advocates from the signing D/hh community, including representatives from the National Association of the Deaf (NAD), held meetings with United States congressional representatives and Department of Education officials, resulting in a reconceptualization of deafness for educational purposes.

In 1997 and 1999 reauthorizations of IDEA, 1975 EAHCA audist practices were revised by deleting references to "speech" and "hearing difficulties" and their role in receiving linguistic information, and by including "language preferences" — sign language — for signing D/hh learners.

The 1999 reauthorization of IDEA included ASL for the first time (U.S. Department of Education, 1999), impacting public education practices for signing D/hh students. Public education found it difficult to ignore sign languages, including ASL, as primary language and preferred mode of communication for signing D/hh students (Rosen, 2006).

ACCEPTANCE OF ASL IN GENERAL EDUCATION

One consequence of altered IDEA practices with signing D/hh learners was an increased presence of sign language interpreters in mainstreamed settings. Their clearly-visual presence in classrooms has generated interest among hearing learners and teachers, many of whom have become "followers" of ASL (Rosen, 2006). Courses in ASL, the American Deaf community, and its culture were requested (Rosen, 2006). The presence of signing D/hh learners in mainstream public education and hearing learners' demand for classes in ASL have opened doors to inside and outside interests, setting in motion the creation of courses and programs, and the acceptance of ASL as a foreign language in public general education (Rosen, 2006).

State legislatures and education departments needed to provide official approval in order for schools to offer ASL courses (which include information on the Deaf community and its culture) for foreign language credit. Beginning in the 1980s, the Deaf community attempted to integrate ASL into public education curricula and initiated the process for meeting with and securing approval from state legislatures and state education departments. However, the process has been idiosyncratic. In New York State, for instance, the Empire State Association of the Deaf, several representatives from the state chapter of the American Sign Language Teachers Association (ASLTA), and other community leaders met with members of the state legislature, received approval, drew up curriculum and assessment materials, and devised examinations for teacher certification and student diplomas (Rosen, 2006). In California (Selover, 1988), Maryland, Nevada (Loux, 1996), Texas, and Washington, consortiums of community organizations, leaders, and faculty from colleges and universities carried out the process. In a few states, the process began at the political level. For instance, a memorandum written by the Virginia Superintendent of Schools led to the passage of a resolution recognizing ASL as a foreign language in the state assembly in 1998 (Pfeffier, 2003; Wallinger, 2000).

Because of this mobilization, a majority of American states now formally recognize ASL as a foreign language (Gallaudet Research Institute, 2004), increased from twenty-eight in 1997 (Kreeft-Peyton, 1998) to thirty-two in 1999 (Jacobowitz, 1999), and thirty-eight in 2004 (Gallaudet Research Institute, 2004). However, the offering of ASL for foreign language credit in high schools has not been predicated on a state education department's recognition of ASL as a language. Several states where ASL has not formally been recognized still have schools that offer ASL for foreign language credit. (High schools offer foreign languages to help its secondary learners gain admission to colleges, which typically require at least two years of foreign language courses in secondary schools.)

The results of the Deaf community's work in ensuring official recognition of ASL at the state level were carried over to public high schools (Rosen, 2006). However, high school principals, foreign language departments, and school districts still need to provide support for *implementing* programs and courses in ASL as a foreign language. In addition, classes need to be offered and students and teachers need to be recruited.

Rosen's (2008) study showed that, nationwide, the process typically begins with ASL interpreters and teachers from other fields who know ASL and want to teach ASL as a foreign language. They take initiative and ask students, either individually or collectively in groups such as an ASL club, about their interest in taking ASL courses for credit. Teachers and learners then request that their principals create these courses and survey parents for their support of ASL foreign language programs. After parents give support, principals request and secure approval from school districts. Districts survey signing community members and give approval for ASL foreign language programs. Rosen (2008) showed that various sources contribute to program implementation: state and community needs, resources, availability, and willingness of players and schools shape the process for the implementation of ASL programs.

Because of these efforts by local Deaf communities, students, parents, and school and district administrative support, an increasing number of American public high schools have established ASL programs and classes over the years. Rosen reported that, based on survey information from thirty-one states (Rosen, 2008), more than seven hundred public high schools offered ASL for foreign language credit during the 2004–2005 academic year. The CAL survey showed thirty-three high schools in 1997 (Center for Applied Linguistics, 1997). The growth rate in the number of high schools with ASL programs from 1997 to 2004 increased more than 2100%.

There have been increases in the numbers, levels, and distribution of ASL programs, classes, and numbers of teachers and learners in public secondary schools. The general hearing public have became "followers" of ASL and reintegrated ASL as a taught language in American public education.

COMMENTARIES ON ASL IN EDUCATION IN NEWS REPORTS

The growth of ASL in public secondary schools has also attracted the attention of mainstream media. The existence of the signing D/hh culture and the increased spread and enrollment of ASL classes for foreign language credit has not been ignored in the media. *The Baltimore Sun* (January 27, 2008), *The Statesman* (Austin, Texas; December 19, 2012), and *The Seattle Post-Intelligencer* (February 18, 2003), have all reported that many hearing high school learners have become aware of ASL due to its increased visibility in movies, television, and public events (conferences, political speeches, church services, etc.). In addition, they have been drawn to ASL classes because of their visual nature and ease in learning as compared to spoken foreign languages. Commentaries in the media on the growth of ASL in public education have helped confirm for the general American public both not only the existence and utility of ASL as a language but also the legitimacy of the signing D/hh community as an American subculture. These commentaries have served to solidify the place of ASL and the signing D/hh community; how news commentaries generate increased enrollment in public secondary school ASL classes has not been investigated in Rosen's (2006, 2008, 2014) studies and remains a fruitful areas for future research.

COMMODIFICATION OF ASL: BETWEEN-LEARNERS USES OF ASL OUTSIDE OF CLASSROOMS

After hearing high school learners acquire ASL, they use it with each other, not only inside but also outside of ASL classrooms. Students who enroll in ASL classes also tend to have some kind of connection with the at-large signing D/hh community. Although they use ASL outside of the classroom with their signing D/hh family and friends (Rosen, n.d.), most students who take ASL as foreign language classes are still largely without connections to the D/hh community (Rosen, n.d.). However, when hearing high school students use ASL with each other and *not* with the signing D/hh people outside of ASL classrooms, ASL becomes a language commodity and is mainstreamed and contagiously diffused into the general American public.

Learners need to construct spaces in the general society outside of ASL classrooms where they can use ASL with each other. Cultural geography studies inform that language, as culture, is imprinted on spaces. Language spaces define and delimit how its occupants should be seen, what meanings to give them, what language(s) to use for communicating, what identities can be developed, the criteria for limiting or gaining access, and how the occupants behave and think within them. Extending cultural geography outside of ASL classrooms is contingent upon enabling hearing foreign language learners use ASL with each other.

There are certain spaces outside of ASL classrooms where learners use ASL with each other. This study looks at the constitution of spaces outside of ASL classrooms where ASL is used between hearing high school foreign language students. More particularly, it examines opportunities and motivation that drives high school students not to use their own native spoken languages but ASL to communicate with each other outside of ASL classrooms.

Rosen's (2014) analysis of learner narratives and observation notes reveals that there are spaces for hearing students outside of ASL classrooms where they can use ASL with each other. In addition, I have observed a wide range of sign language forms, types of interactions, ASL abilities, and forms of mouthing (English or ASL) that are exhibited by the learners in the extra-classroom ASL spaces inside school grounds. The following is an exposition of between-learners extra-classroom ASL spaces.

Interpersonal situations
Some spaces are created by certain interpersonal situations, generated by learners' need for practice, teaching, bonding, sharing knowledge, keeping secrets, and signing songs with each other.

Practice spaces
Some learners set up spaces where they practice signs and sentences they learned in classrooms. Practice spaces are created by learners who forget what they learned in class. Still other learners use ASL if they have questions to their friends who also know ASL. Other practice spaces are created by learners to review ASL vocabulary, numbers, and fingerspelling they learned in class and to practice signs and sentences with each other for recall, comprehension, and examinations. Some learners use spoken English to list vocabulary words and grammar in ASL to practice, and then practice them in ASL. They correct each other in ASL. Some learners mimic receptive tests in class, whereby one signs and the other transcribes in fingerspelling.

Teaching spaces
Students create spaces where they teach ASL signs and sentences. Teaching spaces are created by students when they want to teach what they learn in class to their family and friends. They teach ASL vocabulary, numbers, and fingerspelling. Most students teach their family and friends at their respective homes. Still other learners use ASL to teach ASL to their friends. Sometimes ASL teaching spaces are created by students who have friends and family members who cannot communicate vocally; one student tried to communicate with a baby who had not learned how to speak. Another student explained that she taught family members who had become nonverbal (incidence of stroke or Down's Syndrome).

Bonding spaces

Some students use ASL to communicate outside of ASL classrooms with other students, family, and friends when they wish to bond with each other. Bonding spaces are created either at home, in the hallways, or in other classrooms when they want to use ASL to bond with each other and inquire about their well-being, make plans and gossip, and for fun and pleasure. Learners were observed to do "quick talk" with each other in mini-conversations with simple questioning and answering sentential structures. Other learners were observed to have talked about their weekend activities and future plans. Some learners confided that they converse in ASL with friends who know ASL just for fun, to have conversations, and even to joke with each other. Other students use ASL through video chat and still other learners communicate with friends who are ASL stduents in other schools. Some students use ASL to surprise their friends who did not know they knew ASL and some use ASL exclusively for communication with friends, as if they were in a sign clique group. Other learners remarked that there were give-and-take between learners who took different foreign languages and then taught the languages to each other.

Secrecy spaces

Another interpersonal situation that enables learners to create ASL space is developed when they wish to share secrets or other private communication with each other. Secrecy spaces are created by ASL students for private conversations including gossiping, discussing personal problems, sharing secrets, expressing opinions and feelings about people and themselves with each other that no one else, without a knowledge of ASL, is privy to or can understand. I have observed the use of ASL by student athletes when they need to discuss plays, strategies, or compare team scores so that players from opposing teams can not hear them. In one instance I observed students using ASL in a school hallway to talk about prom because they did not want others to overhear that they were discussing about dates. Some learners use ASL so that they can communicate without anyone else noticing and some even use ASL with each other during testing situations in other classes. ASL teachers confided to me that they knew of learners who used ASL in tests in other classes where they can fingerspell answers to multiple-choice questions by flashing the letters of the alphabet in ASL behind their ears and under desks and out of sight of their teachers.

Expression spaces

Still another interpersonal situation that allows learners to use ASL outside of classrooms is created when they come together and express themselves.

Expression spaces are created by learners when they use ASL to express personal thoughts and feelings, when they sing with signs, and when they try to sync spoken lyrics with the signs they learned in ASL classrooms. Some other learners use ASL to express resentment and anger to get their point across to other ASL students who they suspect of cheating on tests.

Social contexts: Noise-avoidance and Large Distances

ASL students create certain social contexts where they can only use ASL instead of their spoken native languages. These ASL spaces are regulated by the need for silence, greater physical distances, and crowded or noisy environments that precluded the use of speech. I observed in a cafeteria setting where students were seated at several rows of tables apart from each other, discussing plans to meet after school. Because of the ambient noise, students could not hear each other and used ASL. Others comment how they use ASL with friends if they cannot hear them, particularly in noisy environs and crowded places such as parties. Some comment that they prefer using ASL so they can communicate with each other privately in crowded areas. This is in contrast from the situation found in Deaf spaces where side conversations in ASL create visual noise and are often considered impolite.

Quietness spaces

ASL is used in spaces where students are not permitted to use voice (i.e., during class, practice, movies, libraries and study spaces, or even in principal's offices). ASL spaces are created when voicing is not desirable or practical, and students can only use ASL as a non-vocal language with each other.

Did Not Use ASL

Finally, there are learners who do not use ASL outside of the classroom at all. Some feel there are no situations nor contexts that enforce their use of visual-manual ASL with other learners and some students complain that there are no opportunities outside of the classroom to use ASL. Other students explained that ASL is only used for communicating with signing deaf and hard of hearing people and that there are no deaf people with whom to use ASL. Still other students explained that, because all of their family members and friends are hearing, they preferred to speak and hear.

DISCUSSION

This study focuses on the movement of ASL from the American signing D/hh community to its use by high school foreign language learners in the general society outside of ASL classrooms. It covers the development of ASL within the signing D/hh community, its adoption in public high schools in the US, and its utilization by hearing foreign language learners of ASL.

The movement of ASL from the D/hh community to general adaptaion by hearing foreign language learners is similar to the progression of punk subculture products as outlined in Hebdige (1979) and the cultural geography studies of Soja (1989), Lefebvre (1991) and Fouberg, et al. (2009). ASL was developed at the "hearth" of the signing D/hh community first at nineteenth-century residential schools for the deaf that served as "models" of ASL that resisted speaking and hearing cultural values. In the latter part of the twentieth century, ASL was introduced to the public education system and social geographies of ASL classes were created where hearing high school foreign language learners came and learned the language. This "contagious diffusion" of ASL from signing D/hh people to hearing people in high school ASL classes has been noted in the media with commentaries that identified the new D/hh subculture within a social and historical context. After taking ASL classes, high school learners use the language with each other. ASL has become a language commodity and part of the mainstream American culture.

The similarities end here. There are differences between Hebidge's punk subculture model and the steps involved in the development, adoption, and utilization of ASL within general society. There were several steps that were needed after ASL was established within the signing D/hh community before it could be adopted into foreign language classrooms. Before offering it as a foreign language in public school classrooms, ASL needed to be matured through linguistic research that proved it as a language and governmental legislation that recognized its legitimacy.

In addition, for hearing ASL students to use it outside of ASL classrooms, they need to construct spaces where ASL is enforced and native spoken languages are minimized. According to Soja (1989), Lefebvre (1991), and Fouberg, et al. (2009), spaces are imprinted by language when their occupants create language for communication. Language spaces delimit forms of language, topics, identities, and means of access. There are certain spaces where learners need and permit the use ASL with each other. These spaces are created by interpersonal and social conditions outside of ASL classrooms that permit students to elevate a dominant use of ASL.

Whether the steps in the progression of ASL from the signing D/hh community to public school language classes apply to other D/hh cultural products, such as TVs with built-in closed captioning devices in public places, the football huddle, Baby Signs, and educational uses of ASL with children with autism and learning disabilities, is an empirical question. It is hoped that this study initiates future research on the incorporation and utilization of signing D/hh cultural ideas, social structures, and products in general society from their initial development within the signing D/hh community. Various signing D/hh cultural products and processes in its creation, adoption and utilization in the general society need further investigation and theorizing in a systematic way as mechanisms for increased access and assimilation of signing D/hh culture in society.

REFERENCES

Antia, S. D., Stinson, M. S., & Gaustad, M. G. (2002). Developing membership in the education of deaf and hard of hearing in inclusive settings. *Journal of Deaf Studies and Deaf Education*, 7, 214–228.

Baker-Schenk, C., & Cokely, D. (1980). *American Sign Language teacher's resource text on curriculum, methods and evaluation*. Washington, DC: Gallaudet University Press.

Center for Applied Linguistics. (1997). *A national survey of foreign language instruction in elementary and secondary schools: A changing picture: 1987–1997*. Washington, DC.

Charlson, E., Strong, M., & Gold, R. (1992). How successful deaf teenagers experience and cope with isolation. *American Annals of the Deaf*, 137, 261–270.

Cooper, S., Reisman, J.I., & Watson, D. (2008). The status of sign language instruction in institutions of higher education: 1994-2004. *American Annals of the Deaf*, 153 (1), 78–88.

Fischer, S., & Siple, P. (1990). *Theoretical issues in sign language research*. Chicago: University of Chicago Press.

Foster, S. (1989). Social alienation and peer identification: A study of the social construction of deafness. *Human Organization*, 48, 226–235.

Fouberg, E., Murphy, A. B., & de Blij, H. J. (2009). *Human geography: People, place, and culture* (9th ed.). Hoboken, NJ: John Wiley and Sons.

Fromkin, V. A. (1988). Sign language: Evidence for language universals and the linguistic capacity of the human brain. *Sign Language Studies*, 59, 115–128.

Gallaudet Research Institute (2004). States that recognize American Sign language as a foreign language. http://clerccenter.gallaudet.edu/infotogo/index.html.

Gaustad, M. G., & Kluwin, T. N. (1992). Patterns of communication among deaf and hearing adolescents. In T. N. Kluwin, D. F. Moores, & M. G. Gaustad (eds.), *Toward effective school programs for deaf students*. New York: Teachers College Press, pp. 107–128.

Hebdige, D. (1979). *Subculture, the meaning of style*. London: Routledge.

Jacobowitz, E. L. (1999). American Sign Language in higher education: Implications for administrators and teacher trainers. Presented in American Sign Language Teachers Association Professional Development Conference, Rochester, New York, October 7–10, 1999.

Kiger, G. (1997). The structure of attitudes toward persons who are deaf: Emotions, values, and stereotypes. *Journal of Psychology*, 131, 554–560.

Klima, E., & Bellugi, U. (1979). *The signs of language*. Cambridge, MA: Harvard University Press.

Kreeft-Peyton, J. (1998). ASL as a foreign language. K-12 Foreign Language Education, 6, 1–3.

Kusters, A. (forthcoming). Deaf-gain and shared signing communities. In H-D.L. Bauman & J.J. Murray (Eds.), *The new normal: Deaf-gain and the future of humanity*. Minneapolis, MN: The University of Minnesota.

Lefebvre, H. 1991. *The production of space*. Oxford: Blackwell.

Liddell, S. K. (1980). *American Sign Language syntax*. The Hague: Mouton Publishers.

Loux, D. (1996) Report of the legislative task force on American Sign Language to the members of the 69th session of the Nevada Legislature. Nevada (booklet) Cited in Pfeffier, D., op. cit.

Neidle, C., Kegl, J., MacLaughlin, D., Bahan, B., & Lee, R. (2000). *The syntax of American Sign Language: Functional categories and hierarchical structure*. Cambridge, MA: MIT Press.

Padden, C. (1981). Some arguments for syntactic patterning in American Sign Language. *Sign Language Studies*, 32, 239–259.

Pfeffier, D. L. (2003). The implementation and administration of American Sign Language programs for foreign language credit in public secondary schools. Dissertation Abstracts International (UMI No. 3083807).

Rosen, R. (n.d.). Secondary students' motivation for American Sign Language as a foreign language. Unpublished manuscript, Teachers College, Columbia University.

Rosen, R. (2014). Between-learners outside-of-classroom uses of American Sign Language as a foreign language. *Sign Language Studies*, 14(3).

Rosen, R. (2008). American Sign Language as a foreign language in US high schools: State of the art. *Modern Language Journal*, 92(1), 10-38.

Rosen, R. (2006). IDEA and the mainstreaming of American Sign Language, Deaf community and culture in public schools. *Disability Studies Quarterly*, 26(2).

Sandler, W., & Lillo-Martin, D. (2006). *Sign language and linguistic universals*. Cambridge University Press.

Selover, P. (1988). American Sign Language in the high school system. *Sign Language Studies*, 59, 205–212.

Sherley-Appel, C. & Bonvillian, J. (forthcoming). The use of manual signs and gestures by the Inuit of Baffin Island. In H-D.L. Bauman & J.J. Murray (Eds.), *The new normal: Deaf-gain and the future of humanity*. Minneapolis, MN: The University of Minnesota.

Snoddon, K. (forthcoming). Baby sign as Deaf-gain. In H-D.L. Bauman & J.J. Murray (Eds.), *The new normal: Deaf-gain and the future of humanity*. Minneapolis, MN: The University of Minnesota.

Soja, E. (1989). *Postmodern geographies: The reassertion of space in social theory*. London: Verso.

Stinson, M. S., & Kluwin, T. N. (1996). Social orientations toward deaf and hearing peers among deaf adolescents in local public schools. In J. Nash, & P. C. Higgins (eds.), *Understanding deafness socially: Continuities in research and teaching*, 113–134. Springfield, Ill: C. C. Thomas.

Stinson, M. S., & Liu, Y. (1999). Participation of deaf and hard of hearing students in classes with hearing students. *Journal of Deaf Studies and Deaf Education*, 4, 191–202.

Stokoe, W. C. (1960). *Sign language structure: An outline of the visual communication system of the American deaf*. Washington, DC: Gallaudet College Press.

Stokoe, W. C., Casterline, D. & Croneberg, C. (1965). *A dictionary of American Sign Language on linguistic principles*. Washington, DC: Gallaudet College Press.

U.S. Department of Education (1999). Analysis of Final Regulations for Part B of the Individuals with Disabilities Education Act, 64 Federal Register 12527–12656

Valli, C., & Lucas, C. (1992). *Linguistics of American Sign Language*. Washington, DC: Gallaudet University Press.

Wallinger, L. (2000). American Sign Language instruction: Moving from protest to practice. *NECTFL Review*, 48, 27–36.

Wilbur, R. (1979). *American Sign Language and sign systems*. Baltimore, MD: University Park Press.

Watering the Roots of Self-Driven Motivation

A Positive Self-theory and Life-long Resiliency in Deaf and Hard-of-hearing Children

TODD LAMARR, LISALEE EGBERT, JODEE CRACE,
CARRIE DAVENPORT, AND TAMI HOSSLER

DEAF AND HARD-OF-HEARING (D/HH) CHILDREN, LIKE ALL CHILDREN, thrive in environments that support, encourage, and promote a healthy identity. The American Society for Deaf Children (ASDC) has supported families for over forty-five years and believes that with American Sign Language (ASL) and English, D/hh children can learn, thrive, and succeed. Accepting D/hh children for who they are and providing them with full access to language is the beginning of educating their minds and are critical building blocks for raising children who are self-confident, resilient, and willing to reach for the stars.

THE EDUCATIONAL CHALLENGES FOR DEAF OR HARD-OF-HEARING STUDENTS

A D/hh student often faces unique academic challenges that hearing students do not. For example, there are fewer resources, unequal assessment measures, and unequal academic and linguistic access for D/hh students, especially in mainstream environments (Karchmer & Mitchell, 2003; Marschark & Knoors, 2012; Schick, Williams & Kupermintz, 2006). Furthermore, the academic settings for D/hh students vary in degrees of quality. Depending on the D/hh classroom, there can be significant differences in educational philosophy, teacher qualification, language use, and accessibility. Due to these challenges, it is no wonder D/hh students demonstrate lower academic achievement, especially in English reading/literacy knowledge (Easterbrooks & Beal-Alvarez, 2012; Qi & Mitchell, 2012; Swanwick,

Oddy & Roper, 2005). While there may not be a quick and easy solution to the academic challenges faced by D/hh students, how they perceive themselves (their self-theory) is critical for developing self-driven motivation, life-long resiliency, skills, and mindsets that can be imperative for D/hh children throughout their lives.

Self-Theory
Self-theory refers to how individuals implicitly perceive themselves, especially when confronted with a challenging situation (Dweck, 1999). Individuals tend to have one of two self-theories: a *fixed mindse*t or a *growth mindset*. Which mindset someone has is strongly related to the patterns of praise they are given. The purpose of praise is to initiate a response that is positive and beneficial to boosting confidence, self-worth, and motivation in a child; therefore, we must be conscientious of how we give praise.

Fixed Mindset
Individuals with a fixed mindset perceive personal characteristics about themselves, such as intelligence, to be fixed and unable to change. This mindset leads to individuals often quickly giving up on challenging tasks and shying away from future challenges (Dweck & Leggett, 1988; Skipper & Douglas, 2012). Children who are praised for their ability and intelligence tend to pick 'performance-goal' tasks which make them look smart, over 'learning-goal' tasks from which they could develop new skills" (Kamins & Dweck, 1999). This type of praise can be internalized, creating a fixed mindset: "You are so smart for getting an A on your math test today. I'm so proud of you for getting first place." Therefore, when faced with a setback, fixed mindset thoughts take over affecting a child's self-worth and motivation to endure: "I didn't get an A on that test. I must not be as smart as they are telling me." "I only got third place. I guess the high-jump is not my sport."

Growth Mindset
Rather than praising the person, praising the process has a more positive effect on a child. To have a growth mindset is to perceive personal characteristics as not being fixed; they can be changed and improved. Specifically, the "growth" of this mindset comes through persistence, effort, practice, determination, and hard work. Breaking apart the process of the task and praising a child for their effort and hard work can lead a child to value learning opportunities, improve their ability to strategize, and increase their motivation to take on new tasks.

When faced with a challenging math problem, a student with a growth mindset would not equate their struggle to lack of intelligence, but rather with a lack of practice or lack of time management. What can parents and families do to promote a growth mindset?

- D/hh children need to be praised by their parents in ways that can be internalized positively. Praise your children for the process—praise their efforts and persistence (rather than their intelligence or ability). Example: "I just saw your room and I can see that you took your time and worked very hard. Good job!"
- Help your child understand the skills, work and persistence necessary to complete a task or reach a goal. By teaching your child to break a task down into steps/skills, it can help them view the goal as more attainable. Example: "Your job today is to clean your room. What parts of your room need cleaned? In what order do you want to do this? What equipment do you need to clean those areas?
- Discuss setbacks with your child and how to turn them into opportunities to learn and grow. This can be done through 'process chat'. What worked and what was a challenge? Allow the child to share his/her perception and feelings about the experience. Listen and validate the child's thinking. Lead the child to answer questions like: "What did you do well? What would you do differently next time? Would you like to change your strategy?"

	Fixed Mindset	**Growth Mindset**
	intelligence is static	intelligence can be developed
	Leads to a desire to look smart and therefore a tendency to:	Leads to a desire to learn and therefore a tendency to:
Challenges	avoid challenges	embrace challenges
Obstacles	give up easily	persist in the face of setbacks
Effort	see effort as fruitless or worse	see effort as the path to mastery
Criticism	ignore useful negative feedback	learn from criticism
Success of Others	feel threatened by the success of others	find lessons and inspiration in the success of others
	As a result, they may plateau early and achieve less than their full potential. **All this confirms a deterministic view of the world.**	As a result, they reach ever-higher levels of achievement. **All this gives a greater sense of free will.**

Table 1. Differences between a growth mindset and a fixed mindset (Dweck, 2006).

Deaf Culture and Deaf Role Models

Approximately 95% of D/hh children are born into hearing families that have different sensory experiences and do not know sign language (Mitchell & Karchmer, 2004), which can significantly impact a child's well-being (Gascon-Ramos, 2008). One way hearing families can palliate this impact is by incorporating Deaf culture and Deaf role models into their child's life. Deaf role models enrich language development and also have similar experiences with which D/hh children can identify and relate. As a result, Deaf role models are critical to a D/hh child's positive self-perception (Crowe, 2003) and for developing the foundation for a healthy growth mindset (Bat-Chava, 2000; Jambor & Elliott, 2005). What can parents and families do?

- Make communication easy and fun. Make a conscientious effort to include your child in informal and incidental conversations.
- Understand your child's sensory experience and incorporate flashing lights for doorbells, phones, and smoke alarms, use videophones and closed captioning.
- Get involved in the local Deaf community. Learn about Deaf history, culture, and the arts. As a hearing parent, you may feel intimidated by your signing skills, but know that the Deaf community appreciates your willingness to reach out to them. Seek out Deaf/signing friends, playmates, and adult role models for your child.
- Attend the annual conference for the American Society for Deaf Children (ASDC). ASDC's annual conference gives parents an opportunity to network and socialize with other parents and professionals as well as attend workshops that are directly related to raising and educating D/hh children.
- Encourage your child to participate in the Junior National Association of the Deaf (NAD). This is an excellent way to gain leadership and advocacy experience.
- Ask your child's teacher for information on local Deaf events, Deaf mentors, local college ASL classes/clubs, and parent organizations.
- Participate in activities hosted by deaf schools in your state, such as Academic Bowls, Mr. and Miss Deaf Teen Pageants, and camps.

The Individual Education Plan

The Individual Education Plan (IEP) lays out the foundation for educating the student. The role of the IEP team is to develop a plan to address a child's unique academic, communication, cognitive, social-emotional, and physical, needs. Here are some ways to utilize a growth mindset theory in IEP planning so that we can provide D/hh children with the mindset to persist through challenges and the desire to take on new challenges:

- Educate IEP team members on the difference between a fixed mindset versus a growth mindset and how it influences a student's self-theory and motivation.
- Teachers, coaches, support staff, interpreters, and extra-curricular activity sponsors should be cross-trained on how to appropriately support, encourage and adjust their language to praise students in consistent ways that promote healthy social-emotional development and resilience that leads to a growth mindset.
- Students that participate in IEP planning have more positive growth mindsets (Williams-Diehm, Wehmeyer, Palmer, Soukup & Garner, 2008). Find ways to include the participation of D/hh students in developing their IEP.
- Train team members on teaching techniques that incorporate incremental theories that approach a task in parts rather than a whole. Incremental achievement gives a sense of accomplishment without making a project seem overwhelming. Research shows using growth mindsets help students learn to work smarter and harder when faced with a challenge, and their grades tend to improve (Crowe, 2003).
- If the child does not have access to D/hh peers in the classroom, consider ways to make these connections happen (e.g., D/hh staff, online peer-to-peer support through a videophone or other video interplay, playgroups, team events, and social events). Include opportunities for peers to learn ASL and opportunities to practice with each other.

By teaching D/hh children growth mindset skills, supporting them in their endeavors, and instilling a sense of pride in who they are as a people, parents and educators can be positive catalysts for the success of D/hh children. The benefits of a growth mindset and a healthy self-theory extend far beyond the academic setting and continue to impact individuals throughout their lives (Haselhuhn & Burton, 2013; Moorman & Pomerantz, 2010) and give children an opportunity to go through life with high expectations for themselves, the resilience to overcome and persist through challenges, and a sense of confidence in whatever confronts them.

> "If I have the belief that I can do it, I shall surely acquire the capacity to do it even if I may not have it at the beginning" — Mahatma Gandhi

REFERENCES

Bat-Chava, Y. (2000). Diversity of Deaf identities. *American Annals of The Deaf,* 145(5), 420-428

Crowe, T. V. (2003). Self-esteem scores among Deaf college students: An examination of gender and parents' hearing status and signing ability. *Journal of Deaf Studies & Deaf Education,* 8(2), 199-206.

Dweck, C. S. (1999). *Self-theories: Their role in motivation, personality, and development.* New York, NY US: Psychology Press.

Dweck, C. S. (2006). *Mindset: The new psychology of success.* New York, NY US: Random House.

Dweck, C. S., & Leggett, E. L. (1988). A social-cognitive approach to motivation and personality. *Psychological Review,* 95(2), 256-273. doi:10.1037/0033- 295X.95.2.256

Easterbrooks, S. R., & Beal-Alvarez, J. S. (2012). States' reading outcomes of students who are d/Deaf and hard of hearing. *American Annals of the Deaf,* 157(1), 27-40.

Gascon-Ramos, M. (2008). Wellbeing in deaf children: A framework of understanding. *Educational and Child Psychology,* 25(2), 57-71

Jambor, E., & Elliott, M. (2005). Self-esteem and coping strategies among Deaf students. *Journal of Deaf Studies and Deaf Education,* 10(1), 63-81.

Kamins, M. L., & Dweck, C. S. (1999). Person versus process praise and criticism: Implications for contingent self-worth and coping. *Developmental Psychology,* 35(3), 835.

Karchmer, M. A., & Mitchell, R. E. (2003). Demographic and achievement characteristics of deaf and hard-of-hearing students. In M. Marschark & P. Spencer (Eds.), *Oxford handbook of deaf studies, language, and education* (pp. 21-37). New York, NY: Oxford University Press.

Marschark, M., & Knoors, H. (2012). Educating Deaf children: Language, cognition, and learning. *Deafness and Education International,* 14(3), 136-160. doi:10.1179/1557069X12Y.0000000010

Mitchell, R. E., & Karchmer, M. A. (2004). Chasing the mythical ten percent: Parental hearing status of Deaf and Hard of Hearing students in the United States. *Sign Language Studies,* 4(2), 138-163.

Moorman, E. A., & Pomerantz, E. M. (2010). Ability mindsets influence the quality of mothers' involvement in children's learning: An experimental investigation. *Developmental Psychology,* 46(5), 1354-1362. doi:10.1037/a0020376

Qi, S., & Mitchell, R. E. (2012). Large-scale academic achievement testing of Deaf and hard-of-hearing students: Past, present, and future. *Journal of Deaf Studies and Deaf Education,* 17(1), 1-18.

Schick, B., Williams, K., & Kupermintz, H. (2006). Look who's being left behind: Educational interpreters and access to education for Deaf and hard-of-hearing students. *Journal of Deaf Studies and Deaf Education,* 11(1), 3-20.

Schley, S., Walter, G. G., Weathers, R. R., Hemmeter, J., Hennessey, J. C., & Burkhauser, R. V. (2011). Effect of postsecondary education on the economic status of persons who are Deaf or hard of hearing. *Journal of Deaf Studies and Deaf Education,* 16(4), 524-536.

Skipper, Y., & Douglas, K. (2012). Is no praise good praise? Effects of positive feedback on children's and university students' responses to subsequent failures. British Journal of *Educational Psychology,* 82(2), 327-339.

Swanwick, R., Oddy, A., & Roper, T. (2005). Mathematics and deaf children: An exploration of barriers to success. *Deafness and Education International,* 7(1), 1-21.

Williams-Diehm, K., Wehmeyer, M. L., Palmer, S. B., Soukup, J. H., & Garner, N. W. (2008). Self-determination and student involvement in transition planning: A multivariate analysis. *Journal On Developmental Disabilities,* 14(1), 27-29.

Yeager, D. S., & Dweck, C. S. (2012) Mindsets that promote resilience: When students believe that personal characteristics can be developed. *Educational Psychologist,* 47:4, 302-314, doi: 10.1080/00461520.2012.722805

"A Language of Action": James Smedley Brown and the First American Dictionary of Sign Language

DOUG STRINGHAM

JAMES SMEDLEY BROWN WAS A METEORIC YET OVERLOOKED FIGURE IN mid-nineteenth century American Deaf education. Inspired by his wife's familial deafness, he burst on the scene as an instructor at the Ohio Institution for the Education of the Deaf and Dumb in 1841 and, by the time he left the profession, served as the superintendent of two schools for the Deaf, contributed to the emerging national deaf education dialogue, and pioneered vocational education in asylums and institutions for the Deaf in the Midwestern and Southeastern United States.

Although his professional career lasted only twenty years, his contributions were publicly noted by his professional peers and beloved by his students and their communities, but remain largely unknown to history. Most notably, Brown's two attempts at signed language dictionaries in 1856 and 1860 would be the first — and for almost fifty years, the *only* — published reference works on the developing sign language in the United States, pushing back the timeline of exploring lexemic parameters *an entire century before* Stokoe, Casterline, and Cronenberg.

LABELS AND CONTEXTING

In this paper, the historical terms "deaf-mute," "deaf and dumb," or "mutes" which Deaf people of the late nineteenth and early twentieth century were regularly called, are analogous to the contemporary term "Deaf." Though "deaf-mute" and "deaf and dumb" are, without doubt, anachronistic and offensive today, I maintain historicity here where necessary because the people included in this narrative used these labels eponymously. Additionally, "institution" and "asylum" are vestigial and authentic — yet now disrespectful — descriptions from a time when boarded education carried a much different connotation.

And, while the modern descriptor "American Sign Language" or "ASL" has been in use since the 1960s, during the late nineteenth and early twentieth centuries, neither these terms nor any of their associated political connotations existed. The roughly historical equivalent term during this time period would have been "signs" or "the sign language." The earliest attempts at formally naming an American sign language don't even appear until the late twentieth century (cf. Stokoe, Casterline, & Cronenberg, 1965 and Fant, 1972); contemporary to this time period of this paper, authors refer to the "language of signs" (Gallaudet, 1848), "signs" (Ayres, 1849), and "the sign language" (Rae, 1850; cf. Baynton, 2002).

In the instances where signed lexemes and their semantics are discussed, I follow the traditional convention of capitalizing an English word which is a near equivalent to the sign's meaning (e.g. WOMAN or LIBRARY).

FAMILY AND SCHOOLING

Born in Royalton, New York on 10 September 1819 to Nehemiah and Lydia (née Worcester) Brown, James was the youngest of four surviving children; of the eight born to his parents, three sisters and one brother died shortly after birth or in infancy (Wood, 2012). Brown was the grandson of Revolutionary War patriots and renowned New England Universalist/Unitarian pastor and pacifist Dr. Noah Worcester, Jr. (cf. Ware, 1845; Sprague, 1865).

The Brown family moved from New Hampshire to New York in the late 1810s (Census, 1810) and eventually to the Connecticut Western Reserve of northeastern Ohio in the late 1820s (Census, 1820; Wood, 2012). James was closest to his older brother Rollin who survived adolescence; the two of them attended secondary and post-secondary schooling together, co-enrolled at the then newly-founded Oberlin Collegiate Institute (now Oberlin College).

It is still unclear where Brown exactly graduated from university and received his teaching credentials although he initially enrolled at Oberlin as a summer term student in 1834 (Oberlin, 1834) and was listed as a preparatory (Oberlin, 1835), freshman (Oberlin, 1836), and sophomore student through 1838 (Oberlin, 1838); Brown also enrolled in 1837 at The Huron Institute (later Western Reserve Normal School) as a preparatory student in its Classical Department (Huron Institute, 1837). There currently is no extant record of his graduation from Oberlin or Huron/Western Reserve (Oberlin, 1909; Hoffman, 2012).

INTRODUCTION TO THE PARKS AND DEAFNESS

Sometime in 1839, Brown met Theresa (Terrissa or Terrisa) Maria Park, the third of ten children born to Elah and Elizabeth (née Moon) Park. In 1815, Elah had, like the Browns, left Massachusetts to purchase land and settle in the relatively new Connecticut Western Reserve of northeastern Ohio; he soon became a prominent leader in the area, specifically in Avon in Lorain County. By 1819, Elizabeth's father Abraham, along with his brothers Amos, Oliver, and Lodowick (Lodowich), had also left Massachusetts to settle in Lorain County (Wright, 1916).

Born 10 October 1818 in Avon (Brown, 1873), Theresa's pedigree would prove to directly influence her to-be husband James' work for the remainder of their lives. Park's oldest brother Plumb (b. 12 December 1816; Avon, Lorain, Ohio) and younger sister Alice (b. 8 June 1833; Avon, Lorain, Ohio) were Deaf (ancestry.com, 2009a, 2009b), and it is likely that Theresa, though her siblings attended school one hundred and fifty miles south in Columbus, had exposure to signed language and would have at least have a gesture-based relationship with her Deaf older brother and younger sister, uncles, aunts, and cousins.

Plumb, deafened at five months from "swelling under [the] ears" and a student at the Ohio Institution beginning in 1830, graduated in 1836 and took employment as a carpentry instructor at the school from 1838 to 1840. After a four-year hiatus, he returned to the Ohio Institution in 1844 and remained an influential instructor and member of the Columbus Deaf community for the next forty years, eventually retiring in 1883 and relocating to California (Ohio School for the Deaf, 1898). Park's younger sister and Brown's new sister-in-law Alice, born deaf, entered the Ohio Institution in 1843 and graduated in 1851 (ancestry.com, 2009b).

James and Theresa were married 23 February 1840 in Avon (Ohio County Marriages, 1789–1994), and they soon moved to Columbus, Brown taking a teaching position at the Ohio Institution for the 1841–1842 school year (*Fifteenth Report*, 1842). Brown's new relationship to the Deaf-World was not limited, however, to his new bride and his direct in-laws. Plumb's wife Charlotte Peck and sisters were also deaf (ancestry.com, 2009a) and Alice's husband Martin Marshall Hanson, a bright young teacher (and future Brown recruit and colleague), further strengthened the circle of Deaf adults around Brown (ancestry.com, 2009b).

Plumb and Alice's deafness was congenital through their mother Elizabeth Moon; a review of Plumb's, Alice's, and several other 1890 federal *U.S. Special Census on Deaf Family Marriages and Hearing Relatives* self-disclosures indicate cousin and marriage relationships to at least seven other Deaf

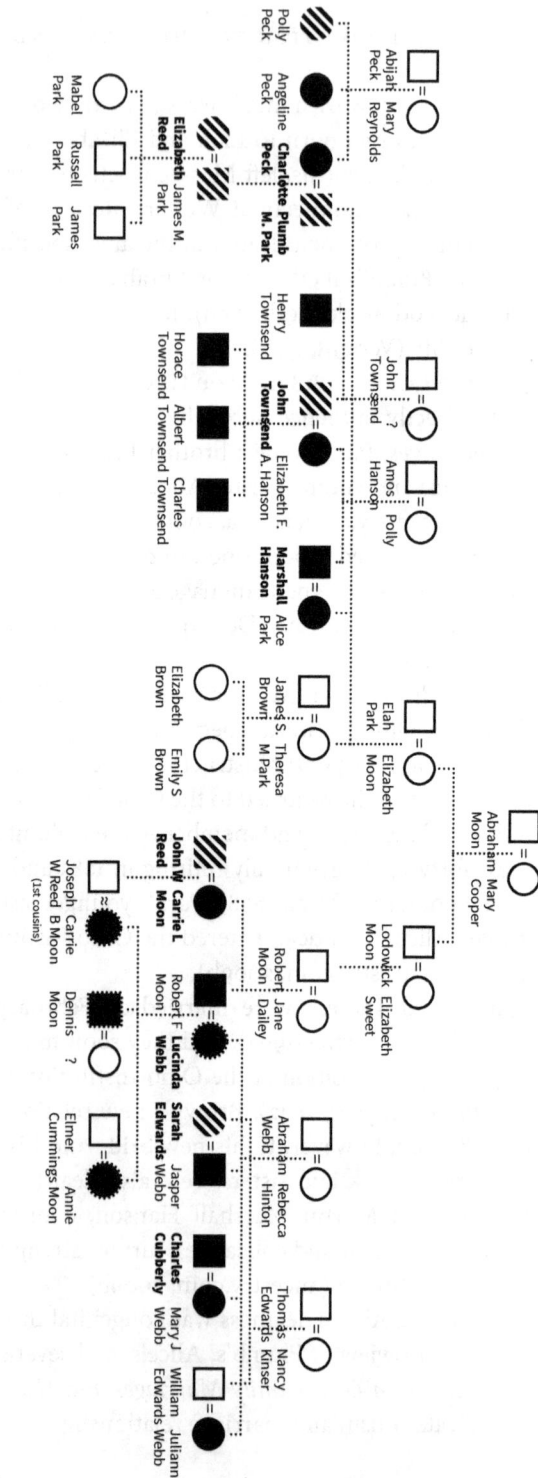

Figure 1. James' wife Theresa had two direct Deaf siblings (Plumb, Alice), second maternal cousins (Robert, Carrie Lorena), and additional Deaf relations by marriage. The Browns and Parks interacted with no less than seven Midwestern and Southern Deaf families (Peck, Reed, Townsend, Hanson, Moon, Reed₂, and Webb; there are additional Deaf in-laws [Edwards, Cubberly] noted in the tree and other cousins not mentioned here); James' career in Deaf education was likely influenced by these associations. (This tree is not representative of all family members; dozens have been removed for space and illustrative purposes.)

Key to symbols: □ hearing male, ○ hearing female, ■ Deaf male, ● Deaf female. Solid shapes indicate self-declared deafness at birth; diagonal lines indicate self-declared deafness caused by illness. Dotted lines around shape indicate deaf-blindness (Webb and Moon families), likely caused by consanguinity.

families in Ohio, Iowa, and beyond (ancestry.com, 2009c, 2009d, 2009e; cf. Figure 1). Along with his in-law families (and Plumb, who it appears to have helped Brown gain employment at the Ohio Institution in 1841), Brown also had exposure to at least twelve to fourteen other Deaf relatives. The Deaf community welcome mat rolled out and a position at the school procured, the Browns began their new life together in Columbus in the fall.

THE TEACHING YEARS: OHIO, INDIANA, AND LOUISIANA

After three years of experience at the Ohio Institution, involvement in a professional teachers' association in Columbus (Lee, 1892), and the receipt of a master's degree between 1842 and 1844 (*Eighteenth Annual Report*, 1844), in a somewhat controversial move, Brown was recruited by the board of trustees of the newly-formed Indiana Asylum for the Education of the Deaf and Dumb and promoted over the then-current deaf superintendent, William Willard, to "take charge of the Institution" (*First Annual Report*, 1844) for the 1844–1845 school year. The Ohio Institution Board of Trustees recommended Brown as "distinguished" and "certif[ied in]...his success as a teacher of mutes, and his thorough qualification in every respect for the responsible station he proposes to fill" (*Circular of the Trustees*, 1844, p. 3–4).

In Brown's first post to a school superintendency, he set himself apart by accelerating school campus building, increasing enrollment, and educating the Board about the cognitive efficacy and ability of Deaf students. Working with his deaf colleague William Willard, the two grew Asylum enrollment from thirty-five pupils in 1845–1846 to one hundred and seventy-two students in 1851–1852. Under Brown and Willard, the Indiana State Legislature appropriated three thousand dollars to procure a one-hundred and twenty-two acre plot on Indianapolis' east side for a new campus to be completed in October 1850 (*Seventh Annual Report*, 1850), just in time for the school year.

Brown used his Superintendent Reports in the school's annual report to the Trustees and state legislature to educate them on the "happiness [found in]...a community of deaf and dumb organized for instruction" (*Fifth Annual Report*, 1848, p. 9) and the importance of trade education for deaf mutes (*Seventh Annual Report*, 1850).

In Autumn 1852, Brown, considered "a gentleman eminently qualified, and occupying in his profession, the very first rank" (*First Annual Report*, 1853) was recruited by the board of trustees of the new Louisiana Institution for the Deaf and Dumb and Blind to assume its superintendency (*Ninth Annual Report*, 1852). Once again, Brown distinguished himself during his tenure through community involvement (*Eighth Annual Report*, 1860), walking streets and knocking doors to recruit deaf students, building state-of-the-art facilities, and pioneering vocational education at the school, including the procurement of state printing contracts and a state-of-the-art printing press to be operated on the Louisiana Institution campus (*Eighth Annual Report*, 1860). During his eight years in Louisiana, Brown spent his own summer vacations to personally canvass miles of streets in Baton Rouge, New Orleans, and other southern states, seeking overlooked Deaf and blind students to attend the nascent school. As in Indiana, James worked tirelessly to grow enrollment, from just eleven students in 1852 to seventy-one by 1859.

Brown announced to the Institution's trustees in the school's 1860 *Annual Report* that plans to have students assist in printing a "Dictionary of Signs for the Deaf and Dumb" had already been proposed, "doubting that your Honorable Bodies will readily see the propriety of this being done by the press of the Asylum" (*Eighth Annual Report*, 1860, p. 7).

Earlier in the year, James had also been publicly praised for his "indispens[ibility]" and "...his untiring attention and industry, and ability, [to which] ... most of the success of the Institution [is] attributable...." (*Eighth Annual Report*, 1860, p. 7). Just weeks later, however, spring state elections and appointments swept in new Republican leadership, and campaign promises of local power were coming due. Despite honest efforts to bring both vocational and financial success to the campus, now in the crosshairs of a newly-appointed school board, and notwithstanding reassurances to the contrary, Brown — and the entire board of trustees — were removed from their posts in May (Porter, 1860, p. 178; *Ninth Report*, 1861, p. 5).

By June, Brown had become the target of Louisiana legislative cronyism, an internal power-grab, and antebellum Civil War sentiment. In a last-ditch effort to fight back, James published an eight-page newspaper article passionately detailing the injustice. Just as swiftly as his extraordinary career began, Brown was forced out of his superintendency of the Louisiana School (Brown, 1860b) and crushed his spirits of a future career in Deaf and other special education.

HOME AGAIN

Defeated and no doubt exasperated, Brown, his wife, and two teenaged daughters retreated to the Indiana homestead (Census, 1860a) they had purchased eleven years earlier while still at the Indiana Asylum. In 1852, before leaving Indiana for Louisiana, Brown had purchased three hundred and fifty acres in southeastern Marion County, renamed it 'Gallaudet Station,' and "granted a diagonal right-of-way through his land to the Indianapolis and Cincinnati Railroad" (Henricks, 1984, p. 472). Upon their return home to Franklin Township, Brown served for a year as the Gallaudet Station postmaster from 3 October 1861 to 28 November 1862 (Henricks, 1984).

Though beaten down, after William S. Marshall, "one of [the Indiana School's] most acceptable and efficient teachers,...tendered his resignation under a conviction of duty in the crisis of the country" (*Nineteenth Report*, 1862, p. 9), Brown was convinced by Superintendent MacIntire in January to accept a substitute teaching appointment for the remainder of the 1862 school year (DeMotte, 1862).

A year later, after executing a simple will giving "my Beloved Wife, Terrisa, my whole estate, Real and personal ... in all things make suitable provision for my dear Daughter Emily...," (Brown, 1863), Brown died of pulmonary disease, fittingly, at his beloved Gallaudet Station on 10 June 1863 at the age of forty-nine (*Indianapolis Journal*, 1863; *Indianapolis Sentinel*, 1863).

MID-NINETEENTH CENTURY DEAF EDUCATION AND RISE OF SIGN LANGUAGE HOMOGENEITY

By the mid-1850s, while the centralization of the American Deaf community (especially in the Northeast) was arising with the formation of the New England Gallaudet Association in 1854 (Lane, Pillard, & French, 2007), a national debate was well underway among instructors of the Deaf over what flavor of signed language had a greater pedagogical advantage.

With the founding of the *American Annals of the Deaf and Dumb* in 1848 by the Convention of American Instructors of the Deaf and Dumb, educators had a forum in which to discuss topics of relevance to the professional field. Articles ranging from approaches to international deaf education and theological considerations as well as state institution histories and alumni listings were commonplace in the *Annals* during its years of publication. However, from 1848 to 1861 (the *Annals* were suspended from 1861 to 1868 because of the American Civil War), no topics were discussed more among educators of the Deaf than 1) the efficacy of colloquial (or "natural" signs) vs. methodical (or "systematic" [*Fourth Annual Report*, 1847, p. 19]) signs and 2) the preservation and consistency of accurate pronunciation of signs among teachers.

To wit, the first day of the 1856 annual Convention featured a provocative paper reading (and subsequent lively afternoon discussion) by Reverend John R. Keep, a professor at the American Asylum in Hartford. Keep's presentation, 'The best method for teachers to acquire the sign-language,' argued that teachers of the Deaf should be "well trained in signs" (Porter, 1857, p. 8) and lamented that the first generation of American educators "were more distinguished for the clearness and elegance of their signs than the present"; they "considered the science of sign-making as of great difficulty and importance, and devoted themselves more zealously to the study of signs than teachers generally do now" (Porter, 1857, p. 8). Others agreed, and at least eight additional delegates suggested that teachers were learning "vulgar and awkward" signs from their uneducated students and that weekly inservice was necessary to keep signs accurately produced. Most convincing, however, was an address by Laurent Clerc himself, who warned teachers against learning signs from "ignorant deaf-mutes," and not "allow[ing] themselves to be corrupted by them" (Porter, 1857, p. 9).

An observation of Brown's efforts on his dictionary projects indicates that he had long been a proponent of sign pronunciation standards. Though he remained focused on school business during the 1856 debates, Brown rarely shied away from teacher activist opportunities, even participating in the formation of a professional teachers' association while a young teacher at the Ohio Asylum in 1842 (Lee, 1892). Brown was already well underway in the development and production of his next major work aimed at the promotion of "teaching the signs carefully to new instructors, so that each generation might be in advance of the one that preceded it" (Porter, 1857, p. 9) although it would be another four years before a version would come off the press.

THE PROLOGUE: *A VOCABULARY OF MUTE SIGNS* (1856)

In an attempt to contribute a voice to the discussion and help create standards around pronunciation among educators of the deaf, Brown published *A Vocabulary of Mute Signs* (hereafter "*Vocabulary*") at the short-lived *Daily Gazette and Comet* newspaper press in Baton Rouge in 1856 (Brown, 1856), the earliest known extant attempt at compiling the American sign language. His motive was simple yet informed by much of the discussion in Deaf education at the time about the use of natural/colloquial vs. methodical/systematic signs; Brown declared in the first line of the preface that "the want of uniformity in signs is a serious inconvenience in all Institutions for the Deaf and Dumb...[however] an identity of signs employed by the different instructors, is absolutely indispensable" (Brown, 1856, p. 3).

Brown and others knew that, even though it would "promote the happiness of American Mutes, were the sign language of all the Institutions in the United States, not merely very much alike, but in all respects identical" (Brown, 1856, p. 5), as with other languages, that the ability for absolute consistency across all possible pedagogy and usage was beyond control, lamenting that, even in "the English language," a sociolinguistic dictionary or lexicon was, as he put it, "still a desideratum [wanted]" for users of English. (Brown, 1856, p. 3)

Brown began assembling *Vocabulary* as early as 1850 ("the result of much labor and study" [Brown, 1856, p. 4]), as a means to somehow provide non-Deaf instructors of Deaf students with a minimum canonical reference to the connotations and pronunciations of then-used signs:

> "Its purpose was not to instruct novices in the sign-language, for its explanations being limited to brief phrases and catch words such as will be intelligible only to educated mutes and their instructors, were not explicit enough for that, but rather to bring about some degree of uniformity among sign makers, and to fix a definite standard of signs" (Fay, 1895, 168–69)

Inspired by the *The School and Family Dictionary and Illustrative Definer*, produced in 1841 by his idol, the Reverend Thomas Hopkins Gallaudet and his colleague Horace Hooker (Gallaudet & Hooker, 1841), Brown deemed the *School and Family Dictionary* "a valuable work, in extensive use in the best schools and academies of the United States" (Brown, 1856, p. 4) and duplicated its contents to inform the list of entries in *Vocabulary*.

Methodology

Vocabulary contained approximately twenty-five hundred signs and focused heavily on compound sign pronunciation (Nover, 2000). A typical entry in *Vocabulary* was very short (Figure 2); to keep the reference at the shortest possible page count ("[had] a detailed description of the signs employed been given, this little vocabulary might easily have been extended to a thousand pages...." [Brown, 1856, 4]), each entry was limited to a single line or line-and-a-half long. Individual pages featured entries in a two-column layout, and heavily abbreviated references to a word's

- grammatical function (e.g. 'v,' for verb, 'n.' for noun, etc.)
- component glosses or English 'equivalents'
- unique connotations and/or parameters (handshapes, movements)

Comprehension of *Vocabulary* is dependent on understanding signs and positions for the listed glosses as well as an obscure appendix ("Abbreviations," p. 47) listing one to three letter contractions for

- prepositions (e.g., ad = 'around,' ag = 'against,' bm = 'bottom,' ro = 'round')
- adverbs (e.g., ady = 'awkwardly,' dw = 'downward,' int = 'intensively,' repy = 'repeatedly')
- nouns or locations (b-s = 'blacksmithing,' carp. = 'carpentry,' c-c = 'coat collar,' fhd = 'forehead')
- verbs (bt = 'brought,' con = 'continue,' ptg = 'pointing,' tk = 'take')
- grammatical denotations (f = 'foregoing,' i = 'intransitive verb,' t = 'transitive verb')

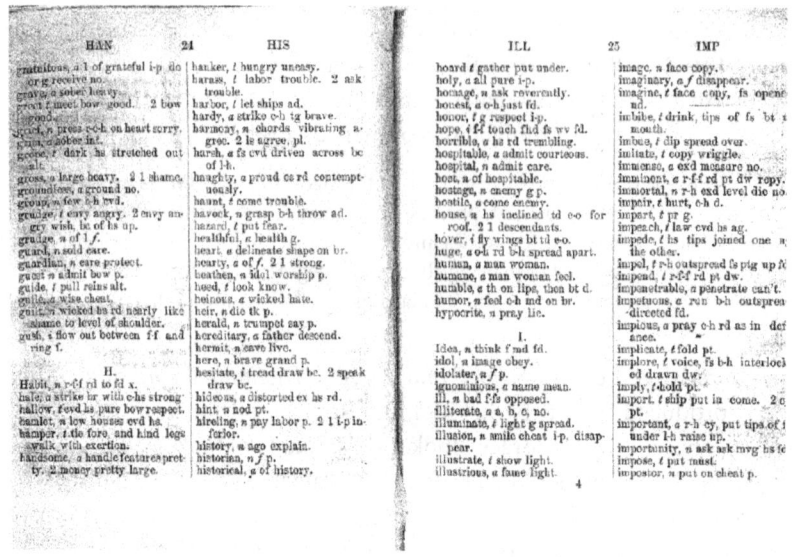

Figure 2. Pages 24–25 of *A Vocabulary of Mute Signs* (Brown, 1856). *Vocabulary* was not a dictionary, per se, but a pronunciation guide based on morphological and lexical sign parts.

The two pages of abbreviations are unfortunately not only not comprehensive but also conflicting in cases (one particular entry uses "1-h" to denote a one-handed pronunciation, but the list of abbreviations indicates that "o-h" should be used).

A few examples provide unique insight into mid-century pronunciations, Brown's understanding of signs, and his intention to preserve their accuracy. The listing on page 25 (Figure 2) for "humble" indicates a 'simple' (or single sign): "…*a* [adjective], *th* on lips, then *bt d*" (Brown 1856, p. 25; italics by author). *Vocabulary*'s rather cryptic abbreviations defines 'th' as 'thumb,' 'bt' as 'brought,' and 'd' as 'down' (47–48), which makes this look like the pronunciation of the modern ASL sign for PATIENCE or a variation on the verb TO-SUFFER. The entry for 'specimen' on page 40, however, indicates the intention to inject multiple semantic concepts into signs: "*n fs of 1-h exe r-th* and *two fs tk one see*" (Brown, 1856, p. 40). Because other contemporary pronunciation references and a comprehensive legend are not extant, in this context, *Vocabulary* often offers more questions than answers.

Observations

There is much more discussion about the linguistics, composition, and structure of *Vocabulary* and Brown's ultimate achievements with this work than can be treated here. However, Brown learned important lessons from his six years of work on *Vocabulary*:

Signed language is more than the sum of its parts. Immediately, a twenty-first century ASL student will recognize that several *Vocabulary* entries highlight not only pronunciation but also Brown's perceived compound structure of signs in the 1860s. A comparison of how signs were written in both his 1856 and 1860 works shows that Brown (and other educators of the time) was learning how the nascent sign language was evolving to more simply and quickly convey complex semantics and salience.

Signed language has an inherent morphology. Secondly, Brown found in Gallaudet & Hooker's *School and Family Dictionary* a replicable and semantic template that would not only structurally inform *Vocabulary* but also his second and greater attempt at a dictionary in 1860. He also began to realize a basic genetic structure for dictionary entries — grammar definitions, abbreviations, etymologies, and sign parameters (movements, handshapes, etc.). As there are no contemporary sources of American signed language production from this time period, it is unknown how accurate Brown's pronunciations of signs were, but as will be shown later in this paper, sign descriptions from his 1860 dictionary are also found in early twentieth-century signed films, which gives some validity to their accuracy.

THE MAIN EVENT: *A LANGUAGE OF ACTION*... (1860)

Brown's second attempt at a dictionary would be much more ambitious and grander in scale. Where *Vocabulary* focused on a preservation of the lexicality and a basic semantic nature of signs as he understood them, his new venture would take him into a much more complex task. There is no evidence that Brown — much less anyone — had *formal* training in the embryonic linguistics or the philology of mid-century sign language, nonetheless, he ventured into conveying its morphology and phonology in his second work. Convinced that the sign language had become, as Laurent Clerc himself put it, "awkward...[and] corrupted," (Porter, 1856, p. 9), Brown picked up the torch and dedicated a significant amount of effort to preserving the language birthed at Hartford.

Brown's work was nothing if not timely — arguably groundbreaking — and spoke to the most critical issue facing Deaf education in the mid-century: the choice of what kind of signed language should be used and promoted in the residential school classroom. Although day schools would slowly begin to gain traction in the 1880s (cf. Van Cleve, 2007 and Reis, 2007), manualism, a healthy respect for natural vs. methodical signs, and its residential/boarding school arena were still clearly the preferred method for Deaf education in the 1850s.

There is, sadly, no known academic discussion or analysis of Brown's 1860 dictionary, but a close reading of an 1895 correspondence between Brown's surviving daughter Emily Brown Robinson and the Indiana Deaf community newspaper *The Daily Hoosier* seems to suggest that she was not fully sure on which project he was working. A full-page article titled "A Dictionary of Signs One Made Fifty Years Ago" appears on page three of the February 14 edition and contains part of a letter to the editor about her father's work. Robinson, who would have only been five years old when Brown began work on *Vocabulary*, discussed his work on the project, recalling that:

> My father did partially write a dictionary of the mute signs, in a large size, but did not live to finish the work. It was a source of great disappointment to him, as he said, not to live long enough to finish it. Some of it is in manuscript and part in printed form. What letter of the alphabet was the last, I do not know. It is not in shape to send it to you — and I do not think can be straightened out. He wrote a little vocabulary once and set the type himself. There were only a few copies printed, and I send you one with my best wishes. Although old and soiled, it is very precious." (Johnson, 1895, p. 3)

The Daily Hoosier article replicated the text of several pages of *Vocabulary* in the article, including the entire preface and the appendix (called "Observations"), abbreviations table, and a selected list of entries from the book. Robinson's recollection of *Vocabulary* is interesting, however, and, perhaps owing to her young age, actually appears to describe Brown's work on his 1860 endeavor, not *Vocabulary*:

- *Vocabulary*, published as a "little book" in 1856 (cf. the page size of the book) was not a "large size," as she told the editor; however, the twenty-four surviving pages of the 1860 work are 25 cm (10 inches) tall
- Robinson said that Brown "did not live long enough to finish the work," however, Brown completed *Vocabulary* in 1856; the first edition of his second dictionary was printed in Louisiana in 1860 shortly before his July 1863 death in Indiana
- that the project was part "in manuscript and part in printed form" seems to suggest that the existing pages of the project may actually be the only completed part and that it was never fully realized
- Robinson remembered that "[h]e wrote a *little* vocabulary once" (italics added), which appears to distinguish it from "a dictionary of the mute signs," implying that Brown's first work on *Vocabulary* had been completed

Although there is no extant evidence for how he determined his new work's ultimate audience, there is little doubt that he considered his fellow Deaf educators and Deaf pupils as the primary audience for his research.

However, Brown also considered a much wider appeal for this new project than for his work on *Vocabulary*, evident in the incredibly verbose but very specific title that he chose for his new work: "A Dictionary of Signs and of the Language of Action, for the Use of Deaf-Mutes, their Instructors and Friends; and, also, designed to facilitate to members of the Bar, Clergymen, Political Speakers, Lecturers, and to the Pupils of Schools, Academies, and Colleges, The Acquisition of a Natural, Graceful, Distinctive and Life-Like Gesticulation" (hereafter, "*Dictionary*") (Brown, 1860a).

Brown was much more purposeful about assigning semantics to entries in *Dictionary* than in *Vocabulary*. In *Dictionary*'s preface, he mentions that the semantics in the entries draw from two sources: Joseph E. Worcester's Boston-published 1860 *Dictionary of the English Language* and an 1860 edition of *Webster's American Dictionary, Pictorial Edition*. Worked into the annotations at the end of each dictionary entry are quasi-cryptic numbers which coincide with definitions, "The expressions 1, 3, 5 : 2, 4 indicate the first, third, and fifth definitions of the word according to Worcester, and the second, fourth definitions according to Webster" (Brown, 1860a, p. vii).

RECONSIDERING STOKOE

Conventional wisdom and lore among contemporary sign language researchers holds that Gallaudet College English professor William Stokoe first unleashed the possibility that a signed language could be described in a phonological and morphological framework (Stokoe, 1960). Along with graduate students Dorothy Casterline and Carl Cronenberg, Stokoe proposed a system for articulating signs in 1965 that introduced *cheremes*, or the parts that make up a sign, and *primes*, or distinct subsets of cheremes, chiefly handshapes, movements, and locations (Stokoe, Casterline, & Cronenberg, 1965). Stokoe is widely considered to have "devised the first system for describing signs" (Valli & Lucas, 2000, p. 26), however, Brown's *Dictionary* has been sorely overlooked in this domain of research.

Well over one hundred years *before* Stokoe, Casterline, and Cronenberg, Brown envisioned a unique triplanal Cartesian morphology and coding and labeling system to enable, he hoped, subsequent generations of signers to preserve correct pronunciations. While no complete volumes of Brown's *Dictionary* are yet extant, the scant pieces that do still exist give users and researchers keen insight into the language's aesthetics a mere forty years past Clerc, Gallaudet, and Hartford.

Brown drew inspiration for his ambitious work from personal heroes Clerc and Gallaudet and the national debate of signed language efficacy, and, from the lessons he learned with *Vocabulary*, had co-opted published works

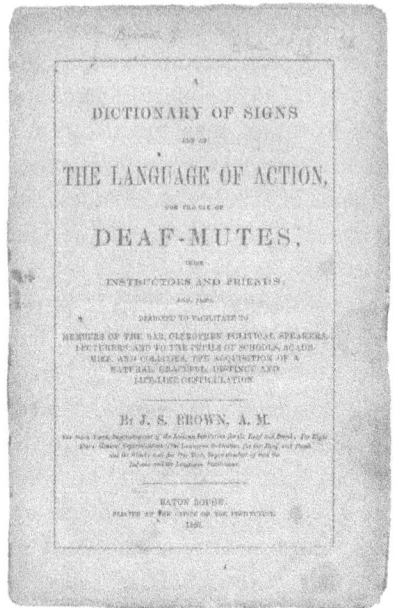 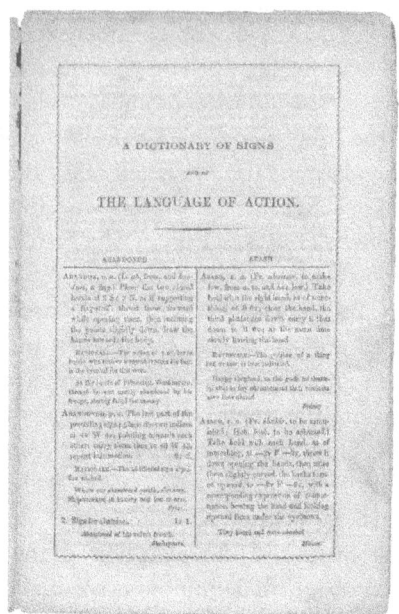

Figure 3a. Title page of A *Dictionary of Signs...* (Brown, 1860a), published at the Louisiana School for the Deaf. The subtitle indicates Brown's desire to inform wide audiences of the linguistics of 'the sign language.'

Figure 3b. The first page of entries to *Dictionary*. The entry structure followed 1860s editions of Worcester and Webster (Brown, 1860a, p. vii).

like *The School and Family Dictionary* (Gallaudet & Hooker, 1841) to inform his book's compositional and semantic structure. He appears to have largely worked alone on *Dictionary*; though blessed with a wife with two deaf siblings (including his good friend, professional Deaf colleague, and brother-in-law Martin Hanson, whom he had convinced to join him at the Louisiana Institution [*First Annual Report*, 1853]) and a large number of extended Deaf family members, there is no other evidence yet that Brown had assistance from or collaborated with any of his various fellow Deaf school teachers nor is the mention of a dictionary present in any of his correspondence or discussions with his national-level colleagues. Brown's own admission that he began concepting *Dictionary* as early as 1850 seems to support this hypothesis as well: though he worked on the project for ten years, his daughter Emily corroborated that he never finished it.

Methodology
In *Dictionary*, Brown proposed a Cartesian framework where sign locations — initial, transitional, and/or terminus — could be plotted, like mathematical formulae, on a dimensional grid. He imagined three perpendicular (x, y,

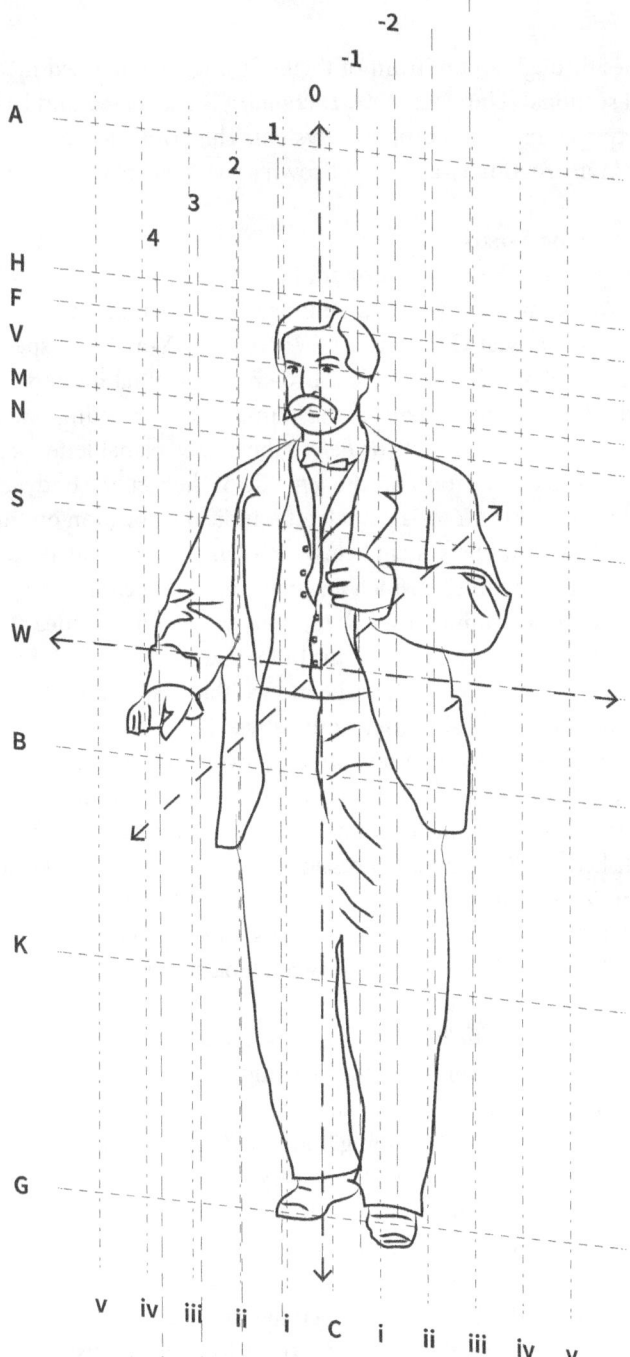

Figure 4. A depiction of Brown's triplanal system for describing sign location. The x-axis is divided into horizontal "palm's breadths" by lowercase roman numerals; the y-axis is divided into eleven vertical sections (A, H, F, V, M, N, S, W, B, K, G); and the z-axis divided by palm's breadths into positive and negative Arabic numbers. 3,564 cubic spaces are possible.

and *z*) planes through and in front of the body and then divided them into meaningful sections. (Unfortunately, *Dictionary* is text-based and lacks any graphical explanation for its proposed system. This paper attempts to add a visual layer of instruction to augment Brown's written explanations.)

The Horizontal, or X-axis

Brown then divided the x-axis (horizontal) in "palms' breadths" (Brown, 1860a, p. iv) determined by Roman numerals, perpendicularly bisecting the center of the body at C (Figure 4). Whereas the Y-axis had specific letters to designate planes (A, H, B, etc.), Brown's horizontal numeric system was dependent on the *placement* of the numeral in the coding system. If "iii," for example, was listed first (or *before* the Y-axis planal letter, e.g. "4iii S 3v"), this indicated a location on the *left* side of the signer's body; alternatively, "iii" listed *after* the Y-axis planal letter indicated location on the *right* side of the body (see coding system below). Brown never indicated exactly in the coding legend the limit to which a signer might stretch his or her signs (..."and by the Roman numerals i, ii, iii, iv, v, vi, vii, viii, ix, measuring to the right or left..."; Brown, 1860a, p. iii) but a scan of the extant dictionary pages shows that "viii," or eight lateral hand widths (assigned to the pronunciations of "abominate," "abstruse," and "abyss") was the widest distance Brown ever indicated in the first seventy-three words of *Dictionary*.

Brown also recognized that a sign might not be pronounced only in neat, fixed widths, but also in "portions of a palm's breadth" and this would be accomplished by "fractional expression[s]; thus i½ W indicates a point on the plane W, one and one-half palms to the left of the Central plane [X-axis center] C. The expression, ¾ S, means on the plane S, three-fourths of a palm to the left of the plane C" (Brown, 1860a, p. iv).

What is a "palms' breadth"? Brown never actually listed a fixed measurement for it in *Dictionary* or any other writings, but a "palm's breadth" or "palm" was a fairly standard linear measurement in the mid-nineteenth century and he used it twice in describing both the X- and Z-axes in *Dictionary*. Measurements of the late nineteenth century were not as yet standardized and still tended to follow anthropometric, or human-based, measuring systems which may have enjoyed popularity in the mid-century because of their use in Biblical texts. (Indeed, the international inch was agreed upon only in 1959 [Astin, Karo, & Mueller, 1959]). Given the wide variety of definitions for "palm," (or "hand") there is some disputation as to its actual distance.

Ancient Egyptians measured a hand/palm at 75 mm (or four 'digits,' the width of a finger, ¼ palm [19 mm]; Clagett, 1999). Roman measuring systems were slightly different, and introduced both a "great palm" (~12 digits at ¼ palm [18.5 mm] = 9 inches [222 mm]) and a "palm" (~4 digits at ¼ palm, or 18.5 mm = 3 inches [74 mm]; Smith, 1851). Still other Mediterranean cities and countries used a "palm" for textiles length based on hand *length*, not width, which introduced variants from 182 mm to 293 mm (Hutton, 1815).

The most contemporary English usage of the word *palm* in the nineteenth century (also called a "handbreadth" or "handsbreadth") calculated the width of a human hand at approximately three inches (76 mm; Mortimer, 1810). Using this measurement, Brown considered that signers would likely stretch laterally no further than twenty-four inches (609 mm) or two feet to either side.

The Vertical, or Y-axis

Brown divided and coded the y-axis (vertical) into eleven salient planes — five focused on head and neck physiology alone — beginning at a point marked by an extended arm (A, "the Arm's length above the head") and ending with a ground plane (G, "l[ying] on the Ground"; Figure 4):

> The plane A is at the Arm's length above the head.
>
> " " H rests on the Head.
>
> " " F cuts the Forehead at half its height.
>
> " " V cuts the Visage or face at half its height, or midway of the nose.
>
> " " M cuts the Mouth between the lips.
>
> " " N cuts the base of the Neck, and rests on the shoulders.
>
> " " S cuts the Breast two palms below the preceding, and is the plane on which more Signs are made than any other.
>
> " " W cuts the Waist two palms below the plane S.
>
> " " B coincides with the Base of the body, or its junction with the lower limbs.*
>
> " " K cuts the Knees.
>
> " " G lies on the Ground.
>
> * Note. — If the arms hang down along the sides of the body, the plane W cuts them at the elbows, and B at the wrists." (p. iii)

It is certainly curious that Brown chose to include anything as high as "A" ("[a]rm's length above the head") or below "W," or the waist (including 'base,' 'knees,' and 'ground') as possible planes for sign production (with rare exception, signs are typically never produced even below the waist because they are out of a conversant's peripheral eyesight) but he may have simply included them as necessary termini.

The Outward, or Z-axis

Finally, Brown determined placements on a z-axis, "measuring forward or backward" (Brown, 1860a, p. iii; Figure 4). Similar to his X-axis coding, the Z-axis centered on a plane envisioned in the fore and aft of the body:

> "The Zero, 0, plane rests on the front of the face, body, and toes, and extends indefinitely to the right and left. Distances from this plane in front, are marked, 1, 2, 3, 4, 5, 6, 7, 8, and 9 : distances in the rear of this plane, are marked by the same numerals with a negative sign prefixed; thus, -1, -2, -3, -4, -5, -6, -7, -8, and -9. Thus, 1 H indicates a point on the plane H, one palm in front of the plane 0; and -4 S means on the plane S, four palms in the rear of the plane 0" (Brown, 1860a, p. iii).

This configuration of a Cartesian system gave Brown a large canvas on which to plot the morphology and lexicality of the sign language of his time. Theoretically, Brown had described 3,564 *whole cubic spaces* (eleven vertical spaces × eighteen horizontal spaces × eighteen outward spaces; not to mention thousands of additional fractional half- or quarter-spaces) which surrounded the body and could map where signs could potentially be placed. The next step in his system was to create a coding method and orthography.

THE CODING SYSTEM

Brown introduced his readers to his unique coding system first with two simple examples:

> "...N v indicates a point on the plane N [base of neck], five palms to the right of the Central plane [that bisects the Y-axis]; while iv N indicates a point on the plane N, four palms to the left of the Central plane." (Brown, 1860a, p. iv)

In the preface, Brown identified four potential locations that his *Dictionary* could display:
- a single hand position on one plane
- simultaneous positions of both hands on same plane
- simultaneous positions of hands on different planes
- continued movement of both hands

Single hand position on one plane

The simplest of the sign positions, Brown defined a simple morphological formula for indicating a point in space — XL Y XR — where (from the signer's perspective) XL represents the distance away from the Central plane on the *left* side of the signer's body or XR represents the distance away from the Central plane on the *right* side of the signer's body, and Y represents the single plane on which the sign is articulated. (It should be emphasized that this is *only a single point in space*, not a sign pronunciation; a handshape and movement still would need to be defined.)

Simultaneous positions of both hands on same plane

Brown also needed a way to describe two-handed signs spaces, or two independent points on the grid and proposed a simple typographic distinction: separate two single hand/single plane point notations with a semicolon (e.g., 4v S 4vi; 3vii 4ii H)

> "The terms, 4v S 4vi, indicate, the left hand placed on the plane S [upper mid-torso], four palms in front of the plane o, and five palms to the left of the plane C; and, at the same time, the right hand placed on the plane S, four palms in front of o, and six palms to the right of the plane C. The series, 3vii 4ii H, indicate both hands placed on H [top of head] at the left of C; the left hand three palms in front of o, and seven palms to the left of C; and the right hand four palms in front of o, and two palms to the left of C." (Brown, 1860a, p. iv)

Simultaneous positions of hands on different planes

When hands are moved to different planes, however, Brown used a different typographic distinction, listing the position of the left hand first, and then the right hand second, separated by a colon:

> "Simultaneous positions of the hands on different planes, arc indicated by writing the numerals and plane letters together, separated only by a colon. Thus 5ii W : 6iii indicate, the left hand on the plane W, five palms in front of o, and two palms to the left of C; and, at the same time, the right hand on the plane H, six palms in front of o, and three palms to the right of C." (Brown, 1860a, p. iv)

Continued movement of both hands

The final concept that Brown created was intended to help a learner be able to reproduce longer and more fluid motion and move signs through multiple points. Brown again used a unique typographic conventions — a comma — to separate discrete movements on either side of a signer's body:

> "A continued movement of one or both hands, may be indicated by the numerals and plane letters marking the points successively passed. Thus: Carry both hands through 4iii S 3i, 3ii M [mouth] 4i, 5i H 5ii, 6v W [waist] : 5ii C, means that the hands are to be carried from point to point, simultaneously and successively, as here stated." (Brown, 1860a, p. v)

HANDSHAPES AND PHONOLOGY

Outside of the ongoing discussions of signed language pedagogy found in the *Annals* between 1848 and 1861 (cf. Baynton, 2002) and even their focus on syntax, the state of sign language phonology in the mid-nineteenth century was largely in infancy. Along with creating his location coding system, Brown attempted to describe various handshapes that could be used in various spaces. Compared to Stokoe, Casterline, and Cronenberg's (1965) nineteen discriminate handshapes ("dez"), *Dictionary* only roughly identifies fifteen shapes, several of them repeated with orientation differences (Table 1).

Brown (1860a) handshapes	Stokoe, Casterline, Cronenberg (1965) handshapes ("dez")
various explanations of 'phalanges'	
'closed hand shut' (A); 'closed shut hand' (S); 'closed hand thumb pointing up' (Å)	A fist
'palm down'; 'palm up'; 'palm out inclining forward about 45°'; 'the tip of the hand'	B flat hand
'extended hand' (B); 'extended hand thumbs up'	5 spread hand
'curved hand' (C)	C cupped hand
'curved hand flattened'	E claw hand
'curved hand, thumb by index'	F okay hand
	G pointing hand
	H index + middle fingers together
'closed hand, little finger down'	I pinkie
	K thumb touches middle finger of V
	L angle hand, thumb + index
	3 (3) vehicle classifier hand, thumb + index + middle fingers
	O tapered hand, fingers curved to touch thumbtip
	R crossed fingers
	V spread index + middle fingers
	W thumb touches pinkie
	X hook
	Y horns
	8 (8) bent middle finger; may touch thumb

Table 1. Comparison of Brown (1860a) handshapes and Stokoe, et al. (1965) ("dez")

Additionally, viewing Brown through the lens of Baker-Shenk & Cokely's (1980) parameter (handshape, palm orientation, movement, and location) taxonomy results in enlightening discoveries. Though not terribly strong in handshape recognition, Brown was surprisingly prophetic in highlighting 'palm down,' 'palm up,' and 'palm out,' or 45°-inclined-forward orientations (Brown, 1860a, p. v). He also recognized the beginning and terminals of sign movement with descriptors like "transversely" (movement along x-axis), "upward" or "downward" (movement along y-axis), "forwards," "backward," or "out" (palm movement along z-axis) (Brown, 1860a, p. vi). Where *Dictionary* excels, however, is in identifying sign *location*; it is apparent from Brown's methodology that he (and perhaps other colleagues) valued and considered location — even granular location — to be a primary feature of preserving the accuracy of 1860s sign language.

THE ENTRIES

Sadly, only twenty-four pages of *Dictionary* are known extant, containing just sixty-eight words with one hundred and three pronunciations (including derivative differences such as noun and adjectival forms along with active and neuter verbs) of words from 'abandon' to 'accroach.' If a word carried multiple definitions, a given description of how to produce the sign was sometimes associated with a coding system reference. Extant 1860 *Dictionary* word entry contents (n = 68) are roughly analogous those of Brown's 1856 *Vocabulary* (n = 47, or a 69.1% similarity). A typical entry in *Dictionary* consisted of several boilerplate features:

- the word entry itself
- an identified part of speech ("grammar, etc.") identified in an abbreviation legend (viii)
- its spoken language etymology (Latin, Greek, French, or otherwise; also identified in an abbreviation legend [viii]) and any identifiable meaningful roots (e.g. 'abandon' was identified as Latin, *ab*, from and *bandum*, a flag); this appears to be a carryover from the 1856 *Vocabulary* which focused on identifying semantic parts of compound signs
- a detailed description of how to produce the sign, including a reference to the coding system
- a 'rationale,' or a visual etymology of what the sign iconically depicts use of the word in an English sentence, often in poetry or literature

TRIANGULATING BROWN

Of course, without other extant contemporary documents and triangulation, it is difficult to determine how accurate Brown was in describing 1860s sign language. Including Brown's 1856 *Vocabulary*, there are few rare published descriptions of *nineteenth-century* American signed language articulation (cf., Mallery, 1881; Clark, 1885; Long, 1909, 1918; Supalla, 1992). There is rather enlightening evidence, however, in Brown's description of the AGENT sign (Brown, 1860a, p. vii). American Sign Language employs a lexemic suffix that a signer can use to designate the actor of a particular activity (the sign AGENT); this sign often functions after the declaration of a verb:

> "thus, by adding this sign to that for the verb serve, we have the sign for *servant*; to legislate, and we have *legislator*; to benefit, and we have benefactor; to law, and we have *lawyer*; to deceive, and we have, *deceiver*, etc. etc." (Brown, 1860a, p. vii, italics added)

Pronunciation of this sign today appears as shown below, but in 1860, Brown described the sign's articulation and etymology as:

> "the personal sign [AGENT]…is made by placing the palms of the extended hands pointing toward each other oi N [neck] oi on the breast, tips of the hands nearly meeting; and thus carrying the hands down the front of the body to oi W [waist] oi. This sign owes its origin to the apron which an artisan wears, which covering as it does the front of the person, becomes a sign for the person. (Brown, 1860a, p. vii)

Figure 5: Robert P. McGregor pronouncing the AGENT suffix in DISCIPLES in "A Lay Sermon" (1913) as described in Brown (1860a)

Figure 6: George W. Veditz pronouncing the AGENT suffix in TEACHER in "Preservation of the Sign Language" (1913) as described in Brown (1860a)

In the 1913 film, "A Lay Sermon: The Universal Brotherhood of Man and Fatherhood of God" produced by the National Association of the Deaf (NAD) as part of its *Preservation* series, Robert P. McGregor provides some serendipitous evidence to Brown's AGENT suffix description. As he questions, in the New Testament, to whom Jesus was indicating should pray to God, McGregor signs FOLLOW + AGENT ("disciples"), and pronounces it *exactly* as Brown elaborates in *Dictionary*.

Even in the most beloved film of the NAD series, "Preservation of the Sign Language" (1913), as George W. Veditz explains the reason for the love that "friends and fellow deaf-mutes" have for the French icon of deaf education Abbe de L'Epee is because he was their first TEACH + AGENT ("teacher"), pronouncing the lexeme *exactly* as Brown describes it in *Dictionary*. A review of other like references to AGENT suffixes in the *Preservation* film series provides evidence that Brown's recorded pronunciation was still present in McGregor, Veditz, and the oratory style of several other contemporaries fifty years *after Dictionary*.

This is significant because comparing and contrasting signs in *Dictionary*, the NAD *Preservation* film series, and modern-day American Sign Language provides rich grounds for research and potential video evidence in observing not only how signed language was pronounced a mere two generations past Hartford but also cataloging how signs have evolved to date.

CONCLUSION

In 1924, editor of the Indiana Deaf community newspaper *The Silent Hoosier* John E. Travis proudly promoted that:

> "It was once thought that there could be no dictionary of the sign-language, as it is so largely ideographic, but we already have two such — the one by Dr. J.[oseph] S.[chuyler] Long of Iowa, and that of Rev. J.[ohn] W. Michaels, recently issued. Now comes another, by Rev. Father D.[aniel] D. Higgins, C. S. S. R, of St. Louis, missionary to the Catholic deaf" (Travis, 1924, p. 4).

In one of the only extant references to Brown's 1860 work, however, Travis rightfully seated *Dictionary* in a rare place in American Sign Language's linguistic and developmental history:

> "There is still another dictionary of the sign language. Perhaps it would be safe to say the first ever undertaken — in America, anyhow. The book is now out of print, it was arranged, edited[,] and published by James S. Brown, the first head of the Indiana School to be designated Superintendent — 1845 to 1853....[T]here remains yet to be printed what should be put into book form, not so much as a dictionary of the sign language as the philology of it." (Travis, 1924, p. 4)

Brown's work on *Dictionary* was, in the chronology of Deaf and sign language studies, one hundred years *ahead* of its time. It pushes the timeline of exploring American signed language lexemic parameters back *an entire century before* Stokoe, Casterline, and Cronenberg. It not only incorporated basic semantics for students and teachers to understand but it also deconstructed composition and skeletal pronunciation while also clarifying etymologies and contexting sign usage. Though tragically shortened and unfinished, better understanding *Dictionary*'s representation of mid-nineteenth century sign language provides researchers with a new tool for triangulating the evolution of signs shortly after their formation at Hartford.

Contributions
Many colleagues have provided valuable assistance to this work; heartfelt thanks to Brandon Scates, Ted Supalla (Georgetown University), Edward Copenhagen (Harvard University), Walker Estes (Louisiana School for the Deaf), Kris Johnson (Indiana School for the Deaf), Elizabeth Dunn (Duke University), Betty Warren and Laura Eliason (Indiana State Library), Connie Swartz (American Philatelic Society), Sylvia Henricks (Franklin Township Historical Society), Frances Wood, Anne Leahy, and research librarians at the State Library of Ohio, Duke University, Gallaudet University, The Ohio State University, and the University of Minnesota.

REFERENCES

Astin, A. V.; Karo, H. A.; & Mueller, F.H. (25 June 1959). "Refinement of values for the yard and the pound." http://www.ngs.noaa.gov/PUBS_LIB/FedRegister/FRdoc59-5442.pdf.

Ayres, J. A. (1849). A complete education for the deaf and dumb. *American Annals of the Deaf and Dumb*, 2(1), 24–32.

Baynton, D. C. (2002). The curious death of sign language studies in the nineteenth century. In W. C. Stokoe, D. F. Armstrong, M. A. Karchmer, J. V. Van Cleve (Eds.), *The Study of Signed Languages* (pp. 13–34). Washington, D.C.: Gallaudet University Press.

Baker-Shenk, C. L., & Cokely, D. (1980). *American sign language: A teacher's resource text on grammar and culture*. Silver Spring, MD: T.J. Publishers.

Brown, J. S. (1856). *A vocabulary of mute signs*. Baton Rouge, LA: Daily Gazette and Comet.

Brown, J. S. (1860a). *A dictionary of signs and of the language of action: For the use of deaf-mutes, their instructors and friends; and, also, designed to facilitate to members of the bar, clergymen, political speakers, lecturers, and to the pupils of schools, academies, and colleges, the acquisition of a natural, graceful, distinct and life-like gesticulation*. Baton Rouge, LA: Louisiana Institution for the Deaf and Dumb and the Blind. Retrieved from http://pds.lib.harvard.edu/pds/view/14809124 16 April 2012.

Brown, J. S. (1860b). *Exposition of the action of a majority of the board of administrators of the Louisiana Institution for the deaf and dumb and the blind*. New Orleans, LA: A. H. Kay.

Brown, J. S. (1863). "Last Will and Testament," recorded in the court 21 Jun 1863. Executed "Galaudet [sic] Marion County Indiana, June 8, 1863." Marion County, Indiana, Will Book C, page 400.

Brown, T. M. (1873). Passport Applications, 1795-1905. Collection Number: ARC Identifier 566612 / MLR Number A1 508; NARA Series: M1372; Roll #: 195: 23 May 1873–10 Jun 1873. Washington D.C.: National Archives and Records Administration (NARA).

Clagett, M. (1999). *Ancient Egyptian Science, A Source Book. Volume 3: Ancient Egyptian Mathematics*. Philadelphia: American Philosophical Society.

Clark, W. P. (1885). *The Indian sign language, with brief explanatory notes of the gestures taught deaf-mutes in our institutions for their instruction and a description of some of the peculiar* laws, customs, myths, superstitions, ways of living, code of peace and war signals of our aborigines. Philadelphia: L.R. Hamersly & Co.

DeMotte. W. H. (1862, April). Indiana Institution for the Education of the Deaf and Dumb. *Indiana School Journal, 7*(4). Indianapolis, IN: Indiana State Teachers' Association.

Fant, L. (1972). *Ameslan*. Acton, CA: Joyce Media, Inc.

Fay, E. A. (Ed.) (1895). Miscellaneous: Mr. Brown's Vocabulary of Signs. *American Annals of the Deaf and Dumb, 40*(2), Washington, D.C.: The Conference of Superintendents and Principals of American Schools for the Deaf. p. 168–169.

Gallaudet, T. H. & Hooker, H. (1841). *The school and family dictionary and illustrative definer*. New York: Robinson, Pratt & Co.

Gallaudet, T. H., Rev. (1848). On the natural language of signs; and its value and uses in the instruction of the deaf and dumb. *American Annals of the Deaf and Dumb, 1*(1), 55–60.

Grover, F. (2013, September 12). Email interview.

Henricks, S. C. (1984, May). Gallaudet: Famous Name and Forgotten Indiana Town. *American Philatelist*, 98, 469-472, 565.

Hoffman, L. (2012, May 29). Email interview.

Hutton, C. (1815). *A philosophical and mathematical dictionary, containing an explanation of the terms, and an account of the several subjects, comprised under the heads mathematics, astronomy, and philosophy both natural and experimental; with an historical account of the rise, progress and present state of these sciences; also memoirs of the lives and writings of the most eminent authors, both ancient and modern, who by their discoveries or improvements have contributed to the advancement of them* (2nd ed). London: the author.

Indianapolis Journal. (1863, June 10). James S. Brown obituary, p 2, c 5.

Indianapolis Sentinel. (1863, June 10). James Smedley Brown obituary, p 2, c 4.

Johnson, R. O. (1895, February 14). A dictionary of signs one made fifty years ago. *The Daily Hoosier*, p. 3. Retrieved from http://indiamond6.ulib.iupui.edu:2011/cdm/compoundobject/collection/ISD/id/1139/show/1137

Lane, H., Hoffmeister, R., & Bahan, B. (1996). *A journey into the Deaf-world*. San Diego, CA: DawnSignPress.

Lane, H., Pillard, R. C., & French, M. (2007). Origins of the American deaf-world: Assimilating and differentiating societies and their relation to genetic patterning. In J. V. Van Cleve (Ed.), *The Deaf History Reader* (pp. 47–73). Washington, D.C.: Gallaudet University Press.

Lee, A. E. (1892). *History of the city of Columbus, capital of Ohio, Volume 1*. Columbus, OH: W.W. Munsell & Co., p. 544.

Long, J. S. (1909). *The sign language: A manual of signs, being a descriptive vocabulary of signs used by the deaf of the United States and Canada*. Washington, D.C.: Press of Gibson Bros.

Long, J. S. (1918). *The sign language: A manual of signs, being a descriptive vocabulary of signs used by the deaf of the United States and Canada* (2nd ed.). Washington, D.C.: Press of Gibson Bros.

Mallery, G. (1881). *A collection of gesture-signs and signals of the North American Indians with some comparisons*. Washington, D.C.: Government Printing Office.

McGregor, R. C. (1913). *A Lay Sermon: The Universal Brotherhood of Man and Fatherhood of God* [Motion picture]. United States: National Association of the Deaf.

Mortimer, T. (1810). *A general dictionary of commerce, trade, and manufactures: exhibiting their present state in every part of the world; and carefully comp. from the latest and best authorities*. London: R. Phillips.

Nover, S. M. (2000). History of language planning in deaf education: The 19th century. Unpublished doctoral dissertation, University of Arizona, Tucson.

Ohio, County Marriages, 1789-1994, index and images, FamilySearch (https://familysearch.org/pal:/MM9.3.1/TH-1-19359-27003-51?cc=1614804&wc=M94Q-VGV:n1424608130: retrieved 16 Feb 2014), Lorain > Marriage certificates 1824-1848, vol 1.

Ohio School for the Deaf. (1898). *Historical and biographical souvenir of the Ohio school for the deaf: Seventy years' history of a notable seat of learning, with personal recollections of its founders and early officials.* Columbus, OH: C. C. Johnston, Publisher.

Padden, C., & Humphries, T. (1988). *Deaf in America: Voices from a culture.* Cambridge, MA: Harvard University Press.

Padden, C. & Humphries, T. (2005). *Inside Deaf culture.* Cambridge, MA: Harvard University Press.

Porter, S. (ed.) (1857). Fourth Convention of American Instructors of the Deaf and Dumb. *American Annals of the Deaf and Dumb,* 9(1). Hartford, CT: American Instructors of the Deaf and Dumb.

Porter, S. (ed.) (1860). Institution Notices: Louisiana. *American Annals of the Deaf and Dumb,* 12(3). Hartford, CT: American Instructors of the Deaf and Dumb.

Rae, L. (1850). Presentation of silver plate to Messrs. Gallaudet and Clerc. *American Annals of the Deaf and Dumb,* 3(1), 41–63. (p. 46)

Reis, M. (2007). The academic integration of deaf children: A historical perspective. In *The Deaf History Reader* (pp. 85–115). John Vickery Van Cleve (ed.). Washington, D.C.: Gallaudet University Press.

Smith, W. & Anthon, C. (1851). *A new classical dictionary of Greek and Roman biography, mythology, and geography partly based upon the Dictionary of Greek and Roman biography and mythology.* New York: Harper & Bros.

Sprague, W. B. (1865). "Noah Worcester, D. D." *Annals of the American Pulpit, Or, Commemorative Notices of Distinguished American Clergymen of Various Denominations: From the Early Settlement of the Country to the Close of the Year Eighteen Hundred and Fifty-five: with Historical Introductions.* Volume 8, p. 191. New York: Robert Carter & Brothers.

Stokoe, W. C. (1960). Sign language structure: An outline of the visual communication systems of the American Deaf. *Studies in Linguistics: Occasional papers (No. 8).* Buffalo: Dept. of Anthropology and Linguistics, University of Buffalo.

Stokoe, W. C., Casterline, D., & Cronenberg, C. (1965). *A dictionary of American sign language based on linguistic principles.* Washington, D.C.: Gallaudet College Press.

Supalla, S. (1992). *The book of name signs: Naming in American Sign Language.* San Diego, CA: Dawn Sign Press.

Travis, J. E. (Ed.) (1924). *The Silent Hoosier,* February 7, 1924. Indiana School for the Deaf: Indianapolis, IN.

Valli, C. & Lucas, C. (2000). *Linguistics of American Sign Language: An introduction.* Washington, D.C.: Clerc Books.

Van Cleve, J. V. (2007). The academic integration of deaf children: A historical perspective. In *The Deaf History Reader* (pp. 116–135.) John Vickery Van Cleve (ed.). Washington, D.C.: Gallaudet University Press.

Veditz, G. W. (1913). Preservation of the Sign Language [Motion picture]. Silver Springs, MD: National Association of the Deaf.

Ware, H. (1845). Memoirs of Rev. Noah Worcester, D. D. *The Advocate of Peace (1837–1845),* 6(3), 33–34.

Wood, F. (2012, May 27). Email interview.

Wright, G. F. (Ed.)(1916). *A standard history of Lorain County Ohio: An authentic narrative of the past, with particular attention to the modern era in the commercial, industrial, civic, and social development; a chronicle of people, with family lineage and memoirs.* Chicago and New York: The Lewis Publishing Company.

Oberlin and Huron College Records

Oberlin College (1909). *Seventy-Fifth Anniversary General Catalogue of Oberlin College, 1833-1908.* Cleveland: Press of The O. S. Hubbell Printing Co. p. 126.

Oberlin Collegiate Institute. (1834). *First Annual Report of the Oberlin Collegiate Institute.* November, 1834. Elyria, OH.

Oberlin Collegiate Institute. (1835). *Catalogue of the Trustees, Officers, and Students of Oberlin Collegiate Institute; Together with the Second Annual Report.* Cleveland: Rice & Penniman's Print.

Oberlin Collegiate Institute. (1836). *Catalogue of the Trustees, Officers and Students, of the Oberlin Collegiate Institute.* Cleveland: Francis B. Penniman.

Huron Institute. (1837). *Catalogue of the Officers and Students of Huron Institute, 1837-38.* Milan, Huron Co. Ohio. Norwalk, OH: Prestons, Printers, Norwalk.

Oberlin Collegiate Institute. (1838). *Catalogue of the Trustees, Officers and Students, of the Oberlin Collegiate Institute.* Cuyahoga Falls, OH: Allison & Mariner, Printers.

United States Federal Census Records

Third Census of the United States. (1810). (NARA microfilm publication M252, 71 rolls). Census Place: Thornton, Grafton, New Hampshire. Records of the Bureau of the Census, Record Group 29. National Archives, Washington, D.C. Retrieved 14 November 2013 from http://ancestry.com.

Fourth Census of the United States. (1820). (NARA microfilm publication M33, 142 rolls). Census Place: Royalton, Niagara, New York. Records of the Bureau of the Census, Record Group 29. National Archives, Washington, D.C. Retrieved 26 April 2014 from http://ancestry.com.

Eighth Census of the United States. (1860a). (NARA microfilm publication M653, 1,438 rolls). Census Place: Franklin, Marion, Indiana. Records of the Bureau of the Census, Roll: M653_280; Page: 891; Image: 268. National Archives, Washington, D.C. Retrieved 26 April 2014 from http://ancestry.com.

Eighth Census of the United States. (1860b). (NARA microfilm publication M653, 1,438 rolls). Census Place: Baton Rouge, East Baton Rouge, Louisiana. Records of the Bureau of the Census, Roll: M653_408; Page: 466; Image: 24. National Archives, Washington, D.C. Retrieved 26 April 2014 from http://ancestry.com.

Ancestry.com. (2009a). Marriage Record of Plumb M. Park and Charlotte Peck: U.S. Special Census on Deaf Family Marriages and Hearing Relatives, 1888-1895 [database on-line]. Provo, UT, USA: Ancestry.com Operations Inc.

Ancestry.com. (2009b). Marriage Record of Martin M. Hanson and Alice M. Park: U.S. Special Census on Deaf Family Marriages and Hearing Relatives, 1888-1895 [database on-line]. Provo, UT, USA: Ancestry.com Operations Inc.

Ancestry.com. (2009c). Marriage Record of Robert F. Moon and Lucinda Webb: U.S. Special Census on Deaf Family Marriages and Hearing Relatives, 1888-1895 [database on-line]. Provo, UT, USA: Ancestry.com Operations Inc.

Ancestry.com. (2009d). Marriage Record of John Wilson Reed and Carrie Lorena Moon: U.S. Special Census on Deaf Family Marriages and Hearing Relatives, 1888-1895 [database on-line]. Provo, UT, USA: Ancestry.com Operations Inc.

Ancestry.com. (2009e). Marriage Record of Joseph Wilson Reed and Carrie Belle Moon: U.S. Special Census on Deaf Family Marriages and Hearing Relatives, 1888-1895 [database on-line]. Provo, UT, USA: Ancestry.com Operations Inc.

Ohio Asylum for the Education of the Deaf and Dumb Annual Reports

Fifteenth annual report of the Trustees of the Ohio Asylum for the Education of the Deaf and Dumb. (1842). Columbus, OH: Samuel Medary, State Printer.

Eighteenth annual report of the Trustees and Superintendent of the Deaf and Dumb Asylum of the State of Ohio. (1844). Columbus, OH: Samuel Medary, State Printer.

Louisiana Asylum for the Education of the Deaf and Dumb Annual Reports

First annual report of the Administrators and Superintendent of the Louisiana Institution for the Education of the Deaf and Dumb, and the Blind. (1853). Baton Rouge, LA: T. B. B. Hatch & Co., Advocate Office, Printers.

Sixth annual report of the administrators and superintendent of the Louisiana Institution for the Education of the Deaf and Dumb, and the Blind. (1858). Baton Rouge, LA: at the office of the Daily Advocate.

Eighth annual report of the Administrators and Superintendent of the Louisiana Institution for the Education of the Deaf and Dumb, and the Blind. (1860). Baton Rouge, LA: at the office of the Institution.

Indiana Asylum for the Education of the Deaf and Dumb Annual Reports

Circular of the Trustees of the Indiana Asylum for the Education of the Deaf and Dumb and the Rules of Internal Economy. (1844). Indianapolis, IN.

First annual report of the Trustees of the Indiana Asylum for the Education of the Deaf and Dumb. (1844). Indianapolis, IN.

Second annual report of the Trustees of the Indiana Asylum for the Education of the Deaf and Dumb. (1845). Indianapolis, IN.

Fourth annual report of the Trustees of the Indiana Asylum for the Education of the Deaf and Dumb. (1847). Indianapolis, IN.

Fifth annual report of the Trustees of the Indiana Asylum for the Education of the Deaf and Dumb. (1848). Indianapolis, IN.

Sixth annual report of the Trustees and Superintendent of the Indiana State Asylum for the Education of the Deaf and Dumb. (1849). Indianapolis, IN: John D. Defrees, State Printer.

Seventh annual report of the Trustees of the Indiana Asylum for the Education of the Deaf and Dumb. (1850). Indianapolis, IN: J. P. Chapman, State printer.

Eighth annual report of the Trustees of the Indiana Asylum for Educating of the Deaf and Dumb. (1851). Indianapolis, IN: J. P. Chapman, State printer.

Ninth annual report of the Trustees of the Indiana Asylum for Educating of the Deaf and Dumb. (1852). Indianapolis, IN: J. P. Chapman, State printer.

Nineteenth annual report of the Trustees of the Indiana Institution for Educating of the Deaf and Dumb. (1862). Indianapolis, IN: Berry R. Sulgrove, State printer.

Directionality of Movement in American Sign Language

KERI BROOKS

AMERICAN SIGN LANGUAGE (ASL) HAS BEEN THE LANGUAGE OF DEAF people in the United States and Canada for over one hundred years: a creole of home signs, Old French Sign Language and Old ASL. It was not until linguist William Stokoe's work in the 1960s that the language was officially recognized as having its own grammar and syntax.

Stokoe (1960) noticed that ASL had grammar feature patterns, specifically position, movement, and orientation of the hands. For movement, he used the word *sig* to code for signification, and recorded movements that consisted mostly of forward, backward, side-to-side, away, or towards signers, and one mention of circular action. There was, however, no indication in Stokoe's system of which direction the circular action should take. Liddell & Johnson later presented the Movement-Hold Model, a more detailed way of recording the movement of signs (Valli, Lucas, & Mulrooney, 2005). This model focuses on the handshape, location, palm orientation, and nonmanual signal changes made during the movement of a sign, meaning one or more of these parameters change. Even with these two ways of recording sign parameters, the directionality of movement is neither mentioned nor emphasized in either model.

Like any other language, ASL is constantly evolving with new vocabulary being introduced as the result of the influences of technology and oralism. Signs such as LIBRARY and COLLEGE are two significant examples of evolving signs. Both LIBRARY and COLLEGE are now being signed more often as an inward movement (towards the signer's body) as opposed to an outward movement (away from the signer's body). According to ASL dictionaries and instructional books published in the 1970s and 1980s, these inward movements are incorrect. At this time, there is no documentation of a set of rules that indicate the directionality of the movements in sign language other than pictures in sign language books that use arrows to indicate directionality and video clips demonstrating how signs are produced. Even with those pictures and videos, there typically is no explanation of the reasoning behind the directionality of the movements.

This evolution of sign directionality has been noted in recent years. As indicated above, LIBRARY has always been signed and published as moving outward away from the body in the older version of the *Signing Naturally: Level 1* book, the *Teacher's Resource* ("Green") books, and *Joy of Signing*. Yet, it is more and more common to see this word signed using the opposite direction, in a circular motion moving towards the body. Even the new *Signing Naturally: Unit 1–6* curriculum shows both directions. This interchangeable sign direction does not change its meaning like it would for other signs that resemble each other, such as COMPUTER, CHURCH, or CHOCOLATE. This merits a discussion on whether the "new" directionality of signs are acceptable or not. There are several possible factors for this trend:

- generational (older signers versus younger signers)
- technological (some video and photography software do not reverse what the camera captures, instead they create a mirrored version of the original source)
- pedagogical (deaf children who are educated in predominantly oral or mainstreamed settings who learn ASL late in life often lack access to native signers and fluency and the ability to reverse what they see being signed in order to reproduce the sign correctly)
- situational (interpreters and teachers produce inaccurate examples)

Something unique to ASL not seen with spoken languages is that oral methods seem to have significantly influenced sign production. More parents have decided to have their deaf children mainstreamed, resulting in a lack of native sign language models for deaf students. A majority of deaf students today learn ASL from their interpreters, teachers of Deaf students, speech-language pathologists, and possibly parents. These people are usually not Deaf and more importantly, they are not always native ASL users. With this in mind, of all the five parameters of ASL (handshape, location, movement, palm orientation and non-manual signals), the directionality of movement seems to be the most impacted by this phenomenon.

What should we do about this phenomenon? While variation is a natural occurrence of human language, it is important for sign language users to understand the difference between pronunciation *variation* and pronunciation *error*. To start with, a set of rules regarding directionality would be beneficial, especially for teaching ASL. With such rules, teachers could explain the rules behind directionality, leading to greater consistency in sign production amongst L2 learners. There are patterns in sign language usage; more specifically, there are patterns in the directionality of sign movements and such patterns need to be documented and shared.

An online survey was created to determine what ASL users believe to be the correct direction for signs. Participants were to be native users, either Deaf or hearing, having used sign language since birth or at least since the age of five. Other participant information was collected: whether they ever had formal ASL instruction and whether they had ever been ASL instructors in community, high school, or college courses. Approximately 50% of the participants had taken a formal ASL course and approximately 48% of the participants did not teach ASL.

A total of twenty-six signs were chosen for this survey based on specific directionality patterns, with two signs presented for each directionality pattern. The survey video presented a right-handed signer demonstrating each sign in opposite directions. Each sign was labeled 'A' for one direction, 'B' for the opposite direction; participants could also choose 'C,' "either."

As expected, the majority of participants shared the same perspective on what they thought was the accurate directionality for each of the twenty-six signs. The patterns of directionality based on the survey results (Table 1) show for either left-handed or right-handed signers with percentages indicating how much that particular directionality was favored.

Palm orientation facing "out" = movement is down-up circular away from body towards dominant side	LIBRARY 82%	SUNDAY 72%
Palm orientation facing "in" = movement is down-up circular towards body, non-dominant side	PLEASE 100%	NAUSEOUS 97%
Palm orientation facing "in," movement is flat circular = towards non-dominant side	MONDAY 93%	SOMETHING 100%
Both palms facing each other and touching, 'U' movement = originates in the non-dominant side and ends at dominant side	UNIVERSITY 95%	COLLEGE 83%
Palm orientation facing "out," 'U' movement = originates in the non-dominant side and ends at dominant side	TRAVEL 72%	ASIA 83%
Both palms facing each other, hands touching, circular movement = movement is towards non-dominant side	WASH 41%	SCOPE 95%

Pattern	Sign 1	%	Sign 2	%
Dominant hand makes movement and then touches non-dominant hand in a flat circular motion = movement is toward dominant side	NATURAL	85%	GRADUATION	100%
Palm orientation facing "in," dominant hand touches non-dominant hand, movement in a flat circular motion = movement is toward non-dominant side	COFFEE	77%	ISLAND	47%
Palm orientation facing "out," dominant hand touches non-dominant hand, movement in a down-up circular motion = movement is toward dominant side	USE	92%	COMPUTER	92%
Movement is horizontal across the chest = originates at the non-dominant side and ends on the dominant side	CONGRESS*	71%	BOARD*	47%
Movement is horizontal across the chin = originates at the non-dominant side and ends on the dominant side	HONEYMOON*	49%	TWINS*	50%
Movement is horizontal across the nose = originates at the dominant side and ends on the non-dominant side	FLOWER	79%	EYES	69%
Movement is vertical on side of face = originates at the side of the chin and ends at the side of the forehead	PARENTS*	67%	HEAD*	47%

Table 1. Patterns of directionality as indicated in survey results. *Signs are noted as having interchangeable beginning locations at the non-dominant side or dominant side, depending on the location of the preceding sign, based on conversations with native users of ASL.

Valli, Lucas, and Mulrooney (2005) indicate additional information about sign movements that are signed across the body, either horizontally or diagonally. For the former, there is flexibility in where the starting point of the sign begins: either on the left or right shoulder. In the survey, horizontal signs signed across the chest (CONGRESS and BOARD) indicated a preference in the starting point of these signs. Seventy-one percent of the participants indicated that the correct directionality for CONGRESS began at the non-dominant side, and 47% (the largest percentage of the three possible answers) indicated the same for BOARD. This contrasts with the information in Valli, Lucas, and Mulrooney (2005), which means an analysis of why survey participants indicated otherwise is crucial.

If one thinks about signs that are signed across the body diagonally, such as KING and LORD, the sign always begins on the non-dominant side and ends on the dominant side. Should the opposite happen, the sign is considered not only incorrect but also uncomfortable to produce. If the rule for diagonal signs across the body has been established as beginning at the non-dominant shoulder, why is this rule not applied to horizontal signs for consistency purposes?

The same issue arises with signs that are signed across the chin, such as HONEYMOON or TWINS. Although a majority of survey respondents participants favored starting at the non-dominant side and ending on the dominant side, the directionality of these signs seem to be interchangeable as well. Interestingly enough, when it comes to signing horizontally across the nose, the opposite direction is preferred: from the dominant side to non-dominant. An overwhelming number of participants responded that signs for FLOWER and EYES began at the dominant side (79% and 69% respectively). The movement directionality across the nose is not as interchangeable as signs produced across the chest or across the chin. Further analysis is needed to determine the reasoning behind this.

In summary, as evident in the survey, there are patterns in directionality of sign movements. By establishing an understanding of these patterns and creating rules or standards for them, it will benefit not only those who teach ASL and interpreters, but also those who teach Deaf children and Deaf adults. With established standards and rules, explanations can be provided to help learners understand the reasoning(s) behind the directionality of sign movements. As a result, these learners will retain what they have learned and apply it to sign production, leading to greater fluency. ASL teachers and interpreters who understand directionality patterns will then be more conscious of their sign production. This, in turn, will produce fewer errors in directionality, thus preserving American Sign Language accurately for years to come.

REFERENCES

Baker, C., & Cokely, D. (1980). *American Sign Language: A teacher's resource text on grammar and culture.* Silver Spring, MD: T.J. Publishers Inc.

Riekehof, L. (1987). *The joy of signing.* Springfield, MO: Gospel Publishing House.

Smith, C., Lentz, E. M., & Mikos, K. (1988). *Signing naturally: Level 1.* San Diego, CA: DawnSignPress.

Smith, C., Lentz, E. M., & Mikos, K. (2008). *Signing naturally: Units 1–6.* San Diego, CA: DawnSignPress.

Stokoe, W. C. (1960). Sign language structure: An outline of the visual communication systems of the American deaf. *Studies in linguistics: Occasional papers (No. 8).* Buffalo, NY: University of Buffalo.

Valli, C., Lucas, C. & Mulrooney, K. (2005). *Linguistics of American Sign Language: An introduction* (4th ed.). Washington, D.C.: Gallaudet University Press.

Introducing the Historical Sign Language Database

TED SUPALLA, PH.D.

THE SHARING OF INFORMATION IS A KEY VALUE WITHIN THE AMERICAN Deaf community, and the information from historical linguistic research may benefit and interest deaf individuals who use American Sign Language, along with hearing and deaf linguists/interpreters who are interested in language change and variation. The deaf community may appreciate learning more about the history of ASL and Deaf Studies scholars may be interested in tools and resources for accessing the language from earlier times.

Because ASL is not a written language, there is very little data available on early forms of the language. These data have previously been available only through rare historical dictionaries and video copies of early motion picture films. This paper describes a new online technology offering sign language researchers, students of sign language and interpreting and Deaf Studies scholars a tool for rapid access to these historical materials.

The Historical Sign Language Database (HSLDB) contains linked, annotated, and cross-referenced corpora, including fourteen National Association of the Deaf films from the early 1900s, as well as the complete entries from three contemporaneous dictionaries of American Sign Language. Background biographical data on the signers and summary information on film content is also included. The HSLDB is now available to the public at hsldb.georgetown.edu.

This digital resource supplements a new textbook, co-authored with Patricia Clark, *Sign Language Archeology: Understanding the Roots of American Sign Language*, published by Gallaudet University Press in 2015. The text reports on analyses of historical documents that included metalinguistic discussions of sign language studies, linguistics, literature, and literacy in America. These documents showed that authors during the early stages of ASL recognized and adapted to natural changes occurring in the language and its community and used this knowledge to develop pedagogical approaches to the instruction of deaf children. Using this knowledge in reviewing historical documents can help to overcome the limitations of materials available for direct historical reconstruction.

HISTORICAL FILM AND BOOK SOURCES

To successfully develop a method for studying change and variation in sign formation, "periodization" is necessary. In our research, we establish the periods of time and use for each of the changing forms of a sign by noting and recording the dates of their use in our primary source materials. Such tokens are cross-referenced whenever the book authors' glosses along with descriptive texts/graphics on sign formation match the actual usage of signs in films.

To date, the HSLDB includes the fourteen NAD films and three sign language dictionaries produced around the same time. Table 1 below shows the total number of signs ("items") glossed. The "metadata" column shows the total number of background, gloss, and additional sign formation information entries for these sources.

Source	Year	Glossed Sign Items	Format	Metadata
14 NAD Films	1910-21	5553	Films	22132
Long book	1910, 1918	1103	Photos, texts	4412
Higgins book	1923	847	Photos, texts	3388
Michaels book	1923	602	Photos, texts	2408

Table 1. Data sources and metadata counts in the HSLDB

From 1910 to 1921, the National Association of the Deaf (NAD) created a set of films to preserve and demonstrate the sign language of the period. They featured speeches, poetry, and stories performed by twelve master signers. The master signers were of different ages, providing a sample of three generations of ASL users at the time. These films have turned out to be a rich source of material for analyses of historical change in ASL.

Year	Signer	Title	Film Length
1915	Bryant, Arthur D.	Introducing Fox in "Lincoln's Gettysburg Address"	29 min
1913	Cloud, James	A Plea for a Statue of de l'Epee in America	6 min
1913	Dougherty, George T.	The Discovery of Chloroform	6 min
1920	Drake, Harley D.	Role of Thomas Hopkins Gallaudet ("A Chapter from the Life of Thomas Hopkins Gallaudet")	6 min
1915	Draper, Amos	The Signing of the Charter of Gallaudet College	5 min
1913	Erd, Mary Williamson	The Death of Minnehaha	14 min
1913	Fay, Edward Allen	Dom Pedro's Visit	5 min
1915	Fox, Thomas H.	Lincoln's Gettysburg Address	10 min
1910	Gallaudet, Edward M.	The Lorna Doone Country of Devonshire England	15 min
1913	Hanson, Olof	Introducing Hubbard in "Address at the Tomb of Garfield"	41 min
1913	Hotchkiss, John B.	Memories of Old Hartford	16 min
1913	Hubbard, Willis	Address at the Tomb of Garfield	9 min
1920	Hughes, Frederick	Role of Edward Miner Gallaudet ("A Chapter from the Life of Thomas Hopkins Gallaudet")	6 min
1920	Knox, Ruth	Role of Mrs. Gallaudet ("A Chapter from the Life of Thomas Hopkins Gallaudet")	6 min
1920	Marshall, Winfield E.	Yankee Doodle	4 min
1913	McCarthy, Michael R.	Reading the printed text for "A Plea for a Statue of de l'Epee in America"	6 min
1912	McGregor, Robert P.	The Irishman's Flea	2 min
1912	McGregor, Robert P.	The Lady & the Cake	2 min
1913	McGregor, Robert P.	A Lay Sermon	16 min
1913	Regensberg, Oscar H.	Introducing Dougherty in "The Discovery of Chloroform"	15 min
1913	Veditz, George W.	Preservation of the Sign Language	14 min

Table 2. Names of dates, signers, roles, titles, and length in NAD Preservation films (in signer alphabetical order).

USING GLOSSES AND FORMATIONAL SYMBOLS IN SIGN LANGUAGE TRANSCRIPTION

Our transcription procedure involved the viewing of a film text first to determine its gist followed by a sentence-by-sentence or phrase-by-phrase rough glossing of each sign. Gloss selection was based on the combination of 1910, 1918, and 1923 dictionary glosses and current generally accepted glosses for most signs. For signs that seemed to be precursors to several current forms, a more generic gloss was selected. The transcription then was expanded and refined by the addition of more specific grammatical information such as beginning and ending location of an inflected sign while re-viewing the film. Our transcriptions of such information were based on descriptive conventions used by Baker & Cokely (1980), and Lentz, Mikos, & Smith (1988) plus a few developed in house.

TUTORIAL GUIDES AVAILABLE IN THE HSLDB

The HSLDB provides a series of guides and tutorials for helping users cross-index different sign forms used by authors in the three book sources and signers in the NAD films. They demonstrate a fundamental technique by which a reference gloss serves as a unique identifier for tracking a particular lexical form across the tokens in the search results.

Viewing Films

The Films tab allows you access to the films, the glossed transcriptions of the sign language in the film, and English translations of what is on the films. The red button in Figure 1 leads the user to the sign language corpus as documented in a particular NAD film. Figure 2 lists a sequence of ASL clauses as presented by Robert McGregor in "A Lay Sermon" film.

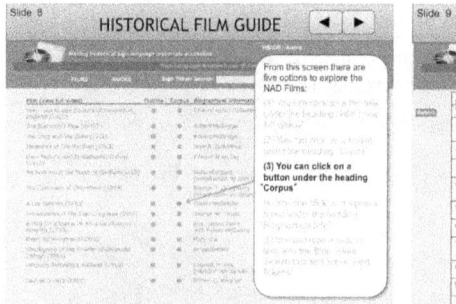

Figure 1. Tutorial slide showing Film access choices

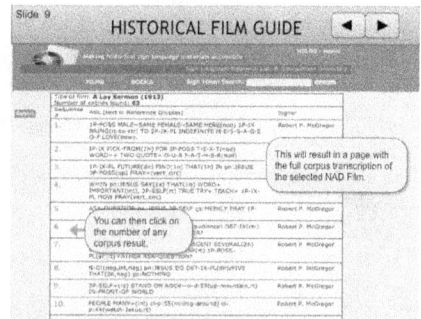

Figure 2. Tutorial Slide showing full corpus annotation for each film segment

Individual segments within a film can be accessed via Token Search results (Figure 3).

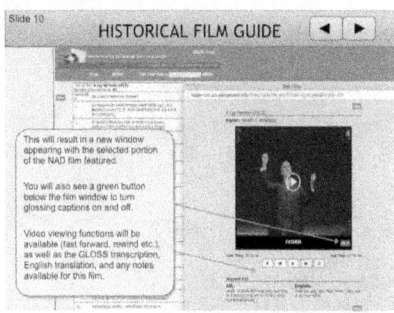

Figure 3. Tutorial slide showing film segment viewing window

Searching Sign Tokens

Glosses, the use of English words to represent signs in written form, are an inherent part of the search function in the HSLDB. Searching a particular gloss for a sign within the HSLDB provides a cross-referenced listing of all tokens that appear in the NAD Films and the three early ASL Dictionaries published during the same era. The Sign Token Search is the tool for viewing all instances (or tokens) of a selected sign in the dictionaries and NAD films.

 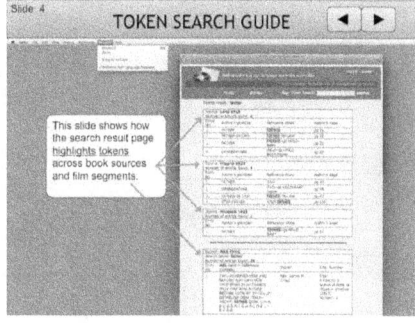

Figure 4. Tutorial slide showing instructions for token searches

Figure 5. Tutorial slide showing HSLDB search result page

Sign tokens are stored and located by the Reference Gloss designed within our lab to link related data through a common and unique identifier for each sign. When you enter an English search term in the Sign Token Search box, you will be taken to a page that lists all tokens in both film and dictionary sources.

This page will also allow you to click and view the actual dictionary descriptions and film clips where that sign appears. Figure 6 below shows how a token window will pop up when a particular row in the search output page is clicked.

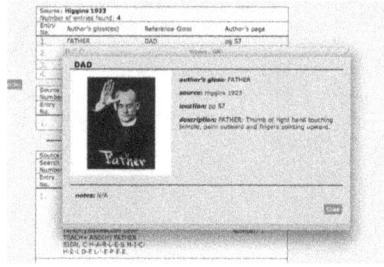 

Figure 6. Tutorial slide showing search result window for a Dictionary entry

Figure 7. Display of grouped dictionary search result viewing windows

The HSLDB token search platform enables synchronic comparison of sign language data from a particular time period. Shown below is a demonstration of how to compare multiple book entry tokens involving the concept of 'fatherhood.' Further comparisons may be made by accessing film segment tokens as shown below.

Figure 8. Display of grouped dictionary and film search result viewing windows

These depictions of search results and comparison of sign language forms for a particular time period have the potential to become an important part of a Deaf Studies/ASL curriculum in the future, enabling instructors to demonstrate and trace the etymology of a modern sign. The electronic articles in ASL mentioned below provide an example of how the HSLDB data can be used in sharing content on ASL history.

Briefly stated here, in the process of building the HSLDB, we discovered various types of signs representing different stages of development in the language that needed to be marked for form as well as content. So when an older gloss from the 1910, 1918 and/or 1923 dictionaries is readily understandable today and uniquely identifies the form, the older gloss will be retained as the reference gloss for FATHER, as shown in Figure 9 below.

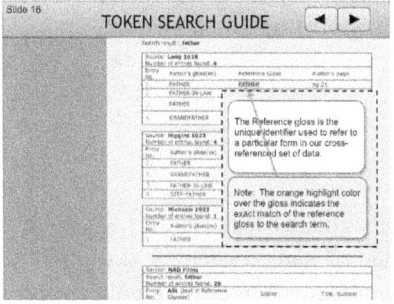 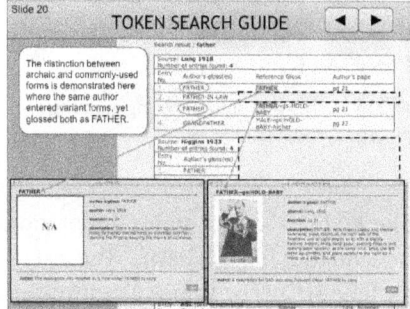

Figure 9. Tutorial slide showing Reference gloss highlighting in search results

Figure 10. Tutorial slide showing glossing of variant forms

There are some occasions where we found more modern variants in the films and books that are distinct from the older forms, like, for example, DAD. Figure 10 below shows two distinctive forms entered into Long's 1918 book for which the same gloss was assigned by the author (see red circles in the figure). Indeed, the abbreviated version described in the left entry would be glossed as FATHER today, due to the process of relexicalization (see Supalla, 2014; Supalla & Clark, 2015, and Supalla, Limousin, & McDonald, in press). The form in the right-hand entry has survived only in formal recitations of the Lord's Prayer.

Meanwhile the three book authors with their different backgrounds do not necessarily abide by common rules for assigning the same gloss, yet they still comply with common principles for deriving or inflecting words. Figure 11 below shows a common derivational process for generating the GRANDFATHER version, in spite of the fact that Long and Higgins each used a different form as the lexical root in the word formation.

Figure 11. Tutorial slide showing glossing of divergent root sign forms

The HSLDB also contains annotation of sign language features within and beyond this lexical level. The categories of sign formation documented include sign type values about the general formation of the sign, pro-form and determiner values, classifier values, specific hand values, specific location values, specific path direction values, body orientation values, manner of movement values, number morpheme values, aspectual morpheme values and non-manual morpho-syntactic inflection values.

The information uncovered through this approach has always been available, but contemporary sign language research has not fully applied the knowledge and principles of language change that historical linguistics can provide in studying the emergence and evolution of lexicon and grammatical morphology (Supalla, 2008; Supalla, 2014; Supalla & Clark, 2015; Supalla, Limousin, & McDonald, in press).

ELECTRONIC ARTICLES IN ASL

A series of articles presented in ASL in the *Deaf Studies Digital Journal* describes the methodology and provides examples of historical reconstruction that establishes etymological relationships between early and modern signs. The search and comparative display functions of the HSLDB enable researchers and teachers to share discoveries on etymological relationships among ASL signs across sources and time periods. Links to each article, with access to an English summary and reference citations is given below, along with the article title and a description of its topic. Below this information, a list of the individual video clips for the sections of each article is given, along with the viewing time for that section. These articles have the potential to be used as a teaching tool for how to use the HSLDB in ASL and Deaf Studies classes. Moreover, these video clips in sequence set forth scientific argumentation leading to the conclusion that Old French Sign Language did indeed function as a protogrammar for ASL. Future versions of the HSLDB will feature ways to insert direct links to HSLDB examples within curricular and academic articles for ease of use and for viewing the actual data in context by teachers, students and researchers.

Sign Language Archeology (Supalla, 2009)
http://dsdj.gallaudet.edu/index.php?issue=1&section_id=9&entry_id=68
Video 1: Introducing Sign Language Archeology (01:39 minutes)
Video 2: Defining Cohort Generations (3:50)
Video 3: Tools for Analyzing Variation (4:00)
Video 4: Integrating Synchronic and Diachronic Approaches (3:49)
Video 5: Digging On Your Own (1:21)
Video 6: Data: NEVER (00:37)
Video 7: Data: STARS (00:21)
Video 8: Data: WATER (00:33)
Video 9: Data: WHO (00:29)
Video 10: Acknowledgements (1:30)

Using Etymology to Link ASL to LSF (Supalla, 2010)
http://dsdj.gallaudet.edu/index.php?issue=3&section_id=9&entry_id=87
Video 1: Recognizing Folk Etymology (5:15)
Video 2: Integrating Etymological Sources (1:48)
Video 3: Seeking the French Connection (6:04)
Video 4: Revealing Periodic Reanalyses (3:18)
Video 5: 'Thumbing' through the Sources (9:54)
Video 6: Accommodating the Outliers (2:09)
Video 7: Contributing Etymologies to Sign Language Archeology (2:39)

Guidelines for the Study of ASL Etymology (Supalla, 2012)
http://dsdj.gallaudet.edu/index.php?issue=4&section_id=9&entry_id=120
Video 1: Introduction: "A Field Guide Companion for ASL Etymology" (00:35)
Video 2: Scrutinizing Etymological Sources (3:32)
Video 3: Sizing up the French Connection (2:25)
Video 4: Ruffling FATHER's Feathers (3:10)
Video 5: Alternative Connections (3:17)
Video 6: Change across Multiple Contexts (3:32)
Video 7: FACE Hidden in Plain Sight (4:50)
Video 8: The Gift of Knowledge (3:58)
Video 9: Lexicography and Homonymy (4:37)
Video 10: Flaws in Lexicography (3:15)

Video 11: Contextual Restraints on Reduction (2:39)
Video 12: Etymological Development in Context (3:48)
Video 13: Summary of Guidelines (1:29)

Tracking our Sign Language Heritage (Supalla, Malzkuhn, & Limousin, 2014)
http://dsdj.gallaudet.edu/index.php?issue=5&section_id=9&entry_id=205
Video 1: Illuminating a 250-year legacy (2:49)
Video 2: The early 20th century sign language campaign (6:50)
Video 3: Further documentation in the 20th Century (2:43)
Video 4: Preserving Deaf folklife films (2:58)
Video 5: Creating a historical film database (3:05)
Video 6: Interpretation of Deaf values in films (6:11)
Video 7: Reconstruction and reenactment of historical signs (4:49)
Video 8: Before the beginning: LSF in France (2:46)
Video 9: The First 50 years of LSF Documentation (2:31)
Video 10: The Etymology for MAN in LSF (4:09)
Video 11: The constructions for BOY in LSF (4:28)
Video 12: The history of ideas in the Deaf Community (5:30)
Video 13: Community epistemology in the NAD films (4:24)
Video 14: Framing ASL as a heritage language (2:22)

SUMMARY

The HSLDB project represents the first major historical linguistic corpus work on a natural sign language with a 250-year evolution, investigating the emergence and change of the lexicon and morphology over the ten generations of its use. The Sign Language Archaeology textbook and online *Deaf Studies Digital Journal* video lectures accompanying the HSLDB platform are the foundation and catalyst for additional resource material and research tools for integrating the linguistic archiving, analysis and reconstruction efforts for early forms of ASL.

Acknowledgements
This research has been supported by NSF Research Grant BCS0925073 to Ted Supalla, NIH Research Grant DC00167 to Elissa L. Newport and Ted Supalla, and by an NEH Fellowship Award to Ted Supalla. Significant contributors to this work include research associates Donald S. Metlay, who programmed the original database architecture using PHP and MySQL software, and Patricia Clark, who completed the original translations and annotations of the historical films and dictionaries. The author thanks Betsy Hicks McDonald for assistance with writing and editing this paper. The author also thanks the Gallaudet University Archives and SignMedia Inc., where the original films were preserved and reproduced. The HSLDB website images in this article are reprinted with the permission of T. Supalla and Georgetown University.

REFERENCES

Baker-Shenk, C. L., & Cokely, D. (1980). *American Sign Language A teacher's resource text on grammar and culture.* Silver Spring, MD: T.J. Publishers.

Lentz, E. M., Mikos, K., and Smith, C. (1988). *Signing naturally teacher's curriculum guide.* San Diego, CA: DawnSign Press.

Supalla, T. (2001). Making historical sign language materials accessible: A prototype database of early ASL. *Sign Language and Linguistics,* 4, 285-297.

Supalla, T. (2004). The validity of the Gallaudet lecture films. *Sign Language Studies* 4: 261-292 (2004).

Supalla, T. (2008). Sign language archeology: Integrating historical linguistics with fieldwork on young sign languages. In R. M. de Quadros (ed.), *Sign Languages: Spinning and unraveling the past, present and future. Proceedings of the Ninth International Conference on Theoretical Tssues in Sign Language Research.* Florianopolis, Brazil, December 2006. Petropolis, Brazil: Editora Arara Azul.

Supalla, T. & McDonald, B. H. (2011). Building an infrastructure to support historical sign language research. *Minpaku Anthropology Newsletter, No. 33, National Museum of Ethnology, Osaka, Japan,* December 2011.

Supalla, T. (2013). The role of historical research in building a model of sign language typology and variation. In Kikusawa, Ritsuko. and Reid, Lawrence. (Eds.) *The Proceedings of the International Conference of Historical Linguistics* 20, 15-42. The Hague: John Benjamins.

Supalla, T. & Clark, P. (2015). *Sign language archeology: Understanding the historical roots of American Sign Language.* Washington, D.C.: Gallaudet University Press.

Supalla, T, Limousin, F. & McDonald, B. H. (in press). Historical change in American Sign Language. In Richard D. Janda, Brian D. Joseph, & Barbara S. Vance (Eds.) *The Handbook of Historical Linguistics Vol. 2.* Hoboken, NJ: Wiley-Blackwell.

Writing Signed Languages:
FOR-FOR? FORM?

DON GRUSHKIN, PH.D.

"After years and years of study, sign language has proven to be extremely valuable.... If we had used sign language, it would have been faster to develop the written language...faster than the transfer of spoken language to written language." (Itard, 1821, p. 325–326)

DESPITE DR. JEAN-MARC ITARD'S SOMEWHAT HYPOCRITICAL PRIVATE musings, the development of a conventionally accepted written system for signed languages has yet to take place. Modern Deaf audiences tend to point to the visual-spatial-kinesthetic nature of signed languages as a rationale for why they believe it is not possible to encode signed utterances in a static format such as writing. What is often overlooked, however, is the fact that spoken languages, being transitory (speech sounds "disappear" almost instantly after being produced) and "invisible" (one cannot see speech) are seemingly equally nonviable candidates for encapsulation in the static, visible format of written languages. Although speech is exceedingly ephemeral, numerous societies have developed a variety of ways to encapsulate the spoken word.

What is the advantage to writing? Carl Sagan put it grandly when he said "Writing is perhaps the greatest of human inventions, binding together people, citizens of distant epochs, who never knew one another" (2011, p. 232). More prosaically, writing allows the easy recording, storage and retrieval of records, history and literature. Writing allows individuals to communicate across distance and time (as mail or e-mail), to share thoughts trivial and major, as shopping lists or grand treatises, news and gossip, mental notes and manuals, books and folklore, and much more. Hagege (1988) observed:

"The intangibility of its contents and its dissimilarity to oral language altered many of the normal circumstances of discourse, creating long-distance dialogues where the usual proximity of the communicators was lacking. Yet precisely because of this, knowledge could become accessible to a far greater number of recipients–writing possessed the advantages of both longevity and range. In spreading to different areas and societies it allowed for all the changes, input and variations that any culture would require, permitting the encoding of new words as well as of already existing ones" (p. 72)

OBJECTIONS TO AND POTENTIAL BENEFITS OF WRITING SIGNED LANGUAGES

Despite the advantages of writing, Deaf communities worldwide have remained predominantly, if not staunchly, "oral," resisting the notion of a written form of their signed language as an impossibility. Objections to the notion of writing signed languages typically follow along the lines presented below. Each argument against writing signed languages will be accompanied by a rebuttal.

Signed languages are not supposed to be written; signed languages are languages in a visual-spatial modality in which elements are presented simultaneously, or nearly so. Moreover, signed languages have features which are not present in spoken languages such as classifiers and spatial morphology that cannot be adequately represented in a two-dimensional format such as writing.
Although in real time, signs may appear to be occurring in time and space, with multiple syntactical and semantic elements embedded within the movements and facial/body grammar, Liddell (1984) and Liddell & Johnson (1989) observed that there is actually an element of sequentiality within signs themselves. Just as consonants are often followed by vowels in many spoken languages, sign movements can be seen to have discrete components. For example, in even a simple sign like "thank you," the hand must first move away from the mouth before beginning its downward (and outward) motion.

Signed languages are best recorded by video technology, since signed language is produced in the visual modality; indeed, video recording is sufficient for instructional, linguistic and social purposes.
While it is true that video technology is probably the best medium for capturing signed utterances exactly as they are produced, the same can be said for audio technology. Yet, audio technology is relatively little-used in comparison to written language. For example, there are books on audio tape. Even so, with the exception of blind people and drivers with long commutes,

most people choose not to listen to a book on tape. This is primarily due to the fact that audio recordings are simply not as convenient as their written counterparts. One must listen to an audio recording sequentially, investing a certain amount of time to hear the message, at the pace the message is recorded. With written works, however, one can skim or read faster than the recorded message might be. Moreover, audio recordings are not easily searchable or scannable; it is difficult to fast-forward through a recording to find a certain word or to search a recording by using a search term to identify instances of a word or phrase.

With writing, however, one can easily skim and search through sections of a written work for those desired words or phrases. The same issues are present in video technology: it takes more time to watch a video than it would be to read (or skim) a transcribed version of the same video, and videos are also difficult to search and scan through. Although most Deaf people presently would likely say they would prefer to watch a video than to read a written version of it, it is probably true that were they to learn and become comfortable with a written form of signed language, they would prefer to read than watch the contents for time-saving purposes.

Developing a written form of signed language will promote the isolation of Deaf people from the "Hearing World": with a written form of their signed language, Deaf people will not need or even want to learn to read and write English.
This is the (monolingual) oralist argument that exposing Deaf people to signed language will prevent them from learning English. This premise has long been found to be false; indeed, research has consistently shown that Deaf children of Deaf adults (whose first language would presumably be a signed language) on the whole outperform their Deaf peers in written language skills (see Stuckless & Birch, 1966; Meadow, 1968; Corson, 1973). If knowing sign language was a deterrent to learning the written form of a spoken language, then one would expect that native signers would not be able to learn how to manipulate a written language. But Deaf people are a small linguistic and ethnic minority (Higgins, 1980; Padden & Humphries, 1988) within the majority "Hearing" society; Deaf people recognize that it is a necessity to be bilingual, to use their signed language for daily communication, yet interact with and contribute to the "Hearing World" through the written form of the majority's spoken language. The same goes for a written form of signed language: although Deaf might read Deaf newspapers, books, stories, and more in a written signed language, Deaf would by necessity also need to be literate in the written form of the majority spoken language, for employment and informational purposes.

Thus, just as certain linguistic minorities like Hispanics, Chinese and Jews can be seen reading materials printed in the written languages of their communities, one also sees these same people speaking and writing in English or other languages spoken by the majority around them. Indeed, in modern society, English has become a global Lingua Franca, and Deaf people will maintain a need to know how to read and write English in order to participate in the global marketplace.

There is no conventionally accepted form of written signed language; moreover, since there is no significant community of written signed language users, there is no need to learn and use a written form of signed language.
It is true there is no conventionally accepted form of written sign language, and it is equally true that there is no significant community of written signed language users. However, this argument is somewhat circular: effect implies cause implies effect. All writing had to be developed at some point, and to find a community of adopters. Due to the utility of writing, writing became conventionalized among early human communities. One can also look to more recent innovations in writing. In 1821, Sequoyah developed his syllabary for use with the Cherokee language. Although his efforts to disseminate this writing system among his tribe were initially resisted, the value of writing their language was realized in less than 10 years, and a community of written Cherokee writers and readers quickly formed. Similarly, Louis Braille's system for encoding written English into a form accessible by blind people had its early detractors, but today is a standard for blind people nearly worldwide.

It is hard enough to learn English, without having to learn and use some newfangled signed language writing system.
It has been argued by advocates of ASL/English Bilingual education that English functions as a second, rather than first language for most Deaf people (Israelite, Ewoldt & Hoffmeister, 1992; Johnson, Liddell & Erting, 1989; Grushkin, 1998). Consequently, any difficulties with developing fluency in written English can be partly attributable to the dysfluencies of expressive English displayed by second language learners. It is well known that children learn to read and write in their first language upon entering school (if not before), and with time, practice and exposure, most become adept at manipulating the written form of their language. Although Deaf people may experience difficulties in manipulating written English as a second language, these difficulties might not be evident given familiarity with a written form of their native (or natural) signed language.

Deaf students need to learn the state-required curriculum; instruction in written ASL takes time away from learning English.
A primary argument of ASL/English Bilingual/Bicultural education has been that as a first (and natural) language of Deaf people, ASL should be used for "through the air" instruction. Krashen (1996) summarizes the rationale for this as follows:

> "When we give students quality education in their primary language, we give them two things:
>
> (1) Knowledge, both general knowledge of the world and subject matter knowledge. *The knowledge that children get through their first language helps makes the English they hear and read more comprehensible*
>
> (2) Literacy, which transfers across languages." (p. 55, emphasis added)

There are a number of studies, such as that of Koda (1988) which indicate that cognitive skills developed in reading a first language do transfer to reading in a second language. Or, as Krashen (1996) says, "Once you can read, you can read. The ability to read transfers across languages" (p. 55). He explains this as a natural consequence of learning in a first language: "…we learn to read by reading, by making sense of what we see on the page…. *If we learn to read by reading, it will be much easier to learn to read in a language we already understand*" (p. 55, emphasis added).

Although most efforts currently focus on pushing Deaf students to read in English, these efforts are somewhat counterintuitive, since as Krashen indicated, Deaf students are being taught to read in English, their second language, without first developing literacy skills in their first, primary language: ASL. If Krashen and his adherents are correct, then it makes sense that Deaf students should instead learn to first read and write in ASL before beginning instruction in written English. It is entirely possible to develop a body of work in written ASL (literary and academic) which can be used to bolster Deaf people's linguistic and cognitive development in that language. Although their development in English would be deferred until a later point in their education, this delay would likely be more than compensated for by increased competence in written English deriving from their increased competence in written and signed ASL.

Written signs cannot adequately record prosody (speed), stress, or accents.
Writing is a limited medium. Utterances in spoken languages likewise cannot be adequately recorded in the static form of writing. Indeed, most writing cannot capture all of the possibilities that one might see in a spoken text. However, writers have often found ways to convey at least some elements of

spoken languages through nonstandard forms. Use of words like "shouted," "screamed," "blurted" give clues to the speaker's tone. A young girl might be depicted as saying "OMIGODJOHHNYCALLEDMEANDHEWANTSTOGOWITH-METOTHEPROM!," which conveys a sense of talking fast, and the use of capitals also gives clues to the loudness of the speaker's voice, or the stress they may place on certain words. The underlining of the word "is" at the beginning of this paragraph is another device to portray stress. Accents are shown through nonstandard spellings such as "y'all," "youse," "pahk your cah." A well-developed system of written signed language would also develop ways which would be conventionally understood to convey elements of signed utterances which would otherwise not appear in the static, two-dimensional format of written language.

Most, if not all, signed languages utilize classifiers, which are often novel forms and might not be understood in writing.
Written language can introduce novel words and forms that are understood through context. One only needs to read Lewis Carroll's poem "Jabberwocky" for an example of written language utilizing a large number of lexical inventions which nonetheless are understood by their syntactic and semantic roles, as well as through the use of metacognitive strategies such as making use of context. Classifiers in a signed language can be treated in the same way–readers would utilize their skills in decoding written signed language to grasp the new word being presented and would likely utilize metacognitive skills to recognize that the writer/signer was likely making reference to a description of the item's size, shape, actions, and so on.

POTENTIAL BENEFITS OF WRITING SIGNED LANGUAGES

Now that we have seen that the typical objections to written signed languages are mostly without merit, it is time to address the potential benefits of developing and accepting a written form of signed language.

Elevation of ASL status
ASL, like many signed languages, exists within a diglossic-like situation (Ferguson, 1959; Stokoe, 1969, 1985, Woodward, 1980) in which the majority spoken language enjoys the status of "prestige language," while ASL and other signed languages are disfavored, or even suppressed, largely due to the efforts of Oralists such as Alexander Graham Bell (Baynton, 1996; Winefield, 1987). Adding to the denigration of ASL is its current status as an unwritten, "oral" language. It is largely true that Western society values literacy, and languages that do not possess a written tradition are often scorned as being

inferior to those with written traditions. Developing a conventionalized and accepted form of the language will place it within the ranks of written languages, and this will remove a major argument for the rejection of ASL as an academic as well as social language.

There are some who will argue that many, or perhaps most, of the world's languages do not have a written form, yet speakers of unwritten languages can become bilingual in two or more languages. This is also true. However, some people, such as Mayer and Wells (1996) have argued that commonly accepted principles, such as Cummins' (1979b) Linguistic Interdependence Theory cannot apply to ASL/English bilingual education, since ASL does not have a written form. That is, they argue that while it is true literacy skills in a first language may transfer into a second language, when there are no literacy skills to be developed in a first language due to its unwritten status, it then stands to reason that there are also no skills to be transferred into the second (written) language. Developing a written form of signed language will go a long way towards eliminating this argument as well. Indeed, this point will be addressed in more detail later in this paper.

The preservation of Deaf history, literature, and language
Written language has provided historians, writers, and linguists with vast amounts of data from which insights into past lives, thoughts, and ways language was used could be gained. Yet, for Deaf people, the lack of a conventionally accepted writing system has led to the loss of an incalculable quantity of similar data on Deaf lives. As Bauman (2002) stated:

> "Tracing early Deaf history is a bit like tracing the path of fireflies. The field is mostly dark, except for scattered moments of illumination. The darkness results in part because manual languages have had no written system, no way of preserving thoughts beyond the moment of utterance. One is always haunted by the sense of how much may have occurred among Deaf individuals and communities throughout history but was never recorded" (452).

Similarly, DeFrancis (1989) observed that writing allows people to "revisit" the earlier forms of their own language. In 1913, George Veditz collected $5000 from the Deaf community to produce a series of films through which the "Sign Language," as it was called then, might be preserved. Yet, with this money, he was able to produce only seven samples of ASL as it existed at that time. If a written form of ASL had existed, one can only dream of how many samples, and the variety of samples that we might have today through which we could better understand the origins and changes that have occurred in ASL over the course of the past 200 years!

With writing, ASL poetry, stories and other forms of literature can be preserved on paper or electronically, as well as on videorecorded media. It is even possible that new forms of signed language literature might arise with the development of a writing system, forms that might not be entirely possible to create "through the air."

ASL instruction

The benefits of a written signed language system do not extend solely to Deaf people alone; non-signers, both Deaf and Hearing, have the potential to gain from the introduction of written signed language into signed language instructional curricula. There are two ways in which this would happen.

First, many teachers, following the lead of several different sign language curricula teach signs and sometimes signed language grammar, through the use of "glossing," which is the representation of words in one language in another. Thus, the French sentence *il fait chaud* would be glossed as "it makes hot," since this is a direct, one-to-one correspondence between the meaning of the lexical terms in French with their equivalent English words. This French-English example illustrates one primary problem with glosses: there is often not a true one-to-one correspondence in meaning between languages; one must often make certain adjustments (translation) in order for an utterance in one language to make full sense in another.

For signed languages, glosses are more problematic due to the diglossic setting in which they are frequently situated. While most people understand that languages such as French and English are separate entities, with signed languages, people often take them to be a form of the majority spoken language. The representation of lexical items in the written system of the majority language adds to this impression. Further, due to the grammatical differences between spoken languages and signed languages, glosses of signed languages make them appear to be ungrammatical and incomplete, and therefore inferior to the spoken language. To illustrate, the signed sentence "I will go to the store, and afterwards, I will come home and take a shower" might be glossed as ME GO STORE, FINISH, COME HOME SHOWER. Although the gloss captured the order of the signs, without facial grammar (non-manual signals) and directional information contained in some verbs and other signs, understanding the semantic intent of the signed utterance is frequently rendered incomplete.

For learners of signed languages, glossing also tends to "lock" students into a one-one correspondence with the gloss and the sign, whereas a sign can often have more than one meaning, especially when modified by non-manual signals and other information. In addition, the glosses are represented in what is usually the students' first language. As a result, signed language students are often led to maintain their thinking in their first language instead of attempting to make the mental translation into the second language. Most sign language dictionaries reinforce this English-dominant pattern by establishing a spoken language (gloss) meaning as the primary means through which a sign can be identified. With a writing system, signed vocabulary can be taught and learned through signs first, before providing students with a possible range of semantic equivalents in their own language.

One notable ASL curriculum, the *Signing Naturally* curriculum, deliberately avoids the use of glosses as an instructional tool for much the same reasons outlined above. Teaching is instead conducted through a notional-functional approach, in which vocabulary and grammar are presented through illustrations and modeling by the teacher. While this approach is effective in its own right, students often do not recognize or remember the grammatical elements being taught and instead maintain their spoken language grammatical patterns.

Moreover, while students may make the semantic connections between a sign as taught "through the air" and their own cognitive understandings of a concept, they may have a limited range of semantic equivalents to draw from, and therefore, may attach an incorrect semantic meaning to the sign. With a written system for signed language, the signs could be taught, with a resource list of the vocabulary provided from which students could study to reinforce their learning. Moreover, students could be provided with worksheets or a textbook in which their learning of grammatical concepts could be taught and reinforced through written explanations and exercises.

Communicate in the language of the community
As members of a linguistic minority situated within a majority group that often does not speak or know our language, Deaf people are frequently taught to read and write in the language of the majority. While this is worthwhile in its own right, this often relegates signed languages to a lesser place, even in the minds of those who value and support the use of their signed language. Most Deaf people feel more comfortable communicating in a signed language; indeed, due to ineffective instructional practices emphasizing spoken language dominance in almost all areas of a Deaf person's educational experience, Deaf people are commonly not comfortable with using the spoken language, in its spoken or written form. Even those who are comfortably bilingual in both signed and written (majority) language often find themselves wishing at times to express ideas or concepts which are present in their signed language but do not have a sufficiently adequate English translation of the sign. As a result, one often has to gloss the sign or resort to a crude means of conveying what sign was intended.

For instance, there is a Facebook page titled "ORANGE-THROAT," a gloss that references an ASL sign which has nothing to do with oranges or throats in general. With a written system of signed language, Deaf (and hearing) signers could communicate with others in their preferred language. Although other technology such as video does exist and can be used, writing offers a quick and easy means of communication that video technology cannot always match, as discussed earlier in "Objection #2."

Discuss signed language in signed language

With Stokoe's (1960) identification of ASL as a language with linguistic principles equivalent to those found in spoken languages, Deaf signers have developed a newfound pride in their language, and there are frequent discussions in the community about signs and signing. Yet too often, these discussions occur in English, with its inherent limitations in representing signed language. In bringing up or referencing a sign, people often resort to a gloss of the sign or provide a lengthy description of the sign such as "hand in 'claw' handshape at throat, palm inwards, hand closes into a fist." In these situations, an extended discussion typically follows in which people ask for clarification about what is meant by the gloss or the linguistic parameters of the sign. With a written system for signed language, the sign could be raised in written signed language, and discussions about the sign could start immediately, and furthermore, the discussions could be entirely in the language which is under discussion. That is, instead of allowing English to maintain its colonization (Ladd, 2003) of signed languages, Deaf audiences could decolonize through their use of their own languages in video and written media without using English.

Standardize an understanding of American Sign Language

Due to the colonization of signed language, especially American Sign Language by English through the introduction of English-based sign systems such as Signing Exact English (SEE2; Gustason, Pfetzing & Zawolkow, 1972) and the push for English monolingualism through Oral instruction, ASL, like many other signed languages have undergone significant changes that some would consider not to be a part of the "natural" evolutionary process that all languages undergo. When this is considered in conjunction with the fact that most Deaf people are not exposed to signed language at an early age, or if exposed to sign language, are not using a "natural" sign language (such as ASL), but rather, a signed version of the majority spoken language, one quickly realizes that most Deaf (and hearing) signers are not native users of ASL or other natural signed languages. As a result, the expressive fluency of signers often varies widely, from heavily spoken language-influenced signing to native fluency, with most falling somewhere in between the two extremes. Lucas and Valli (1992) have argued that these varieties are expressions of language contact between English and ASL, and some have taken this to mean that all ASL signing, whether English-influenced or not, are "ASL." While this may be true, the use of written ASL, like other signed languages, can go a long way towards a standardization and understanding of what "grammatically correct" ASL is, especially among the non-native signing population.

Economics
Writing, for all its drawbacks, is still far less inexpensive than any other recording medium. Video and audio technology require the purchase of equipment to produce and play back recorded information, which can run from the hundreds to thousands of dollars. Writing, on the other hand, requires only a pen and piece of paper, which costs less than a dollar per unit.

Literacy and biliteracy
Many researchers studying the issue of reading skills development in Deaf readers have stressed what they view as the need for phonological encoding strategies for this population. They argue this is important because like many other alphabetically-written languages, the letters of written English represent the phonology of spoken English. Supalla, Wix & McKee (2001) note that for Deaf readers, the focus on English phonology (and therefore the sound base of the English language) is problematic, since Deaf readers do not have full access to the sound system of English, yet "(English) is an alphabetic system, even the visual form of English refers to sound; that is, English graphemes represent phonemes" (p. 178). In response, others have supported alternative strategies to be used for Deaf readers, such as Whole Language and visual and cognitively-based approaches to understanding the written English word (cf. Grushkin, 1998).

If it is indeed true that the development of phonological awareness is important in reading, especially when reading alphabetic languages like English, then it might make more sense for Deaf readers to develop phonological en/decoding skills in their first (or natural) language, ASL, and then according to Cummins' Linguistic Interdependence theory, these skills would likely be more easily transferred toward the en/decoding of written English. Thus, the development and use of written ASL would afford opportunities to study how Deaf readers can learn to read in their first, natural language. Alternatively, it might be the case that phonological encoding is not a requirement for reading in signed languages, in which case the emphasis on phonological en/decoding in English would be de-emphasized in favor of lexical, syntactical, and metacognitive strategies for learning to read and write English, as Grushkin (1998) advocates. An example of such a strategy is the sequential presentation of ASL and English, in order to provide comparisons and contrasts between the grammatical structures of the two languages. While this strategy can be effective, it can be made more effective by making the same contrasts using the two languages in a static format, such as writing. To date, most people have attempted to write ASL in gloss format, however, as discussed earlier, this introduces confusions regarding the relationship between ASL and English. The use of a written form of ASL would provide the benefit of the comparison/contrast approach, while eliminating the potential for confusion as to the nature of ASL. Written ASL can also be a useful tool for developing vocabulary in English as well as signed language, such as through bilingual dictionaries. Most current dictionaries only allow for a unidirectional approach to learning: from English to ASL. *The American Sign Language Handshape Dictionary* (Tennant & Brown, 2010), although it does not utilize written signed language, provides an insight into how Deaf signers (or signed language students) can utilize a signed language dictionary in a bidirectional manner (from sign to spoken language or vice versa), using the handshape as a primary organizing principle for the ordering of signs.

In any case, the development and use of a written system for signed languages would a present a means towards a transformation of Deaf educational pedagogy allowing educators to, as Ceclia Flood, a teacher of the Deaf who uses one attempt at written signed language called SignWriting stated in an interview:

> "...capitalize on language abilities, not language problems. To provide a medium that potentially may enhance linguistic and cultural identity and self-empower Deaf and hard of hearing students. To record the experiential stories of Deaf and hard of hearing... learners that will significantly inform perspectives on the academic literacy learning experiences of Deaf and hard of hearing students, in their own words. (Han, 1999)

Flood goes on to state:

> "Using a yet-to-be tapped resource, signwriting, deaf and hard of hearing students will not only become better signers, but also better readers and writers, plus they will attain membership in the growing club of bilingual readers and writers in the U.S.A."

HISTORY OF WRITING AND WRITING SIGNED LANGUAGES

Diamond (1994) observes that there are three basic strategies utilized by the writing systems of the world which differ in the size of the speech unit signified by a written symbol: a single basic sound (phoneme), a whole syllable, or a whole word. Phonemic systems are typically conventionalized as alphabets, such as found within Hebrew, Cyrillic, and the English alphabet. Within these systems, certain sounds such as /k/, /s/, /i/ are typically represented by a certain written symbol, which we refer to as letters. In contrast, other systems, such as Chinese and Egyptian hieroglyphics, a specific symbol will holistically represent a specific word in its entirety. These systems are referred to as logographic systems. A third, less common approach is to represent words syllabically; that is, syllables such as *ba, be, bo, bu* are each given a character and words are formed through the combination of syllables.

Thus, a word like "family" might be represented as *fa-mi-ly* (Diamond, 1994); examples are the Cherokee writing system developed by Sequoyah or the Japanese Kana. It is important to note, as Diamond does, that although writing systems typically utilize one of these three main strategies, no writing system uses these strategies exclusively. Rather, elements of other strategies are often seen within writing systems; for example, English uses logograms such as letters and arbitrary symbols ($, %, &, etc.) that do not represent phonemes, while Japanese, which primarily uses logograms (derived from Chinese writing) called Kanji, also utilizes a syllabary called Kana as an aid to comprehension of certain words in Kanji which are harder to read, and Chinese ideograms often contain an element which provide information about the phonology of the word.

As stated earlier, to date there has been no conventionally accepted written system for signed languages. This does not mean there is no need for one nor that it cannot be done. Indeed, Fok, Van Hoek, Klima & Bellugi (1991) provide tantalizing evidence that not only do Deaf people have an instinctive desire for representing their own language in writing, but also regarding the means by which it might be done. In a study of young Deaf Chinese and American writers, they found instances where these children attempted to create writing for words or concepts they did not know in their respective languages using principles from their signed languages.

For example, one Deaf child created a representation of the handshape or movement found in the sign DUCK, and at another time attempted to illustrate a two-handed sign, PIE through two drawings, representing the non-dominant base hand of the sign and another showing what appears to be the movement path of the dominant hand. In another case, a Chinese child, given a stimulus picture of a girl opening a door, wrote the Chinese root for a person next to the character for door, which is similar to how he might have signed it, using classifiers and signs in Chinese Sign Language. At another time, this child, writing about a rocket launching, wrote the character "airplane," but added a couple of extra upwards squiggles to the ideogram, likely in expression of the upward movement path and motion of the rocket as it launches, like he might sign this. These examples indicate that

Deaf signers (those without any preconceptions about the nature of writing), do understand the elements of their language, and do have some desire to record their thoughts using their primary language.

With the onset of modern signed language linguistic study, there have been several transcription systems developed for the purpose of recording and analyzing signed languages, such as Stokoe Notation, Hamburg Notation System (HamNoSys), and the Liddell-Johnson Movement-Hold model. However, notation or transcription systems are different from writing in that they are designed to encapsulate fine phonemic differences within a language for the purpose of linguistic study; as a whole, they tend to be too cumbersome, if not arcane for the average layperson to utilize on an everyday basis.

Writing, on the other hand, tends not to attempt to encapsulate every element of an utterance within a language (such as intonation, prosody or variations in regional accents), but rather, to encode just enough elements for comprehension within a static format through which languages were not developed to be expressed. In this way, writing encodes sufficient information for transmission of ideas between members of a linguistic community without becoming too overwhelming for users to learn and manipulate. Or, as Tzeng & Hung (1988) stated:

> "As we look back at these historical changes [in writing systems], we see that the evolution of writing seems to have taken a single direction at every advance, the number of symbols in the script decreases, and as a direct consequence the abstractness of the relation between script and meaning increases and the link between graphemes and phonemes becomes clearer" (p. 275)

Although there is no conventionally accepted written system for signed languages, this is not to say that attempts at creating written signed language have not existed. One of the earliest known attempts was by Roch-Ambroise Bebian, who, as godson to Roch-Ambroise Sicard (the second director of the Royal National Institute for the Deaf in Paris), grew up with Deaf people and became an educator of the Deaf himself. Several examples of his writing system are presented in Figure 1.

  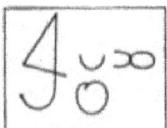

Figure 1. Bebian's Mimographie; (left to right) livre ("book"), cligner ("wink"), clignoter ("flash")

In the 1970s, Valerie Sutton modified the DanceWriting system used to develop choreography for dancing towards signed language. This system consists of drawn symbols representing handshapes, orientations, locations, and movements, and can be modified to portray perspective and other non-standard changes in a sign as well. This writing system has been utilized in several different countries and at a few school programs in the United States. An example of SignWriting is presented in Figure 2.

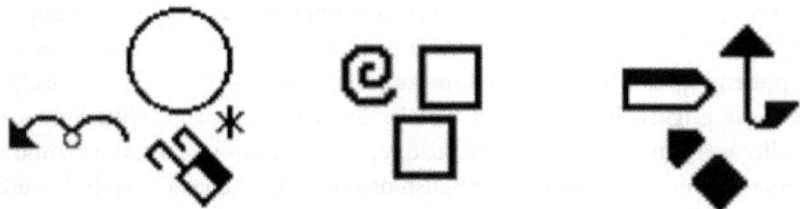

Figure 2. Examples of Valerie Sutton's SignWriting system; (left to right) SNAKE, COFFEE, and ENTER-INTO.

Since the development of SignWriting, others have made attempts at designing a written signed language system. In the 2000s, Robert Arnold created another system, Si5s, which has gained some traction due to his strong promotional efforts. Due to some disagreements about how signs should be written, a member of Arnold's initial group, Adrean Clark, developed a variation on Si5s, which she calls "ASLWrite." Examples of Si5s and ASLWrite are provided in Figure 3, respectively.

Figure 3. Adrean Clark's variation of Si5s (Arnold, 2000; top), ASLWrite (bottom).

What is interesting about all of these systems is that they do not appear to conform to the three basic writing styles identified by Diamond (1994), logographic, syllabic, or alphabetic. Rather, due to the visual-kinesthetic nature of signed languages, they have chosen to represent signs in a manner that might be best described as "iconographic." That is, these systems utilize pictorial (iconic) ways of expressing the elements of a sign, although it should be noted that most, if not all of these do appear to include some phonological information within their "iconograms."

However, it may be possible to encode signed languages more traditionally, utilizing an alphabetic approach. Samuel Supalla and his colleagues working with Deaf children at a Tucson charter school program developed an alphabetic-like system for writing ASL signs based on ASL "graphemes" representing handshapes, locations and movements to be used as a bridge towards English literacy (Supalla, Wix & McKee, 2001). Unlike Stokoe's earlier work in which signs were also represented through a set of symbols, some of which were based on English orthography, Supalla's symbols were based on the appearance of the handshape itself, and are unique to this system. Thus, unlike earlier (notation) systems, Supalla and associates achieved a decoupling of ASL from English orthography, whether partial, as in Stokoe notation, or in whole, as in glosses.

However, Supalla did not appear to envision his system being used as a means for transmitting extended texts, but rather simply as something of a "starter" system towards acquiring English. As a result, the signs are frozen at the lexical level, without much, if any extension toward the syntactical and discourse levels. Grushkin (n.d.), drawing upon Supalla's work, developed a similarly unique set of symbols representing handshape, orientation, location, movement, and non-manual morphemes to be arranged horizontally in a manner similar to English and other orthographies. Unlike Si5s, however, this system has not been widely disseminated. Examples of SignScript are provided in Figure 4.

Figure 4. Grushkin's variation of Supalla (2001), SignScript. (left to right) SNAKE, COFFEE, and ENTER-INTO.

ORTHOGRAPHY AND BILITERACY

If the Deaf community is to develop and accept a system of written signed languages, what then, would be the best approach: iconographic or alphabetic? More important, what will be the impacts upon learning English if signed languages are written using a non-Roman writing (or orthographical) system? Will any differences in orthographical structure negatively affect the acquisition of English as a second (written) language? Perhaps the best way to answer this question is to examine what happens when bilinguals learn to read and write in two different languages, especially when the languages are written in dissimilar orthographical formats. There are two main areas of concern and exploration: first is whether the writing provides readily accessible information to the phonology of the language ("shallow orthography") or the relationship between phonology and the written word is more opaque ("deep orthography"). The second concerns the transfer of reading strategies learned in one language to reading in a second language, especially when divergent orthographies may require the development of different reading strategies.

Hung & Tzeng (1981) note that every orthography transcribes sentences at the level of words, and that this transcription is achieved in a morphemic way. While this is certainly true, differences in the type of script do affect the learning of the script, as well as how readers may process different types of scripts, especially after having learned a differing script type. For example, Geva and Siegel (2000) found that when a script is less complex (in that the relationship between phonology and graphemes are more direct, or "shallower"), children develop word recognition skills with relative ease in comparison to more orthographically complex scripts. However, Hung & Tzeng (1981) state that these effects are somewhat limited: while human visual information processing is affected by orthographic variation, this occurs only at lower levels, which are data-driven (or "bottom-up") processes. At higher levels of reading (concept-driven, or "top-down" processes), reading appears to be immune to orthographic variation.

Reading English involves utilizing an alphabetic orthographical system. An advantage of alphabetic orthographies is that, as Tzeng & Hung (1988) observe, these systems map onto the spoken (or signed) word at the level of the phoneme. Therefore with alphabetic writing systems,

> ...in the ideal case, someone can read words he has never before seen. It is obvious, however, that one can do this only insofar as he is able to map the internal structure of the written word onto the segmental structure of the morphophonological representation of the spoken word he holds in his personal lexicon." (Lieberman, Lieberman, Mattingly & Shankweiler, 1980, p. 149)

Although there are advantages to the alphabetic format of writing, not all alphabets are created equal. For example, Hebrew's alphabet is more "squarish" compared to the Latin alphabet; that is, the letters are more block-like with more horizontal and vertical strokes and fewer curves and diagonals than are present in the Latin alphabet. As a result, it may take readers of

Hebrew slightly longer to recognize differences in letters compared to those reading in English (Share & Levin, 1999).

In addition, although alphabetic orthographies do map onto the phonemic level of language, readers have to be taught to make the connection between the phonemes of a language and the graphemes that represent these phonemes. This task can be complicated in some languages such as English, which has a "deep orthography." That is, one phoneme in English can often be represented in multiple ways. The sound /f/ can be represented as "f" (fish), "ff" (quaff), "ph" (phony) or "gh" (cough); likewise, the sound /n/ can be represented as "n" (need), "kn" (know, knife), "pn" (pneumonia), and "gn" (sign). As a result, beginning readers can experience difficulty decoding English when taught through an explicitly phonics-based approach, which is why Goodman and his associates (1993; 1994) have advocated for the use of Whole Language approaches instead.

In comparison to alphabetic systems, there are logographic systems, such as Chinese or Japanese Kanji (which were borrowed from the Chinese logographs). Whereas alphabetic systems stress the phonemic level of language, reading in logographic systems is primarily established at the lexical (vocabulary) or semantic (meaning) level, since each logogram typically represents a single word or concept. Since logograms represent single words/concepts, this means that learning to read in Chinese involves making associations between the vocabulary in one's linguistic base and the written characters representing the lexical item or semantic concept. Ultimately, this necessitates the memorization of thousands of separate characters. Hung & Tzeng (1988) observed that initially, readers learning logographic systems may have initial success at this task as long as the characters to be learned are distinctly different, however, with the introduction of additional characters, similarities to previously learned characters will begin to appear. At this point, purely visual strategies will become less effective, and the reader must develop other memory strategies to maintain the reading process.

Nevertheless, Tzeng and Hung (1988) hypothesized that since Chinese logographs contain more symbols with similar sounds but different meaning, and since there are often minor differences between logographs, processing of a logographic script would involve more visual/spatial memory than is the case for processing alphabetic scripts. Indeed, Tzeng & Wang (1983) found this to be the case: processing logographs does involve more visual memory than occurs in the reading of alphabetic systems. Although the sheer numbers of logograms to be memorized appears daunting and perhaps cumbersome, Noda (1995) posits one advantage for logographic scripts:

"The phonetic representation systems of Japanese call for a linear approach that slows down the reading process and correspondingly delays understanding of the content, whereas the globality of the logogram means that it can be immediately recognized and understood once it has been memorized" (p. 25)

Advantages and drawbacks of individual orthographic strategies become less clear when one discusses bilingual learning and strategy transfer between languages and scripts. More specifically for our purposes here, what are the effects of nonalphabetic scripts or non-latinate scripts upon learning of an alphabetic script such as that of English?

Kenner, Kress, Al-Khatib, Kam & Tsai (2004) observed that young children, even without prior instruction, can develop understandings of how writing systems operate and can differentiate between multiple orthographies. Further, they found that orthographical knowledge and reading or writing strategies may transfer between languages, even in children who are just beginning to learn to read and write. However, they caution that bilingual literacy development is not a standard one-way path: for each child or person, the process of literacy development can take individual pathways while they are learning about script.

Tzeng & Hung (1988), in their experiment, found some evidence that reading strategy interference does exist between Chinese-English bilingual readers. They attributed this to a transfer of logographic reading processes that were applied (ineffectively) to English (alphabetic) reading. However, Lee, Wee, Tzeng & Hung (1992) conducted Stroop interference tests (in which subjects are asked to name a color presented in a different color) among bilingual subjects whose languages were written in different orthographical systems. Although they hypothesized that a greater difference in orthographic structure would lead to a reduction of interference effects while switching languages, they found that orthographic structure by itself was unrelated to the degree of the interference effect.

Interestingly, Tzeng & Hung (1988) cited research from the Salk Institute, in which Chinese and American Deaf readers were compared in their use of reading strategies. According to the Salk investigators, Chinese Deaf readers tended to explore the spatial layout of logographs, while American Deaf readers focused on the linear arrangements of letter strings. When studied in conjunction with acquisition of a signed language, they noted that Deaf Chinese enjoyed an easier transition from their sign language to the reading of logographs than the Deaf Americans did in transitioning from signing to reading an alphabetic script. This finding has significant implications for the development of a written signed language system, and will be examined in greater detail later in this paper.

Since English script is based on alphabetic principles, and alphabetic writing is strongly associated with the phonemic structure of a language, it comes as no surprise that educators typically stress the need for developing phonemic awareness in readers of English. Indeed, Holm and Dodd (1996) state that the development of phonemic awareness requires alphabetic literacy, not just literacy in general. This assertion is corroborated by both Hanley, Tzeng & Huang (1999) and Cheung, Chen, Lai, Wong & Hills (2001) who indicate that the phonological awareness of Chinese readers is bolstered by the learning of an alphabetic system. These findings are attributable to the fact that logographic systems, which map onto meaning rather than sound, do not provide readers of these systems with experience in consciously identifying the phonological segments of a word, a skill (among others) needed for fluent reading (Holm & Dodd, 1996). This means, according to Holm & Dodd, that those from non-alphabetic written language backgrounds may have difficulties with new or unfamiliar words encountered in English.

However, Holm & Dodd caution that this need for phonological awareness is not absolute, since English spelling can be acquired without phonological awareness, using a "global" strategy, as Whole Language advocates such as Kenneth Goodman (1993, 1994) and his associates have insisted. Further, there are indications that even when children learn to read highly contrasting writing systems, there is still some phonological transfer between languages (Wang, Perfetti & Liu, 2005). Interestingly enough, potential conflicts between reading strategy and learning of a second written system does not appear to be bidirectional: Wang, Perfetti & Liu (2005) found that readers of alphabetic writing systems were able to fairly quickly grasp the orthographic structure of a logographic system such as Chinese, applying their perceptual skills and the mediation of their first language towards the acquisition of Chinese writing.

In an interesting study with implications for written signed language, English biliteracy, Wang, Park & Lee (2006) investigated the development of biliteracy in children whose first language was written in a non-Roman alphabetic system (Korean) who were learning to read English as a second language. The study presents an interesting case because written Korean ("Hangul") has an alphabetic component where the graphemes correspond to phonemes, like English; however, Hangul is laid out in a nonlinear format, like Chinese. This nonlinear aspect is somewhat comparable to the nonlinear aspects of some written signed languages, such as Si5s and SignWriting. It has been established that phonological skills in one language tend to be highly correlated with phonological skills in a second language, and these skills typically contribute to word reading skills in a second language. Additionally, it is known that weak expressive language proficiency in the second language tends to limit the ability to rely on phonological processing for some learners of these second languages. For many Deaf people, English functions as a second, rather than first language (Grushkin, 1998; Wilbur, 2000) and in addition, is less accessible for Deaf people in comparison to signed languages since Deaf people do not typically have complete exposure to English in any form except through writing. What Wang et al. found was that orthographic skills in English and Korean were not significantly correlated; that is, orthographic skills in Korean did not predict English word reading more than possession of English phonological and orthographic skills. The authors suggested that this was potentially due to the difference in visual form and orthographic transparency of the two languages. That is, since English utilizes a linear layout and has a "deep" orthography whereas Korean has a nonlinear layout and a "shallow" orthography, skills developed in Korean did not transfer well to reading in English.

In another interesting note, the authors cited recent neuroimaging work on Chinese-English bilingual adults which indicates these adults experience more activation in the brain areas responsible for coordinating and integrating visual-spatial analyses of logographic Chinese characters in comparison to what was seen when reading English. Similar results for visual-spatial brain activation have been found in Deaf subjects during signed language discourse.

CONCLUSIONS

Does the development of writing for signed languages hold any true benefits for Deaf people, as individuals and as a community? If so, what type of orthographical format should written signed language take, especially when ASL-English biliteracy is a goal?

It has been a long-standing truism that age of acquisition is one of the best predictors of ASL fluency among the adult Deaf population: the earlier one is exposed to ASL, the greater the expressive command of the language one has (Boudreault, 2006; Mayberry, 1993; Newport, 1991; Newport & Supalla, 1990). Yet, even as exposure to ASL is a necessity, simple exposure is not sufficient for mastery. As Singleton, Supalla, Litchfield and Schley (1998) caution, informal exposure to ASL outside of the classroom does not guarantee that a Deaf child will attain a high level of ASL fluency. As is the case with English, Deaf children must be formally taught the structure and rules of the language that they use.

Some teachers of the Deaf have experimented with a variety of ways to provide this formal exposure to ASL. Some, like Snoddon (2010) have turned to video technology in conjunction with a storytelling/writing approach in which student narratives are signed in ASL and then transcribed into English texts which are then revised according to feedback from the teacher. While effective in promoting English literacy, this approach maintains an English-centric dominance in that not only is English the primary focus for improvement, but ASL is not accorded an equal status due to being unwritten. In a similar approach, Susan Mozzer-Mather (1990) utilized glosses to improve and expand written English narratives. In addition to the problems with glosses discussed earlier, the use of glosses like in Snoddon's work also maintains English primacy by representing ASL words in English-seeming format. While the basic technique does foster cognitive comparisons of the structural similarities and differences between the two languages, it is almost certainly the case that written ASL would be more effective at capturing elements which are not easily represented through glosses, and would achieve a true separation between the two languages in the minds of students.

Supalla, Wix & McKee (2001) offer an interesting observation that movement in ASL is comparable to the role of vowels in spoken languages. While it is likely that this statement may very well prove true, it does seem clear that the ability to truly write a signed language offers multiple potentials for developing other insights into the nature of signed languages that might otherwise remain "invisible" to the casual observer. Development of a written system for signed languages also offers alternative ways in which speakers of these languages can examine and stretch the boundaries of their languages. For example, spoken languages have poems and forms of linguistic play such as acrostics and rebuses that are only made possible by being written down. It is reasonable to speculate that the development of written signed language would enable new avenues for exploring the potentialities of signed languages.

The development of written signed language also allows for Deaf speakers of signed languages to communicate with one another in their native/natural language. As one example, social media such as Facebook allow users to switch fonts so they might express themselves in their preferred language. The development of a written signed language font, especially if the font is alphabetic, would allow Deaf interactants to converse with one another, and more importantly, allow discussions about ASL be made in ASL without confusions about the sign referents or the signer's intents.

The most "popular" strategy for writing signed languages is the "iconographic" approach, which utilizes a set of icons representing the parameters of any given sign such as location, movement, and handshape. Like the logographic strategy, iconographic approaches are highly visual in nature, which appeal to Deaf people due to their visual orientation to the world. Noda (1995) notes one advantage of the logographic strategy:

"The phonetic representation systems of Japanese call for a linear approach that slows down the reading process and correspondingly delays understanding of the content, whereas the globality of the logogram means that it can be immediately recognized and understood once it has been memorized" (p. 25)

Evaluation of the several iconographic scripts currently in existence reveals that these systems also present information in a global manner, and therefore hold the potential for more rapid decoding of the sign compared to other possible approaches, such as alphabetic ones. Tzeng & Hung (1988) and Tzeng & Wang (1983) found the processing of logographic scripts to require more visual memory than alphabetic scripts. If iconograpic scripts function similarly, they would be well-suited to Deaf individuals, for whom visual memory tends to be a strength. Indeed, the Salk Institute research cited by Tzeng & Hung in which Deaf Chinese evidenced an easier transition from signed language to reading logographs than American Deaf making the same transition to alphabetic script suggests that Deaf signers might experience an easier transition from sign to iconograph.

The visual nature of iconographic scripts allows for variation in layout, however. While Si5s is arranged in a familiar (for readers of English) left-to-right pattern, its characters are not placed linearly, as is the case of English. Another system, SignWriting, appears to be written in a vertical layout. This is slightly problematic, since Hung & Tzeng (1981) pointed out that studies in perceptual development indicate that writing horizontally, which allows for horizontal scanning, results in faster processing than vertical layouts and scanning. Iconographic scripts, like logographs, may also create problems when readers of these systems attempt to make the transfer towards reading the alphabetic system of English. As Tzeng & Hung (1988) stated:

"Because logographs represent units of meaning rather than units of sound, it has been suggested that logographic orthographies allow more rapid access of meaning than phonetic orthographies...although phonetic orthographies may allow more rapid access of names. Thus, reading Chinese may involve different cognitive processes than reading English." (p. 277-278)

Indeed, Hanley, Tzeng & Huang (1999) found that students from Hong Kong were less likely to utilize the alphabetic information provided within English, preferring to engage the visual strategies learned from reading Chinese logographs. It follows, then, that like Chinese readers, Deaf readers of iconographic writing systems might develop visual strategies for reading these systems that would not be transferable to reading English.

Since English is an alphabetic system which naturally stresses a phonemic relationship between language and writing, it might make more sense, then, to employ an alphabetic approach to writing signed languages in order to facilitate higher transfer of reading skills in the first language (signed) toward the second language (English). Educators of the Deaf have long emphasized what they view as a necessity for Deaf readers to develop awareness of the phonological underpinnings of the majority written language, despite the counterintuitive nature of promoting sound-based phonology in the reading process for Deaf readers (Grushkin, 1998).

As Schwarzer (2001) noted, students can read and write in a second language, even at the beginning of their oral development in that language; speaking is not necessarily a prerequisite for literacy development, especially in a second language. Wilbur (2000), like Holm & Dodd (1996) corroborated Schwarzer's observation, asserting, "However, the absence of an alphabetic writing system, and hence the absence of awareness of individual phonemes, is no detriment to literacy (for Deaf readers), as reflected by the Chinese situation" (p. 88).

Yet, if phonological awareness is important in reading English, might it not make more sense for Deaf readers to develop phonological awareness of their first language (ASL), and whatever skills were developed from reading in this language would be more easily transferred towards the reading of English? Although iconographic systems do contain some elements of signed language phonology, just as Chinese logographs do, an alphabetic system would make these phonological elements more explicit.

Indeed, Hanley, Tzeng & Huang (1999) suggested that phonological awareness in Chinese readers is bolstered by learning an alphabetic system such as the Chinese Pinyin system. Thus, since English is alphabetic, based on phonological principles, it appears logical that if signed language writing were based on signed language phonological principles, there would be positive transfer effects toward reading skills in both languages, although of course due to the different orthographies and phonologies, such transfer would not be entirely direct.

Another point of consideration in favor of employing the alphabetic principle for signed language writing is Goswami's (1999) claim that code acquisition is more rapid in highly transparent orthographies (where phoneme/grapheme correspondences are consistent) than in less transparent orthographies. When one considers that iconographic writing systems do not make the phoneme/grapheme relationship as explicit as an alphabetic system, it would seem to be the case that the development and use of an alphabetic system would be of more utility for Deaf readers, especially when one takes into account the need for development of signed language/spoken language bilingual abilities. Jared Diamond (1994) observed that writing systems, consciously designed by trained linguists, are continually coming into existence. While this can be a good thing, Hagege (1988) warns:

> "The introduction of writing into the heart of an oral society does require certain precautions. Writing has been a progressive rather than a spontaneous development, and important cultural differences separate societies that are literate from those that are not. The latter have over many years developed on the basis of oral language their own modes of expression, their own systems of exchange and balance. To avoid the risks of a dangerous intervention of writing into an oral milieu, these societies must design for themselves the paths through which they hope eventually to accede to the rewards of literacy. (p. 81)

The Deaf cultural community has long functioned as an "oral" culture, even as English is used within the community for interaction among themselves and with others outside of the community. In order to gain acceptance, a writing system must be seen to meet the needs of the community in a variety of ways. Selection of the wrong format would be detrimental to this goal. As Diamond (1994) asks: "Do sub-ideal writing systems really make it harder for adults to read, or for children to learn to read? Many observations make clear that the answer is yes." (p. 113). It has been demonstrated that reading skills developed in one orthography may not be needed in a different orthography, especially if the two orthographies have different script-utterance mapping rules. Thus, as Tzeng (1983) asserts: "…instructional programs for bilingual children whose first language has a nonalphabetic orthography should be carefully designed to facilitate positive transfer and minimize negative interference due to the orthographic factor" (p. 92). If an iconographic system becomes the standard, Tzeng's warning will need to be attended to. Of course, this issue would be drastically mitigated if an alphabetic strategy for written signed languages is chosen by the community.

In sum, a written signed language system should meet these conditions:

1. The written script should be arranged horizontally.
2. The script should be alphabetic for maximal congruence with English learning strategies.
3. The script should not attempt to contain every possible variation in handshape, movement, and location.
4. The script should have a phoneme/grapheme relationship that is as clear as possible.
5. Bilingual instructional strategies should be developed to maximize the ability of a written signed system to induce linguistic transfer towards English literacy.

The reader may at this point, due to the author's arguments for an alphabetic approach to writing signed languages, have obtained an impression that iconographic approaches are ineffective in comparison to alphabetic approaches. This is far from the case. Although the author has some additional "quibbles" about elements of the iconographic approaches created to date (which are outside the scope of this paper), there is no doubt that as writing systems, these approaches do work. It is in the area of biliteracy and skills transfer towards alphabetic languages such as English, that the iconographic approach is being questioned.

While this paper does advocate for an alphabetic approach, it may be the case that the community will prefer to adopt an iconographic approach such as Si5s or ASLWrite. If this does come to pass, Deaf readers can still acquire the biliteracy skills between their signed language and written majority language. However, educators will need to take extra steps in guiding the transition toward learning the written system of the majority, as Tzeng (1983) pointed out above. It is believed, however, that no matter what form written signed language does take, Itard's conclusions about the benefits of signed language could be paraphrased as:

> "With this accomplishment (writing signed languages), the Deaf community could embark just as rapidly on the vast career that this discovery (sign language) opened to his intelligence" (Itard, 1821, p. 325–326).

REFERENCES

Baynton, D. (1996). *Forbidden signs: American culture and the campaign against sign language.* Chicago: University of Chicago Press.

Bauman, H-D. (2002) Book Review, A mighty change: An anthology of Deaf American writing 1816–1864. *Sign Language Studies,* 2 (4), 452–459.

Boudreault, P. & Mayberry, R. (2006). Grammatical processing in American Sign Language: Age of first-language acquisition effects in relation to syntactic structure. *Language and Cognitive Processes,* 21 (5), 608–635.

Cheung, H., Chen, H., Lai, C., Wong, O. & Hills, M. (2001). The development of phonological awareness: Effects of spoken language experience and orthography. *Cognition,* 81 (3), 227–241.

Corson, H. (1973). Comparing deaf children of oral deaf parents and deaf parents using manual communication with deaf children of hearing parents on academic, social and communication functioning. Doctoral dissertation, University of Cincinnati, Ohio.

Cummins, J. (1979b). Linguistic interdependence and the educational development of bilingual children. *Review of Educational Research.* 49 (2), 222–251.

DeFrancis, J. (1989). *Visible Speech: The diverse oneness of writing systems.* Honolulu: University of Hawaii Press.

Diamond, J. (1994). Writing right. *Discover,* (June). 108–113.

Ferguson, C. (1959). Diglossia. *Word,* 15, 325–340.

Fok, A., Van Hoek, K., Klima, E. & Bellugi, U. (1991). The interplay between visuospatial language and visuospatial script. In D. Martin (ed.) *Advances in Cognititon, Education, and Deafness*. Washington, DC: Gallaudet University Press. pp. 127–145.

Geva, E. & Siegel, L. (2000). Orthographic and cognitive factors in the concurrent development of basic reading skills in two languages. *Reading and Writing*, 12, 1–30.

Goodman, K.S. (1993). *Phonics phacts: A common-sense look at the most controversial issue affecting today's classrooms*. New Hampshire: Heinemann Press.

Goodman, K.S. (1994). Reading, writing and written texts: A transactional sociopsycholinguistic view. In R. Ruddell, M. Ruddell, & H. Singer (Eds.), *Theoretical models and processes of reading, 4th ed.* (pp. 1093–1130). Newark, DE: International Reading Association.

Goswami, U. (1999). The relationship between phonological awareness and orthographic representation in different orthographies. in M. Harris & G. Hatano (eds.) *Learning to Read: A cross-linguistic perspective*. 134–156. New York: Cambridge University Press.

Grushkin, D. A. (1998). Why shouldn't Sam read? Toward a new paradigm for literacy and the deaf. *Journal of Deaf Studies and Deaf Education*, 3:3 (Summer), 179–204.

Gustason, G., Pfetzing, D. & Zawolkow, E. (1972). *Signing Exact English*. Los Angeles: Modern Signs Press.

Hagege, C. (1988). Writing: The invention and the dream, in D. Kerckhove & C. Lumsden (eds.), *The Alphabet and the Brain*. New York: Springer-Verlag

Han, A. (1999). A new approach to literacy: SignWriting: Will it work? Silent News (November), http://www.signwriting.org/library/journal/silentnews/sw221.html.

Hanley, R., Tzeng, O. & Huang, H. (1999). Learning to read Chinese. In M. Harris & G. Hatano (eds.) *Learning to read and write: A cross-linguistic perspective*. New York: Cambridge University Press. pp. 173–195.

Higgins, P. (1980). *Outsiders in a hearing world: A sociology of deafness*. Newbury Park, CA: Sage Publications.

Holm, A. & Dodd, B. (1996) The effect of first written language on the acquisition of English literacy. *Cognition*, 59, 119–147

Hung, D. & Tzeng, O. (1981). Orthographic variations and visual information processing. *Psychological Bulletin*, 90(3), 377-414.

Itard, J-M. (1821). *Traite des maladies de l'oreille*. Paris: Chez Mequignon-Marvis.

Israelite, N.K., Ewoldt, C. & Hoffmeister, R. (1992). *Bilingual/bicultural education for deaf and hard-of-hearing students*. Ontario Ministry of Education, MGS Publications (96 pps.)

Johnson, R.E., Liddell, S.K., & Erting, C.J. (1989). Unlocking the curriculum: Principles for achieving access in deaf education. *Gallaudet Research Insitute Working Paper 89-3*. Washington, DC: Gallaudet University Press.

Kenner, C., Kress, G., Al-Khatib, H., Kam, R. & Tsai, K. (2004). Finding the keys to biliteracy: How young children interpret different writing systems. *Language and Education*, 18(2), 124–144.

Koda, K. (1988). Cognitve process in second language reading: Transfer of L1 reading skills and strategies. *Second Language Research*, 4(2), 133–155.

Krashen, S. (1996). The case against bilingual education. in J. Alatis, C. Straehle, M. Ronkin & B. Gallenberger (eds.), *Linguistics, language acquisition, and language variation: current trends and future prospects*, 55–69. Washington, DC: Georgetown University Press.

Ladd, P. (2003). *Understanding Deaf Culture: In search of Deafhood*. Clevedon, UK: Multilingual Matters Ltd.

Lee, W., Wee, G., Tzeng, O. & Hung, D. (1992). A study of interlingual and intralingual stroop effect in three different scripts: Logograph, syllabary, and alphabet. In R.J. Harris (Ed.) *Cognitive Processing in Bilinguals*. Elsevier Science Publishers. 427–440.

Liddell, S.K. (1984). Think and believe: Sequentiality in American Sign Language. *Language*, 60(2), 372–399.

Liddell, S.K. & Johnson, R.E. (1989). American Sign Language: The phonological base. *Sign Language Studies*, 64, 195–277.

Lieberman, I., Lieberman, A., Mattingly, I. & Shankweiler, D. (1980) Orthography & the beginning reader, in J. Kavanagh & R. Venezky (eds.) *Orthography, Reading and Dyslexia*. Baltimore: University Park Press. 137–153.

Lucas, C. & Valli, C. (1992). *Language contact in the American Deaf community*. United Kingdom: Emerald Group Publishing.

Mayberry, R. (1993). First language acquisition after childhood differs from second-language acquisition: The case of American Sign Language. *Journal of Speech and Hearing Research*, 36, 1258–1270.

Mayer, C. & Wells, G. (1996). Can the Linguistic interdependence theory support a bilingual-bicultural model of literacy education for deaf students? *Journal of Deaf Studies and Deaf Education*, 1(2), 93–107.

Meadow, K. (1968). Early manual communication in relation to the deaf child's intellectual, social, and communicative functioning. *American Annals of the Deaf*, 113, 29–41.

Mozzer-Mather, S. (1990). A strategy to improve Deaf students' writing through the use of glosses of signed narratives. *Gallaudet Research Institute Working Paper 90-4*. Gallaudet University, Washington, DC.

Newport, E. (1991). Contrasting concepts of the critical period for language. In S. Carey & R. Gelman (eds.) *The epigenesist of mind: Essays on biology and cognition* (pp. 111–130). Hillsdale, NJ: Lawrence Erlbaum Associates

Newport, E. & Supalla, T. (1990). A critical period effect in the acquisition of a primary language. Unpublished manuscript, University of Rochester, Rochester, NY.

Noda, S. (1995). A four-in-hand script. *The Unesco Courier*, (April) 24–25.

Padden, C. & Humphries, T. (1988). *Deaf in America: Voices from a culture*. Cambridge, Massachusetts: Harvard University Press.

Sagan, C. (2011). *Cosmos*. Random House, p. 232.

Schwarzer, D. (2001). *Noah's Ark: One child's voyage into multiliteracy*. NH: Heinemann.

Share & Levin (1999). Learning to read and write in Hebrew. In M. Harris & G. Hatano (eds.) *Learning to read: a cross-linguistic perspective*. New York: Cambridge University Press. pp. 89–111.

Snoddon, K. (2010). Technology as a learning tool for ASL literacy. *Sign Language Studies*, 10(2), 197–213.

Stokoe, W. (1969). Sign language diglossia. *Studies in Linguistics*, 21, 27–41.

Stokoe, W. (1985). The decoding of simultaneous communication. *Sign Language Studies*, 45 (Summer), 181–187.

Stokoe, W. [1960] (1993). *Sign Language Structure: An outline of the visual communication systems of the American deaf*. Burtonsville, MD: Linstok Press.

Stuckless, R. & Birch, J. (1966). The influence of early manual communication on the linguistic development of deaf children. *American Annals of the Deaf*, 106, 436–480.

Supalla, S., Wix, T. & McKee, R.L. (2001). Print as a primary source of English for Deaf learners. in J. Nicol (Ed.) *One Mind, Two Languages: Bilingual Language Processing*. Massachusetts: Blackwell Publishers, Ltd. 175–208.

Tennant, R. & Brown, M. (2010). *The American Sign Language handshape dictionary*. Washington, DC: Gallaudet University Press.

Tzeng, O. (1983). Cognitive processing of various orthographies. In M. Chu-Chang (ed.) *Asian and Pacific-American Perspectives in Bilingual Education: Comparative Research*. New York: Teachers College Press.

Tzeng, O. & Hung, D. (1988). Orthography, reading & cerebral function. In D. de Kerckhove & C. Lumsden, eds. *The Alphabet and the Brain: The lateralization of writing*. New York: Springer-Verlag, pp. 273–290.

Tzeng, O. & Wang (1983). The first two Rs. *American Scientist*, 71, 238–243

Wang, M., Perfetti, C. & Liu, Y. (2003). Alphabetic readers quickly acquire orthographic structure in learning to read Chinese. *Scientific Studies of Reading*, 7(2), 183-208.

Wang, M. (2005). Chinese-English biliteracy acquisition: Cross-language and writing system transfer. *Cognition, 97,* 67–88.

Wang, M., Park, Y., & Lee, K. (2006). Biliteracy acquisition: Cross-language phonological and orthographic transfer. *Journal of Educational Psychology,* 98(1), 148–158.

Wilbur, R. (2000). The use of ASL to support the development of English and literacy. *Journal of Deaf Studies and Deaf Education* 5(1), 81–104.

Winefield, R. (1987). *Never the twain shall meet: The communications debate.* Washington, DC: Gallaudet University Press.

Woodward, J. (1980). Sociolinguistic research on American Sign Language: An historical perspective. In C. Baker & R. Battison (Eds.) *Sign Language and the Deaf Community: Essays in honor of Wiliam C. Stokoe.* Silver Spring, MD: National Association of the Deaf.

Signed Music: An Emerging Inter-performative Art

JODY H. CRIPPS, PH.D.; ELY ROSENBLUM, AND ANITA SMALL

> "I see little of more importance to the future of our country and of civilization than full recognition of the place of the artist. If art is to nourish the roots of our culture, society must set the artist free to follow [her or] his vision wherever it takes [her or] him." — John F. Kennedy

MUSIC IS ONE FORM OF PERFORMING ART THAT HAS A STRONG CONNection with sound. Sound has typically been identified as music's fundamental medium of expression. Music scholars devote themselves to understanding musical forms, their affect on people and their cultural contexts. At the most fundamental level, musicologists identify musics by the auditory components they are made up of. Though many traditions exist in music, Western and non-Western music have been identified as distinct forms that are both historically and socially divergent. Despite the heterogeneity of musical forms and their respective traditions, it is a small group of researchers in music studies — made up of musicologists, music theorists, and ethnomusicologists — that are entrusted with the task of collecting and analyzing all types of music.

Thaut (2008) noted that music is a highly abstract and non-representational form of art, using sensations of movement, phrasing and motif that reflect thoughts and emotions. Indeed, it is the ever expanding diversity of musical forms that remains mysterious. There are musical performances within the Deaf community that do not rely on audition or auditory culture. Historically, certain Deaf individuals have been creating visual-gestural music performances with the use of their hands to express their works visually. These musical performances have their own artistic style and are highly abstract in their own right. This type of visual-gestural music performance is culturally based in the Deaf experience, and is called Signed Music. For this reason, it is difficult for Music Studies to analyze Signed Music without the aid of socio-linguistics and the Deaf community. Considerations for the evolution and the use of Signed Music performances in the Deaf community are relevant for scholarly and ethnomusicological research, but require an interdisciplinary approach.

MUSIC DEFINED AS AUDIO-CENTRIC

Music is often perceived as exclusively auditory phenomena. Music comprises acoustic properties that include five basic elements: rhythm, timbre, melody, texture, and harmony. However, the incorporation of these musical elements in a performance varies as most of them can be found in Western music; but for some forms of non-Western music, only rhythm, timbre, and texture are found (e.g., Schmidt-Jones, 2007). Melody and harmony tend to be western musical phenomena. Elements of music that are solely based on audition have been central to musical scholarship from its inception. This is a driving force for audism (defined by Humphries (1977) as the notion that one is superior based on one's ability to hear or to behave in a manner of one who hears), whether it be intentional or unintentional. Metaphysical audism is what characterizes this kind of thinking, because music is seen as an "orientation that links human identity with speech" (Bauman, 2004, p. 245) without any consideration for applying these elements to another music modality such as Signed Music.

Maler (2013) noted that Deaf people have mixed feelings when it comes to appreciating or even talking about Signed Music. An example of this kind of mixed feeling among Deaf people is due to auditory culture's historic monopoly over musical practices: those who learn ASL as their second language, translate the spoken language lyrics into signed language, and do so typically without any cultural context mediation. Examples of these performances are frequently found on social media websites, and are often wrongfully presented as a celebration of Deaf culture. This unintentional audism from ASL learners as well as some Deaf performers — who also rely on audible music to create their performances — show that there is an enculturated disregard for the Deaf experience and their relation to sound. The lack of historical and cultural context related to music use with the Deaf community reinforces both external and internal self-imposed barriers for emerging Deaf musicians to express their thoughts, feelings, and sense of movement through Signed Music. The narrow definition of music, as an auditory art form has a significant impact on Deaf individuals and limits our understanding of the full range of human experience and expression. It must be reconsidered in order to understand what music is in all its diversity.

SIGNED MUSIC IN THE PAST

Before analysing contemporary Signed Music performances, it is important to review historic signed music works by deaf groups or individuals. Deaf people in the United States have participated in a variety of performing arts, including music using American Sign Language (ASL).

Their performances can be found either in the Deaf community or on tour performing for the general population. Many of these works have been recorded onto film or videotape. The first recorded signed performance art was of an unknown woman signing "The Star Spangled Banner" in 1902 (Gallaudet University, 1902). The second is a series of films of ASL stories from 1913 to 1915 performed by a number of Deaf and hearing ASL storytellers (Cokely, et al., 2010). The third instance of recorded signed performance documents individuals and groups of deaf performers using music and ASL during the 1930s (i.e., another rendition of "The Star Spangled Banner," "Boat, Drink, Fun, Enjoy…," "Oh Darn, I Hear Nothing!…," and "Yankee Doodle;" T. Supalla, 1994). These signed songs represent both signed translations of songs (i.e., "The Star Spangled Banner" and "Yankee Doodle") as well as percussive elements of songs (i.e., "Boat, Drink, Fun, Enjoy…" and "Oh Darn, I Hear Nothing!…"). However it was not until the 1960s that the National Theatre of the Deaf (NTD) launched and created its popular theater production called "My Third Eye" (Baldwin, 1994). Signed songs can be found in this production as well (i.e., "Three Blind Mice" and "Rescue Story"). There is a unique group performance of Signed Music with choral singing in ASL (discussed in greater detail below). The NTD later recorded this production in 1971.

The rise of ASL poetry in the National Theater of the Deaf (NTD, 1967; 1971–72) inspired Deaf poetic performers such as Clayton Valli and Ella Mae Lentz to expand upon their own work, with a number of ASL poetry performances and publications during the 1980s and 1990s. Signed Music, on the other hand, has only recently received similar attention from Deaf performers and the Deaf community. Ella Mae Lentz performed the poem called "Eye Music" in 1995. In her pre-performance narration, she mentioned that her work is part of translated ASL poetry from written English. At the time it was not even considered to be a musical performance. During her performance, she expressed her poetry in the visual-gestural medium explaining that telephone poles and wires do not require the audible "sounds" from music instruments (e.g., drums, flutes, etc.) to create music (Lentz, 1995).

In her performance, musical sounds were illustrated through visual imagery that served as an analogue of "visual sounds" that Deaf people can enjoy (i.e., as you travel past telephone poles and telephone wires they provide a clear picture to visualize the rhythms and instrumentation of music). Unlike Lentz, Mary Beth Miller (1991) and Bill Ennis (1993) acknowledged their performances as signed music, and told their audiences that they would be signing the songs before they performed them. Mary Beth Miller created a percussion-type signed song, "Cowboy" using signed language classifiers with manipulation of ASL phonological parameters: handshapes, locations and movements. Bill Ennis, on the other hand, performed two "adapted" signed songs and are atheistically pleasing to Deaf people. Both of his performances were adapted from two famous spoken songs, "Mississippi Squirrel Revival" and "Backing to Birmingham" with an emphasis on rhythmic beats in the signed modality (i.e., ASL).

PREVIOUS RESEARCH IN SIGNED MUSIC

When Stokoe and his colleagues (1960; Stokoe, Casterline & Croneberg, 1965) discovered ASL as a human language through linguistic principles, scholarly research on performing arts using ASL followed. During the 1970s, Miles and Fant (1976) published research explaining that Deaf theater had created a new avenue for Deaf performers who use ASL to be present in public on the theatrical stage. Moreover, Klima and Bellugi (1979) noticed that Deaf performers were doing a poetic ASL version when translating spoken songs into signed language and performing some ASL poetry. A number of Deaf linguists in 1990s have explored more about ASL poetry and ASL storytelling using a linguistic framework for such analyses. Valli (1990), who is also an ASL poet, was the first to analyze ASL poetry for lines, meters, and rhythm. Around the same time, Supalla and Bahan (1992), both ASL storytellers, had examined ASL storytelling for its chapters, stanzas, and strophes as found in spoken language storytelling. More recently, Bahan (2006) wrote an article on different genres of ASL literature including percussion and translating songs as found in the 1930s. Research on music in the signed modality has been revisited recently but is limited to translation and percussion songs.

In their first and primarily analysis of music in the signed modality, Klima and Bellugi (1979) explored poetic signs and called it "Art-Sign." They found that there are patterns of linguistic forms that are 'non-conventional' and transformed into musical signed words. They identify three different structures in the different types of art-sign: internal structure, external structure, and superstructure. Internal structure is a musical structure that is loyal to the translation of music lyrics and/or the properties used in acoustic music. "The Star Spangled Banner," "Three Blind Mice," "Mississippi Squirrel Revival," and "Backing to Birmingham" are all examples of signed musical performances that assume internal music structure.

In contrast, art-sign with external music structure is not concerned with translation of lyrics, or the particular acoustic properties of a song. External music structure is unique to Signed Music that involves manipulating the phonological properties of signed language (i.e., handshapes, locations, and movements). "Cowboy" serves as a good example of this practice. Other performances to be considered for external music structure are "Boat, Drink, Fun, Enjoy…" and "Oh Darn, I Hear Nothing!..." The former is part of the percussion songs that use 'one-two, one-two-three; one-two, one-two-three' rhythmic beats and employ external structure as it creates its own rhythm, one of the signed properties characteristic of Signed Music. Likewise, the latter also exemplifies external structure with choral music along with the signed lines of 'DARN, I HEAR NOTHING…' with different sounds created by animals (e.g., 'moo' from cow, 'baa' from sheep, etc). It is important to point out that all of these three signed musics are original without any reliance on auditory musical forms or translations of pre-existing song lyrics.

The uniqueness of signed music is its structure, which includes spatial rhythmic and temporal patterning superimposed on the sequence of signs. "Rescue Story" demonstrates how signed music is performance with simultaneous roles adopted by signers to represent specific things, similar to the roles different musicians take with their respective instruments. An example can be seen as one signer becomes the rhythm of the performance, signing in the percussion mode with rhythmic beats of ocean waves while other performers signed "helicopter," "victim," "rescuer," and "sun" using signed language classifiers. This multi-dimensionality is comparable to a song with a melodic structure adding to the meaning of the lyrics.

Research on the history of musical performances reveals three basic types of music used in the signed modality. First, music that involves *ASL to English translation*, derived from traditional auditory culture. This type of music is still uncertain because too frequently these performances were not considered by the Deaf community to be of high quality. However, there are some translated or adapted musical performances that are considered acceptable and it may be due to the performer's translation skills. These translations tend to embed rhythm into the signs and focus on intent of the lyrics as a good interpretation should, rather than staying too close to the spoken rendition of the lyrics.

The second type of music is *signed percussion songs*, as identified by researchers in signed language literature. As mentioned previously, some

Deaf performers include the unique one-two, one-two-three rhythm beats in their performances. The third type of music in the *signed modality is signed songs that draw upon Deaf cultural experiences*. "Oh Darn, I Hear Nothing!..." is an example of music that incorporates deaf people's lack of experience with audible sounds and a sense of humour. Thus far, no discussion has taken place to examine the basic musical elements except for rhythm in Signed Music. Indeed, more research in this area is necessary.

EVOLUTION OF SIGNED MUSIC

In the last two decades, ASL poetry performances have increased and impacted Deaf performers including musicians. Deaf individuals have come to understand more about what makes signed language poetry 'poetic' which has ramifications for signed language performance arts such as Signed Music. For example, Valli (1990) analyzed ASL poetry for lines, meters, and rhythm and found that poetry in signed language involves rhythmic lines that are analogous to poetry found in spoken languages. This discovery gave license to Deaf poets to explore and produce more poetry in ASL. Moreover, Valli's ASL poetry compositions including rhythmic lines have influenced a new generation of Deaf musicians.

More recently, two young Deaf Canadian performers have produced Signed Music Video performances that involve highly abstract meanings and encourage artistic interpretation. Both of their works include rhythm, and employ audiovisual techniques that emphasize the poetic content of their gestural/signed performances. These videos are created for distribution on YouTube. It can be seen that Signed Music Video participates in the same processes as other musical cultures — like popular music and associated subgenres that have generated a multitude of music videos since the 1980s — while still belonging to the culture of Deaf people.

Janis Cripps created an experimental signed music performance called "Eyes" in 2003. Cripps was raised in a deaf family where she acquired ASL as her native language and attended a residential school for the deaf in Ontario. Though she is Deaf, Cripps enjoyed listen to audible music in her adolescence. In this performance, she expresses her music performance based on her interpretation of audible music that did not have lyrics performed by her hearing cousin. Her work used layers of hands and hand motions to express rhythm with pitches and beats. Similarly, Pamela Witcher created a gestural musical performance "Experimental Clip" in 2009. Witcher also grew up in a deaf family, but attended residential school for the deaf in Quebec and used both ASL and Langue des Signes Québécoise (LSQ) in the home. Unlike Cripps, she began her performance with lyrics that were a mixture of

ASL and LSQ without any reliance on spoken or written English or French. In addition to use of signed lyrics, Witcher uses hand motions to express rhythm in her performance as Cripps does. Witcher composed her Signed Music performance with no auditory component. Audible music was composed later, based on and overlaid onto her Signed Music performance. Using a series of close-up camera angles, Witcher's videotaped performance simulates a "peephole-style" production, as if the viewer is voyeuristically observing her in her home. This visual perspective could be interpreted as a commentary on the authoritarian gaze of auditory cultures: observing and other-ing Deaf individuals and their cultural practices. In sum, it is clear that their musical performances are prime candidates for case studies on the workings of Signed Music.

CURRENT RESEARCH ON SIGNED MUSIC

Ethnomusicological research has proved to be a good theoretical starting point for examining Signed Music, because the discipline infers the musical understanding based on its cultural context. This includes analyses of Signed Music performances from the Deaf community, using ethnographic methodology that compromise a team of insiders, outsiders and mediator. Video clips of Signed Music are being analysed and made to examine the basic musical elements of the signed modality. The authors of this study are currently conducting research based on the two Signed Music Videos mentioned above. This case study uses a mixture of sociolinguistic, anthropological, and ethnomusicological analysis. The goal of this research study is to define Signed Music and its musical elements. Geertz's (1973) Thick Description model is adopted to provide a detailed explanation of Signed Music video clips performed by Witcher and Cripps. Additionally, musical compositions from both of these video clips are subject for comparative analyses with other performing arts such as ASL poetry and dance. The purpose for this is to understand how Signed Music is different from other performing arts that use signed language and how it incorporates other performance arts resulting in a unique inter-performance art. Furthermore, the study of Signed Music encourages scholars to broaden the definition of music by including different experiential and expressive forms of performance. The combination of interdisciplinary studies in Music Studies such as ethnomusicology, studies of cognition, aesthetic, sound, signed language and literature, and Deaf Studies is needed to broaden our understanding of Signed Music as a performance art.

REFERENCES

Bahan, B. (2006). Face-to-face tradition in the American Deaf community: Dynamics of the teller, tale and the audience. In H-D. L. Bauman, J. L. Nelson, & H. Rose (Eds.), *Signing the body poetic: Essays in American Sign Language literature* (pp. 21–50). Berkeley, CA: University of California Press.

Baldwin, S. C. (1994). *Pictures in the air: The story of National Theatre of the Deaf.* Washington, DC: Gallaudet University Press.

Bauman, H-D. L. (2004). Audism: Exploring the metaphysics of oppression. *Journal of Deaf Studies and Deaf Education, 9*(2), 239–246. doi: 10.1093/deafed/enh025

Cokely, D., et al. (2010). *The preservation of American Sign Language.* Burtonsville MD: Sign Media, Inc.

Cripps, J. E. (2003). Eyes. Retrieved from http://www.youtube.com/watch?v=YnwJsFHFebg

Ennis, B. (1993). *Live at SMI!* Bill Ennis. Burtonsville, MD: Sign Media, Inc.

Gallaudet University. (1902). Deaf mute girl reciting "Star Spangled Banner." Washington, DC: Gallaudet Video Library. Retrieved from http://videocatalog.gallaudet.edu/?video=17493

Geertz, C. (1973). *The interpretation of cultures.* New York, NY: Basic Books.

Humphries, T. (1977). Communicating across cultures (Deaf/hearing) and language learning. Ph.D. dissertation, Union Graduate School, Cincinnati, Ohio.

Klima, E. & Bellugi, U. (1979). *The signs of language.* Cambridge, MA: Harvard University Press.

Lentz, E. M. (1995). *The treasure.* In Motion Press.

Maler, A. (2013). Songs for hands: Analyzing interactions of sign language and music. *Society for Music Theory, 19*(1), 1–15.

Miles, D. & Fant, L. J. (1976). *Sign-language theatre and deaf theatre: New definitions and directions.* Northridge, CA: California State University, Northridge, Center on Deafness.

Miller, M. B. (1991). *Live at SMI!* Mary Beth Miller. Burtonsville, MD: Sign Media, Inc.

National Theatre of the Deaf. (1967). *Tyger!, Tyger! and Other burnings.* Indianapolis, IN: Captioned Films for the Deaf, Inc.

National Theatre of the Deaf. (1971–72). *My third eye.* WTTW Chicago.

Schmidt-Jones, C. (2007). *Understanding basic music theory.* Houston, TX: Connexions & Rice University.

Stokoe, W. C. (1960). *Sign language structure: An outline of the visual communication systems of the American Deaf, Studies in linguistics: Occasional papers (No. 8).* Buffalo, NY: Dept. of Anthropology and Linguistics, University of Buffalo.

Stokoe, W. C., Casterline, D. C., & Croneberg, C. G. (1965). *A dictionary of American Sign Language on linguistic principles.* Silver Spring, MD: Linstok Press.

Supalla, S. J. & Bahan, B. J. (1992). American Sign Language literature series: Research and development. In *Gallaudet University College for Continuing Education (Ed.), Deaf Studies for educators. Conference proceedings. March 7–10* (pp. 137–148). Washington, DC: College for Continuing Education, Gallaudet University.

Supalla, T. (1994). *Charles Krauel: A profile of a Deaf filmmaker.* San Diego, CA: DawnSignPress.

Thaut, M. H. (2008). *Rhythm, music, and the brain: Scientific foundations and clinical applications.* New York, NY: Routledge.

Valli, C. (1990). The nature of the line in ASL poetry. In W. Edmondson & F. Karlsson (Eds.), *Signed Language Research '87: Papers from the fourth International symposium on sign language research* (pp. 171–182). Hamburg, DE: Signum Press.

Witcher, P. (2008). Experimental clip 2. Retrieved from http://www.youtube.com/watch?v=zPHraTb36wc

Destination Unknown: The Specialized Field of Designated Interpreting

ANNETTE MINER

IN ANY PROFESSION, RELATIONSHIPS DEVELOP AMONG PEOPLE WHO work together. Vice presidents have working relationships with their administrative assistants; contractors have relationships with vendors and employees who do the work for them, etc. The relationship between Deaf individuals and the interpreters with whom they work is unique in several ways, and is impacted by several factors: the increased access to opportunities currently enjoyed by Deaf individuals due to changes in legislation, the increased demand for interpreters as a result, the power dynamics at play due to a history of oppression of the Deaf community, intercultural competence, the changing role of interpreters, and issues related to language use.

The number of Deaf professionals in the workplace and Deaf individuals accessing services of every type in the United States has been on the rise since the passing of the Americans with Disabilities Act (ADA) in 1990. This legislation "prohibits discrimination against people with disabilities in employment, transportation, public accommodation, communications, and governmental activities" (http://www.dol.gov/dol/topic/disability/ada.htm). This mandated access has given Deaf individuals more access to the work force, to various services, to education, and more freedom to advance to higher professional positions (Hauser, Finch, & Hauser, 2008; McLaughlin, 2010). One way that access is commonly provided to Deaf individuals is through the provision of sign language interpreting services. This increased access has created a greater demand for interpreters.

However, the sharp increase in the need for sign language interpreters has not been met by adequate supply. The shortage of interpreters is well documented and has been an issue since the inception of the sign language interpreting field in the 1960s (McLaughlin, 2010). While interpreters before the passage of the ADA were typically hearing members of the Deaf community (i.e., daughters, sisters, sons of Deaf individuals), as of late, a greater percentage of interpreters have entered the profession without this type of immersion experience in the Deaf community. In addition, training programs for these interpreters are often housed in community colleges, and students complete their entire preparation, from learning the first signs of the language to graduation with the expectation of being able to interpret between American Sign Language and English, in two to three years. This preparation is woefully inadequate; in fact, students of no other language are expected to gain such proficiency in so short a time period.

These historical facts have created a unique dimension in the relationship between Deaf individuals and interpreters. The experience of the Deaf community as a whole is that of an oppressed minority in our society (Lane, 1992; Baker-Shenk, 1985). The experience of many interpreters is that of the privilege of being able to hear in an auditory society. The feeling of the privilege is palpable, as one interpreter recently commented:

> "I'm not sure I'll ever fully understand my duality as both ally and enemy in the lives of Deaf people without some measure of guilt. Like many members of privileged groups, I hope to learn the right way to behave toward an oppressed group — once — and never again have to feel unsure of myself or guilty about my privilege" (Colonomos, 2013, para. Accountability is the Beginning).

The interpreters that work with Deaf individuals are typically not members of their community, but members of the oppressor group (Baker-Shenk, 1985), yet one on whom they depend to achieve their communication goals. This creates a unique dynamic between the Deaf individual and the interpreter, fueled by potential issues of power and intercultural competence.

Another dimension of this relationship is the changing expectation of the role of the interpreter, both by the profession as a whole, and by individual Deaf users of interpreting services. Before 1964, when the profession of sign language interpreters was officially established, interpreters often acted in a helper type role (Humphrey & Alcorn, 2001). They viewed Deaf individuals as limited and not capable of making their own decisions, and thus, became overly involved with the Deaf people they worked with. They viewed their job as a caretaker of Deaf individuals. In the early 1970s, the role of interpreters changed, and they viewed themselves as conduits of messages that simply transformed the words of a speaker in one language to the words of a speaker in another language (Humphrey & Alcorn, 2001). However, as the profession evolved, interpreters began preferring to see themselves as allies to the Deaf community, taking on more of a facilitator role within interpreted interactions. Subsequent research has shown that interpreters often manage turns between speakers in a conversation, create their own utterances, and take responsibility for ensuring smooth interactions between interlocutors (Roy, 2000; Metzger, 1999; Wadensjo, 1998). However, the acceptability of the amount of interaction management by interpreters can vary with each Deaf individual. Some Deaf individuals prefer more independence and want to manage as much of their own interactions as possible, while others require or desire more support. An interesting dimension of the Deaf-interpreter relationship is created by the perception by both the Deaf individual and the interpreter of how much interaction management is expected in any given interaction.

These historical facts about the field of interpreting are only part of the picture. There are other potential factors that can influence how Deaf individuals and interpreters interact and get along with each other. The focus of this study is to learn more about the nature of the relationship between Deaf individuals and the interpreters with whom they work.

DESIGNATED INTERPRETERS

In this study, I report on the results of interviews with a Deaf professional and a *designated interpreter*. Designated interpreters are interpreters who work closely with Deaf professionals; indeed, they are a part of the Deaf professional's team. They must work as one with the Deaf professional, understanding and predicting how the Deaf professional thinks, and work toward the goals of the Deaf professional (Hauser, et al., 2008). It requires intimate understanding of the dynamics of the workplace and the ability to navigate them with the Deaf professionals with whom they work. As Hauser and Hauser (2008) remark in their collection of the literature on this type of relationship, describing it is "almost like describing the concept of marriage with only a few couples to use as examples" (p. 4). This study adds to what we already know based on previous studies of the relationship between Deaf professionals and designated interpreters as it provides more examples to expand the current description of this relationship.

Countless stories are told about the frustrations that Deaf individuals experience in the workplace, regardless of whether they are in positions of power and authority or not. Many stories are related to interpreter issues, such as having to ask an agency not to send an otherwise qualified interpreter to her workplace anymore, due to the interpreter's propensity for arguing with others in the Deaf individual's workplace, or losing access to qualified interpreters right before an important court case simply because they had not shown proof of immunizations to the agency for which they worked. Another story comes from a deaf faculty member who hired an interpreter for the day, knowing that there were only a few hours of actual interpreting work scheduled. To maximize the use of the interpreter, she asked her to assist with other sign language related work that is outside the typical role of an interpreter, only to be met with resistance from the interpreter.

Stories also come from interpreters. They tell stories of the Deaf individuals they work with being rude to them for no apparent reason, insulting them, or admonishing them. Yet, it has been shown that Deaf individuals will put forth considerable effort to get their communication needs met while demonstrating patience when working with interpreters that are not qualified (Brunson, 2011). These are some of the frustrations that may be avoided with a clearer understanding of the Deaf professional/interpreter relationship.

In this study, a designated interpreter who has experience working with Deaf professionals in a variety of settings is interviewed to understand what makes these types relationships successful. A Deaf professional, an academic, who has worked with interpreters in this capacity, is also interviewed. Data from just these two informants reveals that facilitating political relationships with others in the workplace is an important function of a designated interpreter, and that the role of the interpreter and expectations of this specialized type of interpreting is different from interpreting in other, more common settings. Implications for the application of some of the common themes found in this data to interpreting in other settings is also discussed.

LITERATURE REVIEW

There are many factors that can potentially contribute to the success or difficulty of the relationship between Deaf individuals and interpreters in general. This study uncovers some of these factors and how they manifested successfully in a Deaf professional/designated interpreter partnership. Factors that are important to the success of this relationship are issues of power dynamics, concept of the role of the interpreter and interaction management, the interpreter's use of language, and the ever-elusive concept of interpreter attitude. Each of these will be discussed below.

Power dynamics

The interpreter working with a Deaf individual engages in a delicate balance of power. Issues of power arise from the historical oppression of the Deaf community, and can contribute to conflict within the context of interpreting (Baker-Shenk, 1985). The issues of power, oppression and audism, "the hearing way of dominating…over the deaf community" (Lane, 1992, p. 43) are complex and impact the interpreting relationship. They are present in video relay interpreting as well. Deaf individuals accessing telecommunication services through a relay interpreter have been shown to invest time and energy to get their needs met while not upsetting the interpreter they are working with for fear of losing those services (Brunson, 2011).

Role and interaction management
Another factor that contributes to the success of the relationship between interpreters and Deaf individuals with whom they work is the understanding of the expected role and behavior of the interpreter:

> The issue of role conflict and role confusion is one of the difficulties facing sign language interpreters (SLIs) working in employment settings. The source of this conflict is complex, multi-layered, and has its origins deeply rooted in traditional models of interpreting. SLIs are struggling with their roles and responsibilities in relation to their client groups, with all the implications of power and oppression that are grounded in the history of relations between Deaf and hearing communities (Ladd 2003; Cokely 2005). They are also faced with a daily battle, conducted both internally and externally, with the ways in which their role is perceived (Dickinson & Turner, 2008, p. 231).

Interpreters who work with Deaf individuals must make constant, ongoing decisions about their role and level of involvement in any interpreted situation.

Lee & Llewellyn-Jones (2011) visualize a three-dimensional model that defines the level of involvement an interpreter would take in any type of interaction. The first dimension is *presentation of self*, which are utterances or behaviors interpreters make about or for themselves. The second dimension is *interaction management*, behaviors of interpreters that are used to manage the interaction they are interpreting. The third dimension is *participant alignment*, which is how much interpreters seem to align with any specific participant in a conversation. Decisions that interpreters make along any of these dimensions can impact their relationship with the Deaf individual with whom they are working.

Involvement of interpreters has also been studied by Roy (2000), who studied sign language interpreting in a university setting; Wadensjo (1998), who studied spoken language interpreting in a variety of community settings; and Metzger (1999), who studied sign language interpreting in medical settings. Roy's study focused on turn taking in an interpreted event and revealed that speakers were taking turns with the interpreter, who then managed much of the turn-taking process, even generating their own turns.

Wadensjo's research, ranging over twenty interpreted encounters in immigration, medical and community settings, revealed findings in which the interpreters were not only relaying but also managing communication. In Metzger's study, the interpreters not only relayed messages, but also produced utterances of their own as they attempted to respond to questions, offer explanations or repeat information. The level of interpreter involvement in interactions between Deaf professionals and the others in their environment can impact the working relationship between a Deaf professional and designated interpreter.

Use of language

Scholars have discussed the way language is used to convey information cross-culturally in many different ways. Nida (2004) first describes this concept as creating a dynamically equivalent interpretation, that is, "the relationship between receptor and message should be substantially the same as that which existed between the original receptors and the message" (p. 156). Sometimes this means including information that was not actually uttered by the speaker, but is important for the listener to get an equivalent message. Gile refers to this as providing various types of "secondary information" in an effort to preserve the fidelity of the source message (Gile, 1995). In the field of ASL/English interpreting, it has been referred to as expansion and compression of the source message (Lawrence, 1994; Finton & Smith, 2004). In spoken languages, terms such as 'implicature' and 'explicature' (Carston, 2002; Blakemore, 1992) are used, as well as 'enrichment' and 'impoverishment' (Sequeiros, 2002; 1998). The way language is used by designated interpreters including the amount and type of information that is interpreted can have an impact on the relationship of the Deaf professionals and their designated interpreters.

Attitude and Deaf heart

Interpreters with a "good attitude" are valued within the Deaf community. Although this it is considered the most important characteristic of an interpreter, it has yet to be precisely defined. In one study, however, interpersonal skills, such as flexibility, understanding, ability to get along with others, respect, cooperation, empathy, and ability to accept criticism were rated as important by Deaf individuals (Stuard, 2008), and may be what is meant by a "good attitude."

There has been much discussion on recent social networking websites and in both the interpreting and Deaf community (N. Coyer, personal communication, August 31, 2012) about the concept of Deaf heart. The definition of this term is as elusive as the definition of a "good attitude," but it has been described by the executive director of the Registry of Interpreters for the Deaf as the inclusion of the Deaf perspective, and as "shared goals and partnership between interpreters and the Deaf community" (http://rid.org/content/index.cfm/AID/246/content/#SLLIVE1). It has also been described as "caring enough about the well being of Deaf people and their communities to put them above ego, pride, and unwillingness to fight for what is right" (Colonomos, 2013). The extent to which designated interpreters demonstrate the characteristics associated with a "Deaf heart" and "good attitude" can affect their relationships with the Deaf professionals with whom they work.

METHODOLOGY

This study utilizes an ethnographic approach to learning about the nature of the Deaf individual/interpreter relationship. In his text on qualitative inquiry, Creswell describes ethnography as "a description and interpretation of a cultural or social group or system" (1998, p. 58). Ethnographic studies contain "detailed descriptions of behavior, beliefs, and language" (Creswell, 2002, p. 481). Although ethnographies are often thought to explore distinct cultural groups living in discernible territories, they can also be studies of *microcultures* (McCurdy, Spradley, & Shandy, 2005). Microcultures are small pockets of culture that exist within a larger culture. They are distinct from a subculture, however, in that they do not define a way of life, like a subculture does. Examples of microcultures are hobby groups, such as quilters or mountain bikers; sports teams, such as a recreational kickball team or soccer team; and occupation groups, such as grocery store clerks or painters. Individuals from a microculture belong to the larger culture and maintain the characteristics and language of this culture, but also have inside knowledge of their particular microculture and the jargon used within in. For example, mountain bikers know how and when to avoid rocks in a trail, when to shift gears when climbing a hill and when not to, and understand the pros and cons of full-suspension bikes. They share a common knowledge about types of trails, the technical skills required, and the language used to talk about their sport.

For this study, the microculture is the relationship between Deaf professionals and designated interpreters. This study reports the results of two individuals and as such, illuminates only a small section of the larger microculture.

Ethnographic methods for this study consist of interviews with a Deaf professional and a designated interpreter. Since I am seeking to discover the nature of the relationship, an ethnographic approach will be most effective in developing the understanding of the nature of the relationship between

Deaf individuals and designated interpreters. This study is just the first step in a larger project to understand this relationship, which includes participant observations, recurring interviews, video elicitation interviews (Smith, 2013) and participant journals (Dickinson, 2010).

Participants

The participants in this study are a Deaf academic who works for a large California university and an interpreter who has experience as a former designated interpreter in a variety of settings and currently works as a designated interpreter some of the time in his current work setting. Both participants in this study were purposefully selected based on their experience either with or as a designated interpreter. The interpreter is nationally certified as an interpreter and has over twenty years of interpreting experience. The Deaf professional and designated interpreter in this study do not know each other and have not worked together. They each report on independent experiences.

Data collection

Semi-structured interviews were used to collect data (see Appendix A for examples of the type of questions that were asked). Each person was interviewed one time. The interview with the interpreter took place in English at his place of employment, in the researcher's office. The interview with the academic was done remotely, in American Sign Language, through video conferencing technology, while she was in her office. Both interviews were video recorded.

Interviews were unstructured, allowing for development of rapport with the informants, probing for sensitive issues, and for developing subsequent, more structured interviews (Barnard, 1994). Interviews took direction based on the informants. The goal was to provide "a topic of interest and get out of the way" (Barnard, 1994, p. 212).

Analysis

Interviews were analyzed and coded using video analysis software developed for language analysis, regardless of the language in which they were conducted. This method allowed for direct access to the data, as opposed to analysis of a translation (Stone, 2009). This was important so that themes were not lost in the analysis phase. After getting an overall sense of the data collected by viewing the recordings of observations and taking notes, tentative codes or categories were developed. Recordings were viewed again, this time as part of a deeper analysis to identify themes present in both interviews. The initial list of tentative codes or categories was expanded and modified based on the data obtained.

RESULTS

Both the interpreter and the academic discussed the importance of politics in the workplace, and how the designated interpreter can facilitate an understanding of them. They each discussed the unique role of designated interpreters that is in contrast with interpreting in other, more common settings. Both informants shared sets of expectations, both spoken and unspoken, that are required of the designated interpreter. The interpreter also emphasized working as one with the Deaf professional. Further discussion of each of these themes is provided below.

For this report of the interview results, pseudonyms have been given to the informants, for ease of discussion. All quotes from the Deaf academic are English translations of the original statement(s) produced in American Sign Language.

Political relationships

Sometimes even more important than the actual work in a place of employment is the politics. Yet, often the political atmosphere is the most intangible, and can be imperceptible by an outsider. The designated interpreter becomes especially important in meetings where the views of colleagues are important, and it is important to know the perspectives of each participant.

The designated interpreter works with the Deaf professional to figure out the agendas of each person, so that the Deaf professional can decide which participants are allies, or have similar thinking. The designated interpreter in this study, Charles, often worked closely with Deaf professionals at meetings where there were already other interpreters, and his role was strictly to provide extralinguistic information or any other information that was not captured in the interpretation. In this capacity, he reports that "as a designated interpreter, the message is not as important as turn-taking, establishing roles, the power of the room, the relationships of the room...." and these were the cues he made sure the Deaf professionals were aware of. He has been known to sit in a meeting with the Deaf professional he is working with, and text him the information that was missed in the interpretation.

Another benefit is that designated interpreters who work with a specific Deaf professional are still available when the meeting is over. A hired community interpreter will likely be scheduled until the end of the meeting and have another assignment to go to. When there is a designated interpreter, a debriefing meeting can take place to discuss any content of the meeting that could not be interpreted, due to information overload for the interpreter. The interpreter can report any content information that was not interpreted, due to time constraints and can debrief with the Deaf professional about any other politics of the meeting. The designated interpreter has the advantage of attending meetings regularly, knows the politics of the environment, understands the goals of the Deaf professional, and thus, has a better understanding of important subtleties than a community interpreter could possibly have.

An example from the Deaf academic in this study is the Faculty Senate meeting, one of the recurring meetings at institutions of higher learning. These meetings can be very political, and the Deaf academic would not have access to all of the critical information without a designated interpreter.

Elizabeth, the Deaf academic in this study, also discussed the importance of the designated interpreter in facilitating the understanding of political agendas of others. One of her designated interpreters had seen a lot of injustices in the department that Elizabeth had not been privy to. For example, a colleague from another department expressed her concern to the interpreter that some individuals from the Deaf academic's department were not engaging in fair practices toward her and asked the interpreter to pass along her support for Elizabeth. It was part of the interpreter's expectation as a designated interpreter to inform the academic. As a result of her sharing this incidental information, the department has been able to change for the better and experience growth.

Working as the only Deaf individual in a mainstream environment can be a challenge. Other Deaf academics have acknowledged that "all Deaf academics likely fight hard to be accepted by their colleagues as a peer" (Campbell, Rohan, & Woodcock, 2008, p. 93). To Elizabeth, in a place where getting interpreting services is a political issue in itself, "that personal touch (with a colleague) is most important," and she recognizes that others may see the interpreter as reflection of who she is. She has established specific expectations of her interpreter(s) so that conversations and relationships with others are facilitated, rather than hindered. For example, when philosophies among colleagues differ, it becomes especially critical that the designated interpreter understands the perspective of the Deaf professional, so that she knows what *not* to say in certain situations.

While at the workplace, Elizabeth, the Deaf academic, prefers not to engage in conversation with the interpreter: "If I'm talking to the interpreter, fewer colleagues will approach me for conversation. If I'm not talking to the interpreter, more people approach me." She can see the difference it makes, especially at conferences, when there are networking opportunities. She prefers that interpreters remain a step behind her so that they do not engage in conversation and make it appear as though she is too busy to dialogue with her colleagues. Sometimes, however, Elizabeth uses the interpreted situation as a way to make conversations with others that might not ordinarily have happened. For example, when beginning a one-on-one meeting with someone who has never experienced a meeting with an interpreter, she can use positioning of the interpreter as a way to educate others about the interpreting process and break the ice. Political appropriateness is still important, however. During important meetings, she would be less likely to do this.

Interpreter role and expectations
Expectations for a designated interpreter are high and may be unorthodox. For the relationship between Deaf professionals and the interpreters they work with to be successful, there must be a high level of trust. For example, Deaf professionals trust that the designated interpreter can construct their message the way they intend it so they don't have to monitor the interpretation. This frees them to focus on the content of their message or on other things happening in the room, and not on how it is interpreted into English. They trust that the designated interpreter will be assertive enough to take the floor during a meeting when they want a turn to speak. They trust the designated interpreter even when the interpretation takes much longer to deliver than it took for the Deaf professional to say something. They trust the designated interpreter when something is *not* interpreted in the moment; the Deaf professional trusts that the information has already been interpreted, or that it will be discussed after the meeting. Finally, the Deaf professional trusts that the designated interpreter can accurately discuss his or her own strengths and weaknesses so that they can work together most effectively to achieve the Deaf professional's desired outcome. This trust is based on the familiarity that the Deaf professional has with a designated interpreter, and a mutual understanding of and desire for the Deaf professional to achieve his or her goals.

Expectations of interpreter behavior are also high. For example, when working with a team of interpreters, Elizabeth expects that the interpreters will not be together all the time. She prefers that only one of them at a time is with her when she is networking with colleagues, and that the other interpreter will not be present until it is time to relieve the working interpreter. She is also very specific about interpreter positioning when she is communicating with others. She expects that her designated interpreter knows that at the conclusion of meetings, she takes the opportunity to talk to her colleagues. She expects her designated interpreter to understand this goal and be readily available, rather than have to be summoned to interpret. Commenting on the expectations of a designated interpreter, Charles, the designated interpreter in this study, remarked that at times, "as a designated interpreter, you negotiate when you're allowed to leave their side." A designated interpreter understands the context of each situation and "understands when it is an ideal time and when it would be poor timing," even to take a restroom break (Earhart & Hauser, 2008, p. 148). Charles highlighted the level of expectations of the designated interpreter when he remarked, "With a designated interpreter, there is no patience. The expectation is 100%."

Expectations may also be unorthodox. Charles has been in a unique position as a designated interpreter. Charles works as a staff interpreter for a large corporation that employs many Deaf individuals, but also employs individuals who do not use sign language. Representatives from the company often collaborate and negotiate business deals with outsiders, some of whom are Deaf and some who are not Deaf and do not use ASL. Charles often accompanies professionals from his company (both Deaf and not Deaf) to meetings where there are other interpreters already assigned, and is asked to be a second set of ears or eyes and fill in gaps in the interpretation. It is well known that simultaneous interpreting is a difficult task (Christoffels & De Groot, 2005; Green, Vaid, Schwea-Nicholson, White, & Steiner, 1994; Hoffman, 1997; Bajo & Padilla, 2000; Schlesinger, 2003), requiring multi-tasking and the operation of many cognitive activities at the same time. Because of this level of difficulty, it can be a challenge to interpret 100% of the content, interactions and everything else happening in the room. The professionals in these situations where Charles works as a designated interpreter have suspected that they were missing some information, and Charles was expected to watch the interpretation of the other interpreter(s) and fill in for the professionals what was missed.

Working as one
Designated interpreters have a clear understanding of the goals of the Deaf professional they work with. Not only do they understand the goals and their context, they have an equal desire for the Deaf professional to achieve their goals. They work with the professional to accomplish them. They understand what the professional is trying to accomplish, and, in the experience of the designated interpreter in this study, act almost as one entity toward those efforts. They work together to "discover relationships...read people's minds" and navigate meetings together. For the designated interpreter, the work is all about what the Deaf professional is trying to accomplish. They act with "the same mental scope (and) the same emotional scope," almost as a single entity.

The role of the designated interpreter is, indeed, a specialized one. It requires a high level of interpreting skill, commitment to the role, trust from the Deaf professional, open communication, and willingness to be flexible.

IMPLICATIONS

This study is but a first step in the further exploration of the relationships between Deaf professionals and designated interpreters. To continue the exploration, future research is recommended. To gain a more in-depth understanding of the experience, prolonged observations should occur at a Deaf professional's workplace. Repeated observations would be most informative and more interviews should be conducted, beginning as unstructured, then becoming semi-structured, with questions determined by the information gathered from the initial interviews, as well as from observations of the Deaf professional and interpreter(s) in the workplace.

The findings from this study add to the literature currently available on the relationship between Deaf individuals and the interpreters they work with. It has illuminated new roles of the designated interpreter as well as highlighted other aspects with new details. It has implications for interpreter education, especially at advanced levels. The clearer we are on what the expectations are for designated interpreters, the better we can educate and train interpreters to meet the demand.

The unique expectations of a designated interpreter are reminiscent of the unique expectations of educational interpreters in K-12 settings and of the work of Certified Deaf Interpreters. More exploration into the similarities of the three fields may demonstrate that some of the characteristics that exemplify these roles are not so unique after all, and are simply examples of good interpreting; that is, of meeting the needs of the individuals that interpreters work with every day.

REFERENCES

Bajo, M. T., & Padilla, P. (2000). Comprehension processes in simultaneous interpretation. In *Translation in context: Selected contributions from the EST Congress* (pp. 127–142).

Baker-Shenk, C. (1985). "Characteristics of oppressed and oppressor peoples: Their effect on the interpreting context." Paper presented at the conference of the Registry of Interpreters for the Deaf, Alexandria, VA.

Barnard, H. R. (1994). Unstructured and semistructured interviewing. In *Research methods in anthropology: qualitative and quantitative approaches (2nd ed.)*, pp. 208–236. Thousand Oaks, CA: Sage Publications.

Blakemore, D. (1992). *Understanding utterances.* Oxford: Blackwell.

Brunson, J. (2011). *Video relay service interpreters: Intricacies of sign language access.* Washington, D.C.: Gallaudet University Press.

Campbell, L., Rohan, M. J., & Woodcock, K. (2008). Academic and educational interpreting from the other side of the classroom: Working with Deaf academics. In P. C. Hauser, K. L. Finch, & A. B. Hauser (Eds.), *Deaf professionals and designated interpreters: A new paradigm* (pp. 81–105). Washington, D.C.: Gallaudet University Press.

Carston, R. (2002). *Thoughts and utterances: The pragmatics of explicit communication*. Oxford: Blackwell.
Colonomos, B. (2013). Sign language interpreters and the quest for a Deaf heart. Retrieved from http://www.streetleverage.com/2013/02/sign-language-interpreters-and-the-quest-for-a-deaf-heart
Christoffels, I. K., & De Groot, A. M. (2005). Simultaneous interpreting: A cognitive perspective. In J. Kroll, & A. M. De Groot (Eds.), *Handbook of bilingualism: A psycholinguistic approach* (pp. 454–479). New York: Oxford University Press.
Creswell, J. W. (1998). *Qualitative inquiry and research design: Choosing among five traditions*. Thousand Oaks, CA: Sage Publications.
Creswell, J. W. (2002). *Educational research: Planning, conducting, and evaluating quantitative and qualitative research*. Upper Saddle River, NJ: Pearson Education.
Dickinson, J. (2010). Interpreting in a community of practice: A sociolinguistic study of the signed language interpreter's role in workplace discourse (Unpublished doctoral dissertation). Heriot-Watt University, United Kingdom.
Dickinson, J., & Turner, G. H. (2008). Sign language interpreters and role conflict in the workplace. In C. V. Garceas, & A. Martin (Eds.), *Crossing borders in community interpreting: Definitions and dilemmas* (pp. 231–243). Amsterdam, The Netherlands: John Benjamins Publishing.
Earhart, A. D., & Hauser, A. B. (2008). The other side of the curtain. In P. C. Hauser, K. L. Finch, & A. B. Hauser (Eds.), *Deaf professionals and designated interpreters: A new paradigm* (pp. 143–164). Washington, D.C.: Gallaudet University Press.
Finton, L., & Smith, R. (2004). Interpreter discourse: English to ASL expansion/ASL to English Compression [CD-ROM]. Rochester Institute of Technology: National Technical Institute for the Deaf.
Gile, D. (1995). *Basic concepts and models for interpreter and translator training*. Amsterdam, The Netherlands: John Benjamins Publishing.
Green, A., Vaid, J., Schwea-Nicholson, N., White, N., & Steiner, R. (1994). Lateralization for shadowing vs. interpretation: A comparison of interpreters with bilingual and monolingual controls. In S. Lambert, & B. Moser-Mercer (Eds.), *Bridging the gap: Empirical research in simultaneous interpretation* (pp. 331–355). Amsterdam: John Benjamins Publishing Company.
Gumperz, J. J. (1982). *Discourse Strategies*. Cambridge: Cambridge University Press.
Hauser, A. B., & Hauser, P. C. (2008). The Deaf professional-designated interpreter model. In P. C. Hauser, K. L. Finch, & A. B. Hauser (Eds.), *Deaf professionals and designated interpreters: A new paradigm* (pp. 3–21). Washington, D. C.: Gallaudet University Press.
Hauser, P. C., Finch, K. L., & Hauser, A. B. (Eds.). (2008). The Deaf professional-designated interpreter model. *Deaf professionals and designated interpreters: A new paradigm* (pp. 3–21). Washington, D. C.: Gallaudet University Press.
Hoffman, R. R. (1997). The cognitive psychology of expertise and the domain of interpreting. *Interpreting*, 2(1/2), 189–230.
Humphrey, J. H., & Alcorn, B. J. (2001). *So you want to be an interpreter? An introduction to sign language interpreting (3rd ed.)*. Amarillo, TX: H & H Publishers.
Lane, H. (1992). *The mask of benevolence: Disabling the Deaf community (1st ed.)*. New York: Random House.
Lawrence, S. (1994). Interpreter discourse: English to ASL expansion. In E. A. Winston (Ed.), Mapping our course: A collaborative venture. *Proceedings from the convention of the Conference of Interpreter Trainers*. (pp. 205–216), Conference of Interpreter Trainers.
Lee, R. G., & Llewellyn-Jones, P. (2011). Re-visiting role: Arguing for a multi-dimensional analysis of interpreter behaviour. Paper presented at the Supporting Deaf people conference.
McCurdy, D. W., Spradley, J. P., & Shandy, D. J. (2005). *The cultural experience: Ethnography in complex society (2nd ed.)*. Long Grove, IL: Waveland Press.

McLaughlin, J. (2010). Sign language interpreter shortage in California: Perceptions of stakeholders. (Unpublished doctoral dissertation). Alliant International University, California.

Metzger, M. (1999). *Sign language interpreting: Deconstructing the myth of neutrality.* Washington, D.C.: Gallaudet University Press.

Metzger, M., & Bahan, B. (2001). Discourse analysis. In C. Lucas (Ed.), *The sociolinguistics of sign languages* (pp. 112–144). Cambridge, MA: Cambridge University Press.

Mindess, A. (2006). *Reading between the signs (2nd ed.).* Boston: Intercultural Press.

Nida, E. (2004). Principles of correspondence. In L. Venuti (Ed.), *The translation studies reader, 2nd ed.),* pp. 153–164. New York: Routledge.

Roy, C. B. (2000). *Interpreting as a discourse process.* New York: Oxford University Press.

Schlesinger, M. (2003). Effects of presentation rate on working memory in simultaneous interpreting. Retrieved from http://www.openstarts.units.it/dspace/bitstream/10077/2470/1/02.pdf

Sequeiros, X. R. (1998). Interlingual impoverishment in translation. *Bulletin of Hispanic Studies, 75,* 145–57.

Sequeiros, X. R. (2002). Interlingual pragmatic enrichment in translation. *Journal of Pragmatics, 34,* 1069–89.

Smith, M. B. (2013). *More than meets the eye: Revealing the complexities of an interpreted education.* Washington, D.C.: Gallaudet University Press.

Stone, C. (2009). *Toward a Deaf translation norm.* Washington, D.C.: Gallaudet University Press.

Stuard, V. L. (2008). Perception of interpreter qualification by Deaf consumers and hearing interpreters (Doctoral dissertation). Retrieved from http://search.proquest.com.proxyga.wrlc.org/pqdtft/docview/304830326/fulltextPDF?accountid=27346

Wadensjo, C. (1998). *Interpreting as interaction.* New York: Addison Wesley Longman.

Machine Translation: English to ASL Gloss, TRUE-BIZ?

MARY BONHAM

TRANSLATING FROM ONE LANGUAGE TO ANOTHER HAS BECOME EVER more important with increased communication across many languages worldwide. People frequently want to disseminate or assimilate information in their own language and in other languages. The traditional translation industry does not have the means to satisfy the vast needs for translation throughout the world. In an attempt to find a way to translate more material quicker and easier, researchers have developed computer machine translation systems, which have become tools to aid the translation process (Craciunescu et al. 2008).

There are several methods of machine translation (MT), one being statistical machine translation (SMT), the avenue in which the current thesis will proceed. SMT is performed using high volumes of sentences in a parallel corpus with which to train a computer program to translate sentences from the a source language (SL) to a target language (TL) (Koehn 2005; Lopez 2008). Though researchers have been working with MT for many decades using text of spoken languages, sign language MT is less known. Sign languages do not have a widely accepted written form in which to create a parallel corpus, thus sign languages were largely excluded from MT research until the twenty-first century. Today, many researchers worldwide are investigating sign language MT (SLMT) using specialized textual glosses for representing sign languages.

The purpose of this study was to develop and evaluate an SLMT system that translated from English text to American Sign Language (ASL) gloss. We used parallel corpus data that was provided by The Church of

Jesus Christ of Latter-day Saints (the LDS Church). We curated the raw corpus by removing the computer markup language and then aligning the corpus sentence-by-sentence. The result is apparently the largest parallel corpus of text/sign language gloss to date, having over 14,000 sentence pairs. We developed an SMT engine using the Moses open-source toolkit (Koehn, et al. 2007) and used aligned phrases and words to create language models and execute the Moses decoder for the translation stage. To assess the quality of the MT output from the system, we used a state-of-the-art Bilingual Evaluation Understudy (BLEU) scoring protocol.

LITERATURE REVIEW

Translation between languages is not a new phenomenon, but with development and continued expansion of the World Wide Web, the need for translation between languages has grown. Human translators can be expensive and there are not enough translators to satisfy all translation needs (Craciunescu, et al. 2008). It would be impossible to translate all the information available on the Web into even one language, let alone many of them. To aid in the translation process, researchers have developed ways of automating translation. Computer machine translation is one such approach.

Machine translation
Machine translation (MT) is automatic translation from one language to another by computer. Researchers have been studying the process of machine translation for over sixty years. Today, machine translation paradigms include (Koehn, 2010):
- rule-based (RBMT) which uses extensive handwork of human language experts in writing and applying linguistic rules for the translation process in the MT system (Morrissey 2008)
- example-based (EBMT) which tries to match the input sentence with similar phrases and sentences in the corpus, retrieving their translation for the output
- phrase-based (PBMT) which translates small sequences of words or phrases
- statistical (SMT) which analyzes huge amounts of a parallel corpus and finds the highest probability of any given translation
- hybrid MT, a combination of multiple MT approaches

Way (2013) claims that the time for MT is now, arguing that, depending on the requirements for the outcome, MT output can be used solely, or 'raw,' or it can be integrated with either minor or major human editing. He lists a number of people and companies using successful MT, including Stephen Richardson, head of the LDS Church's translation department.

When MT is available for a particular language and particular domain, it can cut the working time of a translator by 50% (Richardson, 2012). Human translators frequently express concern that a machine that can translate between languages will replace them; in reality, MT provides a translator with better tools, which can allow even more translation by increasing productivity and improving quality (Craciunescu, et al. 2008).

Lopez (2008) describes how statistical machine translation (SMT) works with probabilities, using a learning algorithm that computes the probability that a specific word or phrase in the TL is likely to be the best translation of a word or phrase in the SL. The higher the probability, the better is the chance that the match will be correct. SMT was first attempted by IBM in the late 1980s, adding additional features successively, which created a foundation for further SMT research and development (Koehn, 2010).

Researchers found that a large parallel corpus (or *bitext*) of source language sentences and human-translated target language sentences could be used to train statistical models for MT (Brown, et al., 1990). As computers increased in capability of storage, so did the use of larger corpora. Brown et al. (1990) developed a bigram approach, where a computer searched for two contiguous words to see which words were most likely to appear together and then matched them with the most frequent translation. They eventually developed a trigram model based on three contiguous words, that provides and even better translation than the bigram.

In early SMT research, it could take a researcher, starting from scratch, nine months to develop MT algorithms to create a statistical MT system. Koehn and Hoang (2012), developers of the open-source machine translation Moses, explained that their system uses a parallel corpus to analyze and 'learn' the two languages used in the translation process. Moses is an SMT system and does not require the user to input translation rules about the languages. Through annual workshops, researchers worldwide contribute to the development of Moses (http://www.statmt.org/moses), which has become the tool of choice for students and researchers.

This study focuses on the development and evaluation of a Moses/SMT-basded system to translate from English to American Sign Language (ASL) gloss. The current version of the system uses a trigram model. Steps in SMT system development include training Moses to use a parallel corpus in a specific limited domain. Parallel corpora provide data for Moses to create a SL model of correct, grammatically fluent English and a TL model of typical fluent ASL gloss. Moses also created a translation model that demonstrated how English/ASL gloss should be translated. When parallel corpus lines are fed into Moses, it learns models for the two languages, within the specific domain, and determines how the languages relate to each other. Use of narrower domains with limited vocabulary in the parallel corpora achieved better results in the output. Building language models with a larger monolingual corpus within the specific domain of the MT is also helpful (Corbett, 2006). Moses uses the TL language model to simulate the TL when generating translation output. System parameters can be evaluated and readjusted to improve the output. A reordering model resequences words in a SL phrase, word-for-word, and arranges them into proper order for the TL. If words are reordered too much, however, there is resulting TL unintelligibility.

Using a quality human-translator-produced parallel corpus, or bitext, is of utmost importance in preparing the various statistical English, ASL, and English/ASL translation models. The parallel corpus we used was created by translating from English to ASL gloss. The translation was done by a team of human translators who were skilled in both languages. When ten skilled human translators translate a sentence into a TL, the result could be ten different sentences (Koehn, 2010). All the sentences would be considered good sentences, as there are more ways than one in which to translate a sentence and still retain the concept of the original sentence.

Most MT research deals with spoken languages and mentions access to tens of millions of bitext lines of the SL and TL for statistical model development. As sign languages do not have large parallel corpora, researchers view them as low-resource languages. Working with MT for sign languages, most research is being done with only several hundred bitext lines. By contrast, this project involves tens of thousands of bitext lines of English/ASL gloss.

Sign Languages and Glossing
Sign languages are visual. As trying to read lips, ascertain speech, and socialize with individuals who can hear and speak is a difficult, tedious, and tiring task for many deaf people, sign languages have naturally developed throughout the world. There is no one universal sign language.

Sign language poses a challenge for MT. Annotating all the facets of ASL is time-consuming; ASL provides multiple additional variables: facial expressions, eye gaze, mouth movement, hand movement, hand shapes, hand location, palm orientation, and other parameters all require much time to represent orthographically (Morrissey, 2008).

Because of the difficulty in textually representing the various parameters of sign language, SLMT researchers use *glossing* systems. To *gloss* means to use a near-seamantic equivalent written analog in a spoken language to label and identify individual signs and concepts of a sign language.

Sign languages for English, Spanish, Italian, and other languages use glosses with their respective languages in approximately the same manner. For the purpose of this project, I used an English-based system, ASL gloss. To become proficient in ASL gloss, one would need to know ASL, English, and a variety of orthographic symbols that portray hand shape, location, movement of the signs, and non-manual markers.

For transcription purposes, ASL gloss uses English words for each sign or phrase that can be labeled. ASL gloss is represented with small capital letters. The English word 'cat' would be transcribed as CAT in ASL gloss. The English declarative sentence 'The cat was bitten by the dog.' would be transcribed into ASL gloss as DOG BITE CAT. In gloss, transcription symbols express many types of linguistic information (Baker-Shenk & Cokely, 1981):

- the topic of the sentence
- the type of sentence
- the hand shapes
- fingerspelled signs
- compound or contraction signs
- emphasized signs and/or repeated signs
- signs made with one, both and/or alternating hands
- classifier signs
- miming concepts
- arc motion signs
- verb signs that move between objects
- the position of the eye gaze of the signer
- non-manual markers that show adverbial and adjectival information and provide important linguistic information to clarify translations

ASL gloss is not a common orthographic means, and not all deaf people understand gloss. Therefore, gloss is not the end product in translation. Some sign language researchers criticize gloss and express concern that its use cause speople to think the gloss is just a broken spoken language. Table 1 shows examples of English/ASL gloss.

Sentence Type	Written English	ASL Gloss
Declarative	"That is a beautiful cat."	//Cat-it\\ true-biz beautiful.
Yes/No question	"Is this your cat?"	//Cat-it\\ yours?
WH-question	"What is the name of your school?"	//Your school name\\ what?
RH-question	"We go to the temple to seal our family for eternity."	?We go temple for-for? Our family seal-circle always.

Table 1. Examples of sentences in both English/ASL gloss

Though the use of gloss is standard for SLMT, glossing techniques have never been standardized. Researchers use many of the same basic gloss components, but each group of researchers must evaluate current glossing techniques and establish their own conventions for the gloss they use. Regardless of the concerns, SLMT researchers continue to use gloss because of convenience and ease of use.

Morrissey asserts that it requires extensive effort to create and annotate an SLMT corpus and suggests a "central repository with standards" (Morrissey, 2011). She mentions current concerns with evaluation methods and contemplates how accurate MT output must be. Would a gist of the idea be enough? Would the output be helpful to translators? Her questions deserve careful consideration by MT researchers working on SLMT.

LDS Church translation and ASL gloss

ASL gloss helps document ASL in writing and is used academically for learning ASL grammar. However, there are times when a particular entity might use an adaptation of the generally accepted gloss format to meet its own needs. The LDS Church Translation Group (LDSTG) extensively uses ASL gloss in its work and has developed a specific glossing technique that is an amalgamation of several standard accepted approaches. Because their work culminates in filmed, on-screen product, final translation and production processes include the use of teleprompters. Source (English) message is translated into an ASL gloss, put into text files and loaded into a teleprompter, which only accepts ASCII symbols. Signers then read ASL gloss from teleprompter screens, self-convert ASL gloss into a target (ASL) message, and are filmed for live or delayed braodcast.

It is critical that signers, as they are watching the teleprompter, can quickly and easily parse and sign transcriptions for filming. Though typical ASL glosses for lexical items is written in capital letters, the LDSTG has found it is easier to read transcriptions when they are in lowercase letters. For the ease of the signer, glosses are rendered in lowercase letters, using capital letters at the beginning of sentences or for fingerspelled words. They also add punctuation such as periods, commas, and semi-colons to the gloss for signing clarity.

Each ASL translator is given an ASL Translation Guide (LDS Church, 2012) to aid in the process of translating English to ASL gloss. Table 2 lists many of the transcription rules the English/ASL gloss translation department uses at the LDS Church.

Although ASL gloss typically uses capital letters, the LDS Church uses lower-case letters.
LDS ASL gloss does capitalize names, fingerspelled words, and honorific signs.
Paired forward and backward slash marks delimit the topic of a sentence.
Commands, imperative, and emphatic phrases begin and end with an '!'
Signing 'finish' at conclusion of the sentence indicates past tense.
Signing 'will' at the end of the sentence indicates future tense.
The typical gloss for classifiers is CL:. The LDS Church shows a classifier with cl:.
Directional and contracted signs are used when phrases of more than one English word can be signed with one sign. Help-you. Tell-me. Shout-to-him.
Negative sentences are written with a '?' at the beginning of the affirmative sentence, followed by a '?' and then a wave-no.
Yes/No questions and WhQ are shown with the topic and then the question and '?'.
Rhetorical questions are two-part questions. The topic begins and ends with '?', followed by the answer to the rhetorical question. NMM's for RhQ are raised eyebrows.
If a sign-gloss is ambiguous, translators add clarification. 'Run' would be glossed 'machine-run,' nose-run,' 'nylon-run,' 'run-for-office,' 'run-around,' etc.
For pronominalization, the LDS Church does not use IX, which is used generally in glossing. Instead, the gloss would be simply 'he,' 'she,' or 'it.'
Pluralization is done in several ways: child++, or car cl:in-a-line, or cookie cl:stack, or car#3, or children+group.
Some NMMs are italicized and placed within parentheses. Example: //cat\\ (cha) fat! Cha is a mouth movement showing large size.
Body shifts are glossed using arrows: > or < with slight shoulder shift following the arrows.
rs signifies Role Shift – the signer becomes the character or signs a quote: (rs:JS)
Deity is shown with a caret: ^He.
Loan signs and name signs begin with '#' and are capitalized: Relief Society abbreviated #RS or a loan sign of #BANK.
Compound signs are created with a +: true+work (which means 'really' in all its senses).
Information to accompany certain signs is given in parentheses preceding the sign: (1h) one-handed sign, (2h) two-handed sign, (alt) alternate hands, (not) shake head while signing to negate the comment.
Periods end a thought and are signed with a nod.
Commas add a pause in the signing, with a slight nod. Commas replace 'and' or 'or'.

Table 2. List of glossing techniques used by the LDS Church translation group

The LDS Church English/ASL translation corpus contains work both prior to and after the establishment of the revised Translation Guidelines. Due to this discrepancy, existing translation data is not consistent.

For at least two decades, the LDSTG has used human translation of English/ASL in preparation for filming the ASL religious messages. As such, the translation department has hundreds of thousands of lines of English/

ASL gloss parallel corpora. For the current project, we received approximately 20,000 lines, including of translations of several church magazine articles, translations of the *Preach My Gospel* book, and translations of the *Articles of Faith*.

METHODOLOGY

The development of our English to ASL MT system involved five basic steps:
1. Curation of a bitext of the LDS Church human-translated material consisting of English and ASL gloss
2. Downloading and installation of the Moses toolkit
3. Loading of the parallel corpus into Moses and building of English, ASL, and translation language models
4. Partitioning the corpus into three parts (training set, development (dev) set, and test set), training the system to perform a baseline evaluation, and tuning the system improve MT output
5. Decoding and evaluation of the final output and comparison of final results with original baseline score

Corpus curation
As mentioned in the previous section, The LDS Church supplied a religious parallel corpus of thousands of English and human-translated ASL gloss lines for this project. We downloaded and installed Olifant, an open-source translation memory editor and received raw corpus text as translation memory exchange (TMX) files. The TMX format allows for translation memory to be transferred between users and translation tools. The corpus was segmented into paragraphs interspersed with computer markup language.

We loaded the parallel corpus into Olifant. We edited the bitext by splitting paragraphs into sentences and phrases of complete thoughts. As Moses translates raw text, we also cleaned the corpus to remove the markup language from the text. We removed markup language from the bitext and split the paragraphs into sentence/phrases, working on both sides of the sentence pairs, in preparation for MT in Moses, requiring considerable time and effort. Table 3 shows an example of one sequence that needed to be split into sentences, with hand-inserted split markers to divide sentences.

Source language	Target Language
If you are teaching a Melchizedek Priesthood or Relief Society lesson, you should not set this book aside or prepare lessons from other materials. [$SPLIT$] Prayerfully select from the chapter those teachings that you feel will be most helpful to those you teach. [$SPLIT$] Some chapters contain more material than you will be able to discuss during class time. [$SPLIT$] Allow good discussions to continue rather than trying to cover all the teachings.	//if you teach++ lesson\\ for melchizedek priesthood shrug relief-society, //use book\\ (head shake no) put-aside shrug focus other book++for purpose prior prepare not.[$SPLIT$] //chapter list\\ you pray can pick-from-list //that\\ will better help people you teach.[$SPLIT$]//some chapter++ inside\\ have more thing // during class time\\ enough time can discuss all not.[$SPLIT$]//you worry try teach everything\\ not //if have good discussion\\ go-ahead discuss.

Table 3. Source and target sentences with hand-inserted SPLIT markers

Occasional errors in the markup language caused Olifant to display an error message giving the exact location of the mistake. To correct the error, we used Notepad++, an open-source source code editor.

As many of the translations we received in the TMX files contained markup language and several sentences per sequence, the work required more than an hour per one-hundred bitext chunks to divide the paragraphs into separate sentences. To indicate the beginning and ending of chunks of text, we then wrapped the sentences in Standard Generalized Markup Language (SGML), which is a requirement of the NIST scoring tool for evaluation, and prepared the data for training the translation system.

For training and testing an MT system, the parallel corpus must be divided into two or three partitions of randomly selected bitext: the training set for training the MT system, the development (dev) set (optional) for use during development of the system, and the test set for the final evaluation of how well the system was able to translate. Many SLMT articles discuss the percentage chosen for each partition, which typically range from 64–98% for the training set, 2–12.5% for the dev set (when employed), and 2–20% for the test set. Table 1 summarizes corpus size, language, and partitions of SLMT researchers discussed previously (Dreuw, et al., 2008).

After studying how other researchers had partitioned their experiments, we determined our partition approach. Based on Morrissey and Way (2013), we partitioned the corpus into three sets: 70% for the testing set, 10% for the dev set, and 20% for the test set. The corpus partitioned in this manner gives us a large training set with which to train the MT decoder, a sizeable dev set, and a substantial test set containing enough data to give a good indication as to how the MT system performed.

Paper	Language	Quantity	Partition
Almohimeed, et al., 2011	Arabic	203 sentence pairs	-
Bauer, et al., 1999	German	100 signs	-
Bungeroth & Ney, 2004	German	200 sentence pairs	84/16
Dasgupta, et al., 2008	Indian	208 sentence pairs	-
D'Haro, et al., 2008	Spanish	416 sentence pairs	75/12.5/12.5
Dreuw, et al., 2008	English	843 sentence pairs	75/12.5/12.5
Forster, et al., 2014	German	8767 sentences, (6861 DGS)	94/3/3
López-Ludeña, et al., 2012	Spanish	3496 sentences, (820 LSE)	75/12.5/12.5
López-Ludeña, et al., 2013	Spanish	12,741 signs	-
López-Ludeña, et al., 2014a	Spanish	500 sentence pairs	75/12.5/12.5
López-Ludeña, et al., 2014b	Spanish	1364 sentences, (443 LSE)	75/12.5/12.5
Lugaresi & DiEugenio, 2013	Italian	374 sentences, (376 LIS)	-
Morrissey & Way, 2005	English	561 sentence pairs	90/10
Morrissey, et al., 2007	English	595 sentence pairs	-
Morrissey, et al., 2010	English	350 utterances	-
Morrissey & Way, 2013	Several	595 sentences	70/10/20
Othman, et al. 2011	English	431 sentence pairs	-
Porta, et al., 2014	Spanish	229 sentence pairs	15/85
San-Segundo, et al., 2006	Spanish	135 phrases	-
San-Segundo, et al., 2012	Spanish	1,413 sentences, (199 LSE)	75/12.5/12.5
Stein, et al., 2012	German	3077 sentence pairs	83/17
Wray, et al., 2004	English	500 phrases	-
Bonham, 2012 (this study)	**English**	**14,247 sentence pairs**	**70/10/20**

Table 4. Corpus partitions for various spoken language text/sign language gloss MT projects

Toolkit installation and use

Information found in the Moses User's Guide (MUG) on the Moses website helped us establish our SMT infrastructure.

System refinement

To begin the development process, we acclimated Moses on the training set, had Moses translate the English portion of the training set with off-the-shelf settings, and evaluated the MT output. This provided a baseline score on the seen data in the training set. Next, we established a second baseline by partitioning the training set into five equal parts and evaluating the unseen data using five-fold cross validation. We tuned the system and had it retranslate the English portion of the training set, then evaluated the MT output.

We performed a trial run on the dev set as unseen data. We checked the output of the dev set to ensure we had not overtuned the system on the training set. We ran a few development iterations and analyzed the output to determine any MT issues and identify what we could do to generate a better translation. Did the reordering model require more weight, or a higher percentage, or did the translation model need a higher percentage? We adjusted the weights until the right balance and combination of weights produced a better translation (Koehn, 2010). With each iteration of testing, the Moses decoder learned English text/ASL gloss further.

Using the tokenized English text and then the tokenized ASL gloss text, we trained truecase models for each language. Truecasing eliminates most capital letters, keeping only the capitals that are necessary to the translation. The English truecase model changed the capital letters at the beginning of sentences into lower-case letters. Capital letters of proper nouns remained capitalized. The truecase model for ASL gloss recognized which letters in the data should remain capitalized and which letters should be lowercased. Standard ASL gloss is made by capitalizing each gloss word. For the LDS Church, however, capitalization of all words is not the standard and only fingerspelled words are capitalized. Some of the older data we received from the LDS Church was inconsistent with the current translation guidelines and contained capitals for each gloss word. We adjusted the parameters to help the truecasing model recognize only the necessary capitals.

Final evaluation
The best way to determine translation quality is to use human evaluators who are both native TL users/speakers and have bilingual SL skill. (This, of course, is problematic in this study, as there are no native speakers of ASL gloss.) However, there is wide variation among evaluators. Factors that affect translation and translation evaluation include the audience of the translation, the purpose for the translation, the tolerance for complete concept fidelity, and the resources available for the quality check on the translation. Human evaluators can recognize a good sentence, but may vary in word choices and evaluation scores; one might be more critically perfectionistic, whereas another might be more casual and accepting of mistakes; one might be quick in the process, while another might be slow (Papineni, et al., 2002). In any case, human evaluators are expensive and in low supply. Due to the lack of human evaluators, the variance of opinions of evaluators, and the costs in time and money to use them, many researchers opt to use computerized metrics instead.

One such metric is BLEU, which automatically evaluates an MT output (candidate) translation by comparing it to a human translated (reference) translation (Papineni, et al., 2002). The BLEU metric is language-independent, automated, (debatably) accurate, open-source, and widely used as an industry standard in MT output evaluation. For these reasons, we used BLEU to evaluate the MT output frequently throughout the development cycle of the thesis and for the final evaluation. Figure 1 shows the basic steps taken in our system to obtain BLEU scores.

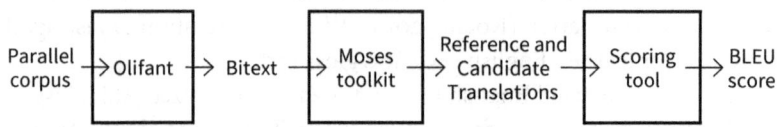

Figure 1. MT and evaluation steps for the current thesis

In assigning a BLEU score to candidate translations, an evaluation tool follows these guidelines:
1. Find and count n-gram matches
2. Penalize sentences that are too short or too long
3. Penalize candidate translation words that are used more frequently than the reference translation
4. Penalize candidate translation when multiple translations are used
5. Prefer a candidate translation that matches the reference translation in length, word order, and word choice

The similarity between the reference and the candidate translation gives a BLEU score ranging between 0–1.0. A score of 1.0 indicates that the candidate translation is an exact equal translation to the reference translation. This rarely occurs, even when comparing human translations. BLEU scores correlate highly with human evaluation scores (Papineni, et al., 2002).

As BLEU measures n-grams, BLEU works best with high quantities of translation material (more reference and candidate sentence pairs) to improve the quality of the score. Having multiple reference translations per candidate translation sentence would also help boost the BLEU score, by adding possible matches to the candidate translation. When an MT system has been trained using a limited corpus of a small domain, the BLEU score tends to be higher (Papineni, et al., 2002). Research with low-resource languages typically yields BLEU scores of between 0–0.2 (Genzel, et al., 2009; Ma, et al., 2011; Irvine & Callison-Burch, 2013). Even an increase of .06 in a BLEU score is discernible by humans.

In summary, to complete the training and evaluation of the SMT we:
- Partitioned the corpus into training, development, and test sets
- Decoded the training set
- Evaluated the output to attain a baseline #1 BLEU score and five-fold cross-validation to attain a baseline #2 BLEU score
- Trained and tuned the system on the training set for several iterations
- Performed system refinement on the training set
- Trained the system with the newly refined training set
- Decoded the dev set
- Evaluated output to attain the BLEU score and ascertain whether the system had improved
- Trained and tuned the system on the dev set through several iterations
- Trained the system with the newly refined training/dev set
- Evaluated the system for the final BLEU score

Sign languages are considered low-resource languages and we had access to a small parallel corpus of English/ASL gloss. We curated the bitext, downloaded and installed Moses, aligned the sentence pairs, created the language models, and prepared Moses to translate. We began a cycle of training, evaluating, tuning, retraining, evaluating, refining, retraining, and evaluating. We did this cycle using two partitions, the training set and dev set. We then combined the two sets into the training+dev set. We translated the final test partition, which was completely unseen data, evaluated the output using BLEU and found the results to be comparable to other low-resource language MT.

RESULTS AND EVALUATION

During the development phase of an SMT system, researchers frequently evaluate the target language output for determining whether the researchers' system modifications have improved the system.

As explained previously, we followed Morrissey and Way (2013) in partitioning our corpus into three sets: 70% for the training set, 10% for the dev set, and 20% for the final test set. This allowed a large training set with which to train the Moses system and establish a baseline score, a good-sized dev set to run an evaluation and to refine the Moses system, and a substantial test set. We thus partitioned the bitext by randomly selecting 9,992 sentence pairs for the training set, 1,427 for the dev set and 2,855 for the test set. After partitioning the corpus, we trained the Moses system on the training set using the Moses default settings.

System evaluations

We then had Moses decode the entire training set and ran an automatic evaluation of the candidate translation to establish a baseline score. We needed a baseline score to determine how well the training set had trained Moses without any user adjustments. We expected that our subsequent improvements would increase the evaluation score at the conclusion of the thesis.

We used a scoring tool provided by the National Institute of Standards and Technology (NIST) (Papineni, et al. 2002), and compared the newly decoded candidate translation of the training set to the human reference translation of the training set. As the machine had been trained using the same bitext sentences, this constituted processing of seen data. Working with ASL gloss is a challenge, such as not sufficient data, multiple translators and word order mismatch. We wanted to see how well the system decoded, so we evaluated the MT output. We achieved a BLEU score of 0.5104. This is an encouraging score, considering that the combination of English and ASL gloss was new to the Moses system. We titled this score Baseline #1.

As the Moses system had seen the bitext data prior to decoding, we decided to run a second baseline using a technique called five-fold cross-validation on the training set. To run the cross-validation (CV), we randomly divided the 9,992 bitext lines of the training set into five partitions, with approximately 2,000 bitext lines in each partition. We trained Moses using default settings on the first four partitions and then had the Moses decoder translate the remaining fifth partition of unseen or unfamiliar data. We did this five times, each time choosing four different partitions to train and leaving one remaining partition of unseen or unfamiliar data for Moses to decode, until all five partitions had been translated.

Experiment	BLEU Score
Baseline #1	.5104
After tuning	.6260
Baseline #2: five-fold CV	.1223

Table 5. Baseline scores on the training set (seen data; 9,992 sentence pairs)

The five-fold cross-validation gave us five sets of candidate translations. We applied the NIST scoring tool to each translation, comparing the candidate translations to the reference translations. This gave us five separate BLEU scores: .1240, .1258, .1228, .1198, and .1193. Averaging these five scores together returned a mean BLEU score of .1223 (baseline #2). We expected baseline #1 to be higher than baseline #2 as we included only four portions of the training set each time we ran the five-fold cross-validation, and thus the fifth partition of the test would be unseen data for that round. Table 2 shows the baseline scores.

Moses has an automatic tuning feature. To tune automatically, Moses makes a copy of itself, checks the candidate translation against the reference translation, and determines where it can improve in translating by adjusting its own parameters. After establishing the two baseline BLEU scores, we automatically tuned the system using the full training set. This included:

- Automatically tuning the system
- Updating the system with the new tuning weights
- Retranslating the training set using the new weights
- Evaluating the output

After tuning, the BLEU score was .6260, an increase of .1156.

Development and dev test phase

After the automatic tuning, we ran two rounds of hand refinements and adjustments to fine-tune the SMT system. By running iterations of evaluating, adjusting parameters and decoding, we expected to be able to improve the SMT system and increase the BLEU score further.

We loaded the candidate and corresponding reference translation into Notepad++ and hand compared the translations line-by-line. After analysis of several issues in the initial translation, we prioritized adjustments that we expected could substantially improve the translation system. Next we then refined the translations, adjusted the weights of the models, decoded, automatically evaluated the new candidate translations, and calculated new BLEU scores through both iterations.

After the first iteration, we noticed a few tokenization issues that could be changed:

- The ASL gloss for the concept of 'tithing' is a written fraction '1/10'; the fraction was split (+ + 1 / 10 pay-to-Lord)
- The deity reference caret modifier (^) was separated from its subject
- Topic markers (//) were separated from themselves and the topic
- Plural (++) sequences were separated.
- Fingerspelling hashtags (#) were separated from the word, but fs- for fingerspelling was not
- Classifier referencing (cl:) was separated
- Non-manual markers or explanation words were placed within parentheses, which were separated from their subjects/objects
- ASL gloss uses > or <, which the tool does not accept; instead, we used markup language (< – tokenized - & lt;)
- Compound signs joined by (+) were separated.

We made several changes related to these tokenization issues to enable reference and the candidate translations to be similarly tokenized:
- We added spaces after specific characters, such as , / ? . + ( ) # and ! from their words.
- We added a space to separate topic markers // and \\.
- We space-delimited non-ASCII characters, such as exotic encodings for quote marks, ellipses, etc.
- We removed the space after the deity reference caret modifer (^)

The candidate translation had more frequent capital letters in the data than did the reference translation. Because of the variation in upper and lower case, we did not include case sensitivity when using the scoring tool.

The first round yielded a higher BLEU score, reflecting improvement in the SMT system. Making the few adjustments explained above, we increased the BLEU score to .6726. When we eliminated case sensitivity, the BLEU score increased to .6749.

In Round 2 we corrected further tokenization discrepancies in the reference and candidate translations. The second round yielded a BLEU score of .6761. With the iterations of evaluation, adjusting parameters and decoding of the training set, the BLEU scores showed that our training set refinements and parameter adjustments we made to the MT system had a positive impact on the candidate translation.

Table 3 shows the various BLEU scores we received when we evaluated the development (dev) set. After automatic tuning of the SMT system we ran a test of Moses decoding the English portion of the dev set. The dev set was 10% or, 1,427 sentence pairs of unseen data. The candidate translation of the dev set was evaluated by comparing it to the reference translation of the same set using the NIST scoring tool. We obtained a BLEU score of .1454 on the dev set. We then used the hand-refinements to test the dev set, applied the first set of refinements, and increased the BLEU score to .1677. We then applied the second set of refinements and got a BLEU score of .1678.

These values are substantially lower than the Baseline #1 previously cited because the data in the dev set was unseen by Moses and by us. The 1,427 sentence pairs had been randomly selected prior to any training and set aside for translation and evaluation during the development phase.

We then combined the training and dev sets (training+dev), which totaled 80% of the data, or 11,419 sentence pairs. We completed a baseline training and translation on the combined sets (seen data) and got a BLEU score of .5634. This represents a substantial improvement over Baseline #1.

Finally, using the manual refinements we developed in the development phase, we had Moses tune its parameter on the training+dev set. This tuning took approximately twenty hours of processing time on a dedicated server. We then had Moses retranslate the training+dev set and we ran the scoring tool on the result, which yielded a BLEU score of .6666, an increase of .1032.

Experiments	# of sentence pairs	BLEU score
Baseline Dev test (10% of data, unseen)	1,427	.1454
Round 1 (1st set of refinements)	1,427	.1677
Round 2 (2nd set of refinements)	1,427	.1678
Training+dev set (80% of data, seen)	11, 419	.5634
After tuning on training+dev set (80% of data, seen)	11,419	.6666

Table 6. Evaluation scores on dev and training+dev sets

Final evaluation

When we had refined and adjusted the SMT system, thus completing the development phase, it was ready for final evaluation. This involved training Moses on the training+dev set (80%) of the corpus, and then decoding on the last 20% of the corpus, the evaluation/test set. This was unseen data for us and for Moses. This consisted of 2,855 sentence pairs.

Experiments	BLEU score
Evaluation of final test set (20% of data) (unseen data)	0.1765
Evaluation of final test set five-fold cross-validation	0.1606

Table 7. Final evaluation of unseen data of the test set (2,855 sentence pairs)

As before, our final evaluation compared the candidate translation of the test set with the human-produced reference translation of the same set. The results of our final evaluation are shown in Table 4. We again used the NIST scoring tool and received a BLEU score of .1765, which is as good as or even better than other low-resource languages using Moses. Since the paucity of parallel corpora for low-resource languages typically yields BLEU scores of .08–.12 in SMT research, our final BLEU score of .1765 was clearly a state-of-the-art result.

CONCLUSIONS AND DISCUSSION

We trained a Moses MT system using an English text/ASL gloss parallel corpus within the religious domain of The Church of Jesus Christ of Latter-day Saints. We curated the parallel corpus, hand-separating multiple-sentence paragraphs into single sentences and phrases. We also hand-separated the extensive markup language from the parallel corpus. After weeks of cleaning the English/ASL bitext with the Olifant tool, we had created apparently the largest parallel corpus, thus far, of any sign language worldwide.

We then downloaded and installed the Moses toolkit on a dedicated computer on the BYU campus. Loading the bitext into the Moses toolkit, we trained and tuned the system through several iterations. Each time we evaluated the output using automatic scoring tools. Each iteration yielded increasingly better output results with increasing BLEU scores. We attained a BLEU score on unseen data that was comparable to, and even better than, typical BLEU scores for low-resource languages.

FUTURE WORK

Continuing this research with additional quality data, if available, would improve the MT output. Follow-up research could involve a thorough, systematic linguistic evaluation of the output results to consider ways the MT system might be improved, such as using constituent reordering models to compensate for syntactic differences between English and ASL gloss.

Instead of using humans to convert the MT output to sign language, extra steps could be taken that would include an additional intermediate representation of HamNoSys to the final output for programming a computer avatar that would sign the message in sign language.

This project included automatic evaluation using BLEU. Future work might include human evaluation of the output. That would entail incorporating people skilled in reading ASL gloss and English to evaluate the output. Or the output can be converted to sign language and a target audience skilled in ASL and English could watch the ASL message and compare it with the English to analyze the output. These human evaluation options were beyond the scope of the thesis.

REFERENCES

Almohimeed, A., Wald, M., & Damper, R. I. (2011). Arabic text to Arabic sign language translation system for the deaf and hearing-impaired community. In *Proceedings of the Second Workshop on Speech and Language Processing for Assistive Technologies*, 101–109.

Baker-Shenk, C. & Cokely, D. (1981). American Sign Language: A teacher's resource text on grammar and culture. Washington, D.C. Gallaudet University Press.

Bauer, B., Nießen, S., & Hermann, H. (1999). Towards an automatic sign language translation system. In *Proceedings of the International Workshop on Physicality and Tangibility in Interaction: Towards New Paradigms for Interaction Beyond the Desktop*, Siena, Italy.

Brown, P. F., Cocke, J., Della Pietra, S. A., Della Pietra, V. J., Jelinek, F., Lafferty, J. D., Mercer, R. L., & Roossin, P. S. (1990). A statistical approach to machine translation. *Computational Linguistics* 16(2), 79–85.

Bungeroth, J., & Ney, H. (2004). Statistical sign language translation. In *Proceedings from the LREC Workshop On Representation and Processing of Sign Languages*, 105–108.

Corbett, C. (2006). 23C3: Open source machine translation. 23rd Chaos Communication Congress, presentation. https://www.youtube.com/watch?v=mnOrCnSh7z8

Craciunescu, O., Gerding-Salas, C., & Stringer-O'Keeffe, S. (2008). Machine translation and computer-assisted translation: a new way of translating? *Translators and Computers*, 8(3).

Dasgupta, T., Dandapat, S., & Basu, A. (2008). Prototype machine translation system from text-to-Indian sign language. *IJCNLP 2008: Proceedings of the Workshop on NLP for Less Privileged Languages*, 19–26.

D'Haro, L. F., San-Segundo, R., de Córdoba, R., Bungeroth, J., Stein, D., & Ney, H. (2008). Language model adaptation for a speech to sign language translation system using web frequencies and a MAP framework. *Proceedings of the 9th Annual Conference of the International Speech Communication Association*, 2199–2202.

Dreuw, P., Neidle, C., Athitsos, V., Sclaroff, S., & Ney, H. (2008). Benchmark databases for video-based automatic sign language recognition. International Conference on Language Resources and Evaluation.

Forster, J., Schmidt, C., Koller, O., Bellgardt, M, & Ney, H. (2014). Extensions of the sign language recognition and translation corpus RWTH-PHOENIX-weather. *Proceedings of the 9th Language Resources and Evaluation Conference*, 1911–1916.

Genzel, D., Macherey, K., & Uszkoreit, J. (2009). Creating a high-quality machine translation system for a low-resource language: Yiddish. *Proceedings of the Twelfth Machine Translation Summit*, 41–48.

Irvine, A. & Callison-Burch, C. (2013). Combining bilingual and comparable corpora for low resource machine translation. *Proceedings of the Eighth Workshop on Statistical Machine Translation*, 262–270.

Koehn, P. (2005). Europarl: A parallel corpus for statistical machine translation. *Machine Translation Summit* 5, 79–86.

Koehn, P. (2010). *Statistical machine translation*. New York: Cambridge University Press.

Koehn, P. & Hoang, H. (2012). Open source statistical machine translation. The Tenth Biennial Conference of the Association for Machine Translation in the Americas. Presentation. 139 slides.

Koehn, P., Hoang, H., Birch, A., Callison-Burch, C., Federico, M., Bertoldi, N., Cowan, B., et al. (2007). Moses: Open source toolkit for statistical machine translation. In *Proceedings of the 45th Annual Meeting of the ACL: Interactive Poster and Demonstration Sessions*, 177–180.

Lopez, A. (2008). Statistical machine translation. *ACM Computing Surveys*. 40(3), 1–49.

Lugaresi, C. & DiEugenio, B. (2013). Translating Italian connectives into Italian Sign Language. *Proceedings of the 51st Meeting of the Association for Computational Linguistics* (ACL-2013). 270–280.

Morrissey, S. & Way, A. (2013). Manual labour: tackling machine translation for sign languages. *Machine Translation* 27(1), 25–64. doi:10.1007/s10590-012-9133-1.

Othman, A. & Jemni, M. (2011). Statistical sign language machine translation: from English written text to American Sign Language gloss. *International Journal of Computer Science*. vol. 8, 5(3), 65–73.

Papineni, K., Roukos, S., Ward, T., & Zhu, W-J. (2002). BLEU: A method for automatic evaluation of machine translation. *40th Annual Meeting of the Association for Computational Linguistics (ACL)*. 311–318.

Porta, J., López-Colino, F., Colás, J., & Tejedor, J. (2014). A rule-based translation from written Spanish to Spanish Sign Language glosses. *Computer Speech and Language* 28, 788–811.

Richardson, S. (2012). Using the Microsoft translator hub at The Church of Jesus Christ of Latter-day Saints. In *AMTA 2012: Proceedings of the Tenth Conference of the Association for Machine Translation in the Americas*. San Diego, California.

Richardson, S. (2014). Translation systems at the Church of Jesus Christ of Latter-day Saints. BYU Translation, Interpretation, & Localization Event.

San-Segundo, R., Barra-Chicote, R., Fernando D'Haro, L., Montero, J. M., de Córdoba, R., & Ferreiros, J. (2006). A Spanish speech to sign language translation system for assisting Deaf-mute people. *Proceedings of the Ninth International Conference of Spoken Language Processing*, 1399–1402.

San-Segundo, R., Montero, J. M., de Córdoba, R., Sama, V., Fernandez F., Fernando D'Haro, L., López-Ludeña, V., Sánchez, D., & García, A. (2012). Design, development and field evaluation of a Spanish into sign language translation system. *Pattern Analysis and Applications*, 203–224.

Stein, D., Schmidt, C., & Ney, H. (2012). Analysis, preparation, and optimization of statistical machine translation. *Machine Translation* 26(4), 325–357. doi:10.1007/s10590-012-9125-1.

Way, A. (2013). Traditional and emerging use-cases for machine translation. Presentation at Translating and the Computer 35, London.

Wray, A., Cox, S., Lincoln, M., & Tryggvason, J. (2004). A formulaic approach to translation at the post office: reading the signs. *Language & Communication* 24, 59–75. doi:10.1016/j.langcom.2003.08.001.

ASL Cinema: An Exploration of a Genre

BRIDGET KLEIN

TO TELL THE TRUTH, I NEVER ENVISIONED STUDYING FILM WHEN i enrolled in Gallaudet University's American Sign Language (ASL)/Deaf Studies master's degree program. One required course for that program was ASL 709, ASL and Deaf Studies Visual Media Production. My first teacher was Facundo Montenegro, who encouraged me to capture more images, create more film work, and who gave me feedback on my shooting and editing skills. Little did I know that the following year he would pass away. It was an honor to have him as my film teacher; without him I would not be creating ASL Cinema as a new genre.

In investigating ASL Cinema, it is helpful to also examine both the role of English language in film and ASL as art in language. Anatol Knotek's work with English language and film is foundational and overlooking his work would would certainly warrant an apology. Regarding ASL as art in language, there are rules for various genres in language in art. One art form, ASL literature, has several genres: storytelling, poetry, and folktale; an emerging genre, however, is ASL Cinema. In his work on ASL poetry, Valli initially noted limited references to and discussions about ASL poetry, so he first looked at spoken language poetry to understand how its properties of sound and rhythm helped a poem 'sound' good. Valli then applied similar properties in developing ASL poetry with rhythm and meter. "Rhythm and handshape rhyme help create clear and simple lines" (Valli, 2003, p. 40). He also suspected that there had been ASL poems since the 1840s; however, at the time, few acknowledged ASL as a potentially poetry-rich language. Valli noted, "These poems were overlooked or disregarded" (Valli, 2003, p. 10).

At the time, there were few producing research into ASL literature. Today, there exists a much more substantial body of ASL literature and poetry research across several signed languages, including Italian Sign Language (LIS), Sign Language of Netherlands (NGT), Brazilian Sign Language (LIBRAS), and British Sign Language (BSL) (Sutton-Spence & Muller de Quadros, 2005).

ASL Cinema is actually an emerging genre that combines ASL literature with film. In this study, I have analyzed three films — "Hands," by Clayton Valli; "Eye Music" by Ella Mae Lentz; and "Groei," ("Growth") by Dutch artist Wim Emmerik — and then began experimenting how film could combine with ASL literature. The result of this study was the creation of two originally conceived and produced films, "The Unnoticed Life" and "The Hitchhiker." As a followup to these experimental films, Ted and Samuel Supalla created "Story-telling Duo" and Ian Sanborn produced "Caterpillar."

In an attempt to explain filmmaking conception and ideation, I use diagrams below. The location of the camera is indicated with an X; it can be in a single or multiple positions throughout the entire film. The square around person's body, head, and hand indicate specific shots (close-up or wide-angle shots). Finally, pictures from the video are used to show examples of production of ASL cinema (see Figures 1 and 2 for examples).

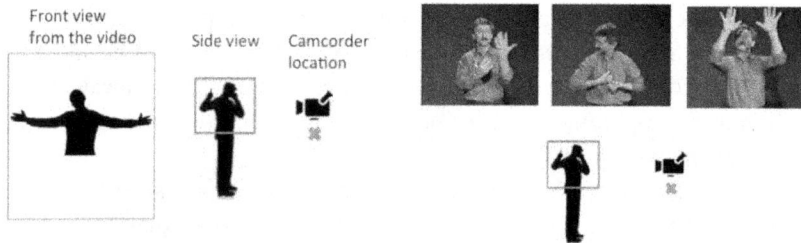

Figure 1. Graphical symbols used to show where signer view and camera location/angle for individual shots.

Figure 2. Shot setup for "Hands" (Valli, 1990)

Perceived differences between ASL literature and film have seemingly kept the two apart but can this separation be overcome to allow the two to work together? The traditional approach for capturing ASL literature with film has been to place the camera in a stationary, straight-on, medium shot at the person while he or she is signing. Historically, the purpose for most ASL films has been to record the signer's ASL literature to allow for the fine tuning of skills and language. Valli said that he used film to see his work in order to improve his poetics (Valli, 2003, p. 2). An example of this traditional film approach is in "Hands" (Valli, 1990), with the traditional camcorder shot of the signer, as shown in Figure 2. Although the major reason for this traditional view was for signers to use video recordings to help improve their skills in their literature, I submit a challenge to utilize film to actually become a new genre, ASL Cinema.

What limits can we push to enable the two distinct art forms of film and literature to overlap? I have noticed hints of this in several previous works, including Ella Mae Lentz's "Eye Music." In this poem, Lentz produces signs up over her head in a neutral place and the camera swings along with her signing (Figure 3).

Figure 3. Eye Music (Lentz, 1995)   Figure 4. Groei (Growth) (Hiddinga & Pot, 2005)

Examples of ASL Cinema have also emerged in experimental film festivals and then, just as quickly, disappear. At the 2005 Deaf Rochester Film Festival, "Groei" ("Growth") premiered, directed by Anja Hiddinga and Leendert Pot. The film cast a deaf person, Wim Emmerik, performing a poem in Dutch Sign Language. Standing in front of the camera (Figure 4), the videographer, Stef Tijdink, took multiple shots of Emmerik, close ups of hands, Emmerik's face, and full shots of Emmerik's upper torso. The producer, Leendert Pot, brought together all of the multiple shots to create the final film. ASL/Sign Language Cinema requires two important components: the literature of sign language and film language.

Inspired by this possibility, I began experimenting with the overlap between literature and film and created two films, "The Unnoticed Life," about the combination of ASL poetry and the film language of image shots, and "The Hitchhiker," exploring the combination of ASL storytelling and folklore and film editing.

"The Unnoticed Life" explored the overlap of ASL poetry and the film language of wide, medium, and close up shots of an image that matched with my signing. I edited the film to ensure that my signing was synchronized with the display of the images to produce rhythm. Paul Filiatreault was the videographer for this film and we worked together to create multiple shots of the poem. Shawn Broderick worked with me in creating the poem, and Ben Bahan worked with me focusing on the timing of signing with B-roll. I worked as producer and editor of "The Unnoticed Life" project, which received several awards across American Deaf film festivals. This work was first published in *Deaf Studies Digital Journal* (2009; see Figure 5).

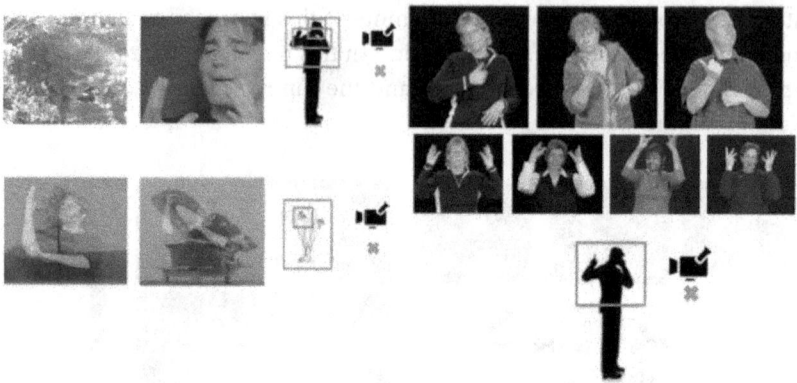

Figure 5. The Unnoticed Life (Klein, 2009)   Figure 6. The Hitchhiker (Klein, 2009)

Another ASL literature genre is folklore, the stories that a community tells and passes down over generations. In her work on American Deaf folklore, Rutherford explains about "how folklore mirrors the culture of a people," and examines how people use folklore to both release community aggression and anxieties (Ruthford, 1993). Folklore in the Deaf community consists of stories that have been known for many years, passed down from generation to generation; one of the most beloved and best known stories being "The Hitchhiker," a story about a deaf driver and a hearing passenger and how they deal with speeding and an interaction with a police officer. This story has been in the community for many years, yet no one knows who originated the story or when the story appeared. Regardless, this piece of folklore is a hallmark of ASL literature.

This story led to my second film, produced with and directed by Dr. Ben Bahan. The idea was to reimagine "The Hitchhiker"; this version, however, uses thirteen different characters composited together to tell the same story. Interestingly, each person created their own sign for the hitchhiking "thumb" and I purposefully built a range of feelings from stoic to hyperemotional by capturing facial expressions and sign size representative of the officer's flashing lights. At the beginning of this version of "The Hitchhiker," Bahan explains about collectivist cultural norms and how the passing down of this story inspired us to create a film integrating these ideas. This film also received awards from various America Deaf film festivals and was published in *Deaf Studies Digital Journal* in 2009.

I returned to the Rochester Film Festival in 2011 to see more ASL Cinema genre films. Ted and Sam Supalla were also exploring ASL Cinema; when they were younger, the Supallas experimented with an 8mm movie camera. Ted was in his early twenties and Sam was in his late teen years. They played with film language and literature and produced ASL Cinema. Like my version of "The Hitchhiker," the Supallas also created film projects with multiple tellings of the same story, a translated version of "The Sorcerer's Apprentice." For the 2011 Rochester Deaf Film Festival, they returned to their untouched film and redited it to show both characters telling the same story, alternating back and forth between the two (see Figure 7).

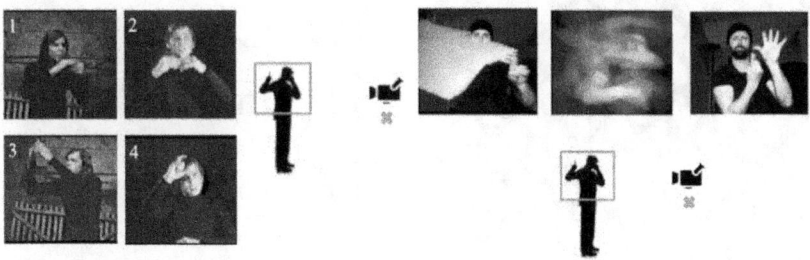

Figure 7. Story-telling Duo   Figure 8. Caterpillar

"Caterpillar," created by Ian Sanborn, is another example of ASL Cinema. Sanborn's story depicts a caterpillar's metamorphosis, adding several visual effects and speed modulation. The ASL literature aspect of this film focused on creative storytelling and the film aspect included the use of visual effect and speed of the film (see Figure 8). Table 1 shows a comparison of the use of ASL literature and film language in ASL Cinema. ("Hands" was a traditional documentation while the others represent ASL Cinema, see Table 1.

Title	ASL Literature genre	Film
Hands (1990)	Poetry	Traditional medium shot
Eye Music (1995)	Poetry	Camcorder movement
Groei/Growth	Poetry	Camcorder frames and editing
The Unoticed Life (2005)	Poetry	Camcorder frames, editing, and images
The Hitchhiker (2006)	Folklore	Editing
Story-telling Duo (2011)	Translated story	Editing
Caterpillar	Storytelling	Visual effect

Table 1. Chart of ASL Cinema

ASL cinema is not just about signing and film. Written poetry often adds concrete styles or shapes which focus on the topographical aspects of the text, or on changing the font to produce shapes with additional meaning. Knotek's poetry work is identified by the use of letterforms to create clever representations; "Rain" uses the negative space of the lowercase 'a' to reproduce the shape of a raindrop (Figure 9) and the animation "Just in Time" rotates the latter half of a lowercase 'm' every second to function as the second hand of an analog clock (Figure 10).

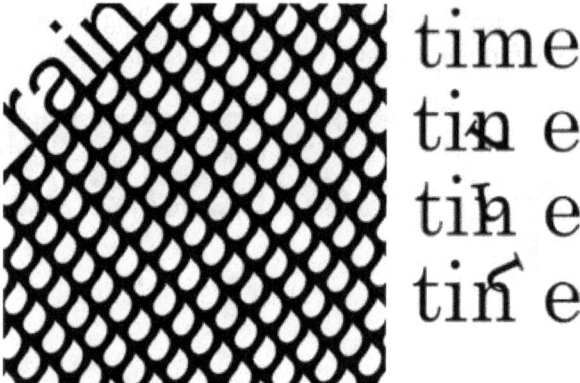

Figure 9. Rain (http://www.anatol.cc/concrete_poetry/rain.html)

Figure 10. Just In Time (http://www.anatol.cc/textanimations.html#.U5Xc1xZI6zA)

Understanding and creating ASL Cinema requires artists to understand the boundaries (and ways to push those boundaries) of literature and film. We need to know what a camcorder offers (angles, zoom, shutter speed, exposure) and also explore what literature offers (ABC, handshape, and personal experience stories). Hopefully, more ASL cinema will appear and will use beautiful and creative ways of overlapping literature and film. The future creation of ASL Cinema also prompts the need for recognition and discussion at Deaf film festivals and in social media. Art never ends; ASL Cinema is a new genre and needs more experimentation with ASL literature and film.

REFERENCES

Poetry in Motion, Hands (1990). VHS. Burtonsville, MD: Sign Media Inc.
The Treasure, Eye Music (2006). DVD. San Diego: DawnSign Press.
Sutton-Spence, R., & Muller de Quadros, R. (2005). Sign Language Poetry and Deaf Identity. *Sign Language & Linguistics* 8(1/2), 177-212.
Rutherford, S. D. (1993). *A study of American Deaf folklore*. Maryland: Linstok Press, Inc.
Valli, C. (1993). Poetics of American Sign Language poetry. Unpublished doctoral dissertation, Union Institute Graduate School.
Valli, C., Lucas, C., Mulrooney, K. J., & Rankin, M. (2011). *Linguistics of American Sign Language: An introduction (5th ed)*. Washington DC: Gallaudet University Press.

What Successful Deaf Readers Can Tell Us About Deaf Studies

AARON KELSTONE, ED.D.

AS THE FIELD OF DEAF STUDIES CONTINUES TO EVOLVE, ITS ORIGINAL role and purpose may need to be reconsidered. The establishment of Deaf Studies programs across the United States has served the Deaf community, educators, and scholars well. This is especially true over the past fifteen years, however, the current state of Deaf Studies fields may find it beneficial to conduct some form of reassessment. This is needed in order to remain relevant to today's students, educators, and scholars. By recognizing the current state of affairs, it will be possible to foster changes that will support the sustainability of Deaf Studies through the twenty-first century.

One way to reassess the Deaf Studies field is to consider how successful deaf readers have managed to cope with their experiences in English and American Sign Language (ASL). Their bilingual and bicultural experiences have influenced how they develop skills to address bimodal experiences, leading to successful outcomes in reading fluency. As they work through language duality, they have also discovered new solutions for effectively living in bilingual and bicultural worlds. Understanding this etymology offers a useful perspective for developing similar solutions to support a viable future for Deaf Studies fields.

Before delving into the relationship between successful deaf readers and Deaf Studies, it is beneficial to explore factors that have led to the establishment of Deaf Studies. An understanding of these early historical influences helps clarify why, at this particular waypoint, it is important to reassess the field of Deaf Studies. The primary historical influence was, and remains to some extent, the federal government. The rise of federal interventions through congressional legislation that created specific statutes (Public Law 93-112) were later interpreted by the Rehabilitation Services Administration (RSA). As RSA established regulations, one regulation, Section 504, would generate the most impact on individuals with disabilities and deaf people. Over time, this would lead to the provision of interpreting services, which would result in greater ramifications than the original intent.

Not only did Section 504 support improved communication access and other services designed to support the needs of various disabilities, it also indirectly created the need for a variety of professionals in the Deaf education field. As a result, sign language interpreters face requirements for educational training and certification that, to some degree, became one of the rationales for the establishment of Deaf Studies programs at the college or university level. As a result, federal intervention through specific statutes lead to the creation of a new service industry focused on accommodating the needs of deaf people.

Consequently, when Congress passed additional statutes (Public Law 94-142 or IDEA), interpreting programs were needed to provide sufficient numbers of interpreters to support the transition of deaf students to the public school system. Other sections from these statues, particularly language regarding 'least restrictive environments (LRE),' also helped accelerate the flow of deaf students away from the residential deaf schools.

This directly had a national impact on the deaf community. No longer could the Deaf community depend on the traditional role of residential schools to provide community and cultural sanctuaries. The ability for deaf people to locate a common community where they could easily socialize, become educated, find a common language, and to be exposed to the enculturation process within a specific geographical boundary was disrupted.

This educational diaspora was discussed during a prior Deaf Studies conference at Gallaudet University in 1999. In her keynote address, Dr. Carol Padden proposed that the traditionally fixed boundaries of deaf schools, deaf clubs, and borrowed spaces used by deaf people for educational purposes, conferences, sports tournaments, and Expo events were changing (Padden, 1999, p. 8-9). She proposed that, because of the specific federal interventions mentioned earlier, these geographic spaces were becoming fluid and social and cultural boundaries were increasingly becoming blurred. The Deaf community was placed in a lifeboat and cast into a sea of change. As a consequence, Padden explained, "[w]e still talk about spaces and boundaries to ourselves and others, but we use language and culture, not fences, to mark out the edges" (p. 9).

Imagine traveling to Gallaudet University or the American School for the Deaf in Hartford. Upon arrival, one can see the stone walls and iron fences surrounding each school clearly demonstrating visually the essence of those historical boundaries. One can feel the essence of being able to enter into a safe harbor. If a person would take a similar journey to locate a mainstream program within a local public school system often this kind of geographical definition would be lacking. Thinking of it in this manner can then support the idea that the early establishment of Deaf Studies programs was needed to serve as a substitute home in support of the declining influence of the residential deaf schools.

This perfect storm was helped along further by acts of social change primarily focused on civil and disability rights. These social changes would lead, for example, to the formation of Black Studies programs that in turn induced the establishment of Deaf studies (Katz, 1999, p. 121). As language and culture created new abstract boundaries, they also needed to reframe the deaf experience. Deaf Studies programs became the new 'geography' where the values and norms of the Deaf community could be preserved in lieu of the social, athletic, political, and organizational efforts of deaf people at residential deaf schools and after graduation in the deaf clubs.

An entry gate, a doorway, a wall, or fence traditionally guarded these communal spaces and provided a mechanism for granting membership entry into the Deaf world. These communal spaces would now be controlled through language and culture. By establishing their credentials based on their knowledge of the language (ASL) and Deaf culture only then could they gain entry into the Deaf world to experience the benefits that Holcomb calls "the most powerful solution for effective living among Deaf people" (Holcomb, 2013, p. 224).

The early efforts to establish Deaf Studies programs began at residential deaf school settings. However, as residential school enrollments declined this became problematic. To compensate for this, Deaf Studies programs transitioned to post-secondary programs at the California State University at Northridge (CSUN), Gallaudet College, Boston University, and Rochester Institute of Technology (RIT) (Katz, 1999). As this transition occurred, Deaf Studies classroom compositions began to change. The original purpose to preserve and to educate deaf people about their language and culture now began to split away to a secondary duty: to educate hearing people.

As Deaf Studies was emerging at the post-secondary level, there became growing interest in ASL courses at the secondary level, that in turn would create demand from these students for higher-level ASL courses at colleges and universities. As the demand for classes, teachers, and cultural courses increased, it fostered the transition of Deaf Studies from a deaf-centric activity to one where the focus shifted to a diverse classroom environment involving both deaf and hearing students. Deaf Studies programs needed to shift their focus from the exclusive enculturation of deaf students to the education of both hearing and deaf students. With this shift it now becomes important to reassess the current state of affair within Deaf Studies.

Over the past twenty-five years, course enrollments have increased from 1,602 courses to 91,763. By 2009, ASL had become the fourth most studied language in the United States (Furman, Goldberg, & Lusin, 2010). Deaf studies programs now experience an increasing pressure from these high levels of enrollments to provide a dual focus. The original intent was to support deaf students with the cultural and language knowledge they needed to navigate through the various stages of their Deaf identity (Holcomb, pp. 67-77). A new requirement has arrived to support the education of hearing students being trained in the interpreter, audiology, and secondary teacher fields to understand. The need is not only to preserve but also to clarify why Deaf culture and ASL remains relevant to their fields of study.

The use of waypoints as a theme for this conference is appropriate. A waypoint is often is defined as a stopping point on a journey that allows a person or a group to gain their bearings before departing on to the next waypoint. What mechanism could help us as a program and a profession to gain our bearings in a manner that will allow us to confidently proceed on to the next waypoint? What do we need to understand about these processes that will support the growth and maturation of Deaf Studies?

Observing how Deaf people have navigated their way through bimodal experiences provides one method. While looking through the lens of successful Deaf readers, their experiences can frame our thoughts about Deaf Studies. This can be based on how successful Deaf readers have navigated their way between bicultural and bilingual experiences as they work through bimodal processes with English and ASL. Interviews conducted by this author with successful deaf readers discover that certain experiences help them navigate within their bilingual spaces. These Deaf readers explain that their experiences with English and ASL involve the use of transitions and making associations utilizing inference techniques. To further support their process they developed bridging techniques using repetition and active use of a bi-directional translation process (Kelstone, 2012).

Why is an understanding of these qualities useful to Deaf studies? First of all, when both Deaf and hearing individuals participate in the field of Deaf studies as students, educators, and scholars, a distinct polarity between the two groups exists, similar to the bimodal experiences of deaf readers with English and ASL. Serving the needs of two distinct groups with oppositional perspectives requires some form of transitioning between the two. It even requires us to recognize the need to incorporate this transitioning effort into our existing Deaf Studies program so that each group has their needs satisfied as they gain an understanding of Deaf culture.

For example, successful Deaf readers place equal value on both ASL and English. Their transitions between both languages create cognitive, emotional, and perceptual shifts in their learning process (Kelstone, 2012). Peter Cook's performance of "My First Word" offers a dramatic example of his discovery and comprehension of the word 'snake' while playing outside with another child. Within the performance, we are shown the memories of countless hours of speech therapy, the action of the snake slithering past him, and the excited mouthing of the word 'snake' by his childhood friend. Within the context of that moment, transitioning between word, image, and repetitive speech practice, comes the illuminating moment that connects him visually and linguistically with the word 'snake.' Would a similar process that incorporates effective use of transitional experiences between hearing and deaf students, educators and scholars lead us to new places of illumination about the meanings contained within Deaf Studies?

Within this context, successful deaf readers place equal value on experiences gained from exposure to both languages. As they effectively interact within a bilingual framework, it enables them to more fluidly navigate their bilingual/bicultural experience. They also begin to infer what these trans-itional experiences mean to them, expanding the boundaries of their Deaf-world. What can Deaf Studies infer from these transitional experiences towards a common understanding of the purpose and use of Deaf Studies in a world rapidly becoming globalized?

Can deaf and hearing people begin to acknowledge that identity is not bound to a specific cultural experience? Perhaps identity can be blended in ways that offer a more balanced perspective on being Deaf and Hearing in modern society. Membership within the Deaf-world no longer remains tied to a geographical experience. As ASL spreads beyond the hands and eyes of deaf people, signed language is no longer exclusively in use by deaf people. Instead, membership is based on the role one has within the Deaf-world as a deaf person, a supporter, an ally, or as an active servant to the community in ways that we have not anticipated yet.

What it means is that participation benefits all members separate from any ability to hear or sign. Changes in laws, technology, and other societal conventions continue to foster life experiences that are no longer bound to a geographical location. In its place is a virtual smorgasbord of options that allow an effective means of bridging these experiences in ways that offer positive outcomes for all participants.

As this becomes increasingly comfortable, each member has the ability to manage his or her bilingual/bicultural life into an organic experience within the Deaf-world. Successful deaf readers achieved a similar bilingual experience by using repetition to maintain a constant interaction with both languages. Likewise, there is a need to maintain a similar repetitive process that keeps both deaf and hearing participants engaged with one another to effectively make new advances in the field of Deaf Studies.

Interestingly, successful Deaf readers engaged in a translation exercise, translating stories between English to ASL (or ASL to English). By alter-nating the translating process for both languages, they gained a greater appreciation for the structure of both languages. Over time, as they persisted in applying this alternating translation approach, they became increasingly adept at using both languages. This is similar to how deaf signers code-blend while conversing with others in a bilingual setting (Emmorey, Petrich, & Gollan, 2012). In these situations, the Deaf person is not simultaneously communicating (sim-com) nor are they alternating between both languages as they interact with others. What happens in this code-blending process is that the Deaf person begins to skillfully use their cognitive abilities to find parallel meaning in both languages within this bimodal process.

As classrooms become increasingly diverse and populated by both Deaf and hearing students, a similar kind of code-blending seems to occur. However, in this context, the switching moves beyond language. Individuals find themselves moving between languages, cultural perspectives, various norms, and values. For Deaf Studies, it may be beneficial to explore these intersectional experiences between hearing and deaf people as students, educators, and scholars.

An open dialog — and effective scholarship — related to these experiences can lead to a better understanding of the field of Deaf Studies, and, in turn, offer solutions how new curricula can provide even more enriching experiences for everyone involved in Deaf Studies. Moving in this way may offer a 'Deaf gain' effect that supports a better understanding of multicultural roles within a future global society.

REFERENCES

Emmorey, K., Petrich, J. A., & Gollan, T. H. (2012). Bilingual processing of ASL–English code-blends: The consequences of accessing two lexical representations simultaneously. *Journal of memory and language*, 67(1), 199–210.

Furman, N., Goldberg, D., & Lusin, N. (2010). *Enrollments in languages other than English in United States institutions of higher education, Fall 2009*. New York: Modern Language Association of America.

Holcomb, T. K. (2013). *Introduction to American deaf culture*. New York: Oxford University Press.

Kelstone, A. (2012) Understanding deaf readers: an interpretative phenomenological analysis. Education Doctoral Theses. Boston, MA: Northeastern University.

Katz, C.N. (1999) A partial history of deaf studies (pp. 119–135). *Deaf studies VI: Making the connection: conference proceedings, April 8–11, 1999, Oakland, California.* Washington, D.C: Gallaudet University, Continuing Education.

Martin, E., Martin, R., & Terman, D. (1996). The legislative and litigation history of special education (pp. 25–39). *The Future of Children: Special Education for Students with Disabilities*, 6(1). New Jersey: Princeton University

Padden, C. (1999). Future of deaf people (pp. 1–15). *Deaf studies VI: Making the connection: conference proceedings, April 8–11, 1999, Oakland, California.* Washington, D.C: Gallaudet University, Continuing Education.

Petitto, L. A., Katerelos, M., Levy, B. G., Gauna, K., Tétreault, K., & Ferraro, V. (2001). Bilingual signed and spoken language acquisition from birth: Implications for the mechanisms underlying early bilingual language acquisition. *Journal of child language*, 28(2), 453–496.

Deaf Education in the United States and Morocco

KRISTINA DOMANEY, JENNY SIPIORA, AND JOHN PIRONE

IN THE UNITED STATES, TWO FEDERAL EDUCATIONAL LAWS PROTECT the rights of individuals with disabilities, including deaf individuals, and their access to support services. However, inconsistencies in how these federal mandates are applied create challenges for students and educators. An investigation of how these laws are applied is needed in order to gain a better understanding of the impact of the interpretation and application of these laws on deaf education.

Section 504 of the Rehabilitation Act of 1973 took effect in May 1977. This section protects the rights of people with disabilities in programs that receive federal fiscal aid and funds (U.S. Department of Education, 1999). Section 504 requires that students with disabilities receive a "free appropriate public education" and protects students whose disabilities do not adversely affect their educational performance. For example, deaf students who may need accommodations in their general education classes, such as having interpreters, are protected under this law.

Under Section 504, teams are created to plan how the needs of deaf students are met. These 504 teams typically consist of legal guardians, general education teachers, representatives of the Local Education Agency, and specialists such as deaf schoolteachers, interpreters, and speech pathologists (U.S. Department of Education, 1999). 504 teams meet and develop Individual Accommodation Plans (IAPs), which outline the services needed by students in order to meet the legislative requirements for "least restrictive environment." Least restrictive environment aims to provide students with disabilities with the opportunity to be educated alongside their peers whenever possible. For elementary students, legal guardians have a significant role in determining accommodations for their children. Once an IAP is finalized, the services identified in the plan are provided to the student and the 504 team meets on a regular basis thereafter to evaluate the student's academic progress.

Another law, the Individuals with Disabilities Education Act (IDEA), is modeled after aspects of its state law precursor, Massachusetts Public Education Law Chapter 766. The act, which was signed into law on October 30, 1990, is a U.S. federal law that requires that specific educational services be provided to students with disabilities. The law has two parts: Part B, which gives infants and toddlers with disabilities (up to two years of age) the right to receive early intervention services, and Part C, which provides special education and related services to children and youth (three to twenty-one years of age; U.S. Department of Education, 2006).

Similar to Section 504 of the Rehabilitation Act of 1973, IDEA ensures that children with disabilities receive a "free appropriate public education" in the least restrictive environment (U.S. Department of Education, 2006). IDEA requires that children be evaluated to determine their present level of performance. However, unlike Section 504, these students must be diagnosed as having a disability that adversely affects their educational performance in order to qualify for support services. Individualized Education Programs (IEPs) must be created for children to receive these services. IEPs are developed by IEP teams, which usually consist of legal guardians, special education teachers, specialists, and a representative of the Local Education Agency. Legal guardians advocate children to decide what services are necessary. Thereafter, placement and educational services must be based on the IEP (U.S. Department of Education, 2006). For example, IDEA requires that deaf children receive appropriate modifications and/or accommodations as outlined in their IEPs. The purpose of IEPs is to ensure that students with disabilities have equal opportunities to receive an education.

In theory, Section 504 and IDEA are meant to benefit all individuals with disabilities. However, the provisions in these laws may not consistently serve the needs of such individuals. People with disabilities have special needs that are specific to each individual; therefore, one policy or law may be insufficient to assist such a large and diverse group of people. These federal legislations do not focus on specific communities, such as the deaf community; however, they do provide states with the opportunity to create more detailed laws. Nevertheless, not all states have further developed the legislature regarding the education of students with disabilities.

PURPOSE OF STUDY

The present study seeks to compare the processes and services provided by Section 504 and IDEA to deaf elementary school students (Kindergarten to Grade 5) in Maryland and Massachusetts. These two states were selected because they are each home to well-known deaf schools. One deaf school from each state was selected for examination. The two selected schools employ a bilingual approach in that all academic and social activities are conducted in American Sign Language (ASL) with an emphasis on English reading and writing. This approach is an effort to help students acquire ASL as a first language and English as a second language. Unlike Maryland, Massachusetts has several other deaf schools that use different communication methods (oral and total communication approaches).

Researchers established two hypotheses. First, that public schools in close proximity to a deaf school are more likely to have 504 and IEP teams consisting of deaf teachers, interpreters, or other members of the deaf community, while schools farther away from a deaf school are more likely to have speech pathologists and audiologists on their 504 and IEP teams. Second, that public school districts are more likely to refer deaf public school students to a deaf school if it is located in close proximity to the public school (i.e., commute time less than one hour) than if the deaf school is located farther away (i.e., commute time greater than one hour). The two deaf schools in this study offer residential programs for middle and high school students, but not for elementary students. Therefore, the presence of residence halls should not influence placement decisions made by public school districts in regard to deaf and hard-of-hearing elementary school students.

METHODOLOGY

This study reviewed educational laws and collected data from interviews with members of the deaf community and one representative from each of the ten selected public elementary schools in each state. Interviews were conducted by telephone and in person. Consent forms and a series of interview questions were developed and approved by the Institutional Review Board at the College of the Holy Cross. Public elementary schools were selected based on their geographic location. Ten public elementary schools were selected in each of the two states: five were located in close proximity to the deaf school and five were located farther away from the deaf school. For the purposes of this study, close proximity is defined as a commute time of one hour or less, while farther away is defined as a commute time greater than one hour. Educators (special education teachers, principals, and assistant principals) who are familiar with 504 and IEP processes were asked about the composition of the 504 and IEP teams in their school, how they determine what constitutes the least restrictive environment in terms of accommodations and modifications, and what alternatives are considered if accommodations and modifications are not readily provided.

RESULTS

Maryland

The state of Maryland has no educational laws concerning individuals with disabilities. The only protections offered to deaf students are those under Section 504 and IDEA. Nevertheless, the Maryland Department of Disabilities is tasked with editing the State Disabilities Plan at least once every four years (Maryland Department of Disabilities, 2012). Maryland's State Disabilities 2012–2015 Plan includes an education section that highlights a number of goals that are consistent with the requirements of Section 504 and IDEA. One goal of the State Disability Plan is to provide students with disabilities with assistance as they transition from high school to post-graduation life (higher education or employment; Maryland Department of Disabilities, 2012).

Based on information collected in the interviews, many of these goals and laws are applied in Maryland. Three out of five public elementary schools located in close proximity to a deaf school expressed their willingness to send deaf students from their schools to the deaf school. The 504 and IEP teams at these public schools included deaf advocates and teachers from deaf schools. Strategies employed by these schools in order to create the least restrictive environment include the rearrangement of seats in order to visually assist deaf students.

Educators from public elementary schools located farther away from the deaf school were more hesitant about sending deaf students to the deaf school; only one teacher mentioned the possibility. Educators prefer to either make accommodations and modifications within their schools or to send deaf students to nearby county programs that will provide them with free appropriate public education. The county program referred to by interview participants is another school that is located within the region but may not be in the child's own school district. Deaf or hard-of-hearing children are sent to these programs by school district teachers.

Participants felt that deaf schools and county programs provide appropriate forms of education for deaf students. These educators also noted that their 504 and IEP teams typically consist of legal guardians, general education teachers, special education teachers, audiologists, speech pathologists, and teachers who work with deaf students. Depending on circumstances, psychologists and social workers may also attend team meetings.

One Maryland special educator from a school located farther away from a deaf school shared that the IEP or 504 team meetings for deaf students at her school involved specialists working with deaf students, general educators, special educators, and other professionals (such as occupational or physical therapists), depending on the needs of the children. This same participant also noted that the proceedings of IEP meetings were overseen by a facilitator, a member of the community who is trained to assist with 504 and IEP team meetings. According to "Facilitated IEP Team Meetings in Maryland," published by the Maryland State Department of Education (2007), a facilitator may be employed to prevent and help resolve miscommunications between parents and school officials (Maryland State Department of Education, 2007). Parents or school systems can request the involvement of a facilitator.

When this same participant was asked if her school district sends students to the deaf school (farther away), she explained that the school first tries to provide the least restrictive environment, and only in extreme cases (that she did not define) would students be sent to the deaf school. In that case, the local school district is legally required to alleviate the costs involved. If students remain within their local school district, then accommodations and modifications (such as testing accommodations, supplemental resources, and/or assistive technology) are required, depending on students' needs. Examples of modifications include altering the curriculum and providing captions on videos.

Another educator from a school located farther away from a deaf school explained that hearing devices influence 504 and IEP processes. Just as the use of ASL influences the composition of 504 and IEP teams, hearing aids and cochlear implants play a crucial role in the composition of the team. If deaf students wear hearing aids or have cochlear implants, then audiologists and speech pathologists are more likely to be present at IEP meetings. Audiologists and speech pathologists encourage the oral method, which ultimately makes it less likely for deaf students to be placed at a deaf school.

To provide the least restrictive environment, special educators employ sign language interpreters, assistive technology, FM systems, visual support, preferential seating, technological software, captioning, volume augmentations, and books on tape. The researchers noted that the use of books on tape may not be considered applicable to deaf students in the eyes of some educators. Inappropriate accommodations and modifications were a main concern of an educator who works with deaf students in Maryland and who felt that schools too often attempt to keep deaf students in public schools even when a deaf school would provide a more accessible learning environment. According to this interviewee, such circumstances were common because sending students to schools outside their local school district creates a financial burden. This educator explained that there were instances where public elementary schools provided deaf students with certified interpreters who lacked fluency in ASL, resulting in incorrect interpretations and ineffective communication in the classroom.

Furthermore, she explained that in classrooms containing only one deaf student using ASL, that student often spends most of his or her time interacting with one adult, the interpreter, which presents challenges to language and social development. Instead, if that student were attending a deaf school, he or she would not have to rely on an interpreter who is not completely fluent in ASL, but would have direct access to the deaf community.

This same educator explained that, in order to improve the education of deaf students, federal laws need to be changed. She argued that the current interpretation of 'least restrictive environment' was ineffective and unfair because deaf students do not receive appropriate accommodations. In her opinion, giving more attention to IAPs and IEPs and analyzing them for appropriate accommodations could improve the learning environment. She noted that all students at the deaf school have IEPs, and the IEP teams consist of legal guardians, students, teachers, administrators, and (sometimes) speech therapists. With appropriate and consistent reviews of IAPs and IEPs, deaf students may encounter fewer challenges in mainstream and special education classrooms because their needs are correctly accommodated.

Providing accessible resources to deaf students will allow for a free appropriate public education regardless of geographic location. Until then, public school professionals are likely to continue making accommodations and modifications within classrooms in an effort to create what they consider to be the least restrictive environment, sending students to county programs, or sending students to deaf schools. Of the Maryland public elementary schools involved in this study, more were willing to send deaf students to a deaf school than keep them in the public school with accommodations and modifications.

Massachusetts

Massachusetts, unlike Maryland, has a mandate that is specific to the education of deaf students. The Massachusetts Fair Educational Practices Law provides limited protections in the area of education. Under this law, excluding citizens from receiving an education (defined as any institution for instructing or training) because they are blind, deaf, or require the use of a guide dog is illegal (Massachusetts Office on Disability, 2012).

Massachusetts is the first state to have an educational law targeting deaf people, according to one study participant who is a former educator of deaf students. However, the act does not ensure that deaf students receive the same *quality* of education as their hearing counterparts. Therefore, like Maryland, deaf students rely on the provisions of Section 504 and IDEA for the protection of their rights.

Educators from five public elementary schools located in close proximity to the deaf school were interviewed. Participants were asked about the composition of 504 and IEP teams at their respective schools. Four of the five educators interviewed reported that 504 and IEP teams typically consisted of legal guardians, general or special education teachers, and deaf teachers or interpreters. One educator did not mention the inclusion of members of the deaf community in these processes.

Educators from five schools located farther away from the deaf school were also interviewed and asked about the composition of 504 and IEP teams at their respective schools. Similar to the first group, the principals and special education teachers at these schools reported that 504 and IEP teams for deaf students consisted of legal guardians, general education teachers, and special education teachers. However, none of these participants mentioned members of the deaf community, such as deaf teachers, interpreters, and deaf advocates. Instead, respondents focused on the inclusion of audiologists and speech pathologists in the meetings. One principal stated that the speech pathologists that attended their 504 and IEP meetings were often from the nearby oral school because of its close proximity.

Participants from all ten schools were asked about classroom accommodations and modifications for deaf students that are based on 504 and IEP meetings. A majority of respondents reported that their schools had FM systems to accommodate deaf students (with specialists to check if the systems are working properly). Some participants from schools located in close proximity to the deaf school stated that the deaf school provided interpreters when requested. Almost all participants reported that modifications were made on a case-by-case basis, but they did not provide specific examples.

All participants reported that deaf students had attended, or were attending, their schools. A follow-up question was then asked about where these students were sent if IEP or IAP teams determined that support services could not be properly provided within the public school. Nearly all participants were reluctant to respond to this question and explained that they almost always managed to figure out ways to serve the needs of their deaf students. They explained that since accommodations and modifications could usually be made, they tended not to focus on the option of education at a deaf school because of the heavy costs involved. One participant who was previously an elementary special education teacher reported that the public school system in which he worked unquestionably preferred to keep deaf students within the public school system due to monetary reasons.

Another educator of deaf students explained that when the costs associated with education become the primary focus, public school systems tend to forget that the most important part of the process is to ensure that *students* are provided with correct accommodations and modifications in order to receive the education to which they are legally entitled. This educator shared that, throughout his years of service, he had witnessed deaf students being misplaced in public classrooms on numerous occasions. Sometimes students were placed in classes with teachers who did not know sign language and/or with interpreters who had limited or no credentials and fluency in sign language. Another participant, a public school principal, stated that deaf students did not need to be on par with their hearing counterparts, they only needed to show some type of progress. These findings suggest that the "appropriate" aspect of free appropriate public education is not always fulfilled, regardless of what is mandated by law.

Teachers who have rarely, if ever, encountered deaf students and are then placed in a classroom with deaf children pose another dilemma. Such educators have little to no experience teaching deaf students and may struggle to make accommodations and modifications for these students. While special education teachers are recertified every five years, suggesting they have the credentials to teach in the classroom, it appears that these credentials may not include the specific skills necessary to teach deaf children. One participant suggested that these credentials may not be sufficient since deaf students often suffered academically in these classrooms and missed out on vital information that was being taught. According to this educator, a deaf school can better provide such students with a free appropriate public education than the public school.

Participants in this study tended to veer away from answering questions about student placement in the deaf school. However, after explaining that deaf students were sent to deaf schools only in very rare situations, nearly all participants reported that they preferred to make accommodations and modifications to provide the least restrictive environment because sending students to the deaf school was more expensive. On the infrequent occasions when participants admitted to sending deaf students to other schools, the schools to which students were sent varied. All five public schools located in close proximity to the deaf school sent their elementary students there, albeit only when absolutely necessary (e.g., services could not be provided in the public schools). Four of the five public schools located farther away from the deaf school, but closer in geographical proximity to the local oral school, typically sent their students to the oral school when absolutely necessary. A participant from the one remaining school explained that student placement depended on the individual. Many participants explained that the choice of where to send the deaf student was generally made based on proximity. Arguably, distance should not be the only factor in the selection process.

The majority of participants in this study shared the view that if public schools cannot provide appropriate services for deaf students, then these children are likely to receive a better education at a deaf school, where services are more accessible. However, not every deaf school can serve the needs of all deaf students because they do not all apply the same methods of teaching. Thus, perhaps 504 and IEP teams should consider not only the geographical locations of the schools but also the pedagogies that they use.

Based on information from phone calls and interviews, the researchers concluded that public elementary schools in Massachusetts typically try to keep deaf children within their public school systems. These schools prefer to make numerous accommodations and modifications as needed rather than send students to deaf schools. However, the schools tend to vary in terms of IEP team composition and placement choices based on their proximity to deaf schools.

ANALYSIS

A comparative analysis was conducted for the information obtained from participants in Maryland and Massachusetts. Participants from public elementary schools in both Maryland and Massachusetts were certain that their schools were following Section 504 and IDEA by providing accommodations and modifications. Despite the insistence that appropriate measures are taken, the collected information arguably shows that these accommodations and modifications may vary in regard to how well they suit the needs of deaf students in creating the least restrictive environment. Almost all of the public school educators contacted in either state mentioned amplification systems as an accommodation, implying that there were more hard-of-hearing than deaf students in these schools. However, these professionals also explained that 504 and IEP teams vary from one student to the next and, therefore, accommodations and modifications vary.

The two hypotheses formulated for this study are supported by the data. In both states, if a public elementary school is located farther away from a deaf school, then the school district generally prefers to keep deaf and hard-of-hearing students within the local public school system. Therefore, distance may influence the decisions of public school professionals concerning the appropriate environment for deaf students. Furthermore, there is a positive correlation between proximity to a deaf school and the composition of 504 and IEP teams. Those schools located in close proximity to a deaf school include deaf advocates and interpreters in their 504 and IEP team meetings. On the other hand, those schools that are located farther away from a deaf school, but closer to an oral school, tend to involve speech pathologists and audiologists in 504 and IEP team meetings.

Educators from deaf schools in both states emphasized the necessity for legal changes. They explained that creating legislation specifically for deaf students is necessary in order to improve the education of these students. Another common theme that emerged in the interviews was the importance of deaf schools. Participants admitted that although accommodations and modifications are often sufficient to fulfill the needs of students, the most accessible and appropriate services are typically found at a deaf school.

Accommodation issues were also a main concern of participants. They all mentioned that one of the most serious concerns was public schools providing interpreters in mainstream classrooms who lack experience in the field of education and fluency in ASL. Such interpreters may be unfit to interpret for students, which could explain why some of these students suffer academically. Participants also referred to programs at deaf schools in Maryland and Massachusetts that provide additional services for deaf and hearing families, such as home visits, play groups, support groups for parents and legal guardians, and meetings with speech-language pathologists.

When educators from both states were asked to provide further examples of modifications, the educators from Massachusetts said that they could not do so because every student was different and modifications were provided based on the needs of the individual. In contrast, educators in Maryland provided multiple examples, such as visual assistance in the classroom and changes to the curriculum to make it more accessible to deaf students.

Another trend discovered during the interviews was the focus on finances. Public school educators frequently mentioned that they preferred to keep students in their respective schools because doing so placed a smaller financial burden on the district. In addition, interviewees reported that, instead of hiring experienced educational interpreters, professionals at public schools chose to hire relatively new and low-paid interpreters in order to save money. The practice of making choices based on financial considerations is questionable as it may distract from considerations of what is best for deaf students and their education.

The dissimilarities between the two states reported here demonstrate that the education of deaf students is inconsistent across the United States. A specific example is that in Massachusetts, proximity to an oral school versus a deaf school seems to influence the decisions made by public elementary school educators. In contrast, there are no oral schools in Maryland, so this issue does not apply.

In Massachusetts, public elementary schools located farther away from a deaf school are more likely to have speech pathologists and audiologists on their 504 and IEP teams. On the other hand, schools located in close proximity to a deaf school are more likely to include deaf advocates and interpreters on their 504 and IEP teams. Besides proximity, educators emphasized the importance of keeping students within their home school districts due to financial reasons.

In Maryland, proximity does not appear to be a factor, possibly due to the fact that there is no oral school in the state of Maryland. In fact, many public school educators in Maryland explained that 504 and IEP teams usually include teachers from deaf schools and interpreters, regardless of location. Unlike Massachusetts, public elementary schools in Maryland appear to be more willing to send deaf students to deaf schools.

CONCLUSION

A number of conclusions may be drawn from the results of this study. While Section 504 and IDEA enable states to create more specific laws, neither Maryland nor Massachusetts has a particular mandate to protect the rights of deaf students to access support services. In addition, these laws are interpreted and applied differently in Maryland and Massachusetts. Educators at public elementary schools tend to interpret the meaning of free appropriate public education differently. Some interpretations consider free appropriate public education to mean the provision to deaf students of all services requested by 504 and IEP teams, while others interpret it to mean that only some services need be provided, regardless of whether these services best suit the needs of deaf students.

The distance between public elementary schools and deaf schools was found to relate to the composition and decisions of 504 and IEP teams. In Massachusetts, educators at public elementary schools that are located in close proximity to a deaf school typically have teams that include members of the deaf community and tend to be more willing to send children to deaf schools. Meanwhile, schools located farther away from a deaf school generally do not include members of the deaf community in 504 and IEP teams, nor are they as willing to send students to deaf schools. In addition, 504 and IEP processes and decisions depend on the proximity of the public school to a deaf school that employs a bilingual approach versus an oral school.

In Maryland, most of the schools surveyed include members of the deaf community, such as deaf schoolteachers and other various specialists, in their 504 and IEP teams. However, schools in close proximity to a deaf school are more willing to send their students to the deaf school than are public schools located farther away from a deaf school.

RECOMMENDATIONS

The findings of this study suggest several ways to improve and expand upon this research in future studies. In an effort to improve the current study, more interviews can be conducted by the researchers. This addition would allow for a wider variety of perspectives and input on the research topic and questions and provide more information to support the common themes that have been identified. Visits to special and general education classrooms and deaf schools in the US could be beneficial in understanding what educators consider to be the least restrictive environment. Specific to the states of Maryland and Massachusetts, a future study should investigate financial cost in regard to their deaf schools. The deaf school in Maryland is public while the deaf school in Massachusetts is private, so an analysis of the costs associated with sending students to these locations should be conducted. Also, more public schools could be contacted to assess the influence of cost on the placement of deaf students.

Future studies can expand upon previous research by conducting longitudinal studies that focus not only on elementary school children but other age groups as well. Deaf children, who have a legal right to support services, could be monitored from kindergarten until completion of high school and the effectiveness of laws and services could be assessed based on their academic success. To evaluate success, researchers should meet with students and their legal guardians to discuss grades, services, accommodations and modifications, and satisfaction throughout the years of the study. Additionally, researchers could administer an annual survey to legal guardians and students to evaluate their thoughts and experiences.

Improving and broadening this research will potentially raise more awareness about the deaf community. Perhaps with a better understanding of this population, individuals may be more inclined to advocate for the educational rights and needs of Deaf people. Ideally, this will improve the quality of deaf education.

COMPARISON OF DEAF EDUCATION IN THE UNITED STATES AND MOROCCO

Although interpretations of federal law seem to vary by state, all states are required to comply with federal laws, specifically Section 504 of the Rehabilitation Act of 1973 and IDEA. The existence of IAPs and IEPs in the United States raises the question as to whether equivalent laws exist in Arabic countries that are less developed than the United States.

PURPOSE OF STUDY

This study seeks to compare educational legislation and implementation in the United States and Morocco. These two countries were selected for investigation based on their varying levels of development according the Human Development Index (HDI) and Gross Domestic Product (GDP) per capita. The United States is considered a more developed country than Morocco based on these two categories, as it ranks in the top 35% for both. The HDI is calculated based on statistics in the categories of health, education, and income. The United States is ranked third out of 186 countries, with an HDI of .937, according to the 2012 Human Development Report. The GDP per capita measures a country's overall economic output. The GDP per capita in the United States is $50,700, which puts it in fourteenth place out of 229 nations, as reported in 2012 by the CIA World Factbook.

In contrast, Morocco is ranked in the bottom 35% for both of these indices. The HDI for Morocco is .591, which puts it in 130th place out of 186 countries. The GDP per capita in Morocco is $5,400, which puts it in 155th place out of 229 nations. The variation in rankings for these two countries make them ideal for this comparative analysis of educational laws and services for deaf students, since the research aims to investigate countries with different levels of development.

Another reason for selecting Morocco for this study is the fact that it has laws concerning people with disabilities, including deaf people, that are similar to U.S. laws concerning people with disabilities. In addition, Morocco is in the process of raising awareness for the deaf community and Moroccan Sign Language (MSL). The country has deaf schools, some of which use MSL as the primary language in the classroom. This investigation explores the assumption that educational laws and services for deaf youth in the United States surpass those of Morocco.

METHODOLOGY

The researchers collected data through a literature review, a review of Moroccan laws concerning individuals with disabilities, and interviews. Legal investigations in the previous study determined the rights of people with disabilities in the United States. In this second study, information will be examined in relation to the legal findings in Morocco. Interviews in Morocco were conducted with professionals in the field of deaf education. All participants in this research have been de-identified for confidentiality purposes. A series of questions and consent forms were developed for the interviews and approved by the Institutional Review Board at the College of the Holy Cross.

Morocco

Legislation for individuals with disabilities is not unique to more developed countries, as demonstrated by the fact that Morocco, a lesser developed nation, has such laws. According to a report created in the early 2000s by the Ministry of National Education in Morocco, various laws exist to improve the education of people with disabilities; however, whether those laws are fully applied is debatable.

The Moroccan Ministry has adopted a national approach to school integration that is similar to that of the United Nations Educational Scientific and Cultural Organization (UNESCO). This approach strives to obtain precise diagnoses of students with disabilities and then place them into mainstream classes where they can pursue their studies. Another law, Joint Circular No. 130, revised on March 30, 2004, intends to create awareness campaigns for the inclusion of children with disabilities and to establish criteria for integrating them into classes and selecting teachers for such classes (Ministry of National Education, 2004). None of these laws mention any sort of IEP or 504 equivalent. Thus, there are no legal documents entitling deaf students to support services.

Although these mandates exist in legislation, there are few specific mentions of the deaf community at the public level in Morocco. Individuals who are familiar with the deaf community do not appear to be aware of legislation concerning the education of deaf students. The former head of a deaf school and two school professionals in a town near the city of Fes who were interviewed for this study explained that they and many other educators are unaware of the rights of children with disabilities. These three interviewees worked at a deaf school that recently closed, and although it received government funding, the amount was not enough to keep the school open. They explained that their lack of awareness was common not only for educators in deaf education but also for the majority of workers involved in public education in Morocco. From their perspective, education laws (and laws in general) are difficult to implement because people are unaware of them.

The former professionals from the deaf school stressed that the most important way to improve the educational rights of people with disabilities, specifically deaf individuals, was to promote awareness of sign language and deaf culture. Better awareness could help raise funding to establish deaf schools. A study by the Dutch foundation Het Marokko Fonds found that 68% of deaf children in Morocco between the ages of four and fifteen years did not go to school, and 87% of the parents of these children considered their children's disability as the reason (Bernichi, 2010).

The three workers explained that there were no educational options at the secondary school level (ages fifteen through eighteen) or the university level (age eighteen or older) for deaf people. Therefore, opportunities for deaf people to further their education are almost non-existent. As docu-mented in the World Federation of the Deaf survey (2008), education for deaf people in Morocco is only available at the primary level (ages five through twelve). The lack of access to formal education for all age groups in the deaf community could explain the high percentage of deaf children who do not attend school.

While an increase in the number of educational opportunities is arguably beneficial, the limited availability of teachers who use MSL and have experience working with deaf students is an issue. The three interviewees stated their concerns for mainstream public classes. Deaf students are placed in these classes but, as supported by previous findings from the World Federation of the Deaf survey (2008), few services, if any, are provided to include deaf students in the learning process. Re-arrangement of seats in classrooms in order to provide visual assistance to deaf students was the one accommodation noted by the interviewees.

The three workers agreed that in order to improve the quality of education for deaf students, public schools should create training centers geared toward teachers of mainstream classes, teachers working with deaf students, interpreters, parents and legal guardians of deaf children, and any other interested members of the community. Such centers could provide training in MSL and instruct teachers in effective pedagogical techniques for teaching deaf students. Unfortunately, few people in Morocco have a sufficiently extensive understanding of MSL to interpret or teach at deaf schools or in mainstream classrooms, much less at training centers.

According to the interviewees, given that fluent signers are scarce, the requirement that educators have prior experience working with deaf students is not considered important. This situation is not surprising given that

MSL interpreters are extremely rare in Morocco. A survey by the World Federation of the Deaf (2008) reported finding only five interpreters in Morocco, and deaf people or their families use their own personal wealth to pay for such services. Because of the small number of interpreters, the interviewees explained that even a person with very limited experience with MSL is allowed to interpret or teach at a deaf school (The National Academies, 2013). According to the interviewees, public elementary schools in more rural areas do not have sufficient resources or teaching materials. These circumstances make learning a challenge for deaf students, since their needs are not being met.

While the Ministry of National Education instituted criteria for creating mainstream classes for deaf students and selecting teachers for them, such actions are arguably of no use if people do not know they exist. The criteria also seem to be insufficient for providing a free appropriate public education equivalent to deaf students, according to the interviewees. The protections do not outline any steps that deaf students may take to access supplemental services in the classroom.

ANALYSIS

The findings from this study and the findings from the previous study of public elementary schools in the United States make it apparent that neither the United States nor Morocco provide specific laws or guarantees for specialized services for deaf students. However, deaf students in the United States seem to receive more support services than children in Morocco. Morocco appears to be in the formative stage of developing a prominent deaf community and stable deaf schools. Although MSL is a legally recognized language, as stated in the World Federation of the Deaf survey (2008), the workers at deaf schools in Morocco do not consider MSL to be as accessible as ASL. Fewer Moroccans are fluent in MSL, so some workers at deaf schools who are not fluent in MSL have created their own sign system.

In Morocco, deaf children in mainstream classrooms do not necessarily receive interpreter services or other accommodations and modifications. While similar situations happen in the United States, the existence of 504 and IEP teams are meant to limit such occurrences. Since there are no 504 or IEP equivalents in Morocco, preventing these situations can be difficult.

Deaf children generally do not have interpreters, deaf teachers, amplification systems, or any other additional services, making learning in mainstream classrooms extremely difficult. Also, when services are requested, they cannot always be provided, since there is not enough financial support from public schools to provide them. According to the report by the World

Federation of the Deaf (2008), if deaf students request an interpreter, they or their relatives must pay for the service. Funding issues also occur in the United States, but not in the same manner. In the United States, public school officials are generally hesitant to provide services for deaf students because they are expensive. In some cases, school districts hire low-paid interpreters with less experience in order to save money.

Another difference between the US and Morocco is related to exposure to deaf culture. In the United States, deaf schools (such as those in Maryland and Massachusetts) offer classes for legal guardians of deaf children to learn about the deaf community. In Morocco, interviewees explained that such classes are rare and a number of deaf schools focus only on teaching spoken language to deaf students. They also explained that students (especially young ones) benefit more from learning to speak, their reasoning being that this will make them more successful in the mainstream setting.

Furthermore, according to interviewees, few deaf people sign in public because they are ashamed of being recognized as deaf. Since MSL is not well-recognized by the public, it might be difficult for society to treat MSL with respect, as they do with other languages. This lack of acceptance may explain why MSL, although a recognized language under law, is not widespread or uniform. Although a similar social stigma used to exist in the United States, those sentiments are much less prominent today. In regard to schools practicing the oral method, they are not unique to the United States or Morocco. In both countries, educators at schools using the oral method have the same goal: teaching students to speak. However, in the United States, they exist not because of a lack of sufficient interpreters, but because some legal guardians prefer their children to become proficient in spoken English. Thus, in the United States, students have the choice to attend a school that focuses on spoken or signed language. In Morocco, depending on location, such a choice is not always available.

Although some may assume that there are no similarities between deaf education in the United States and Morocco, the two countries are not entirely different from a legal perspective. In Morocco, the Ministry of National Education does not appear to have any laws that specifically pertain to improving the quality of education for deaf students. Federal laws in the United States also lack regulations and statutes that are specific to the deaf community.

The progress of deaf education in each country, although at different levels, shares a fundamental similarity. Both Morocco and the United States are working to improve the quality of education for deaf students. Therefore, regardless of what stage each nation is at in achieving this goal, they are both looking to accomplish the same objective.

CONCLUSIONS

After a thorough analysis of literature reviews, legislation, and interviews, a number of conclusions may be drawn. The United States has two federal laws that protect the rights of individuals with disabilities and provide them with access to services. However, not all states in the country have specific legislation for the education of deaf individuals. Similarly, Morocco has laws that establish educational rights for children with disabilities. However, these rights are not as extensive and developed as Section 504 of the Rehabilitation Act of 1973 or IDEA in the United States. Morocco lacks any sort of 504 or IEP equivalent that allows for accommodations and modifications for students who need them. Consequently, services for deaf children are not always provided, leaving these students to fall behind in classrooms that do not represent the least restrictive environment. Thus, whether implemented well or not, the United States appears to have more educational laws than Morocco in regard to protecting the rights of children with disabilities.

Although legally provided services in the United States are not always the most well-suited options (such as interpreters who lack experience in the field of education), services are given to those who request them. In contrast, in the less-developed country of Morocco, such services are very scarce and not often provided in classrooms. In this case, the more developed country has more services and easier accessibility.

DISCUSSION

There are a number of ways to improve and expand upon this research for future studies. With the goal of enhancing the current study, regions of the United States and Morocco could be separated to explore whether certain geographic locations provide more (or fewer) support services than others. Also, additional educators could be interviewed to provide more information and perspectives.

Future studies can expand upon previous research by including more states in the United States and/or additional Arabic nations. The inclusion of other locations would grant researchers the ability to conduct a wider comparative analysis. Also, the original intention to compare educational legislation and its application in a more developed country to that of a less developed country could be eliminated or broadened. This change would create a different context and perhaps lead to more research topics and questions. Improvements and expansions on this research could increase awareness about the deaf and hard-of-hearing community. Perhaps with a greater understanding of the population, individuals may be more willing to promote the educational rights and needs of people with disabilities. Ideally, the quality of deaf education will improve.

REFERENCES

Bernichi, P. L. (2010). Handicapés: Les négligés du maroc. Maroc Hebdo International, 914. http://www.maroc-hebdo.press.ma/Site-Maroc-hebdo/archive/Archives_914/pdf_914/page51.pdf.

Central Intelligence Agency. (n.d.). The world factbook. https://www.cia.gov/library/publications/the-world-factbook/rankorder/2004rank.html

Maryland Department of Disabilities. (2012). Maryland: State disabilities plan 2012–2015. http://www.mdod.maryland.gov/uploadedFiles/Publications/2012-2015%20State%20Disabilities%20Plan%20for%20IADB%20Approved%20Final.pdf

Maryland State Department of Education. (2007). Facilitated IEP team meetings in Maryland: An introduction and frequently asked questions for parents and public agency/school personnel. http://www.marylandpublicschools.org/nr/rdonlyres/5f4f5041-02ee-4f3a-b495-5e4b3c850d3e/13899/facilitatediepmeetingfaq.pdf

Massachusetts Office on Disability. (2012). Disability rights laws in Massachusetts. http://www.mass.gov/anf/docs/mod/disability-law-booklet-2012-revision.pdf

Ministry of National Education. (2004). The education of disabled children. Retrieved from http://www2.men.gov.ma/viescolaire/Documents/Education%20des%20enfants%20handicap%C3%A9s%20En.pdf

The National Academies. (2013). Assistive technology for improving literacy among the deaf and hard of hearing. http://sites.nationalacademies.org/PGA/dsc/peerscience/PGA_069374

United Nations Development Programme. (2012). Human development report. http://hdr.undp.org/en/countries

U.S. Department of Education. (2006). Building the legacy: IDEA 2004. http://idea.ed.gov/

U.S. Department of Education. (1999). Free appropriate public education for students with disabilities: Requirements under Section 504 of the Rehabilitation Act of 1973. http://www2.ed.gov/about/offices/list/ocr/docs/edlite-FAPE504.html

World Federation of the Deaf. (2008). Global survey report: WFD interim regional secretariat for the Arab region (WFD RSAR) global education pre-planning project on the human rights of deaf people. http://www.wfdeaf.org/wp-content/uploads/2011/06/7.-RSAR-Regional-Survey-Report-No-7-English-Version.pdf

American Sign Language: An Advertising Tool?

REBECCA CLARK

TELEVISION COMMERCIALS INVOLVING AMERICAN SIGN LANGUAGE often catch my eye. Advertisements involving American Sign Language and Deaf actors have become a trend in marketing since McDonald's created the first television advertisment featuring sign language in 1986 (Riley, 2005, p. 124). Since then, companies such as Crest, Citibank, Levi's (Farnall, 1999, p. 316), AT&T, Bell Atlantic (Levitan & Moore, 1990), Snap.com, Wal-Mart, Nabisco/Oreo, Walt Disney (Walt Disney World Public Affairs, 2008), Kellogg (Carroll, 1994), Kraft Singles, Whiska's, Bayer (DeafLife, 1995), Saturn (Suggs, 1996), Mutual of Omaha, PepsiCo, American Heart Association, Kay Jewelers, McDonald's (Riley, 2005, p. 124) and Apple, have continued the trend, with some companies using the tactic more than once.

As a signer, it seems obvious why these ads would intrigue to me, but are they equally appealing to non-signers? This was one of the fundamental questions of my work, "American Sign Language and the Desire to Buy" (Furland, 2011). This study investigated the effectiveness of commercials involving sign language compared to those without sign language, but that were closed-captioned, as well as to commercials without sign language that were not closed-captioned. Focus groups were set up to represent two separate language and culture affiliations, signing individuals involved in the Deaf community and non-signing individuals with little to no exposure to Deaf culture. The results of that study illustrate that commercials involving sign language are successful in both groups but for different reasons. The commercial's success was measured by the participant's intent to purchase. Furland (2011) demonstrated that both signing and non-signing individuals' intention to buy a product increased after watching a commercial involving sign language representing that product. This paper will expound upon one of the television ads that incorporated sign language, Kay Jeweler's "Signs." After a brief description of the commercial, the focus group participants' reactions will be discussed, as well as an interview with Stern Advertising, responsible for creating "Signs."

Kay Jewelers Inc. has long utilized the tagline "Every Kiss Begins with Kay" in its advertising campaigns. The thirty-second television spot "Signs" (Figure 1) is one of the many ads to conclude with this slogan. The commercial opens to a scene with a well-dressed, heteronormative Caucasian couple in their twenties or thirties, rushing excitedly into a room with several Christmas-related decorations. As they sit on the floor near the Christmas tree to converse, quality furnishings are visible behind them, exemplifying a stereotypical white, middle-class, Christian, heterosexual couple. Until the dialogue begins, there is nothing distinctive about this advertisement. With the onset of conversation, however, the ad differentiates itself slightly from the typical holiday ad. The man, hearing and learning ASL, starts the conversation using simultaneous-communication (Sim-Com), speaking and signing at the same time, to apologize for his lack of sign skills. The Deaf woman responds using ASL accompanied with subtitles for any non-signing audience. After a brief conversation regarding learning new signs ("Merry Christmas"), the man presents a jewelry item to the Deaf woman as a Christmas gift. The man Sim-Coms, "Do you like it?" She responds by signing LIPREAD, (subtitled "Read my lips") and the commercial concludes with the couple kissing and the popular slogan flashing across the screen.

Figure 1. Scene from Kay Jewelers' 30-second television Spot "Signs."

After only a quick glance, it is clear the ad above does not break the mold with regards to race, gender, age, class, or sexual orientation. Instead, it is quite similar to most other ads, homogeneous in terms of diversity. The only aspect of the ad that breaks the advertising norm is the inclusion of ASL. One would think that it might parallel advertising in foreign languages (i.e., any language other than English). This type of advertisement is fairly rare in America mainstream media, but it does exist. Often the reason for incorporation is clear: the language or associated culture directly relates to the product or company, e.g., the incorporation of Spanish subtly authenticates a product such as tacos shells. Thus far, ASL has not been used in this fashion, unless we argue that technology such as the iPhone and FaceTime are Deaf culture products. More often than not, there is no direct relation to Deaf culture or deafness and the product represented in the ad.

Another possible overlapping category would be disability in advertising. In research, for this study most publications categorized the inclusion of sign language in advertising in this way (as disability), regardless of whether the advertisement featured a deaf actor/actress. There are several ads that involve sign language, but do not use deaf individuals. From instances such as those, it is clear that it was sign language that marketing firms were after, rather than deafness itself. Another common use of disability in marketing is in cause marketing, or advertising that garners support for an organization related to a disability, giving a portion of their profit to the organization. While ads in this category can vary widely, I have yet to find an ad involving sign language that concurrently garnered profit for an organization through sales. Thus, when ASL appears in a television advertisement, deafness is not the main focus. Sign language in advertising is unique in that it is a foreign language to the majority of Americans and closely related to deafness, but it neither acts like a foreign language advertisement nor an advertisement involving a disability. Advertisements involving sign language, in this way, arguably make up their own genre of ads. The reasons Stern Advertising includes ASL in their thirty-second spot "Signs" is discussed later in this paper.

FOCUS GROUP RESPONSE TO "SIGNS"

As mentioned before, reactions of signing and non-signing audiences to "Signs" differed. The average non-signing group participant responded that his/her intent to purchase increased after watching the ad (demonstrated by a mean of 1.18) while the average signing group participant's intent to purchase slightly decreased after watching the ad (a mean of .95; Table 1). The responses from the two focus groups show a statistically significant difference at a 90% confidence level, with a t value of -1.680 and significant level of .097 at a 90% confidence level, t(78)=-1.680, two-tailed p=.098, α=.10 (Appendix A, Table 2, cf. Furland, 2011, p. 80).

Likeliness to	Focus Group	N	Mean	Std Deviation	Std. Error Mean
Purchase Apple, Inc.	Signing	43	1.53	.505	.077
	Non-signing	38	1.58	.500	.081
Purchase Key Jewelers	Signing	42	0.95	.697	.108
	Non-signing	38	1.18	.512	.083
Purchase McDonald's	Signing	43	1.28	.666	.102
	Non-signing	38	1.03	.492	.080
Purchase Pepsi	Signing	43	1.26	.581	.089
	Non-signing	37	1.03	.600	.099
Remember American Heart Association	Signing	42	1.31	.749	.116
	Non-signing	38	1.74	.503	.082

Table 1. Group statistics for commercials involving sign language. (Note: Data was originally coded as 'Deaf' and 'Hearing,' but has since been converted to 'Signing' and 'Non-signing' to better reflect the linguistic and cultural affiliation of the individual. 'Signing' Participant 30 did not circle a response on the "likeliness to remember" scale for American Heart Association. 'Deaf' Participant 16 did not circle a response on the "likeliness to purchase" scale for Kay Jewelers. The missing responses are visible in their respective graphs.

Thus, the results from Furland (2011) illustrate that "Signs" influenced non-signing individuals significantly more than it did signing individuals. A closer look at Table 1 shows the positive impact of this type of advertising on non-signing individuals. All of the means of the non-signing focus group were above 1.00; for all commercials involving sign language, the average non-signing participant responded with an increased likeliness to purchase. (Responses of "increased likeliness to buy" were coded as 2.00, "likeliness to buy" coded as 1.00, and "decreased likeliness to buy" coded as 0.00; a mean score greater than 1.00 indicates participants responding favorably with an stronger likeliness to buy.)

This was not the case for either of the other two sets of commercials (closed captioned and non-closed captioned). Kay Jeweler's is but one of the five ads involving sign language to prove effective in a non-signing focus group, but the only ad to result in a mean of below 1.00 from either group.

Why was there a discrepancy between signing and non-signing audiences for the Kay Jeweler's ad? The best clues seem to lie in the short answer portion of the survey. I hypothesized that it was related to the phrase, "Read my lips," utilized as a plot device for Kay's tagline and quite obviously playing heavily off the common misconception that all deaf individuals read lips.

I hypothesized that the wide dissemination of the ad would continue to cultivate this stereotype causing signing individuals to dislike the ad; however, not one participant directly commented on that controversial catchphrase in his/her written responses. Instead, the negative feedback centered around the deaf/hearing relationship and lack of genuineness. In fact, there was a wide range of both positive and negative comments within each group.

(Participant comments here are unattributed; for a complete reading of all the Stern Advertising "Signs" focus group comments and attributions, see Furland, 2011.) One signing focus group participant stated that the "Kay's commercial was not what I liked. I already don't like them and this commercial just make me don't [sic] like them more. I['m] not a supporter for deaf/hearing relationship[s]. It [that type of relationship] almost never works out." Similarly, a non-signing participant expressed concern for the success of the relationship stating, "I don't know how a person like in the Kay commercial would have a serious relationship without being able to communicate." These comments are indicative of some hesitation from both language orientations toward a Deaf and hearing (i.e., signing and non-signing) individual's romantic involvement.

Aside from that critique, eight non-signing individuals identified "Signs" as one of the most visually attractive ads they were shown, compared to the same response from only two signing participants. Furthermore, only signing participants commented on the incorporation of a deaf actress as a reason to support the production, writing "Kay Jeweler's Products, McDonald's product, and Pepsi Product because they showed deaf actor involved for commercials that's what I want to see from that" and "Kay Jewelers because they have respect for deaf [to] include [him/her in their] commercial, that was so nice of them."

Another divisive result centered on whether or not the company's interest in the Deaf community was genuine or not. With some participants of each group on either side, the overall consensus was that more non-signing individuals perceived the ad as a genuine interest in the signing community. One participant wrote, "I think to Kay's and Heart Assoc. were the most genuine because they were about helping I think the others were genuine, but more of an advertising ploy." Interestingly, this non-signing participant recognized the incorporation of sign language as an advertising tactic, Also, his views on the productions were the exact opposite of those of the signing focus group; he found the ads identified as the worst by the signers to be the most genuine. Furland (2011) indicated that cultural affiliation influenced a consumer's perception of advertisements. The wide range of written responses from the signing focus group makes it difficult to pinpoint why "Signs" was the only ad to indicate a decrease in intent to purchase.

THE MAKING OF "SIGNS"

I conducted an interview with Stephen Romanenghi, Executive Vice President and Executive Creative Director at Stern Advertising and co-author of "Signs." With his partner, Robert Felty, the Art Director and Creative Director at Stern Advertising, they brainstormed holiday commercial ideas. Working with Kay Jeweler's, they knew the commercial's concluding line would be "Every Kiss Begins with Kay" and likewise, the action, a kiss. In this fashion, Romanenghi contends that the ad "Signs" was almost "reverse engineered" (Furland, 2011, p. 126).

The idea to involve ASL in the ad did not originate with an interest in the Deaf community; rather, it spawned from Vice President George H. W. Bush's now-famous one-liner at the 1988 Republican National Convention, "Read my lips: no new taxes" (Bush, 1988). It was Bush's remark that actually prompted Romanenghi and Felty to consider the phrase in the Kay advertisement, dropping the last half to have "Read my lips" lead into a kiss. Once that was decided, the rest developed naturally, but in reverse. Romanenghi recalled the thought process: "wait a minute, read my lips…sign language… hearing impaired…sign language…what if we did the spot in sign language, so then we did that" (Furland, 2011). This thought process is interesting for two reasons. First, it relies heavily on the popular misconception that all Deaf people read lips, which reflects the amount of interaction with the Deaf community they had prior to the creation of this ad. Second, it was sign language, rather than deafness, that came to mind first. Interestingly, if they wanted the "Read my lips" line to be more accurate, they could have incorporated a non-signing deaf individual with extensive oral communication training. Instead, the implication is that sign language was the sought after feature, rather than deafness itself.

It is clear that the popular misconception of lipreading was actually what fueled Felty and Romanenghi's creativity, leading them to involve a Deaf actress and ASL in the ad. The inclusion of a minority group, disability, or foreign language was not the goal of the ad, however. Romanenghi mused:

> "[W]hat we try to do is tell these very sweet, condensed, romantic love stories in thirty seconds. It ['Signs'] was almost reverse engineered. It wasn't like 'Hey, you know [what] we need in this spot? We need a deaf girl in this spot.' It wasn't about that."

If the inclusion of ASL happened without prior thought and attention, it is not surprising that the Deaf community was not being targeted directly by the ad. Romanenghi admitted that "the goal wasn't necessarily to reach out to that [the Deaf] audience. We naturally assumed it would and we hoped that it would be a positive portrayal and we wanted to make sure that we got it right." It is important to emphasize Romanenghi's prior thought and consideration of a positive media portrayal as that is not always a concern of individuals who are not participants of the minority.

Stern Advertising hoped a positive representation of the Deaf community would attract signers and that added business would be "a happy byproduct of it [a good ad involving ASL]."

In an attempt to create a realistic, positive portrayal, a specific casting session was conducted in search of a deaf actress. Romanenghi explained, "we probably saw about thirty actresses. We were actually kind of blown away that there were thirty hearing-impaired working actresses in Hollywood. That was kind of an education in and of itself." This comment furthermore illustrates how little experience Romanenghi had with the Deaf community and became more informed as the filming process progressed. Having previously produced television spots in Mandarin and Cantonese, Romanenghi reflected on the experience of filming in ASL. He compared the filming of "Signs" to the other productions involving foreign languages. In all cases, an interpreter or language consultant was hired and depended upon to ensure smooth filming. Great trust was given to that individual to monitor and approve that each shot was completed with accuracy in the target language. Stern Advertising took several measures to ensure that the representation of the Deaf actor and ASL were accurate. The concluding line, "Read my lips," however, was never addressed as a potential hazard to supporting stereotypes.

From a business and marketing perspective, "Signs" was wildly successful. Kay Jewelers' sales during the two years the spot aired were very good and positive feedback was received. "Signs" aired for the maximum advertising length — two years — before it was retired. In fact, Romanenghi asserts that Kay Jeweler's was so pleased with the ad that they would have run the advertisement for a third year, but that it was against their advertising policies. Essentially, "[t]hey [Kay Jewelers] were extremely happy with how it turned out, as were we," declared Romanenghi.

From a business standpoint, "Signs" was an unmitigated success and the non-signing focus group reflected this enthusiasm by indicating an increase in likeliness to purchase after watching the ad. However, the signing focus group's response, a slight decrease in likeliness to purchase, contradicts both of the above positive findings. Aside from a general critique of the ad, the reasons behind this aversion remain a mystery. A lot can be speculated, but the end results from the research data are inconclusive, with positive and negative comments regarding this specific ad from both focus groups. Romanenghi spoke of no negative feedback received. When I asked if Kay Jeweler's had received any, he assured me that if they had received "any negative emails, the agency would have heard about it very quickly. We didn't."

Most marketing involving sign language is effective for both signing and non-signing audiences. Therefore, this trend is likely to persist. As it does, so can the analysis, critique, and development of positive deaf representation in mainstream media.

REFERENCES

"Aha moment: We're all the same." Mutual of Omaha, n.d., http://www.ahamoment.com/pg/moments/view/22891. Retrieved April 22, 2011.

Bush, G. H. W. (1988). Address accepting the presidential nomination at the Republican National Convention in New Orleans, August 18, 1988. Retrieved from http://www.presidency.ucsb.edu/ws/?pid=25955.

Carroll, C., (1994). "Taking off: From Cereal commercials to plays and dance, MSSD Grad's Career Hits High Gear," *Preview: Pre-College Programs*, 10. Jane Norman Media Collection.

DeafLife. (1995, November). "Maximum impact: Jackie Roth stars in a new Bayer aspirin commercial — in ASL," *DeafLife* 8(5).

Farnall, O. (1999), "Invisible no more: Advertising and people with disabilities." In Dawn O. Braithwaite and Teresa L. Thompson (eds.) *Handbook of communication and people with disabilities: Research and application*, New York: Routledge, 307–318.

Furland, R. (2011). "American Sign Language and the desire to buy: A study of sign language in TV advertisements." Unpublished thesis, Gallaudet University.

Haller, B. & Ralph, S. (2001, Spring). Profitability, diversity, and disability images in advertising in the United States and Great Britain. *Disability Studies Quarterly*, 21(2), http://dx.doi.org/10.18061/dsq.v21i2.

Levitan, L, & Moore, M. S. (1990, May). "Bell Atlantic has 'Gotten It Right.'" *DeafLife*, 2(11).

Lipman, J. (1990, February 28). "Deaf consumers aren't ignored anymore." *Wall Street Journal*, p. B6.

"Marlee Matlin Apple Macintosh Commercial," YouTube, n.d., http://www.youtube.com/watch?v=yr618Y73sJQ.

Quinn, J. (1995). "Able to buy," *Incentive*, 169(9), September 1995, 80.

Riley, C. A. (2005). *Disability and the media: Prescriptions for change*. Hanover, NH: University Press of New England.

Suggs, T. (1997, June). "Faking it: How a hearing woman fooled thousands of people into thinking she was Deaf — and how she was unmasked by a Deaf reporter," *DeafLife* 9(12).

Walt Disney World Public Affairs (2008, January 22). "Disney wins prestigious award for TV ad," https://web.archive.org/web/20101226204200/http://www.wdwpublicaffairs.com/ContentDrillDown.aspx?DisplayItem=96372a81-8fb2-4062-81e8-095d848cce47.

Appendix A, Table 2. Independent Samples Test

Likliness to		Levene's Test for Equality of Variances		t-test for Equality of Means					95% Confidence Interval of Difference	
		F	Sig	t	df	Sig (2-tailed)	Mean Diff	Std. Error Diff	Lower	Upper
Purchase Apple, Inc.	Equal variances assumed	.567	.454	-.394	79	.695	-.044	.112	-.267	.179
	Equal variances not assumed			-.394	77.939	.695	-.044	.112	-.267	.179
Purchase Key Jewelers	Equal variances assumed	1.459	.231	-1.680	78	.097	-.232	.138	-.506	.043
	Equal variances not assumed			-1.706	74.973	.092	-.232	.136	-.503	.039
Purchase McDonald's	Equal variances assumed	14.065	.000	1.920	79	.058	.253	.132	-.009	.515
	Equal variances not assumed			1.955	76.701	.054	.253	.129	-.005	.510
Purchase Pepsi	Equal variances assumed	1.745	.190	1.729	78	.088	.229	.132	-.035	.492
	Equal variances not assumed			1.725	75.430	.089	.229	.133	-.035	.493
Remember American Heart Association	Equal variances assumed	12.659	.001	-2.964	78	.004	-.427	.144	-.714	-.140
	Equal variances not assumed			-3.021	72.217	.003	-.427	.141	-.709	-.145

Table 2. SPSS output for commercials involving sign language

Tracing Deafhood:
Exploring the Origins and Spread of Deaf Cultural Identity, Part III

JORDAN EICKMAN, PH.D.

THIS PAPER REPRESENTS THE THIRD PART OF THE TRACING DEAFHOOD project presented at the Deaf Studies *Today!* Conference series. Selected European data is the focus of the map data presented in this paper.

Previous public Tracing Deafhood project presentations covering different geographic regions and types of data were made at various conferences and sites, and published as part of the Deaf Studies *Today!* (2006) and Deaf History International (2006) conference proceedings. Most of the basic foundational information of the Tracing Deafhood project is the same here as in these other sources, so for simplicity's sake, citations to this type of information will not be included here. However, a list of these presentations and publications are included as part of the reference list to acknowledge these works.

The Tracing Deafhood project aims to identify how the formation and worldwide spread of Deaf cultural identity has occurred by utilizing a Geographic Information System to map and visually determine the chronological sequences of and patterns in the establishment and spread of schools for deaf children, Deaf clubs, Deaf sport clubs, national Deaf associations, Deaf churches, and other Deaf community 'pillars' worldwide.

Understanding three key concepts are the key to understanding and analyzing Tracing Deafhood project data and maps. The three key concepts are Deafhood, Deaf community 'pillars' and ArcGIS analysis. Each concept will be briefly defined.

Deafhood

Ladd (2003, p. xviii) defines the concept of Deafhood, which he describes "as the process by which Deaf individuals come to actualise their Deaf identity." This term seeks to define the essence and existence of Deaf identity (Ladd 2003, p. xviii, 3, 4).

Deaf community 'pillars'

Eickman (2004, p. 34, also see p. 190, 264) broached the concept of Deaf community 'pillars.' Generally, Deaf community 'pillars' (henceforth referred to as pillars, for short) include schools for deaf children, Deaf clubs, Deaf sport clubs, national Deaf associations, and Deaf churches. Each pillar has a role in maintaining the Deaf community's existence and serve educational, social, and political purposes. Lane, et al. (1996, p. 131-137; 137-138) describes how American Deaf schools, Deaf clubs and Deaf sport have impacted the acculturation process of deaf people into the American Deaf community and the National Association of the Deaf's socially significant role.

ArcGIS analysis

ArcGIS is the name of a ubiquitous Geographic Information System (GIS) software program used by geographers. After feeding geographic data and other data variables into ArcGIS, maps can be generated to determine and/or illustrate patterns. Multiple map layers can be plotted on a single map. For example, one map layer can show where schools for deaf children have been established while another map layer can show where Deaf clubs have been founded. Both layers can be placed on the same map to determine which cities have both a school for deaf children and a Deaf club.

Data collected on pillars and their characteristics is plotted on a single map using multiple map layers and their geographic origins, spread, and interplay can be studied. Multiple maps representing different specific years or time periods in history are compared against each other as another way of determining and/or illustrating patterns. The potential power of multi-dimensional analysis of Deaf community pillar data using ArcGIS is great.

ANALYSIS OF DEAF COMMUNITY PILLAR MAPS: WHAT CAN WE LEARN?

We can learn patterns from the connections between pillars and locations of high and low degrees of Deaf community activity. The maps also illustrate the geographic impact Deaf-centered leadership, sign language usage, pro-Deaf rights legislation (all which are positive impacts) and oralism, audism, and the Milan 1880 conference (all negative impacts). Locations having high and low degrees of Deaf community activity, evidenced by the formation and existence or absence of the pillars, will be indicators of where Deaf identity has been/is strongest or weakest, representing possible manifestations of an 'ideal' Deaf community or forces of audism.

INSPIRATION

The inspiration for the Tracing Deafhood project came from *The History of Deaf People* (Eriksson, 1998). Eriksson offered two different maps: one showing the location of early European schools for deaf children (pp. 60-61) and the other showing the spread of the two major teaching methods used at early European schools for deaf children (p. 65). Analysis of geographic patterns to determine how Deaf identity has spread globally can be made as the pillars serve as Deaf identity development venues. If one accepts Ladd's (2003, p. xviii, 3, 4) aforementioned definition of Deafhood which essentially states that Deafhood is equal to Deaf identity actualization, then one can accept that the pillars influence Deafhood. Thus, the compilation and analysis of the origins and spread of the pillars is vital to understand the origins and spread of Deaf identity.

DATA COLLECTION

Data collection focused on gathering names, locations and founding years for each pillar. For schools for deaf children, the number of students and instruction method (when available) were also collected. For schools for deaf children, this paper drew on five main sources:

- the *Troisième Circulaire* issued by the l'Institut Royal des Sourds-Muets de Paris (hereafter cited as *Troisième Circulaire*, 1832)
- Tabular statements of schools for deaf children issued by the *American Annals of the Deaf and Dumb* (Fay, 1882; Fay, 1883). Fay (1883) is mainly a supplement to correct and fill in gaps from Fay (1882) according to Fay (1883, p. 47–48).
- Circulars of Information issued by the Volta Bureau (Volta Bureau, 1896; Volta Bureau, 1902)

For Deaf sport clubs and Deaf national sport organizations, this paper drew on three main sources, decennial "handbooks" produced by Comité International des Sports Silencieux (CISS) roughly every decade, covering the periods of 1924–1958:

- *Liste des Nations au CISS...*, n.d.; hereafter cited as *CISS HB*, 1934; *Liste des Nations en instance...*, n.d.)
- *Nations Affiliées...*, n.d.a; hereafter cited as *CISS HB*, 1949)
- *Nations Affiliées...*, n.d.b.; hereafter cited as *CISS HB*, 1958)

For Deaf national organizations, this paper drew on *World Federation of the Deaf: A History* (Gannon, 2011). In support of the above data, other sources were also utilized:

- www.findlatitudeandlongitude.com/batch-geocode was used to batch geocode latitude and longitude coordinates of pillar locations.
- translate.google.com was used to assist in city name translations/identifications, including determining city names in different languages and to translate and understand non-English written source material.
- www.wikipedia.org was used to determine locations and names of cities listed in source data with different names than they have today. Most such cases involved cities that formerly were Prussian, but now belong to various countries, as the nation of Prussia no longer exists (i.e., Apparent Prussian cities are listed in *Troisième Circulaire*, 1832, p. 170, 172; Fay, 1882, p. 37-39; Volta Bureau, 1896, p. 10, 12, 14; and Volta Bureau 1902, p. 20, 22). An example of this determination is the city currently known as Wrocław, Poland, which was formerly known as Breslau. This was deduced by accessing http://en.wikipedia.org/wiki/Breslau.
- Matthews (1996) was used to verify the location of an Irish school for deaf children.
- *The Traveler's Atlas: A Geographic Handbook* (1996) ensureD correct plotting of cities when producing maps.

It must be emphasized that the data collection is not claimed to include every European Deaf community pillar being examined in this paper (Deaf schools, Deaf sport clubs, Deaf National Sport Association, Deaf National Organizations). It is certain that other sources exist that have information on additional pillars. Over time, it is hoped that all pillar locations will be identified and combined into truly complete and accurate-as-can-be maps.

DATA COLLECTION ISSUES

Several issues arose while evaluating collected data:

City Names and Locations

- City names changes over time. As territory changes hands, city names do change. As aforementioned, the majority of these cases involved formerly Prussian cities that now have different names. This added more time and difficulty in determining latitude and longitude coordinates.
- At times, educated guesses and making slight modifications in city name spelling were utilized in an attempt to identify the most likely correct current name.
- It is possible to have a country that has two or more cities with the same name. When a pillar is identified as being in a city of that name, using educated guesses and Wikipedia resources and other information from the source data informed choosing the most likely location of the pillar amongst the cities of the same name.

Data Presentation

- Sometimes the source itself did not provide enough data to identify exact pillar locations or did not include additional information about pillars (i.e., number of school pupils) so those pillars could not be included in the maps in this paper. This is particularly true in the case of the Soviet Union which *CISS HB,* 1958, p. 56 lists as having 450 clubs but no information is given to their location, and to a lesser extent Yugoslavia from *CISS HB,* 1949, p. 37–38 where five clubs are mentioned but no further information was provided to CISS.
- Data sometimes was combined into one report for two different schools or campuses (e.g., boys and girls schools or separate manual and oral sections at a single school), thus it was not always possible to represent each piece of information separately on the map.
- Sometimes, a pillar may be listed in one source then disappear in the subsequent source, and then return in being included in a third, later source. This might be due to lack of contact with the pillar in question (e.g., the Spanish Deaf national sport association, see *Liste des nations en instance...* (n.d., p. 20), *CISS HB,* (1934, p. 15–38), and *CISS HB,* (1958, p. 21–22)) or in the case of war (e.g., German Deaf sport clubs, contact with the German Deaf national sport association was halted for a period of time due to World War II, see *CISS HB,* (1949, p. 15)).

- Some source data in the form the author accessed them was not always legible due to notbeing able to fully flatten source data book binding for photocopying. This problem can be rectified in the future by hand-copying data from source data books rather than photocopying.

Data Reliability
- Even some sources themselves indicate that the source data is not completely perfect (Fay, 1882, p. 32 and Fay, 1883, p. 47–48).
- Even some sources themselves indicate that the source data is not all-inclusive (Volta Bureau, 1896, p. 3–4); Volta Bureau (1902, p. n.p.a.— "Introduction" page).
- Sometimes, two different sources may differ on a pillar's founding year.
- Source data within a source may differ in the year of report among themselves (e.g., reports from different years may be consolidated into one source data as in the case of French data in Fay (1882, p. 36–37 and actually throughout Fay (1882) and Fay (1883)) and Italian and German data in Volta Bureau (1896, p. 5, also see pp. 13 and 21). If and when maps are produced for each year, rather than over time intervals, then the maps will need to be more precise in distinguishing between and reflecting the actual year of report of data.

ArcGIS technical issues
- Scaling of proportional circle symbols representing numbers of students at each school differs across maps due to different high and low number marks. This is a technical issue that needs to be made more consistent, so one can accurately gauge the actual numbers as schools grow in enrollment across time. It is anticipated that as the author gains more proficiency in using ArcGIS, this issue will be resolved.

Terminology and classification of teaching methods
- Sources differed in how they classified teaching methods. The next section discusses this important issue in depth.

Thus, as a disclaimer, the data and maps are not perfect. Corrections to and additional information to fill in missing information on the presented data and maps are welcome.

TEACHING METHOD TERMINOLOGY AND CLASSIFICATION

Teaching method terminology differed between the two main publishers (the American Annals of the Deaf and Dumb — for Fay (1882) and Fay (1883), and the Volta Bureau — for Volta Bureau (1896) and Volta Bureau (1902)) of data that included teaching methods used by schools for deaf children. Fay (1882, p. 32–33) described the difficulty of ensuring consistency in classifying schools by teaching methods in his explanation of the four categories (manual, oral, combined, and transition). The Volta Bureau sources (1896, p. 3, 5 and 1902, p. n.p.a., "Explanatory" page) generally were the same, using seven different categories.

For the purposes of this paper, Fay's (1882, p. 32–33) categories were followed when generating maps and including a fifth category named 'no information' to indicate when no teaching method data was given for a particular school. For Fay (1883), a similar approach was taken, with a sixth category named "other" to classify other teaching method data that was not compatible in some way to classify among the other five categories.

The Volta Bureau (1896, 1902) data was simplified by evaluating the teaching methods data for each school and classifying them into six categories: manual, combined/mixed, separate departments/student designations, oral, other, and no information. The oral category covered all schools reported as either 'oral' or 'pure oral' as listed in Volta Bureau (1896, p. 5) and Volta Bureau (1902, p. n.p.a., "Explanatory" page). This was done to make the data simpler and easier to read on maps with fewer categories. Even with this reclassifying of the data, at times, judicious choices had to be made where a school was placed in the category that appeared to most fit the school's "slant" toward a particular category.

RESULTS

The results are presented in a series of twenty-two maps. The maps are classed in six groups: school locations, student population, teaching methods, Deaf sport clubs, Deaf national sport associations and Deaf national organizations. Maps for Fay (1883) combined both Fay (1882) and Fay (1883) data.

School Locations
Each Deaf school included in the data set whose location could clearly be identified is marked on maps by an icon of a colored box with a flag post on top, symbolizing a school. An accompanying legend shows the icon shape and color used for that particular map.

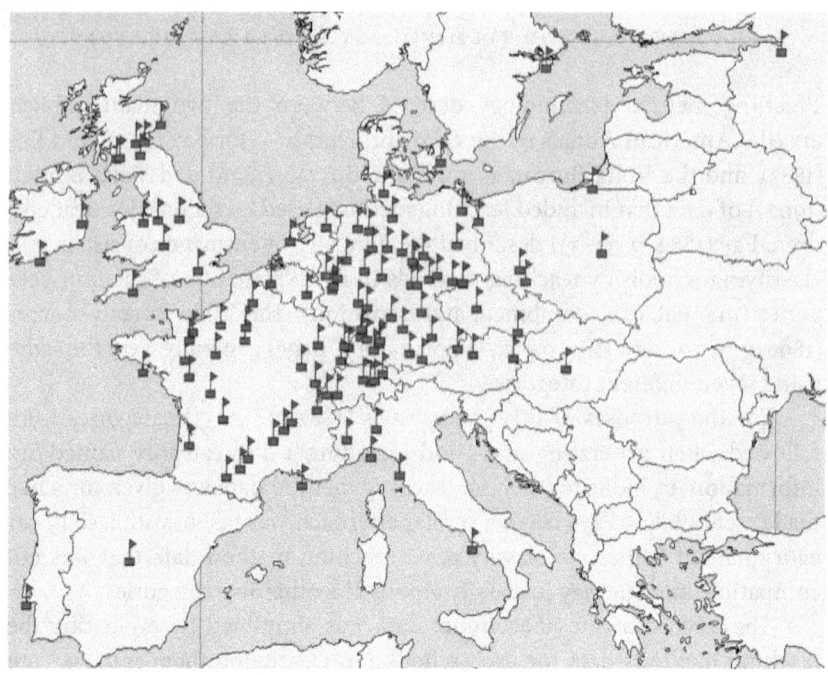

Map 1. European Deaf Schools (*Troisième Circulaire*, 1832)

Map 1 shows many early European schools for deaf children. It appears that the majority of schools are concentrated in France, Germany, and to a lesser extent, Great Britain. A few other countries are shown as having schools.

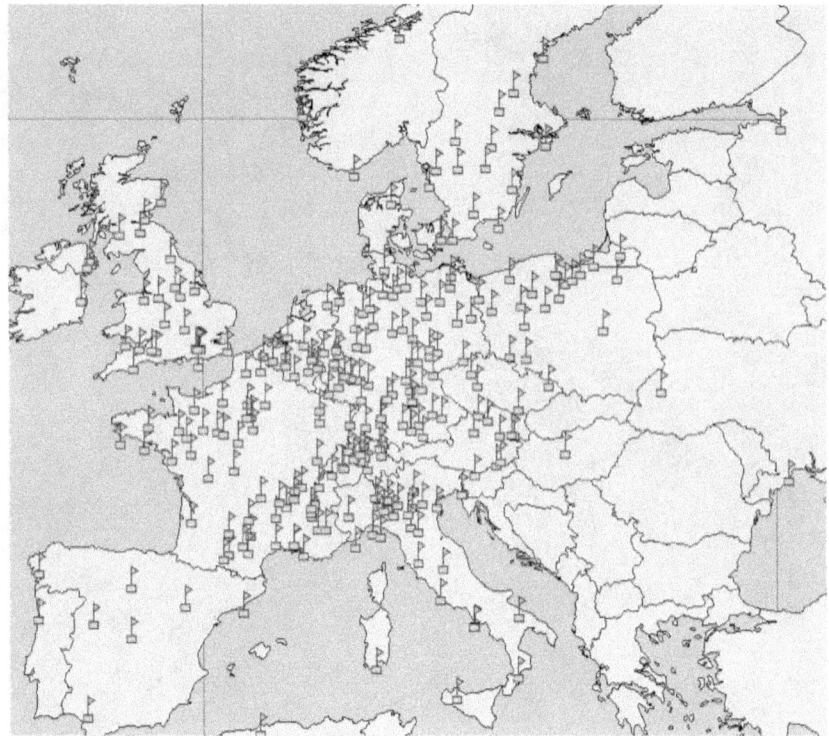

Map 2. European Deaf Schools (Fay, 1882)

Map 2 shows substantial growth in the number of reported European schools for deaf children in the fifty years since the *Troisème Circulaire* was published in 1832. Again, France and Germany have many schools, but significant increases in school numbers occurred in Great Britain, Italy, Belgium, Sweden, Switzerland, Spain, and in central-eastern Europe.

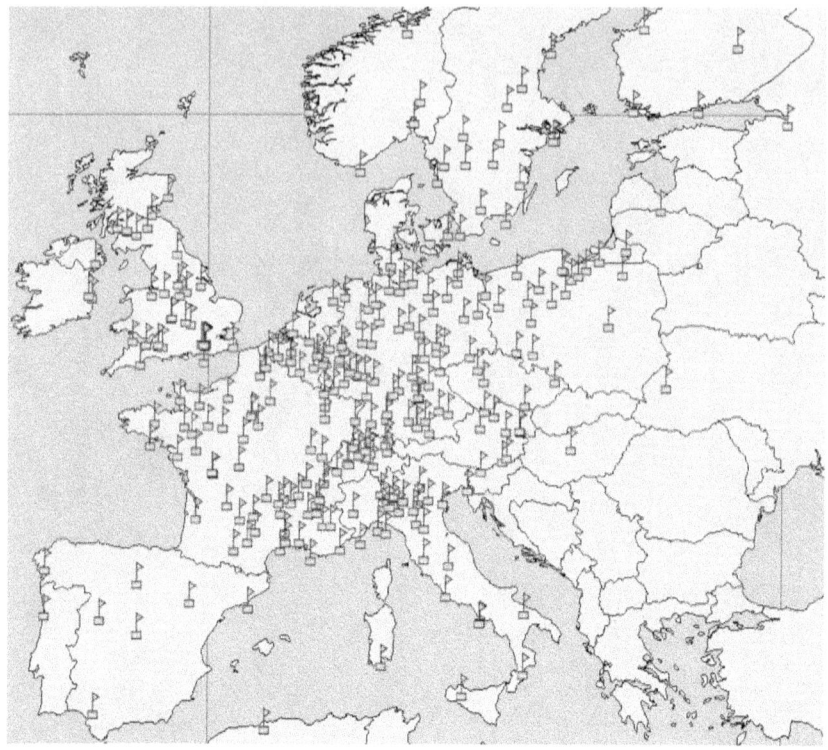

Map 3. European Deaf Schools (Fay 1883)

As mentioned earlier by Fay (1883, p. 47–48), Fay (1883) is mainly an improved version of Fay (1882), so no great changes are immediately noticeable in Map 3 except that a few schools "disappear" and noticeable additions of schools occur in Finland, Norway, Great Britain, and France.

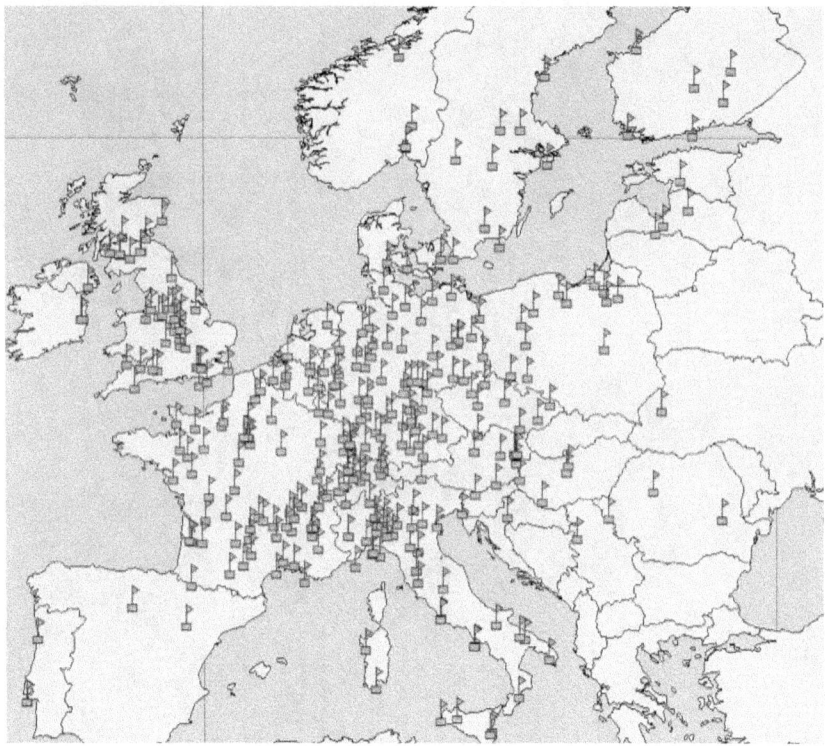

Map 4. European Deaf Schools (Volta Bureau, 1896)

Map 4 shows some disappearing schools, particularly in Spain, Sweden, and Poland, but growth appears to take place in the Balkan and Baltic regions along with Great Britain and Italy.

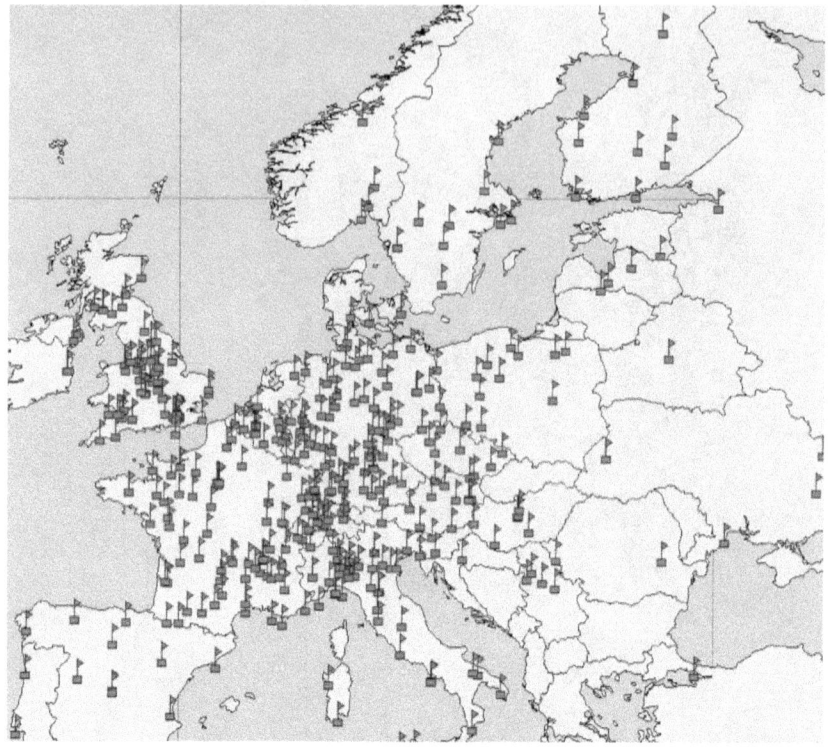

Map 5. European Deaf Schools (Volta Bureau, 1902)

Map 5 shows some changes in schools within Germany, France, and Great Britain. Growth in school numbers occurs in Spain, Ukraine, Serbia, Sweden, and Finland. Schools are reported in Algeria, Turkey, and Belarus.

Student Populations

Each Deaf school included in the data set whose location could clearly be identified is marked on maps by a colored circle. The circles vary in size, with larger circles denoting larger student populations and smaller circles denoting smaller student populations. The circles were scaled into five different sizes, each size representing a range of numbers within the student population. The scale differed for each map and a legend for each map's scale is provided. City names are those listed in the source and included for those schools whose student population was among the two largest size ranges. When possible, circles representing schools with smaller populations are placed in front of circles representing schools with larger populations so data for both schools are visible, without the larger circle "blocking" the smaller circle. Analysis commentary focuses on where the largest schools are in terms of student population, rather than the actual student population numbers themselves.

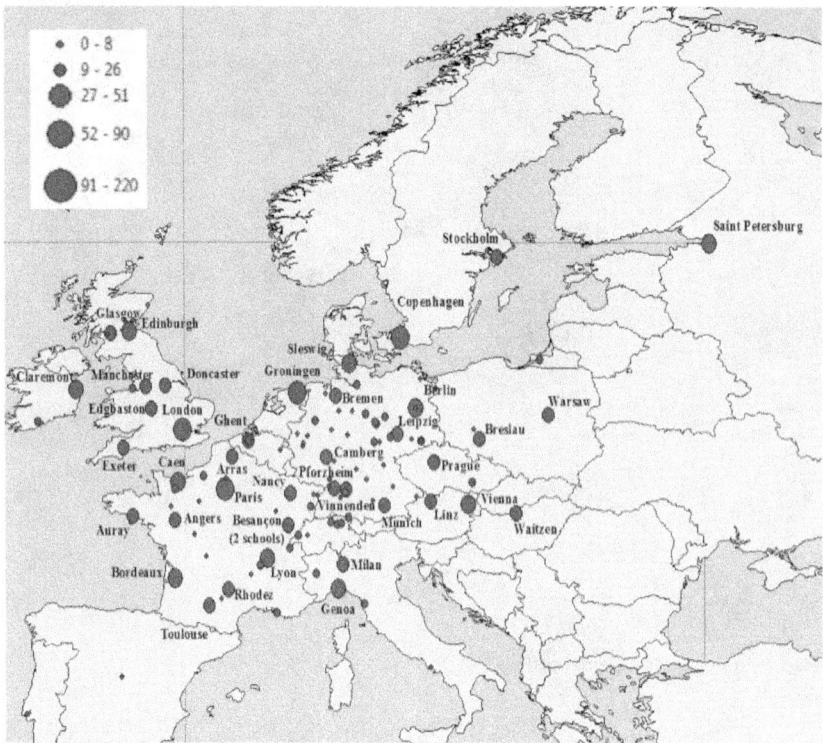

Map 6. European Deaf Students (*Troisième Circulaire*, 1832)

Map 6 indicates that the largest schools in terms of student population are in Great Britain, France, Germany, in central Europe, and a few schools further away from central areas (Copenhagen, Stockholm, Milan, Genoa, and Saint Petersburg).

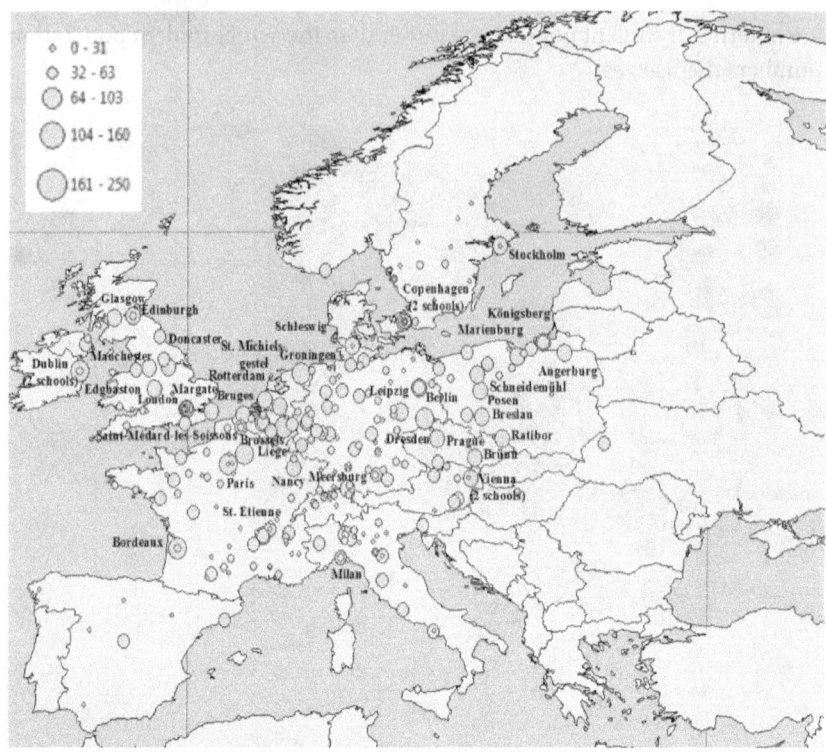

Map 7. European Deaf Students (Fay, 1882)

Map 7 shows a large overall shift in a northeastern direction from the previous map in where the largest schools are. The larger schools are found in Germany, Poland, Czech Republic, Austria, Belgium, and Great Britain. There is a noticeable overall decrease in France, much overall growth in Great Britain, Belgium, Germany, Poland, Austria, and Czech Republic, and some growth in Italy.

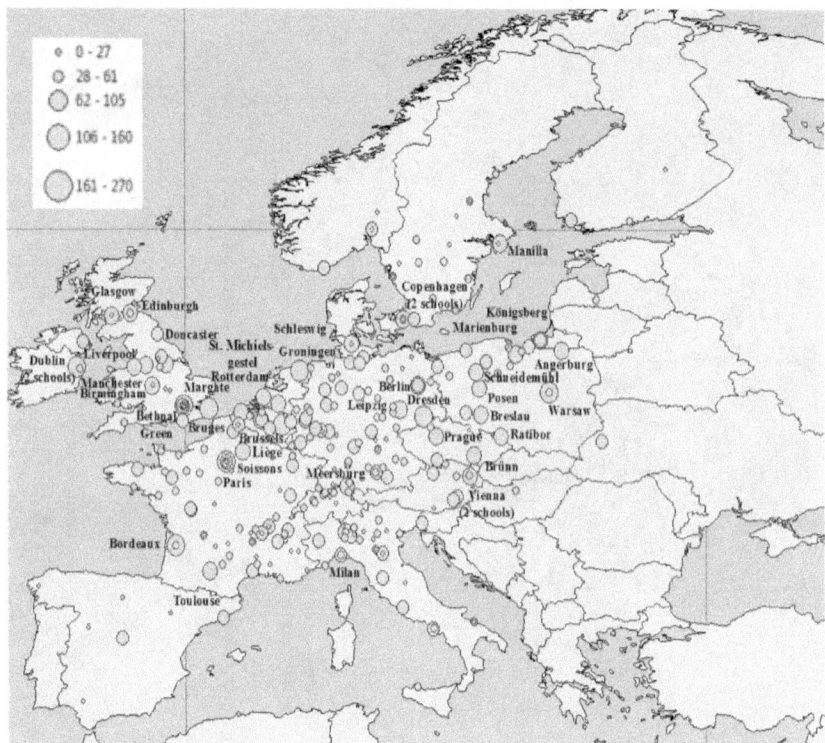

Map 8. European Deaf Students (Fay, 1883)

Map 8 is similar to Map 7 but noticeable growth is indicated in Warsaw and Toulouse. France sees a few changes.

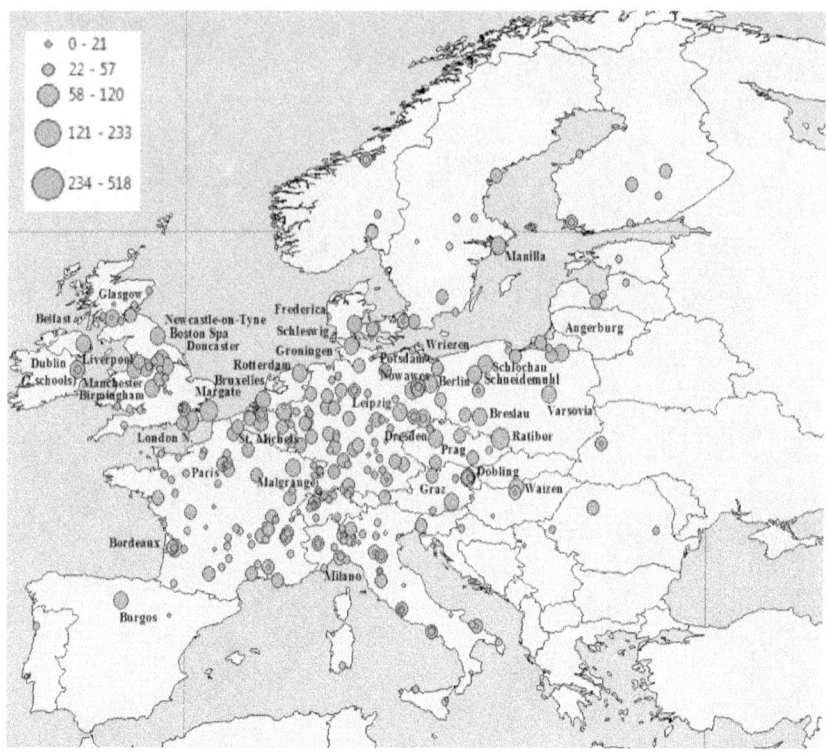

Map 9. European Deaf Students (Volta Bureau, 1896)

Map 9 sees some changes in Great Britain, Spain, and Poland. Hungary and Finland also see growth.

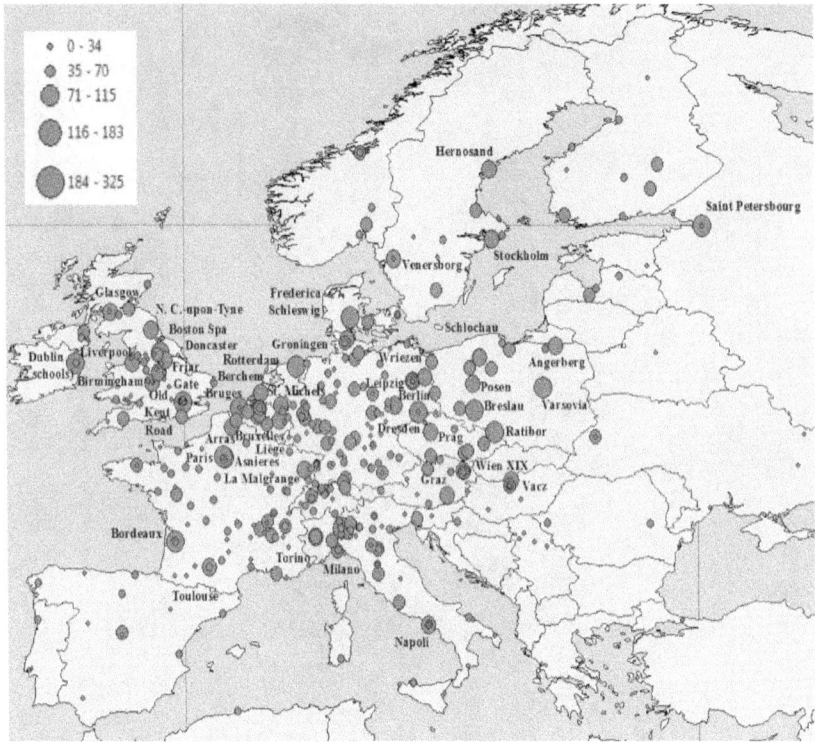

Map 10. European Deaf Students (Volta Bureau, 1902)

Map 10 is similar to Map 9. However, growth is indicated in Napoli, Saint Petersburg, Hernosand, and Venersborg. There are changes in Poland and an overall decrease in Germany.

Teaching Methods

Each Deaf school included in the data set whose location could clearly be identified is marked on maps by a colored circle. The circles' colors vary depending on the type of teaching method used at that particular school. Due to different systems being used within the sources to classify teaching methods, which the author adapted and simplified (as explained in an earlier section), each map has its own legend, but as a general rule, schools using the manual method are identified by larger green circles with the city name, as listed in the source, also included. The other teaching methods are indicated by smaller circles with differing colors. When possible, circles representing schools with smaller populations are placed in front of circles representing schools with larger populations so data for both schools are visible, without the larger circle "blocking" the smaller circle.

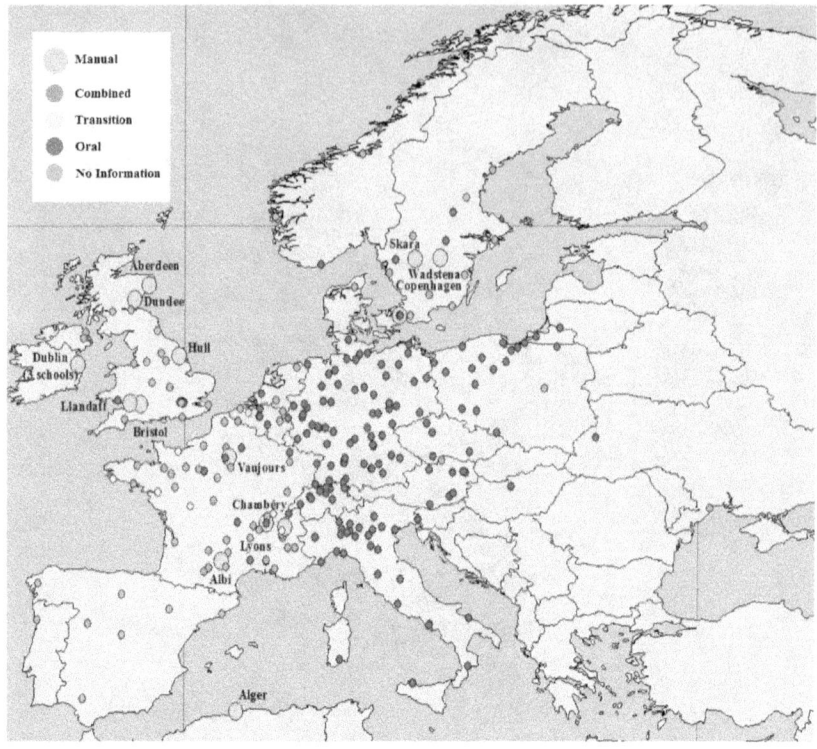

Map 11. Teaching Methods (Fay, 1882)

Map 11 clearly shows three trends in teaching methods. Oralism is prevalent in central and eastern Europe. The combined method is mainly found in Spain and Great Britain. Manualism is mostly found in Great Britain, France, and Sweden, with the other manualist schools in Ireland, Denmark, and Algeria.

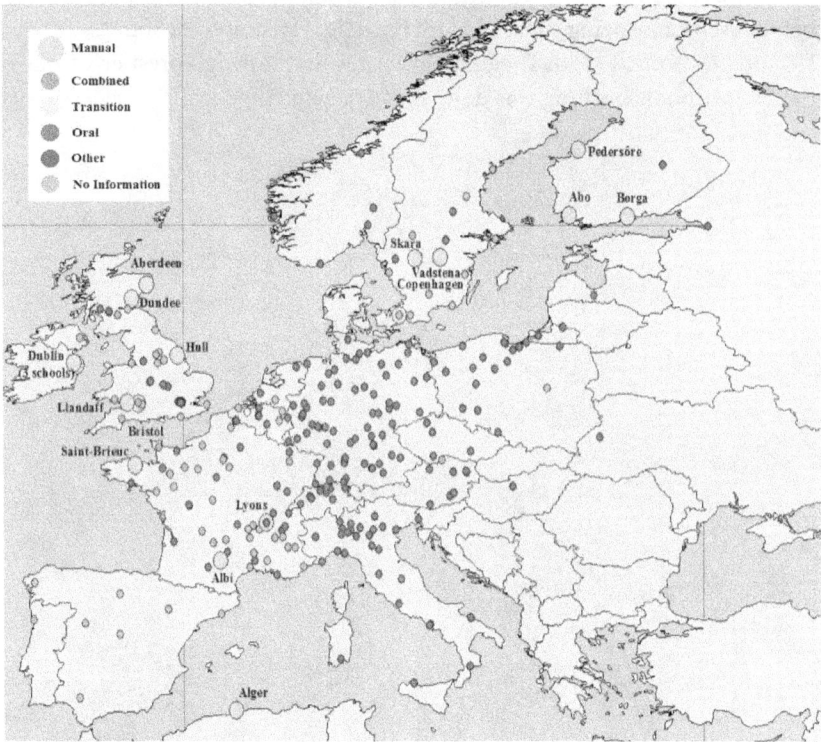

Map 12. Teaching Methods (Fay, 1883)

Map 12 shows the same general results as Map 11, although a few more manualist schools are reported in Finland and that the combined method is not prevalent in Great Britain.

Might the schools in Abo and Borga be manualist due to the influence of Carl Oscar Malm? Malm was a deaf teacher who taught through manualism with the aim of pupils acquiring "both sign language and written language at the same time," founded a school for deaf children in Porvoo, and advocated for the formation of a school for deaf children in Turku (Finnish Museum for the Deaf, n.d.). Also, Eriksson lists a 'Malm' as the founder of the school in Borgå; this Malm is assumed to be the same Carl Oscar Malm (1998, p. 61, 65).

Might also the school in Lyon be manualist due to the influence of David Comberry and Claudius Forestier? *Histoire des Sourds* (2002a) and *Histoire des Sourds* (2002b) both indicate that both men were involved in the school at Lyon and that both men were apparently deaf due to their schooling at the Bordeaux and Paris schools, respectively. Comberry initially ran the St. Etienne school which later moved to Lyon, where he was the director, before eventually being succeeded by Forestier (Histoire des Sourds, 2002b). *Histoire des Sourds* (2002a) clearly indicates that during Forestier's time at the Lyon school, teaching was done through sign language.

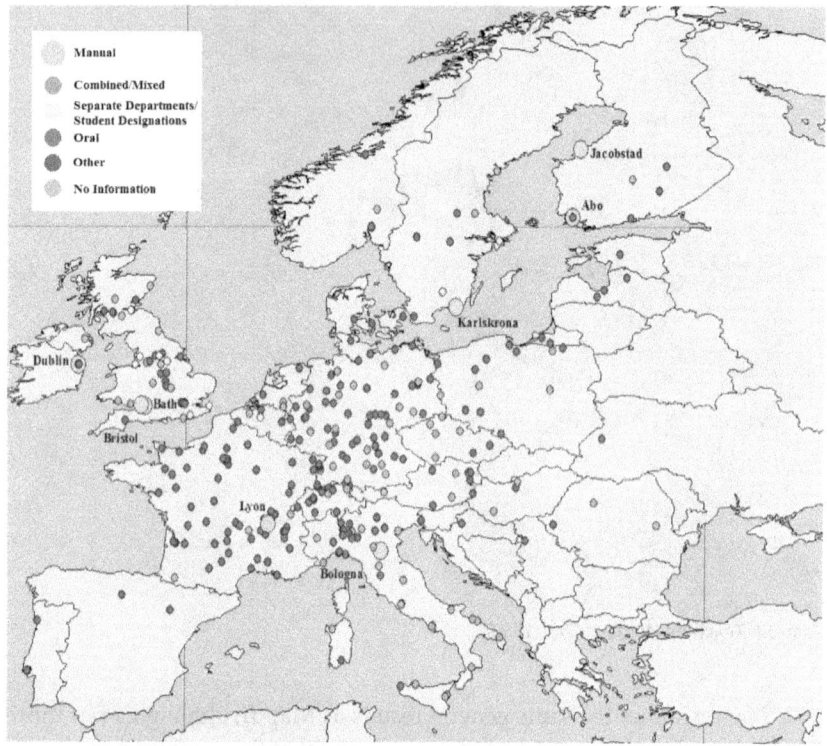

Map 13. Teaching Methods (Volta Bureau, 1896)

Map 13 shows clearly that oralism has made inroads into Great Britain and especially France. There are fewer manualist schools. Interestingly, there is no information in this source on teaching methods for a lot of schools in Germany and elsewhere in central and eastern Europe.

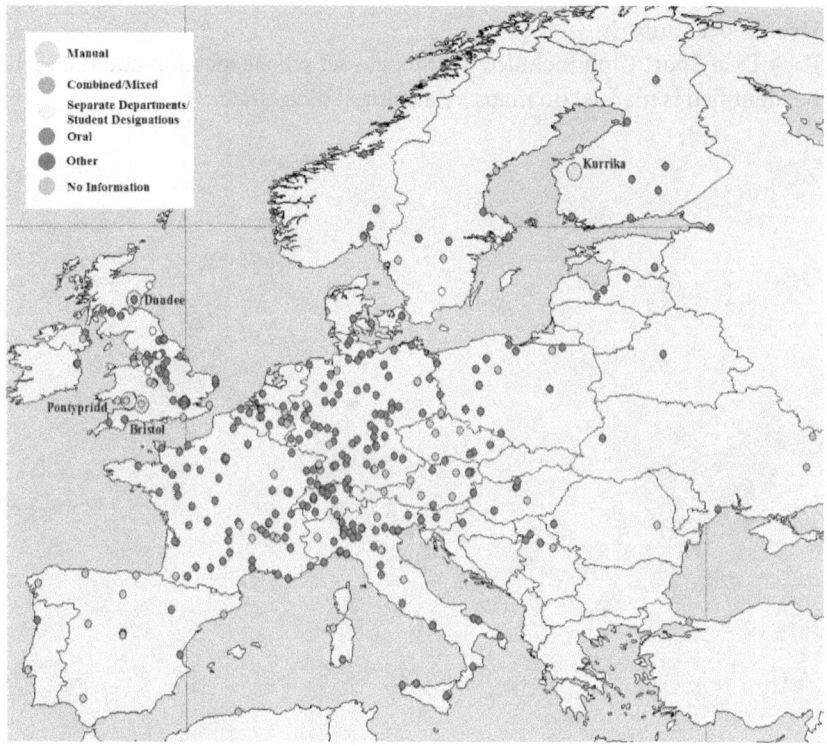

Map 14. Teaching Methods (Volta Bureau, 1902)

Map 14 shows more clearly that oralism is prevalent throughout Europe. Only four schools are manual (Bristol, Dundee, Kurrika, and Pontypridd). Might the reason for Bristol and Dundee being manual be due to their origins with Matthew Robert Burns and Alexander Drysdale? Matthew Robert Burns was a deaf man who was involved in founding various schools for deaf people, including in both Bristol and Dundee, but whose impact for our purposes here was probably greatest in Bristol (Jackson, 2001, p. 63-64). Alexander Drysdale was a Deaf man who established the longest-existing school for deaf children in Dundee, and served along with his wife as its leaders for thirty five years, before being succeeded by James Barland, another Deaf man and alumnus of the same school (p. 64). Might Kurrika have had some influence from Carl Oscar Malm?

It would be very interesting to examine the history of each manualist school shown in Maps 11-14. This is an area for further research, along with the individual histories of Carl Oscar Malm, David Comberry, Claudius Forestier, Matthew Robert Burns, and Alexander Drysdale.

Deaf Sport Clubs

Each Deaf Sport Club included in the data set whose location could clearly be identified is marked on maps by a colored blue circle.

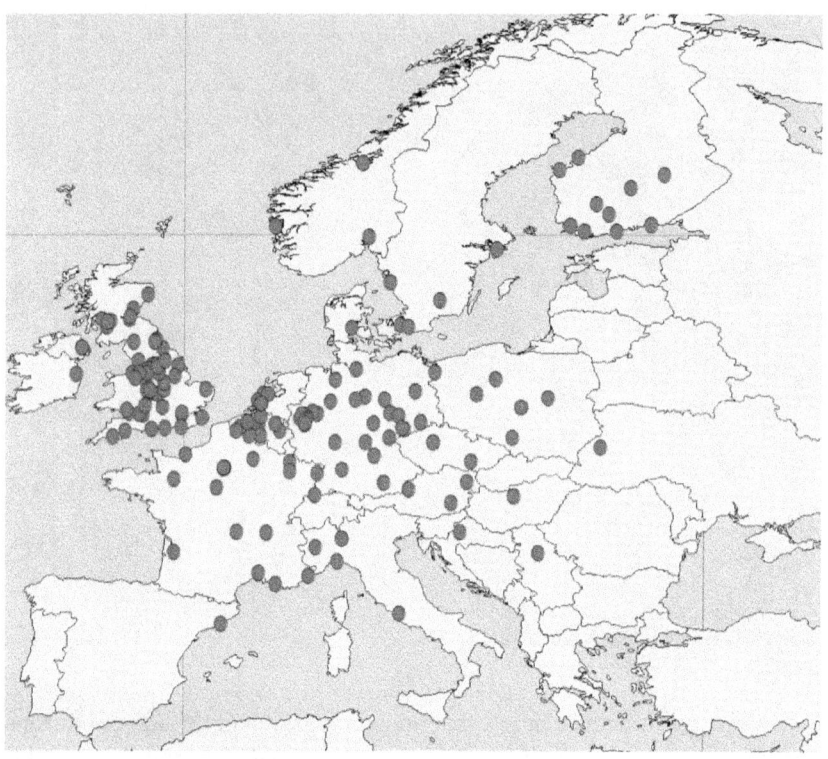

Map 15. European Deaf Sport Clubs (CISS HB 1934)

Map 15 clearly indicates that the highest concentration of Deaf sport clubs are found in Great Britain, Belgium, Germany, Finland and to a lesser extent, France and Poland.

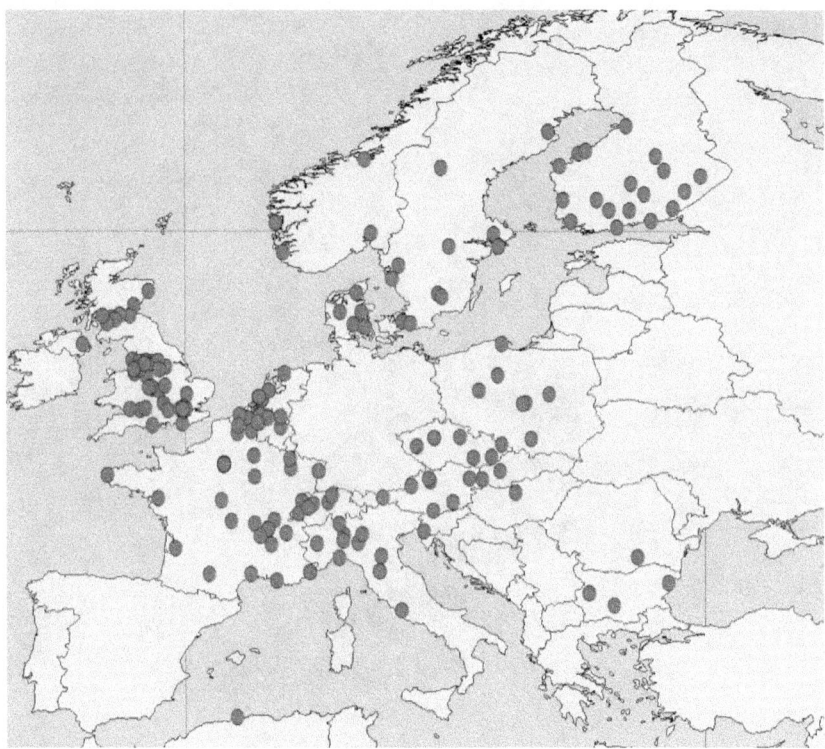

Map 16. European Deaf Sport Clubs (CISS HB 1949)

Map 16 shows the same trend of a high concentration of Deaf sport clubs in Great Britain, Belgium, and Finland as in Map 15. Increases are noticeable in France, Italy, Switzerland, Austria, Czech Republic, Sweden, Bulgaria, and Denmark. Germany is noticeably absent from this map due to the aforementioned interruption of contact due to World War II (CISS HB, 1949, p. 15) along with the aforementioned lack of location information from Yugoslavia in *CISS HB*, 1949, p. 37–38 for the five Yugoslav Deaf sport clubs.

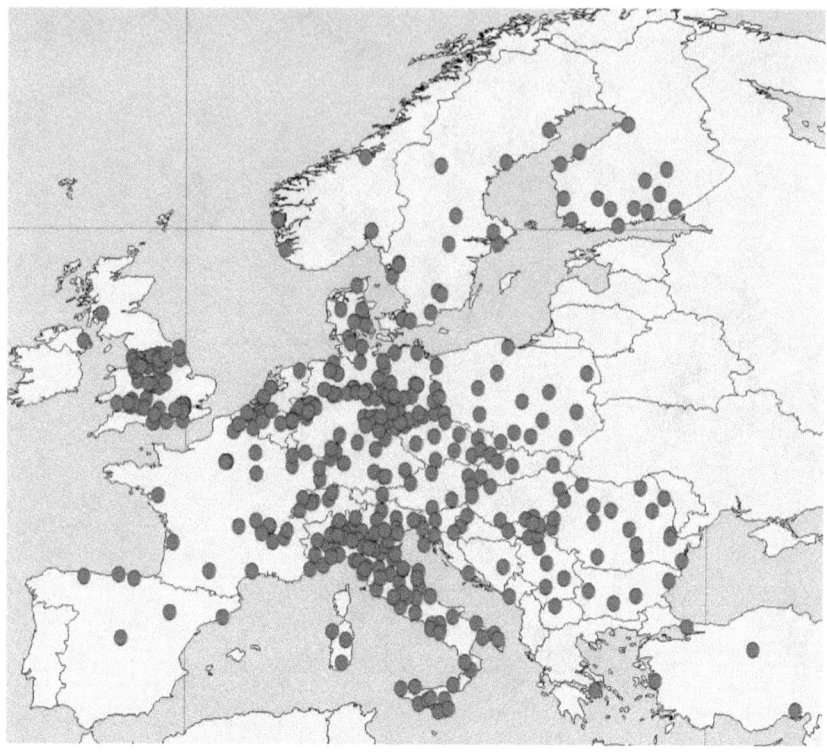

Map 17. European Deaf Sport Clubs (CISS HB, 1958)

Map 17 shows huge growth in the number of Deaf sport clubs reported, particularly in central and eastern Europe. It is interesting that Scotland only has one Deaf sport club included in this map. The aforementioned absence of location information from the Soviet Union for their 450 Deaf sport clubs mentioned in *CISS HB*, 1958, p. 56 is noticeable here.

Deaf National Sport Associations
Each Deaf National Sport Association included in the data set is identified by placing a green circle where the national capital city is located. When known, the founding year of that Deaf National Sport Association is adjacent to the green circle.

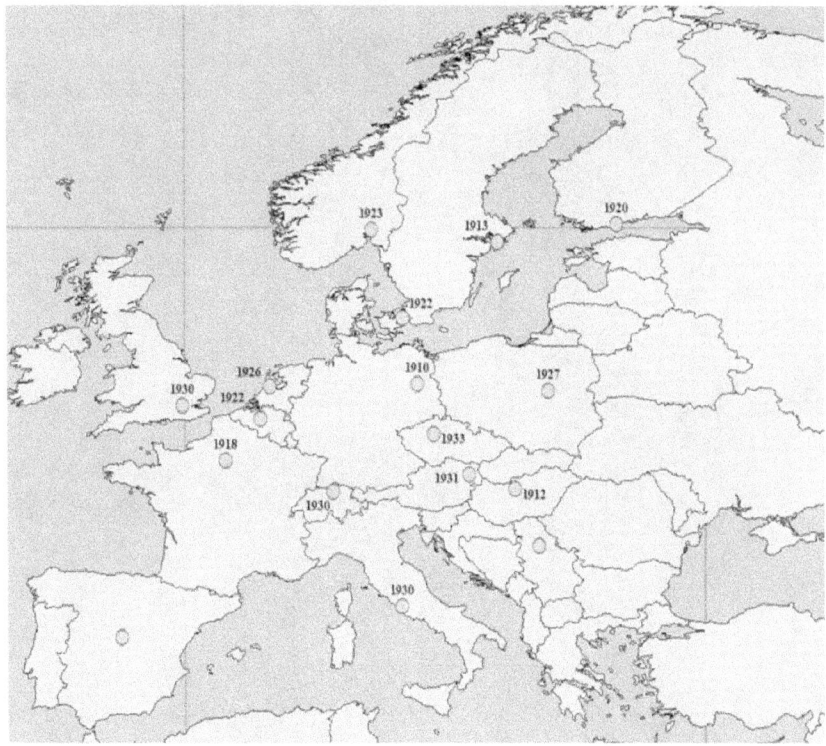

Map 18. European Deaf National Sport Associations (CISS HB, 1934)

Map 18 indicates that the earliest Deaf national sport associations appeared in Germany, Hungary, Sweden, France, Finland and Belgium. All Deaf national sport associations shown here with a definite founding date were founded prior to 1933. The two without founding dates (Spain and Yugoslavia) are listed because they are included in a list of nations whose affiliation with CISS were pending (*Liste des Nations en instance...*, n.d., p. 20), so it is assumed that CISS recognized some kind of Deaf sport organization in existence in these countries at this time.

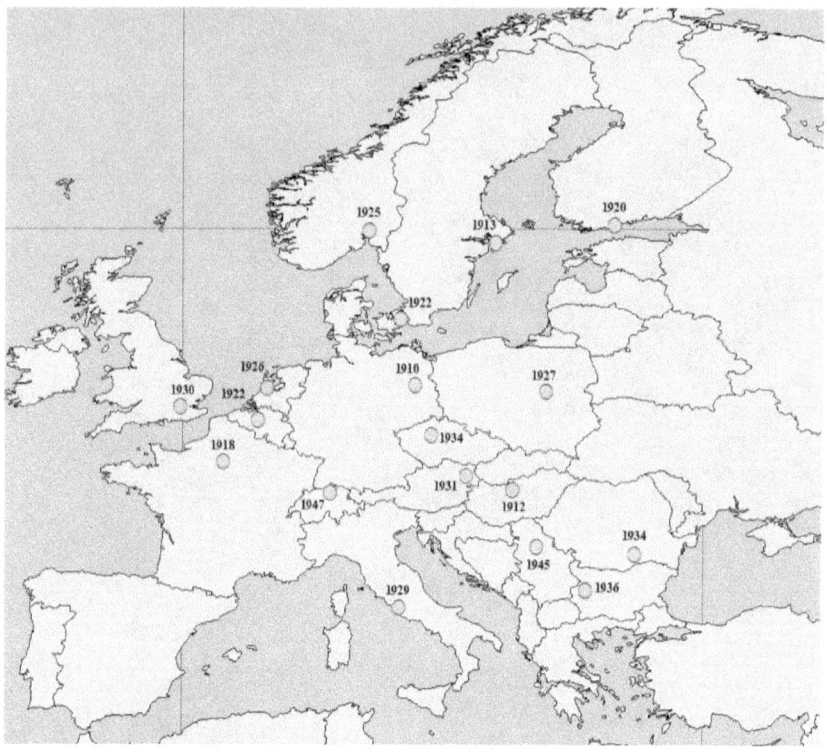

Map 19. European Deaf National Sport Associations (CISS HB, 1949)

Map 19 generally only differs slightly from Map 18 in growth in the Balkans and a change in the Swiss association's founding date. The latter merits further investigation.

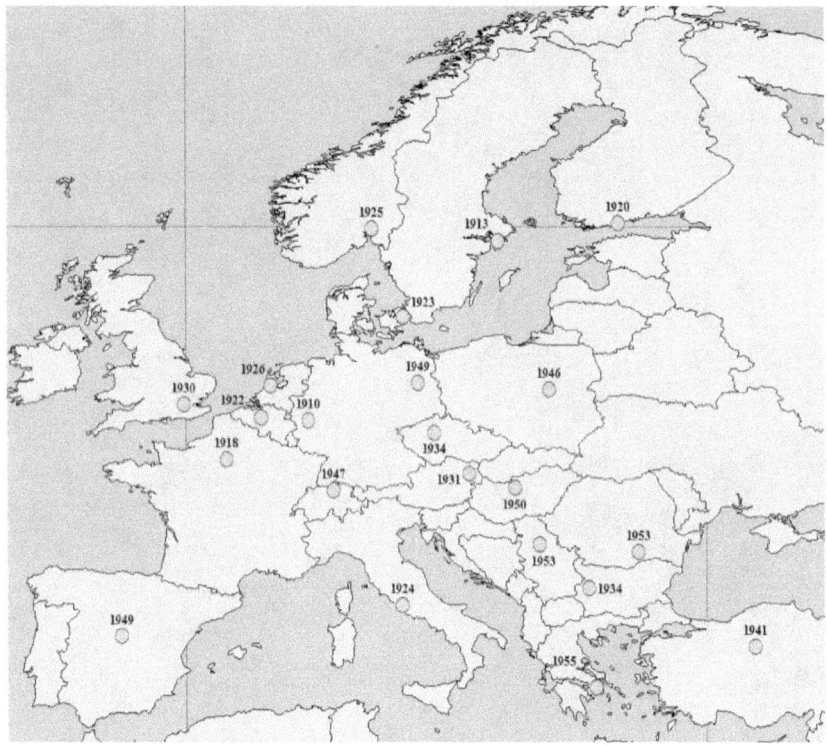

Map 20. European Deaf National Sport Associations (CISS HB, 1958)

Map 20 again generally differs only slightly from Map 19, with additions in the southeastern Balkans, the appearance of Spain and East Germany and a change in the Romanian founding date (which also merits investigation). Unfortunately, the Soviet Union data was inadvertently omitted; the founding date is given as 1926 in *CISS HB*, 1958, p. 56.

Deaf National Organizations
Each Deaf National Organization included in the data set is identified by placing a blue box where the national capital city is located (with the exception of Belgium, which has two Deaf national organizations; two separate blue boxes are placed in different parts of Belgium to distinguish between the two organizations). When known, the founding year of that Deaf National Organization is adjacent to the blue box.

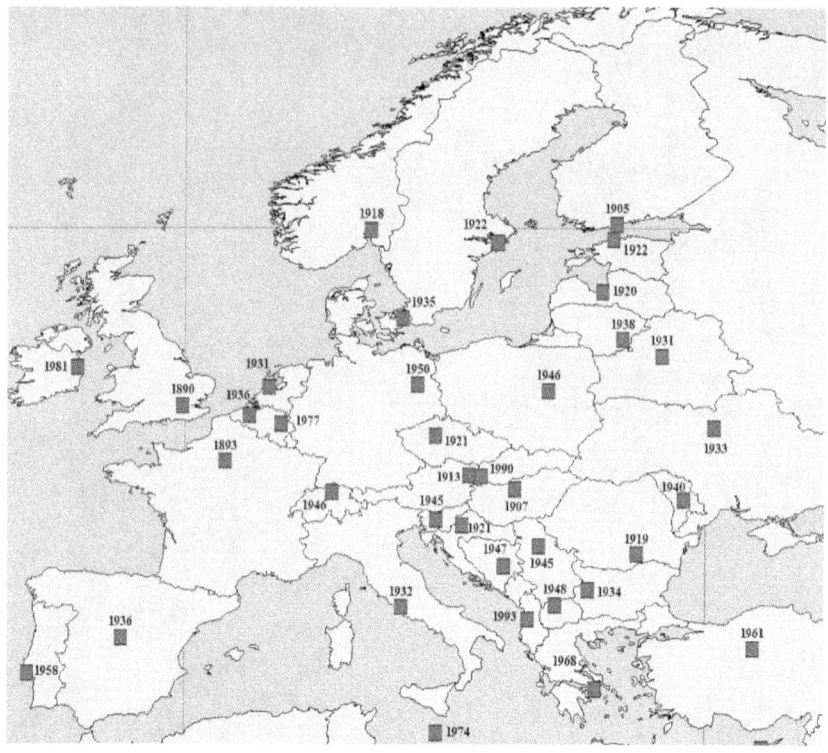

Map 21. European Deaf National Organizations (Gannon 2011)

Map 21 indicates that by 2011, virtually all European nations included in this field of view have established a Deaf national organization. The earliest Deaf national organizations are reported as Great Britain, France, and Finland. It then appears that Scandinavia, central Europe, and the Balkans gradually saw more Deaf national organizations set up with countries further away from the center of Europe, with the exception of Scandinavia and the former Soviet Union, generally establishing their Deaf national organizations later in time. It is also interesting that 1950 is listed as the founding year for the German Deaf national organization, when an earlier organization is known to have existed (Worseck, et al., 2008, p. 3, 5), thus this also merits further investigation and future modification of this map.

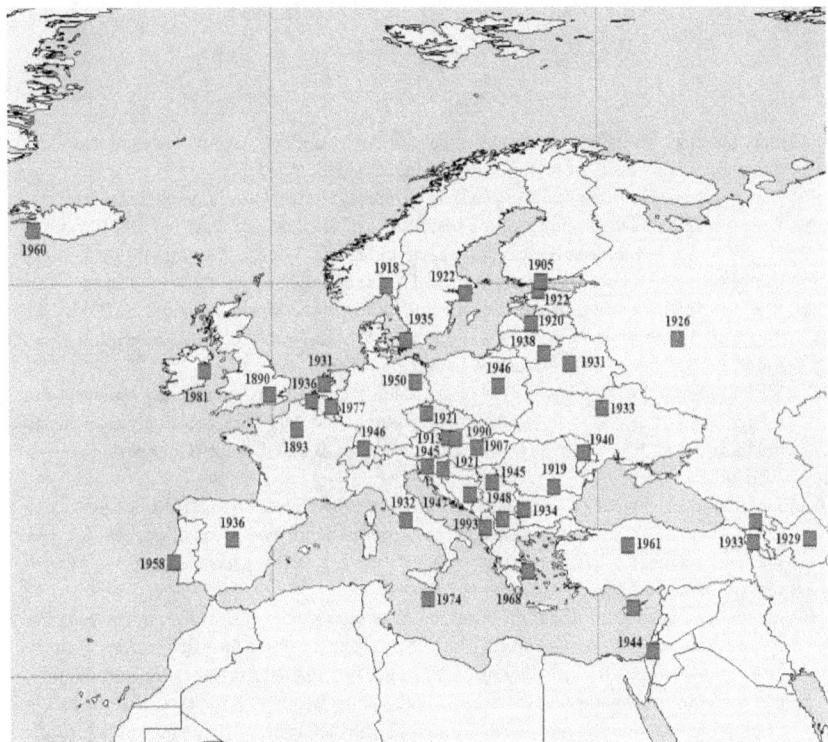

Map 22. European Deaf National Organizations (Gannon 2011)

Map 22 is the same as Map 21, except that the field of view is expanded to include Iceland, Israel, Russia, Armenia, Georgia, and Azerbaijan. Russia has the earliest founded Deaf national organization from this group.

Potential Future Directions

There are several potential future directions to pursue with the Tracing Deafhood project. These include documenting impact of heads on Deaf pillars' membership/development, identifying patterns in developed/developing countries, identifying patterns in highly/sparsely populated countries, and conducting further research into correlation of various variables!

Special Thanks
The author wishes to give special thanks to Dr. Steve Graves, Jason Mejia, Patrick Kahn, and Henry Durand, CSUN Department of Geography, for ArcGIS assistance; and Anthony Ivankovic, Christine Firkins, Gregorio Nieto, and Grady at the National Center on Deafness Library at CSUN for data collection assistance.

REFERENCES

Eickman, J. (2004). The role of deaf sport in developing Deaf identity. Unpublished doctoral dissertation, University of Bristol, Bristol, United Kingdom.

Eriksson, P. (1998). *The history of deaf people* (J. Schmale, Trans.). Örebro, Sweden: Daufr.

Fay, E. A. (1882). Tabular Statement of the Institutions of the Deaf and Dumb of the World. In Fay, E. A. (Ed.). *American Annals of the Deaf and Dumb*. Vol. 27. Washington, D.C.: The Convention of American Instructors of the Deaf and Dumb. pp. 32–53.

Fay, E. A. (1883). The Institutions for the Deaf and Dumb of the World. In Fay, E. A. (Ed.). *American Annals of the Deaf and Dumb*. Vol. 28. Washington, D.C.: The Convention of American Instructors of the Deaf and Dumb. pp. 47–61.

Finnish Museum of the Deaf. (n.d.). Carl Oscar Malm. Accessed 3-31-15 from http://www.kl-deaf.fi/Page/3b3c3115-afce-4ca7-999f-6ca74337a2ae.aspx (Note: March 16, 2010 is given as the last modification of this page at http://www.kl-deaf.fi/en-GB/searchresult/?QueryString=carl+oscar+malm)

Gannon, J. R. (2011). *World Federation of the Deaf: A History*. Silver Spring, MD: National Association of the Deaf. pp. 293–389. Note: European nations on pp. 295, 296, 298–301, 304, 306–307, 314, 315–318, 321, 324–331, 333–334, 337–339, 343, 344–345, 348, 349, 353–354, 357, 361–362, 363–365, 366–367, 369–376, 378–381, 383–385.

Histoire des Sourds. (2002a). Claudius Forestier. Accessed October 11, 2013 from http://hids.free.fr/hids/Personnage/ClaudiusForestier.htm (Note: Actual website does not indicate author or date, but by going to hids.free.fr, one obtains the copyright date, organization author and that the website is by Pierre-Yves Bagur. On the actual webpage, it indicates that the text is from the Association Etienne de Fay without any further acknowledgment. translate.google.com was used to translate the content from French to English.)

Histoire des Sourds. (2002b). David Comberry. Accessed March 30–31, 2015 from http://hids.free.fr/hids/Personnage/DavidComberry.htm (Note: Actual website does not indicate author or date, but by going to hids.free.fr, one obtains the copyright date, organization author and that the website is by Pierre-Yves Bagur. On the actual webpage, it indicates that the text is from the Association Etienne de Fay without any further acknowledgment. translate.google.com was used to translate the content from French to English.)

Jackson, P. (2001). *A pictorial history of Deaf Britain*. Winsford, England: Deafprint Winsford.

Ladd, P. (2003). *Understanding Deaf culture: In search of Deafhood*. Clevedon, United Kingdom: Multilingual Matters Ltd.

Lane, H., Hoffmeister, R., & Bahan, B. (1996). *A journey into the Deaf-world*. San Diego, CA: Dawn Sign Press.

Liste des Nations affiliées au CISS. et leurs addresses.: (Liste der dem CISS. angeschlossenen Länder und Anschrift ihrer Vereine.) (n.d.). In A. Dresse (Ed.), Comité international des sports silencieux Recueil des Renseignements Statistiques et Administratifs, 1924–1934 Internationales.

taubstummen-sport-komitee Statistische Zusammenstellung derVerwaltungsarbeiten, Satzungen und Regeln. Printer: Essen: Druckerei Siepmann. pp. 12–20. (Note: Antoine Dresse (compiler) and Heinrich Siepmann (French-German translator). I credit Dresse as the editor.)

Liste des Nations en instance d'affiliation au CISS.: Liste der noch nicht dem CISS. angeschlossenen Länder, die mit dem CISS. in Verkehr stehen. (n.d.). In A. Dresse (Ed.), Comité international des sports silencieux Recueil des Renseignements Statistiques et Administratifs 1924–1934 Internationales taubstummen-sport-komitee Statistische Zusammenstellung derVerwaltungsarbeiten, Satzungen und Regeln. Printer: Essen:

Druckerei Siepmann. p. 20. (Note: Antoine Dresse (compiler) and Heinrich Siepmann (French-German translator). I credit Dresse as the editor.)

Matthews, P. A. (1996). *The Irish Deaf Community: Volume 1: Survey Report, History of Education, Language and Culture.* Dublin: The Linguistics Institute of Ireland. (Note: Used to verify location of Claremont school on pp. 67–68.)

Nations Affiliées: avec addresses et liste de clubs: Affiliated Countries: with addresses and clubs list. (n.d.a) In *Comité international des sports silencieux Annuaire – handbook 1935–1949 (2nd ed).* Printer: Gand: L. Vanmelle, S. A. pp. 15–38. (Note: European nations on pp. 15-18, 23–38.)

Nations Affiliées: avec addresses et liste des clubs: Affiliated Countries: with addresses and clubs list. (n.d.b) In *Comite International des Sports Silencieux: Annuaire - Handbook: 1950–1958 (3rd ed.).* Gand: L. Vanmelle, S. A. pp. 9-59. (Note: European nations on pp. 9–14, 16–22, 28–39, 41–59.)

The Traveler's Atlas: A Geographic Handbook. (1996). 2nd ed. New York: Graphic Image, Inc. (Note: Alternate book title is The Traveler's Atlas (Compass Rose).

Troisième Circulaire de l'Institut Royal des Sourds-Muets de Paris, a Toutes les Institutions de Sourds-Muets de l'Europe, de l'Amérique et de l'Asie. (1832, September). Paris: Imprimerie Royale. pp. 169-175. (Note: Editor name apparently not available. Electronic version digitized by Google obtained on October 7, 2013 at http://babel.hathitrust.org/cgi/pt?id=mdp.39015063 049525;view=1up;seq=1)

Volta Bureau. (1896). *Circular of Information, No. 3: International Reports of Schools for the Deaf: Made to the Volta Bureau: December, 1895.* Washington, D.C.: Gibson Bros., Printers and Bookbinders. (Note: Electronic version, digitized by Google, obtained on October 7, 2013 at http://books.google.com/books?id=bIs4AQAAIAAJ&pg=PR3&lpg=PR3&dq=circular+of+inf ormation+no+3+volta&source=bl&ots=0GRFhsGpvv&sig=0qTXlpgPz8gFutIM3FQHNstUx 2w&hl=en&sa=X&ei=6-JSUtDKC8G1iwK8_oHIDQ&ved=0CCkQ6AEwAA#v=onepage&q= circular%20of%20information%20no%203%20volta&f=false)

Volta Bureau. (1902). *Circular of Information, No. 6: International Reports of Schools for the Deaf: Made to the Volta Bureau: January, 1901.* Washington, D.C.: Gibson Bros., Printers and Bookbinders. (Note: Electronic version, digitized by Google, obtained on October 7, 2013 at http://books.google.com/books?id=bIs4AQAAIAAJ&pg=PR3&lpg=PR3&dq=circular+of+inf ormation+no+3+volta&source=bl&ots=0GRFhsGpvv&sig=0qTXlpgPz8gFutIM3FQHNstUx 2w&hl=en&sa=X&ei=6-JSUtDKC8G1iwK8_oHIDQ&ved=0CCkQ6AEwAA#v=onepage&q= circular%20of%20information%20no%203%20volta&f=false)

Worseck, T., von Borstell, F., & Vogel, H. (2008). *Die Geschichte des Deutschen Gehörlosen-Bundes e.V.* Publisher appears to be Deutscher Gehörlosen-Bund e.V. Accessed March 31, 2015 from http://www.gehoerlosen-bund.de/images/stories/pdfs/dgbhistorie2008.pdf. (Note: Used translate.google.com on March 31, 2015 to translate partial content for needed information from German into English. Date assumed to be 2008 from weblink name.)

Research Tools

https://translate.google.com. Used to assist in city name translations/identifications and to understand source material not written in English.

http://www.findlatitudeandlongitude.com/batch-geocode. Used to batch geocode latitude and longitude of pillar locations.

http://www.wikipedia.org. Used to determine locations and names of cities listed in source data with different names than they have today.

References used to determine location of cities/locations known by different names:
(Note: Tabular presentation is used for convenience, to save space, and to quickly direct interested persons to the correct website; multiple references are shown for certain locations as they were used to make an overall choice on the best placement for each location on the map or location name for geocoding purposes)

City	Old Name	Website(s)	accessed
	Aachen	http://en.wikipedia.org/wiki/Aachen	4/8/2014
	Aachen	http://en.wikipedia.org/wiki/Rhine_Province	4/8/2014
	Alger	http://en.wikipedia.org/w/index.php?search=Alger%2C+France&title=Special%3ASearch&go=Go	4/8/2014
	Alger	http://en.wikipedia.org/wiki/Alger_(department)	4/8/2014
	Alger	http://en.wikipedia.org/wiki/Algiers	4/8/2014
Anklam	Anclam	http://en.wikipedia.org/wiki/Anklam	11/21/2013
Anklam, Germany	Anklam	http://en.wikipedia.org/wiki/Anclam	4/4/2014
Ansbach	Auspach	http://en.wikipedia.org/wiki/Ansbach accessed 11/21/13	11/21/2013
Barciany, Poland	Barmen	http://en.wikipedia.org/wiki/Barten	11/21/2013
Barciany, Poland	Barmen	http://en.wikipedia.org/wiki/List_of_cities_and_towns_in_East_Prussia	11/21/2013
Barmen		http://en.wikipedia.org/wiki/Barmen	4/4/2014
Barmen, Germany	Barmen	http://en.wikipedia.org/wiki/Barmen	4/4/2014?
Berlin		http://en.wikipedia.org/wiki/Berlin	4/4/2014
Braniewo, Poland	Braunsberg	http://en.wikipedia.org/wiki/Braunsberg	4/4/2014
Brühl, Germany		http://en.wikipedia.org/wiki/Br%C3%BChl	4/4/2014
Brühl, Germany		http://en.wikipedia.org/wiki/Br%C3%BChl_(Rhineland)	4/4/2014
Brühl, Germany		http://en.wikipedia.org/wiki/Br%C3%BChl_(Baden)	4/4/2014
Buchholz (Alternate to Wąsosz, Poland)	Bruchhof	http://en.wikipedia.org/w/index.php?search=Principality+of+Lippe-Schauenbourg&title=Special%3ASearch	11/21/2013
Buchholz (Alternate to Wąsosz, Poland)	Bruchhof	http://en.wikipedia.org/wiki/Principality_of_Schaumburg-Lippe	11/21/2013
Buchholz (Alternate to Wąsosz, Poland)	Bruchhof	http://en.wikipedia.org/wiki/Lower_Saxony	11/21/2013
Buchholz (Alternate to Wąsosz, Poland)	Bruchhof	http://en.wikipedia.org/wiki/Schaumburg_Land	11/21/2013
Buchholz (Alternate to Wąsosz, Poland)	Bruchhof	http://en.wikipedia.org/wiki/Landkreis_Schaumburg	11/21/2013
Büren	Bueren	http://en.wikipedia.org/wiki/B%C3%BCren_(Westfalen)	11/21/2013
Büren	Bueren	http://en.wikipedia.org/wiki/German_cities	11/21/2013
Büren	Bueren	http://en.wikipedia.org/wiki/Bueren	11/21/2013

Büren, Germany		http://en.wikipedia.org/wiki/Bueren	4/4/2014
Büren, Germany		http://en.wikipedia.org/wiki/B%C3%BCren,_Westphalia	4/4/2014
Büren, Germany		http://en.wikipedia.org/wiki/Lotte,_Germany	4/4/2014
Büren, Germany		http://en.wikipedia.org/wiki/Neustadt_am_R%C3%BCbenberge	4/4/2014
Büren, Germany		http://en.wikipedia.org/wiki/B%C3%BCren_(Neustadt_am_R%C3%BCbenberge)	4/4/2014
Cologne		http://en.wikipedia.org/wiki/Cologne	4/4/2014
Człuchów, Poland	Schlochau	http://en.wikipedia.org/wiki/Schlochau	4/4/2014
Elbląg, Poland	Elbing	http://en.wikipedia.org/wiki/Elbing	4/4/2014
Erfurt, Germany		http://en.wikipedia.org/wiki/Erfurt	4/4/2014
Gdańsk, Poland	Danzig	http://en.wikipedia.org/wiki/Danzig	4/4/2014
Gorizia, Italy	Gorz	http://en.wikipedia.org/wiki/Gorizia	11/7/2013
Grudziądz, Poland	Graudenz	http://en.wikipedia.org/wiki/Graudenz	4/4/2014
	Gumpetan	http://en.wikipedia.org/w/index.php?search=Gumpetan&title=Special%3ASearch&go=Go	4/8/2014
	Gumpetan	http://en.wikipedia.org/w/index.php?search=Gumpetan%2C+Sweden&title=Special%3ASearch&go=Go	4/8/2014
	Gumpetan	http://en.wikipedia.org/w/index.php?search=Gumpeten%2C+Sweden&title=Special%3ASearch&go=Go	4/8/2014
	Gumpetan	http://en.wikipedia.org/w/index.php?search=Gumpeten&title=Special%3ASearch&go=Go	4/8/2014
	Gumpetan	http://en.wikipedia.org/wiki/Kil,_V%C3%A4rmland	4/8/2014?
	Gumpetan	http://en.wikipedia.org/w/index.php?title=Special%3ASearch&profile=default&search=Kil%2C+Sweden&fulltext=Search	4/8/2014?
	Gumpetan	http://en.wikipedia.org/w/index.php?title=Special%3ASearch&profile=default&search=Kil&fulltext=Search	4/8/2014?
	Gumpetan	http://en.wikipedia.org/wiki/Kil_Municipality	4/8/2014?
	Gumpetan	http://en.wikipedia.org/wiki/V%C3%A4rmland_County	4/8/2014?
	Gumpetan	http://en.wikipedia.org/wiki/Grums_Municipality	4/8/2014?
Halberstadt, Germany		http://en.wikipedia.org/wiki/Halberstadt	4/4/2014
Jelgava, Latvia	Mitau	http://en.wikipedia.org/wiki/Mitau	4/8/2014
Jelgava, Latvia	Mitau	http://en.wikipedia.org/wiki/List_of_German_names_for_Latvian_places#F (correct apparent error, this is listed under Knopia, Finland)	11/7/2013

Kaliningrad, Russia	Königsberg	http://en.wikipedia.org/wiki/K%C3%B6nigsberg	4/4/2014
Kikinda, Serbia		http://en.wikipedia.org/wiki/Kikinda	4/8/2014
Königsberg	Koenigsburg	http://en.wikipedia.org/wiki/K%C3%B6nigsberg	11/21/2013
Königsberg	Koenigsburg	http://en.wikipedia.org/wiki/German_cities	11/21/2013
Königsberg	Koenigsburg	wiki search for Koenigsburg directed to Königsberg page; replicated search on 3/31/2015 at http://en.wikipedia.org/w/index.php?title=Special%3ASearch&profile=default&search=Koenigsburg&fulltext=Search and got first hit as http://en.wikipedia.org/wiki/K%C3%B6nigsberg which is the same webpage as the first Koenigsburg entry listed above	11/21/2013 & 3/31/2015
Kosovska Mitrovica, Kosovo		http://en.wikipedia.org/wiki/Kosovska_Mitrovica	4/8/2014
Kosovska Mitrovica, Kosovo		http://en.wikipedia.org/w/index.php?search=Kosovska+Mitrovica%2C+Serbia&title=Special%3ASearch&go=Go	4/8/2014
Krefeld	Crefeld	http://en.wikipedia.org/wiki/Crefeld	11/21/2013
Krefeld, Germany	Crefeld	http://en.wikipedia.org/wiki/Crefeld	4/4/2014
Kristiansand	Christiansland?	http://en.wikipedia.org/wiki/Kristiansand	10/3/2013
Legnica, Poland	Liegnitz	http://en.wikipedia.org/wiki/Liegnitz	4/5/2014
Magdeburg, Germany		http://en.wikipedia.org/wiki/Magdeburg	4/4/2014
Malbork, Poland	Marienburg	http://en.wikipedia.org/wiki/Marienburg	4/4/2014
Malbork, Poland	Marienburg	http://en.wikipedia.org/wiki/Malbork	4/4/2014
Malbork, Poland	Marienburg	http://en.wikipedia.org/wiki/Al%C5%ABksne	4/4/2014
Malbork, Poland	Marienburg	http://en.wikipedia.org/wiki/Feldioara	4/4/2014
Meersburg, Germany		http://en.wikipedia.org/wiki/Meersburg	4/5/2014
Mikkeli, Finland	St. Michel	http://en.wikipedia.org/wiki/List_of_Latin_place_names_in_Continental_Europe,_Ireland_and_Scandinavia#Cities_and_towns_in_Finland	4/8/2014
Mikkeli, Finland	St. Michel	http://en.wikipedia.org/w/index.php?search=St.+Michels%2C+Finland&title=Special%3ASearch&go=Go	4/8/2014
Mikkeli, Finland	St. Michel	http://en.wikipedia.org/wiki/Mikkeli	4/8/2014
Münster, Germany		http://en.wikipedia.org/wiki/M%C3%Bcnster	4/4/2014
Oliwa, Poland	Oliva	http://en.wikipedia.org/wiki/Oliwa	4/4/2014
Pedersore		http://en.wikipedia.org/wiki/Pedersore	4/8/2014
Pedersöre (municipality)	Pedersôre	http://en.wikipedia.org/w/index.php?search=Peders%C3%B4re&title=Special%3ASearch&go=Go	4/8/2014
Pedersöre (municipality)	Pedersôre	http://en.wikipedia.org/wiki/Peders%C3%B6re	4/8/2014

Pétershagen, Germany		http://en.wikipedia.org/wiki/Petershagen	4/4/2014
Piła, Poland	Schneidemühl	http://en.wikipedia.org/wiki/Schneidem%C3%BChl	4/5/2014
	Polva, Belarus?	http://en.wikipedia.org/w/index.php?title=Special%3ASearch&profile=default&search=Polva%2C+Belarus&fulltext=Search	3/31/2015
Põlva, Estonia	Polva, Estonia?	http://en.wikipedia.org/wiki/P%C3%B5lva	3/31/2015
	Polva, Estonia?	http://en.wikipedia.org/w/index.php?title=Special%3ASearch&profile=default&search=Polva%2C+Estonia&fulltext=Search	3/31/2015
	Polva, Latvia?	http://en.wikipedia.org/w/index.php?title=Special%3ASearch&profile=default&search=Polva%2C+Latvia&fulltext=Search	3/31/2015
	Polva, Lithuania?	http://en.wikipedia.org/w/index.php?title=Special%3ASearch&profile=default&search=Polva%2C+Lithuania&fulltext=Search	3/31/2015
	Polva, Russia?	http://en.wikipedia.org/w/index.php?title=Special%3ASearch&profile=default&search=Polva%2C+Russia&fulltext=Search	3/31/2015
	Polwa, Belarus?	http://en.wikipedia.org/w/index.php?title=Special%3ASearch&profile=default&search=Polwa%2C+Belarus&fulltext=Search	3/31/2015
	Polwa, Estonia?	http://en.wikipedia/org/w/index.php?title=Special%3ASearch&profile=default&search=Polwa%2C+Estonia&fulltext=Search	3/31/2015
	Polwa, Latvia?	http://en.wikipedia.org/w/index.php?title=Special%3ASearch&profile=default&search=Polwa%2C+Latvia&fulltext=Search	3/31/2015
	Polwa, Lithuania?	http://en.wikipedia.org/w/index.php?title=Special%3ASearch&profile=default&search=Polwa%2C+Lithuania&fulltext=Search	3/31/2015
	Polwa, Livonia	Polva, Estonia or Polva, Russia. Tried other former Soviet Republics in same area, with no success. Changed all spellings back to Polwa and got success but different coordinates with Estonia, Belarus, and Russia. Going with Estonian one as think would be closest to Livonia plus same coordinates if Polwa or Polva. Note: Repeated search as best as could do on 3/31/15 as data for this search was lost. Confirmed that this location is probably best placed in Estonia, although the map was already constructed using Polwa, Estonia coordinates, rather than Polva, Estonia.	Lost initial date for search; Repeated on 3/31/15
	Polwa, Russia?	http://en.wikipedia.org/w/index.php?title=Special%3ASearch&profile=default&search=Polwa%2C+Russia&fulltext=Search	3/31/2015
Poznań, Poland	Posen	http://en.wikipedia.org/wiki/Posen	4/5/2014
Poznań, Poland	Posen	http://en.wikipedia.org/wiki/Pozna%C5%84	4/5/2014
Quedlinburg, Germany		http://en.wikipedia.org/wiki/Quedlinburg	4/4/2014

Racibórz, Poland	Ratibor	http://en.wikipedia.org/wiki/Racib%C3%B3rz	4/5/2014
	Rephutt	http://en.wikipedia.org/w/index.php?search=Rephutt&title=Special%3ASearch&go=Go	4/8/2014
	Rephutt	http://en.wikipedia.org/w/index.php?search=Rephutt%2C+Sweden&title=Special%3ASearch&go=Go	4/8/2014
	Rephutt	http://en.wikipedia.org/w/index.php?search=Rephult%2C+Sweden&title=Special%3ASearch&go=Go	4/8/2014
	Rephutt	http://en.wikipedia.org/w/index.php?title=Special%3ASearch&profile=default&search=Rephult&fulltext=Search	4/8/2014
Reszel, Poland	Rossel	http://en.wikipedia.org/wiki/Rossel	4/5/2014 & 4/8/2014
Reszel, Poland	Rossel	http://en.wikipedia.org/wiki/Reszel	11/7/2013 & 4/5/2014 & 4/8/2014
Reszel, Poland	Rossel	http://en.wikipedia.org/wiki/Warmia	11/7/2013 & 4/5/2014 & 4/8/2014
Reszel, Poland	Rossel	http://en.wikipedia.org/w/index.php?search=Rossel%2C+Prussia&title=Special%3ASearch	11/7/2013
	Schleswig	http://en.wikipedia.org/wiki/Schleswig,_Schleswig-Holstein	4/4/2014 & 4/8/2014
	Schleswig	http://en.wikipedia.org/wiki/Schleswig	4/8/2014
	Schleswig	http://en.wikipedia.org/w/index.php?search=Schleswig%2C+Denmark&title=Special%3ASearch&go=Go	4/8/2014
	Schleswig	http://en.wikipedia.org/wiki/Schleswig,_Germany	4/8/2014
Senta, Serbia		http://en.wikipedia.org/wiki/Senta	4/8/2014
Senta, Serbia		http://en.wikipedia.org/w/index.php?search=Senta%2C+Croatia&title=Special%3ASearch&go=Go	4/8/2014
Sovetsk, Russia	Tilsit	http://en.wikipedia.org/wiki/Tilsit	4/4/2014
Speyer	Spire	http://en.wikipedia.org/wiki/Speyer accessed 11/21/13	11/21/2013
Szczecin, Poland	Stettin	http://en.wikipedia.org/wiki/Szczecin	4/4/2014
Vändra, Estonia	Fennern	http://en.wikipedia.org/wiki/List_of_German_exonyms_for_places_in_Estonia; "Alt-Fennern" translated as Old-Fennern (at translate.google.com on 11-7-13?)	11/7/13?
Wąsosz, Poland	Bruchhof	http://en.wikipedia.org/wiki/W%C4%85sosz_(disambiguation)	11/21/13?
Wąsosz, Poland	Bruchhof	http://en.wikipedia.org/wiki/W%C4%85sosz,_West_Pomeranian_Voivodeship	11/21/13?

Węgorzewo	Angerberg	http://en.wikipedia.org/wiki/East_Prussia	4/4/2014
Węgorzewo, Poland	Angerburg	http://en.wikipedia.org/wiki/Angerburg	4/4/2014
Weissenfels, Germany		http://en.wikipedia.org/wiki/Weissenfels	4/4/2014
	Wriezen	http://en.wikipedia.org/wiki/Wriezen	4/5/2014
Wrocław, Poland	Breslau	http://en.wikipedia.org/wiki/Breslau	4/4/2014
Zlín, Czech Republic	Gottwaldov	http://en.wikipedia.org/wiki/Zl%C3%ADn	4/8/2014
Zlín, Czech Republic	Gottwaldov	http://en.wikipedia.org/w/index.php?search=Zl%C3%ADn%2C+Slovakia&title=Special%3ASearch&go=Go	4/8/2014
Zlín, Czech Republic	Gottwaldov	http://en.wikipedia.org/wiki/Gottwaldov	4/8/2014
Zlín, Czech Republic	Gottwaldov	http://en.wikipedia.org/wiki/List_of_historical_German_and_Czech_names_for_places_in_the_Czech_Republic	4/8/2014

Writing a Visual Language: A Method for Writing Signed Languages

MARY SHAWVER

"The crucial factor that promotes or hinders success in today's society is the ability to access, understand, and use different types of information. Our job as educators is to help students develop the appropriate attitudes, knowledge, and skills that will enable them to become proficient readers and writers" (Cooney, Good-Muir, Luckner, Sebald & Young, p. 456)

IMAGINE A DAY WHEN OUR DEAF CHILDREN PICK UP A BOOK AND READ with ease the story before them. Their mind leaps through page after page excited to see what stories unfold. However, instead of bounds of success, many deaf students struggle to read and write. This difficulty confounds practitioners and other professionals as an educational community gropes for a method that will serve as a key to unlock the wealth of knowledge kept captive within the sounds of the page. Frequently reported literacy issues relating to deaf and hard of hearing students are partially caused by the discrepancy between an incomplete spoken language and a speech-based reading system (Mayer, 2007, p. 412). But, what if the deaf didn't need those sounds. Writing is visual, right? What if the deaf child's own innate language could unfold the mysteries held within the page.

The goal is to create a system for teaching the deaf to read and write by using an ASL orthography, namely the system contained in *Writing a Visual Language: A method for writing signed languages.* By combining current best practices with the new ASL orthography, a system to teach ASL reading and writing can be realized. This requires that we scaffold instruction to the deaf by using a written form of ASL. "But as native sign languages do not have widely accepted forms, deaf students cannot acquire these literacy skills in their first language to transfer in the written form of a second spoken language." (Mayer & Akamatsu, 1999, p. 2)

Writing a Visual Language: A method for writing signed languages describes an orthography, Deaf Write, designed for the native signer. The system uses the visual representation of sign language by incorporating the different parameters and features necessary to read and write the equivalent information communicated with sign production. The orthography uses common media, a keyboard. This study will review the symbols and basic word development from this orthography, and then identify if a written word in ASL would have production equivalence with readers who were unfamiliar with sign language.

Data was collected from two college students who were taught at different times; lessons were given privately. Non-signers were chosen, because someone learning the orthography who is unfamiliar with American Sign Language would evaluate the writing system based on the method presented and read a true representation of the written word. Their sign production of the written word would provide data as to whether an anticipated sign production would be equivalent or deviate for each of the written words. The results for both students found similar information for basic word production, but for simplicity, this analysis will describe the findings from the research done with just one of the students. ASL production combined with ASL orthography will hopefully give way to a written form of ASL that is easy to write, read, learn, and use, promoting free expression and literacy.

DEFINING THE CHARACTERS

Specific keyboard symbols are paired to the different parameters of ASL by character selection. This process involved giving special consideration to potential outcomes. The choices made for assigning keys on the keyboard needed to be evaluated in terms of ease and accuracy with creating words. Evaluation of sign parameters and symbol correlation were based on five main considerations: Iconic Selection, Familiar Concepts, Patterned Methods, Functional Variance and Ergonomic Choices.

Iconic Selection
First, selections needed to be made by choosing symbol representation that would associate a visual image with the selection. By being conscious of what visual representation might be inherent in a keyboard character, iconic symbols were chosen. Keys that have a conceptual or inherent meaning promote comprehension of the writing system. For example, the arrow symbol (<) represents the arrow pointing to the non-dominant side. This is iconic

for assisting in palm orientation. An example of a conceptual representation includes the ampersand symbol (&), which joins features to convey that signed parts occur simultaneously.

Familiar Concepts
Building on this idea of familiar concepts, manual alphabet characters allow users to pull from what they already know.

Patterned Methods
Considerations were also made to find patterned methods that could be easily repeated in constructing written words. Visual repetition of numbered grids was established, and these pattern grids were repeated in several areas: the hand, arm, head, and body locators. This repetition of the grid also repeated within itself; this made the ability to pinpoint locations easier than having a straight count of 729 areas within a grid.

Functional Variance
Obviously, the choice made to correlate the keys to the sign language parameters had to be done in such a way that the character was flexible enough to allow for functionality variance. An example of a selection with this consideration occurred with the handshapes association to letters. Capital letters correlate to the Head Locator area, and lower case letters correlate to the Body Locator area. This gave functional clarity to the grid areas. Functionality took precedence in the overall decisions. The symbols needed to be placed in an order that would line up in such a way that ease of accurately reading the different characters was achieved. The variance needed to include flexibility that would allow for details to be signed with precision.

Ergonomic Choice
Finally an effort was made to create ergonomic choices so that ease of typing the information in ASL would be achieved. Consideration was given to commonly used features in ASL so that the writer would be able to type with minimal movements.

PARAMETERS

Handshapes
An obvious resolve for grouping letters is to use the alphabet for the handshapes. The manual alphabet was easily identified, however other significant handshapes also needed to be represented. Classifiers and numbers needed to take on handshapes that did not have a direct correlation to the keys like

the manual alphabet. In order to accommodate this difference, digraphs were used and the paired letters assigned a new meaning. A 'wy', for instance, became a representation of the '5' handshape. This was done for several handshapes. All handshapes became a part of the letter keys. Currently, there are about fifty primary handshapes listed. This list is not exhaustive; new handshapes may be added to this list as they are deemed necessary and useful.

Location
The next parameter to address was location. Location must be precise to the size of the fingertip; signed languages use space in explaining details. This parameter includes several areas encompassing the signing area. The location parameter was expanded to identify the 3D space. The graphs show a 3D figure to assist in identifying specific areas. This 3D space is also incorporated in zones.

Zones. Measurements of space that are incrementally identified by moving in hand lengths forward from the body, are defined as *zones* (see Figure 1).
- **Proximal Zone.** The first zone is determined by placing a '5' or 'wy' handshape on the center of your chest. The distance away from your body between your thumb to your pinky is zone one, called the *Fine Zone*. This proximal zone extends outward and in a parallel plane in front of the body. Zone 1 or the *Fine Zone* is considered the default zone, so no keyboard character is given to identify this space.
- **Medial Zone.** The second zone or *Car 1 Zone* is identified by starting at the end of the Fine Zone and moving forward the distance from your wrist to the end of your longest finger. This medial zone is represented by using the apostrophe '.
- **Distal Zone.** The third zone or *Car 2 Zone* begins at the end of the Car 1 Zone. It is also the distance from your wrist to the end of your longest finger. This distal zone is represented by using the symbol ".

Writing a Visual Language: A Method for Writing Signed Languages

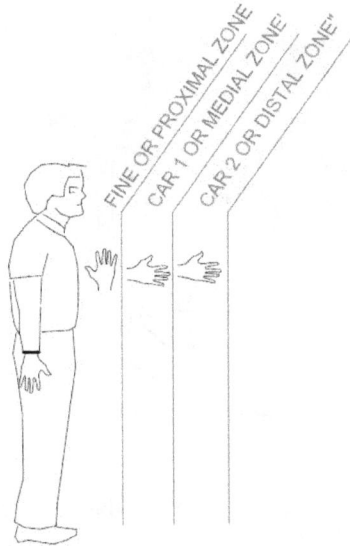

Figure 1. The Zone indicator

These three zones make up the area in front of your head and body by going out to the length of your arm with a slightly bent elbow. This gives the sign depth; it adds the 3D element.

Body Locations. A numbering system that works like a grid is used to define the area in front of the body and to the sides of the body. The grid incorporates nine main sections. The area chosen within the grid extends to outer regions of the body. It should be noted here, that the area at and below the knees can be added by using the bar symbol '|' prior to identifying the grid in front of the legs and feet. This grid would be available to use when needed, but the tendency would be to use this grid in gesturing more often than signed communication. Also the back of the head and body can be identified by incorporating the letter 'Zz' to identify this area in the rare occasions that it may be needed. Once the main nine areas are identified, another equal division of nine squares is made within each of the nine main sections. These nine squares get divided a third time (see Figure 2). This allows for 729 specific areas to be identified in the sign space directly in front of and adjacent to the body. When identifying a specific spot on the grid, you start by calling out the biggest square. For example, the heart is in the large/main **2** square. The second set of squares show that the heart is within the number **6** box. This would be written **26**. Finally, the third set of squares pinpoint the heart's location in the center area on the left pectoral muscle. Hence, the heart location is called out as **265**.

Figure 2. Body locator grid   Figure 3. Head locator grid

Head Locators. Head Locators work in a similar fashion as the Body Locators (see Figure 3). For example, in this Head Locator grid, the dominant eye is **548**, the nondominant eye is **568**, the chin is **858** and so on.

Hand and Arm Locators. The final locator area to define is the hand and arm. The hand is divided into several sections.

Finger Locators. These areas include the sides of the fingers, the areas between and including the knuckles, and the identification of the fingers themselves (see Figure 4).

- **Finger Sides Identifiers.** The sides of the fingers are identified by the numbers 1–3. The first area is the inside or palm side of the finger. This is the assumed part of the finger, so no number is assigned to this part. Next to the inside of the finger, on the radial side or the side closest to the body, is side number **1**. The back of the finger is **2**, and the side farthest away from the body or ulnar side is identified as number **3**.
- **Knuckle and Division Markers**. The area between the knuckles are differentiated by using the letter(s) 'N' and/or 'n' in different combinations. The base of the finger to the bottom knuckle is represented with a lowercase 'n.' Moving up the finger to the medial area, that section is identified with both a capital 'N' and a lowercase 'n,' namely 'Nn.' The upper section of the finger or distal area is defined with a capital 'N', and the tip of the finger is represented with two capital 'N's, namely 'NN.'
- **Finger Identifier.** The final part of the finger locator method includes identifying which finger will be used in the sign. The fingers are numbered starting with the index finger as number **1**; **2** is the middle finger. **3** is the ring finger, and **4** is the little finger or pinky. The thumb is **5**.

Writing a Visual Language: A Method for Writing Signed Languages

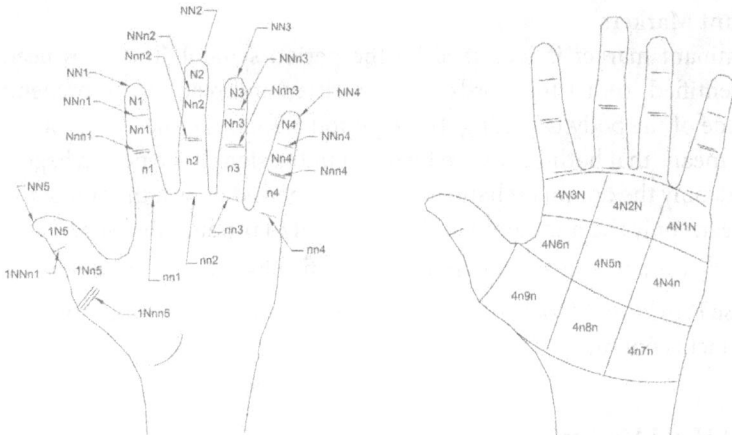

Figure 4. Finger locator. Front of hand view. Figure 5. Hand locator. Front of hand view.

Hand Locators. The remaining hand areas need to be defined.

- **Hand Identifier.** This part of the hand area is first identified by the number 4.
- **Hand Division Markers.** The distal area of the hand or the back of the hand is identified by the letter combinations namely NN, Nn and nn. The grid is used to identify a specific square on the palmar or dorsal area of the hand. The grid number is written between the N's to show the specific place on the palm (see Figure 5). The letters are also placed in the same position as the finger locators, namely NN, Nn, and nn. This is done to simplify the writing.
- **Hand Side Indicator.** The sides of the palm are identified by the numbers 1–3. The first area is the palm. This is the assumed part of the palm, so no number is assigned to this part. Next to the inside of the palm, on the radial side, is labeled with the number **1**. The dorsal or back of the hand is **2**, and the side farthest away from the body or ulnar side is identified as **3**.

The arm is a continuum of the same method as used to identify the hand. It begins with the wrist, and it works its way up to the shoulder. These parts include: the locators for the wrist **5**, forearm **6**, and elbow **7**. The tricep/bicep **8**, and shoulder **9** can be identified in this same method, or by using the Body Locator grid.

Dominant Markers

The dominant marker is identified by the period symbol. The sides need to be identified so that the words can be written and read to comprehend which side of the body is signing. If the period is found in the center of the word, it means that both hands are involved in the sign. If the period begins the word, only the dominant hand is signing. A period only at the end of the word means only the nondominant hand is used to produce the word.

- *Touch Marker.* The touch marker is identified by the colon : symbol.
- *Close Proximity Marker.* This is used the same way as the touch, but contact is not made. The symbol is the asterisk *.

Referent Hand Marker

The referent hand is identified by the **0** symbol. A referent hand stays stationary. It is used to assist the 'reader' in identifying previously given information that remains constant.

Palm Orientation Markers

There are six main palm orientations:

=   Palm In
+   Palm Out
<   Palm Face Toward Nondominant
>   Palm Face Toward Dominant
-     Palm Down
_   Palm Up

Shift Marker

The shift marker is identified by the comma , . The shift is used to identify different stages of signing a word. The comma is used to aid the reader in making these shifts. It breaks the sign into syllables.

Movement Markers

The way a sign is being produced determines if the sign has movement or instead, it has a shift of location, palm orientation, or handshape. These shifts may look like movements, but for this orthography, a movement happens in a more localized area. This would include an isolated movement, or a movement that occurs during a shift. The symbols for movement include the following two keys.

~   Wiggle fingers: a flutter motion of the fingers
@   Arc or circle movements: changes in location that do not connect from the first position to the second position in a straight line.

When the @ symbol is used, it informs the reader that the hand will be making an arc or circular movement in space. The locations that are placed between the @ symbols are the points that need to be located within the arc. If there is only one point given, that means that the hand circles at one point. The default for this movement is a movement circling toward the dominant side of the body.

Frozen Text Marker

The keyboard is convenient for writing lexicalized words that are fingerspelled. The Manual Alphabet pairs with the keyboard, so fingerspelled words can be typed just as they are written in English, Spanish, French, and so on. This ability to switch to a fingerspelled word can be done at any time; it can also be used with any character on the keyboard. For example instead of writing out longhand .wy1+ you could write {5} instead. These curly brackets around the 5 are the frozen text markers.

Timing Markers

Timing can be identified in two different ways. The first way creates a timing option by speeding up the signing. This option is done in lieu of the comma or shift marker. This symbol is represented by the semi colon ;. Parenthesis ( ) are used to show that a section of the sign needs to be repeated. This helps in writing repetitive parts of a sign.

Non Manual Marker (NMM)

Using the same considerations as listed for the Manual Markers, the NMMs were developed. One way of isolating a locator is to use the brackets][to specify a physical feature. For example the eyes can be specified by using the locations for the eyes **56** and **54**. The eyes can be further distinguished by using the dominance marker, e.g., **56.54**.

Now, suppose that the eye gaze shifted from looking at the person you are signing to, to setting up space. This change in eye gaze would be shown by first isolating the eyes with the location marker as in this example [**56.54**]; next to these parentheses is the second part of the location identifier where the number associated to the direction the eyes are shifted is written.

For this part, the location is divided into the area as it relates to an assumed forward position. These NMM locators are structured by coordinating two points of variance. Both of these variances range from one to seven. The first number identifies the direction from the dominant to the nondominant side by counting in equal increments from **1** to **7**. Number **4** is the area directly in front of the signer and the assumed position (see Figure 6).

Figure 6. The positions dominant to non-dominant

Figure 7. The positions of NMMs up to down

Using the same principle, increments are established from the highest overhead position down to the floor numbering from 1 to 7. These two number sets of seven can be used together. The first number will identify the horizontal direction and the second number the vertical. Assuming to our previous example, I again establish what feature will be doing the action, the eyes, by writing [56.54]. Then by adding the number next to it, I write where the eyes are looking. Suppose I am looking slightly to my dominant side; I would write [56.54]3. If I am looking slightly to my dominant side and slightly downward, I would write [56.54]35. This can also be done with movement at joints. For example, the head (at neck) and body (at waist) can be positioned this way (see Figure 7).

The tongue and eyebrows play an important role in communicating facial NMMs:

!   the tongue
?   lowered eyebrows
/   represents raised eyebrows

These symbols are initiated at the point in the sentence or question when the NMM would begin and are marked again in the notation at the end of the duration. This feature is used in a similar way to how quotes are used in the English language. *Writing a Visual Language: A method for writing signed languages* has an entire chapter dedicated to writing NMMs.

READING WORDS IN ASL

The order of the parameters for a basic word is $H(l)(z)LPD(t/c)H(l)(z)LPS$. These initials represent words that coincide to parts of the sign. These basic word parameters are listed below. The breakdown here is limited and does not include the full extent that the signed word can be broken down. Again, *Writing a Visual Language: A method for writing signed languages* has dedicated several chapters to this topic, but for the purpose of this summary, this initial break-down can assist with writing basic words:

H   Handshape for the nondominant hand including the capitalization for the (l) locator identifier,
L   Location as found on the correlating grid after the (z) zone is identified for where to put the nondominant hand
P   Palm orientation for the direction the nondominant hand is facing
D(t) Dominance and (t) touch identifier. This marker separates the dominant hand from the nondominant.
H   Handshape for the dominant hand including the capitalization for the (l) locator identifier
L   Location as found on the correlating grid after the (z) zone is identified showing where to put your dominant hand.
P   Palm orientation for the direction the dominant hand is facing
S   Shift for the change in one of the parameters of the sign

An example of a word with a shift is $H(l)(z)LPDH(l)(z)LPSTPDP$ The S represented by the comma is used as the shift symbol unless there is a (T) timing piece. The timing for a fast shift is represented with a semicolon;. The breakdown for the above parameter listing includes a shift with the palm orientation for both hands. Assume the sign **d'6>.d'4<,-.-**

The non-dominant hand starts first with the 'd' handshape. It is a lower case 'd,' so that means the sign will take place in the Body Locator grid. The Location is at the large square number **6** with the zone marker shown as an apostrophe. This means the sign is in the medial zone or Car 1 zone. The palm orientation is pointing to the dominant side. Next the dominant marker is shown. The period separates the nondominant and dominant hands. The dominant hand also has a 'd' handshape. This hand is located in front of the body at the main 4 square in the medial or Car 1 zone. This hand is facing toward the non dominant side of the body. Next the shift shows that certain parameters will be changed. Only the items that change in the sign are identified after the shift marker. In this sign, the dominant and nondominant hands both change palm orientation from facing each other to facing palm down. The above example of the glossed word HAPPEN shows that both hands are shifted by incorporating the second dominant marker. This completes the sign.

FINDINGS

The reader, Emily, began by learning the manual alphabet. We discussed the grids and how the location interacted with the handshapes. I also introduced the zones and palm orientation characters at the initial meeting. We formed some basic sign morphemes, then I introduced the shift. Emily was able to read these basic signs and also signs with a shift. Complete words were achieved at this point. Amazingly this was completed in two sessions. Emily was reading basic signs after about two-and-a-half hours of training.

Emily was given a list of nine words. The list of words were new to her, and she had to use the charts and follow the method to read these on her own. She video taped her responses. The words and results are listed below.

Word One: .f1+,=
The sign was executed perfectly. Again Emily had created these videos on her own after only a couple hours of training. In this video she used the correct hand, handshape, location, zone, palm orientations, and shift.

Word Two: :D82<,:49
This sign is done with the dominant hand touching the spots located on the head. It has a shift. The rule for writing the words is that the uppermost part of the hand is to be placed in the locations given unless the word specifies an exact location. In this example and in a similar sign that repeats these sign features only with a different handshape, I noticed that the exact location of the hand part that touches the head or body needed to be specified. This sign was acceptable, and would probably be understood by the majority of fluent signers, but without an exact location identified on the head the sign for 'deaf' was not as clear. I made the adjustments to specify the location of where the hand touches. It now is written .:1N1:D82<,:49.

Word Three: .D4=,V7
This sign was executed perfectly. It is the sign for 'half'. The number 1 is shown over the number 2. Clearly read and an exact representation.

Word Four: .s1+,-,+,-
Emily used the correct hand, handshape, palm orientation and shifts. This sign production however was positioned in the 'S' placement rather than the 's' placement. The reader overlooked the lowercase letter and placed this sign

in the Head Locator area instead of the Body Locator. Interestingly enough, at a later date, a fluent signer asked Emily to read the words; she read him this word, and the fluent signer showed her the correct way to sign it. When Emily looked at the word to check it, she replied that he was correct; that was the right way to sign it.

Word Five: .h'1-,ho
Again this sign was executed perfectly. The proper hand, handshapes, location, zone, palm orientation and shifts were performed.

Word Six: :B[469]=
This sign was a contact sign with the forehead area. The production of this sign was skewed. The reader's perception of the face as a 2D drawing influenced the sign production. The side of the face, such as the temple, is contoured. This distinction needed to be emphasized with the reader either by offering 3D drawings or by a more thorough explanation of the method of writing regarding this difference with the reader. Emily tried to lay her hand in a flat position on the side of her face, rather than following her face contour. This and the way the sign was executed with the side of the pinky finger touching rather than the first four finger tips, created an unreadable distorted sign. Training including a 3D diagram and contact identification of the hand should resolve this confusion. This sign is now written as .:N1234:B469=.

Word Seven: :BA854<,:515
The contact location was correctly identified, but the specific place on the hand to touch the face was not identified, therefore the signer read the word with not enough direction to create a recognizable sign. This written word was intended to have the first, second and third fingers touch near the fingertips on the locations identified on the head. Instead Emily followed the rule to touch the head or body with the finger part that is closest to the body before contact. It was clear from the sign production, that Emily read it correctly because she used her thumb rather than her fingertips to make contact. This error in production of the written word is now corrected by using the Finger Locator information. This was a valuable finding in the research. Now the word is written .:NN123:BA854<,:515.

Word Eight: :O52<
In this sign I wanted to see if the correct placement of the hand could be achieved with the combination of just a placement. Emily signed this word exactly as written; it was a perfect execution of the sign.

Word Nine: .lb'8-;'5;'2
This final word was also produced accurately. This sign included the semi colon. The semicolon directs the reader to speed up the sign through the movement. This adjustment in the shift was smoothly executed and the concept of 'childhood' was clearly conveyed.

CONCLUSION

The signers in this study were not familiar with how signs are developed, and still they were able to learn the material at a very accelerated rate. Since this research was completed, Deaf signers were taught the writing system. Fluent Deaf signers were able to comprehend this orthography and accomplished the equivalent amount of information in about a fifth of the time. The college students that were unfamiliar with sign language required more time for them to learn the orthography.

The findings from this study were encouraging. Further development of this orthography will provide an opportunity for literacy in a linear written form of signed communication that is convenient, programmable, and accessible to both the Deaf and Deaf-blind community. Updates will be given as they become available at https://sites.google.com/site/writingasl.

Acknowledgements
This research could not have been completed without the contributions from the professional linguists who share an interest in seeing writing systems developed for sign languages, and the dedicated students who committed invaluable time toward this discovery. In gratitude, I recognize Carole Brenton, Stuart Thiessen, Albert Bickford, Stefanie Saltern, Theresa Fargher, Emily Moes, Amy Lytle, Jayme Christensen, Saraa Kastning and all the support from the Idaho Association of the Deaf. Drawings were done by J. Scott Shawver.

REFERENCES

Aitken, S., Buultjens, M., Clark, C., Eyre, J. T., & Pease, L. (2013, October 28). *Teaching children who are deaf-blind: Contact communication and learning*. Routledge.

Bickford, J. A., & Fraychineaud, K. (2006, December). *Mouth morphemes in ASL: A closer look*. Paper presented at the 9th Theoretical Issues in Sign Language Research Conference. Retrieved from http://www.editora-arara-azul.com.br/ebooks/catalogo/3.pdf.

Brauer, J. (2013). Dorsal and ventral pathways in language development. Retrieved from http://www.sciencedirect.com/science/article/pii/S0093934X13000709.

Brose, N. (2013, February 8). Italy: Sign language. Retrieved from http://german3510europe2013blog.wordpress.com/2013/02/08/italy-sign-language/.

Corina, D. P., & Sandler, W. (1993). On the nature of phonological structure in sign language. *Phonology*, 10(2), 165–207.

Dotless Braille.org. (2005). Transcribing codes versus computer Braille. Retrieved from http://www.dotlessbraille.org/compare.htm.

Ebbinghaus, H., & Heßmann, J. (1996). Signs and words: Accounting for spoken language elements in German Sign Language. *International Review of Sign Linguistics*, 1(1), 23-56.

Hodges, L. (2000). Effective teaching and learning. *Teaching children who are deaf-blind: contact, communication and learning,* 167.

Lentz, E. (2010). Poem-Dew on Spiderweb.mov. Retrieved October 5, 2013, from http://www.youtube.com/watch?v=YaHChvFWegQ.

Luckner, J. L., Sebald, A. M., Cooney, J., Young, J., & Muir, S. G. (2005). An examination of the evidence-based literacy research in deaf education. *American Annals of the Deaf,* 150(5), 443-456.

Mayer, C. (2007). What really matters in the early literacy development of deaf children. *Journal of Deaf Studies and Deaf Education,* 12(4), 411-431.

Mayer, C., & Akamatsu, C. (1999). Bilingual-bicultural models of literacy education for deaf students: considering the claims. *Journal of Deaf Studies and Deaf Education,* 4(1), 1-8.

Wheeler, L., & Griffin, H. C. (1997). A movement-based approach to language development in children who are deaf-blind. *American Annals of the Deaf,* 142(5), 387-390.

A Preliminary Report on Initialized Signs Accepted and Used in the Deaf Community

DAISY CARTWRIGHT

MY MOTIVATION FOR INVESTIGATING THE NATURE OF INITIALIZED signs in American Sign Language (ASL) lies in the recognition that, although this type of sign is not always popular, deaf signers use them on a daily basis. There has been reluctance among sign language scholars and researchers in ASL linguistic literature to examine initialization in-depth (Cagle, 2010). I am interested in understanding how and which initialized signs are accepted and used in the Deaf community. Many Deaf community members understand that the source of many initialized signs is the educational system, where some educators tried to facilitate the instruction of English language to deaf children through the invention of English-based sign systems. Signing Exact English (SEE), first introduced in the 1970s (Gustason, Petzfing, & Zawolklow, 1972), serves as a good example. Developers of SEE-type systems created many signs to ensure that they had the vocabulary necessary for the representation of English lexicon through a visual/gestural modality.

SEE signs include one or two handshapes or contact with the signer's body (like what one would expect for a word in ASL). However, unlike their ASL counterparts, *most* SEE signs are initialized. In a typical initialized sign, one alphabetic handshape is used to represent the first letter of an English word that is chosen to represent an intended sign. Some initialized signs are created 'from scratch' and therefore artificial and difficult to produce (i.e., violating linguistic principles concerning the production of ASL signs). Several SEE signs are similar to signs for profanity in ASL, and some signs have been subject to ridicule within the Deaf community for their poorly conceived forms. Many signs in SEE are unnecessarily initialized. For these reasons, SEE signs are frequently rejected and looked down upon by ASL users in the Deaf community.

Deaf community members recall a time when SEE and other similarly-conceived sign systems were confusing and resembled a modern Tower of Babel. Educators fought among themselves about which system (and related inventory of signs) should be adopted. The negativity that the Deaf community experienced with invented signs was especially prevalent in the 1970s and 1980s. With SEE, educators went as far as creating signs to represent the morpho-syntactic structure of English in the visual/gestural modality (e.g., IS, WERE, THE, -ING, -S, DIS-, EN- etc.). This was done with hopes that, like hearing children, deaf children would learn and use signed (and spoken) English. This language planning effort was not successful; Deaf children did not acquire or use English as they did ASL. English-based signing has been cumbersome and ineffective based on what is known for a natural language like ASL (see Supalla & McKee, 2002 for a review of problems plaguing English-based sign systems).

Fortunately, English-based signing is not something contemporary educators pursue in schools and programs for the deaf. However, many SEE signs have found their way into the lexicon of ASL. I am aware that some Deaf community members have argued that ASL should be made 'pure' through the exclusion of initialized signs from its lexicon (c.f. Padden, 1998). However, I respond that ASL had initialized signs long before the introduction of SEE and other English-based sign systems. Historically, ASL is related to French Sign Language (LSF), introduced by Laurent Clerc, one of the founders of the country's first permanent school for the deaf in 1817. What contemporary American Deaf community members frequently do not realize is that some ASL signs are initialized based on eighteenth and nineteenth century LSF sign creation; French "methodical signs" were promoted by educators, analogous to the American creation of English-based signs..

Although Clerc was fluent in LSF, it is likely that he also used initialized French signs. Three ASL sign examples that were subject to French initialization are WITH, GOOD, and SEARCH. WITH is produced with two A handshapes, referring to the initial of the French word *avec*. GOOD consists of two B handshapes that refer to the initial of the French word *bien*. Finally, SEARCH utilizes a C handshape that refers to the initial of the French word *cherche*. Deaf Americans are often unaware that many ASL lexical items were originally initialized LSF signs. Many ASL users have an unfavorable attitude toward initialized signs and borrowing from English due to the minority's social perspective about borrowing from a majority language, similar to French Québécois who resist borrowing from the English majority around them. Years of observation has led me to conclude that, although

ASL signers tend to reject the use of initialization and borrowing consciously, they use initialized and borrowed lexical items unconsciously (Cagle, 2010).

Initialized signs appear to function much like native signs, depending on how they are formed; many initialized signs involve the appropriate use of movement and locations in front of or on the signer. A sign cannot be so drastic with movement that it appears odd or that the sign produced in a location that would be hard for the signer to do.

Moreover, native signs are supposed to originate in the classifier system of ASL (Padden, 1998 and Valli & Lucas, 2005 for a review of the classifiers in the signed language). In ASL, the classifier system is used to describe things or actions. Signs are rather like words, but many words in ASL are originally a product of the classifier system.

- The sign ROOM is natively pronounced with two flat B handshapes depicting the walls of a room, where contemporary initialized systems specify an O handshape for OFFICE
- The sign INSPECT or INVESTIGATE uses a 1 (one) handshape against the flat handshape of another hand depicting the action of inspecting or investigating; initializing the 1 handshape with a D becomes DISSERTATION and with an R becomes RESEARCH.

These classifier productions have gradually become part of the ASL lexicon. Research conducted by Lillio-Martin (1988) is insightful on how classifiers are manipulated to create a new sign and more work is needed to understand how 'native' signs are created and used in the Deaf community. Additionally, there are several initialized signs created *after* the introduction of SEE systems that have found their way into common ASL usage. Unlike the artificial signs promoted by educators who intended to replace ASL with SEE or some other English-based sign system, these initialized signs seem to help with lexicon building and increase the number of signs for potential use in ASL (Padden, 1988). It is important to maintain, however, that the contrived morphemic and syntactic signs developed for SEE are not generally acceptable.

Prior to the 1980s, there was no standarized sign for 'culture'; about this time, the current initialized sign for CULTURE began to appear in the community. Historically, Deaf people would fingerspell the English word if they needed to talk about culture in ASL. (Fingerspelling in general can be sometimes taxing to a signer, especially when a word is repeatedly used in the context of a discussion.) The pressure for a sign apparently caused the development of the initialized signs. I believe that someone who first came up with the sign for 'culture' had thought about what the native sign should be and then had it initialized. The classifier system (in ASL) would be first employed for the creation of C̲ULTURE. It involves the use of a straight index finger that represents a person and a spread out handshape moving around (which is similar to how the number 5 is expressed in ASL) representing the surrounding.

When these two classifier handshapes are put together to create the natural sign, it would make sense to a signer (associated with the relationship of a person and the surrounding). This sign then underwent the initialization process instead. The spread-out 5 handshape was replaced with C, the first English letter of 'culture.' Other signs with similar semantic intent followed this pattern: E̲NVIRONMENT, using an E handshape, and O̲RIENTATION using an O handshape.

SOME PRELIMINARY FINDINGS ON THE NATURE OF INITIALIZED SIGNS

At this point, I was determined to create a database on initialized signs in ASL. I checked with other culturally Deaf colleagues and community members who are fluent in ASL to authenticate initialized signs. In addition, I collected initialized signs through observations of other signers in the Deaf community and reviewed several printed ASL dictionaries (Table 1) and ASL teaching materials and websites. to identify almost 1,000 initialized signs. (Please see Appendices A & B for the listing of initialized signs divided into various word groups, noting that some words such as C̲ERTIFY/C̲ERTIFICATE, E̲MOTION/E̲MOTIONAL, E̲VALUATE/E̲VALUATION, and U̲NIVERSAL/U̲NIVERSE utilize the same sign).

Based on the numbers displayed in Table 1, I found that 6% to 22% of the current ASL sign vocabulary (according to the five ASL resources) is initialized. With the average rate being 13%, the initialized signs make up a small but sizable percentage of the ASL lexicon.

Within this database, I was curious about which initialized signs could be categorized as nouns/verbs, adjectives, adverbs, prefixes, and contractions. How did this list of initialized signs break down into these categories? According to my analysis, an overwhelming majority of initialized signs are either nouns or verbs. Approximately eighty-three initialized signs are found to be adjectives, six adverbs, two prefixes, and one contraction. It appears that ASL signers rely on many initialized nouns and verbs to create semantic and vocabulary expansion in ASL.

Year	Title/Author	Number of initialized signs of total	Percentage of total
1964	*Talk with Your Hands* (David O. Watson, Jr.)	138/1,000	14%
2004	*Learning American Sign Language* (2nd ed.) (Tom Humphries and Carol Padden)	126/2,000	6%
2005	*The Gallaudet Dictionary of American Sign Language* (Clayton Valli (ed.))	444/3,000	15%
2010	*The American Sign Language Handshape Dictionary* (Richard A. Tennant and Marianne Glusak Brown)	304/3,000	10%
2011	*Signs of the Times* (2nd ed.) (Edgar H Shroyer)	283/1,300	22%

Table 1. Number and representative percentage of initialized signs found in American Sign Language dictionaries.

I also subcategorized these signs as 'initialized signs' and 'abbreviation signs.' Padden (1988) and Brentari & Padden (2001) have explained that abbreviation signs are quite different. For example, 'closed captions' is signed as #C-C in the neutral signing space in front of the signer. Initialized signs, however, move and make contact with the signer's body. Understanding that a vast majority of signs in my list are initialized, approximately 213 signs that have more than one alphabet handshape in use, e.g., LANDLORD, BACKGROUND, PAJAMA, REFRIGERATOR, and DISQUALIFIED.

Approximately 454 initialized signs existed *before* ('pre-SEE') the introduction of SEE to deaf education and 531 signs were created *after* ('post-SEE') the introduction of SEE to deaf education. This suggests that SEE did not play the only role in the growth of initialized signs for ASL (that many in the Deaf community believe to be true). Instead, initialized signs have been part of ASL for a long time. It is also interesting that out of those two hundred and thirteen signs with more than one alphabetic handshape, one hundred and sixty one are pre-SEE list and fifty two are post-SEE signs. Pre-SEE and post-SEE signs are best characterized as 1) individual signs, 2) topical groups, and 3) sign categories (Table 2):

Title/Author	Pre-SEE	Post-SEE
Individual Words	106	9
Topical Groups	43	8
Sign Categories	23	177

Table 2. Categorization of pre-/post-SEE signs

In Table 2, the majority of pre-SEE initialized signs are introduced into the Deaf community as individual signs or in topical groups. 'Individual signs' refers to the creation of the sign for a single concept (e.g., FREQUENCY, INSURANCE, VERY etc.). There are also multiple initialized signs that share a common topic (e.g., math, rulers, time). Table 2 gives examples of initialized signs that are 'individual signs' or 'topical groups' or another:

Individual words	Topic Groups (Art History)	Directionality	Sign Categories
HURRY	BAROQUE	LEFT	BUTTER → JELLY
HARD OF HEARING	BYZANTINE	RIGHT	HONOR → RESPECT
INTEREST (money)	GOTHIC	EAST	MOUSE → RAT
ISLAND	RENAISSANCE	WEST	
KEEP		NORTH	
LAZY		NORTHEAST	
PEOPLE		NORTHWEST	
RESTAURANT		SOUTH	
VINEGAR		SOUTHEAST	
VISIT		SOUTHWEST	

Table 3. Examples of individual words, topic groups and sign category initialized signs. Underlined letter indicated initialized handshape (this convention is used throughout this paper).

In contrast, the majority of post-SEE initialized signs belong to 'sign categories' (instead of individual signs or topical groups). It appears that, after SEE was introduced to deaf education, the Deaf community shifted how it accepted new initialized signs. Deaf people appear to prefer the use of 'native' or legacy signs as the root for the creation of initialized signs and that they are somewhat uncomfortable with creating new initialized signs from 'scratch.' There are several examples sign categories shown below where a native sign was initialized for a different, but related concept:

ADMINISTRATOR	CHANGE	COLD	COME-BACK
DIRECTOR	ADJUST/MENT	REFRIGERATOR	REIMBURSEMENT
	CONVERT/SION	WINTER	
	EVOLVE/EVOLUTION		
	MODIFY/ICATION		
	REPENT/ANCE		
	REVISE/ION (with repetition)		
	TRANSLATE/ TRANSLITERATION		
	TRANSITION		

DEAF	LESSON	RING
DOWN'S SYNDROME	AGENDA	DIAMOND
RETINA PIGMENTOSA	COURSE	ENGAGE/MENT
USHER SYNDROME	LESSON	FIANCE/E
WARRDENBERG SYNDROME (two signs for this term)	REGiSTER/ REGISTRATION	

Table 4. Creation of additional related signs from a native or root sign.

Pre- and post-SEE initialized sign introduction and usage has changed dramatically and strategies for vocabulary expansion are quite distinct.

There are additional interesting patterns of initialized signs creation and evolution that are worthy of mention, but for brevity and space, here are thirteen patterns.

1. Initialized signs plus agent suffix	AUDIOLOGIST, DIRECTOR, FOREIGNER, VEGETARIAN
2. Negation using movement	EXPIRATION (license), ILLEGAL, MISCOMMUNICATION, UNFAIR
3. Incorporated NEW	NEW LONDON, CT., NEW YORK, NEW ORLEANS
4. Written abbreviations	COMPANY, DX (diagnostic), JUNIOR, NORTHWEST
5. One sign for compound word	FOSTER-PARENT, GOOGLE-SEARCH, NATIVE-PEOPLE, ROUND-OFF
6. Parameters changed	FEEDBACK (handshape), IDIOM (movement), USE (palm orientation), VICE PRESIDENT (location)
7. ASL puns	BUREAUCRAZY, WEIRD, NORDSTROM, SEARS (S on both ears)

8. One initialized sign requiring mouthing	REACT, REPLY, REPORT, RESPOND
9. Two initials for compound word	HEADQUARTERS, KNOCKOUT, LANDLORD, VIDEOPHONE, WITHDRAW,
10. Two initials for word phrase	CLOSED CAPTION, FRENCH FRIES, POWER POINT, MILITARY POLICE, BED & BREAKFAST, STAFF & FACULTY, CODE OF ETHICS, BOARD OF TRUSTEES
11. Combining a native sign with an initialized sign	TEACHER'S AIDE, OLD TESTAMENT, HOLY SPIRIT, WATERMELON, CANDY M&Ms, WASHINGTON DC, CLASSROOM (2), LIVING ROOM (2), FRENCH TOAST (2), X-RAY (2), E-MOTION, T-SHIRT
12. Unique X	EXECUTIVE BOARD, FAX, TRANSSEXUAL, TEXAS, XEROX-COPY, PHOENIX, AZ
13. Unique influence Z movement	ALZHEIMER'S DISEASE, BRAZIL, FUZEMEETING, SCHIZOPHRENIA, VERIZON (sign formed in a Z movement)

Table 4. Additional patterns, types, and categories of initialized signs.

CONCLUSION AND FUTURE RESEARCH

Given that most of the 985 initialized signs are nouns and verbs, they appear to be informative rather than descriptive in nature. Initialized and abbreviation signs tend to refer to community, education, employment, religion, health, and technology. Both Brentari and Padden (2001) have written that initialization has been a productive way to build ASL words, especially in technical and professional domains. The Deaf community has found initialized sign development strategies to be helpful in creating domain-specific language.

Areas of future research emerged from this study. One is tracing the influence of French methodology in the education of deaf students transplanted to the United States in the early nineteenth century. More historical research is needed on how French methodical signs were developed in France and its impact on the lexicon of LSF. How did initialization take place in French signs that later became part of ASL? Additionally, Cagle recommends a further study on initialization in French Sign Language (LSF) and how ASL has borrowed from initialized LSF lexical signs. I must note that this research has limitations. Although I categorized initialized signs as 'pre-SEE' and 'post-SEE' for my data (based on personal experiences), additional research is needed in the verification of initialized signs related to these two time periods.

A framework for signs that involve alphabetic handshape(s) (regular fingerspelling, fingerspelling abbreviations, name signs, lexicalized fingerspelling, initialized signs, and abbreviation signs) could be created. I hope future researchers will take this study into consideration and pursue new and different questions related to how signs are created and accepted in the Deaf community.

Special Acknowledgements
I would like to thank Dr. Keith Cagle, Gallaudet University, Washington, D.C., and Dr. Sam Supalla, University of Arizona, Tucson, Arizona. or their review, consultation and support for this project. I want to thank my husband, Alan Cartwright, for helping me with this project.

REFERENCES

Bragg, B. (1995). Sign initialization/fingerspelling in ASL: Its impact on Deaf people. *Deafness: Life & Culture II*, 45, 7-9.

Bragg, B., & Olson, J. R. (1994). *Meeting halfway in American Sign Language: A common ground for effective communication among Deaf and hearing people* (D. F. Moores, Ed.). Rochester, NY: Deaf Life Press.

Brentari, D., & Padden, C. A. (2001). Native and foreign vocabulary in American Sign Language: A lexicon with multiple origins. In D. Brentari (Ed.), *Foreign Vocabulary in Sign Languages: A Cross-Linguistic Investigation of Word Formation* (pp. 87–120). Mahwah, NJ: Lawrence E. Associates.

Cagle, K. (2010). Exploring the ancestral roots of American Sign Language: Lexical Borrowing from Cistercian Sign Language (doctoral dissertation). University of New Mexico, Albuquerque, NM.

Gustason, G., Pfetzing, D., & Zawolkow, E. (1972). *Signing Exact English* (C. B. Norris, Illustrator). Los Alamitos, CA: Modern Sign Press.

Humphries, T., & Padden, C. (2004). *Learning American Sign Language (2nd ed.)* (R. Hills, P. Lott, & D. Renner, Illustrator). Des Moines, IA: Pearson Education, Inc.

Lepic, R. (2014, July). The phonology and morphology of initialized signs in American Sign Language [Chart]. Presented at Theoretical Issues in Sign Language (TISLR) Conference in London, England.

Lillo-Martin, D. (1988). Children's new sign creations. In Michael Strong (Ed.), *Language learning and deafness*, 162–183. Cambridge: Cambridge University Press.

Padden, C. A. (1998). The ASL lexicon. *Sign Language and Linguistics*, 1, 39–60.

Shaw, E., & Delaporte, Y. (2010). New perspectives on the history of American Sign Language. *Sign Language Studies*, 11(2), 158–204.

Shroyer, E. H. (2011). *Signs of the times (2nd ed.)* (S. P. Shroyer, Illustrator). Washington, DC, USA: Gallaudet University Press.

Supalla, S. J. (1992). *The book of name signs: Naming in American Sign Language*. San Diego, CA: Dawn Sign Press.

Supalla, S. J., & McKee, C. (2002). The role of manually coded English in Language development of Deaf children [Chapter 6]. In R. P. Meier, K. Cormier, & D. Quinto-Pozos (Eds.), *Modality and Structure in Signed and Spoken Languages* (pp. 143–165). New York, NY: Cambridge University Press.

Tennant, R. & Brown, M. G. (Eds.) (2010). *The American Sign Language handshape dictionary (2nd ed.)*. Washington, DC: Gallaudet University Press.

Valli, C. (Ed.). (2005). *The Gallaudet dictionary of American Sign Language* (P. S. Lott, D. Renner, & R. Hills, Illustrator). Washington, DC, USA: Gallaudet University Press.

Valli, C., Lucas, C., & Mulrooney, K. J. (2005). *Linguistics of American Sign Language (4th ed.)*. Washington, DC: Gallaudet University Press.

Vicars, B. Lifeprint.com: ASL University. (Notes on initialized signs and lexicalized fingerspelling).
Watson, D. O., Jr. (1964). *Talk with your hands*. Menasha, WI: George Banta Company, Inc.
Woodward, J. (1973). *Manual English: A problem in language standardization and planning*. In Department of Education, Gallaudet College, Recent Developments in Manual English. Washington, D.C.: Gallaudet College, 1–12.

Appendix A
Initialized signs and abbreviation signs used before the development of Signed Exact English (SEE); topical groups, sign categories, and individual words

TOPICAL GROUPS

(any + ___)
anyone
anything
anywhere

(appliances)
air conditioner
refrigerator (1 of 2)

(art history)
Baroque
Byzantine
Gothic
Renaissance

(beverages)
beer
juice
water
wine

(buildings/places)
apt   apartment
aud   auditorium
BB   bed & breakfast
dept   department
dorm   dormitory (1 of 2)
co   company
ds   drugstore
HQ   headquarter
ICU   intensive care unit
lab   laboratory
PO   post office
PX   post exchange
rec   recreation

(colors)
blue ^
brown ^ (2)
green ^
pink ^
purple ^
red ^ {regional?}
tan ^
yellow ^

(days of the week)
Monday
Tuesday
Wednesday
Thursday (1 of 2)
Thursday (2 of 2)
Friday
Saturday

(days: every+___)
every+Monday
every+Tuesday
every+Wednesday
every+Thursday
every+Friday
every+Saturday

(degrees)
AA, AS
BA, BS
MA, MS
Dr., Ph.D.

(directions)
east
north
northeast
northwest
south
southeast
southwest
U-turn {U+turn}
west

(elements)
{alphabetic / numeric codes}
CO2 [carbon monoxide]
H2O [water]
NaCl [salt]
O [oxygen]

(food)
barbeque (BBQ)
cream
MMs
French+toast (2)
lemon
mayonnaise
Pepsi
Seven-up {7+UP}
vanilla (1 of 2)
vegetable (1 of 2)

(functions)
role
character

(grades)
A
B
C
D
F
'all grades A'
'all grades F'

(holidays)
Columbus Day
Easter
Merry Christmas
Veterans' Day

(identity)
gay
lesbian

(interjections)
damn
NG   no good
OK   okay
TB   too bad
wow

(math)
X-axis
Y-axis
Z-axis
X-number
Y-number
integral
differential
DX   derivative
fraction
use of greek symbols (e.g., α, β, π, φ, Σ)

(measurements)
doz   dozen
ft   foot, feet
gal   gallon
inch   inch, inches
kg   kilogram
km   kilometer
lb   pound
m   meter
mcg   microgram
mg   milligram
mm   millimeter
oz   ounce
qt   quart
tbs   tablespoon
tsp   teaspoon

A Preliminary Report on Initialized Signs Accepted and Used in the Deaf Community

(medical terms)
d<u>x</u>   diagnostic
<u>R</u>x   prescription

(months)
<u>Jan</u>   January
<u>Feb</u>   February
<u>Aug</u>   August
<u>Sept</u>   September
<u>Oct</u>   October
<u>Nov</u>   November
<u>Dec</u>   December

(physical conditions)
<u>a</u>rthritis
<u>c</u>erebral palsy
<u>c</u>holesterol
<u>d</u>evelopmentally disabled
<u>d</u>iabetes {sweet+D}
di<u>s</u>abled, di<u>s</u>ability
handi<u>c</u>ap/ped
<u>i</u>nfection
<u>m</u>uscular <u>d</u>ystrophy
<u>m</u>ultiple <u>s</u>clerosis
<u>p</u>neumonia {PN+lung}
<u>t</u>uberculosis {TB+lung}
<u>v</u>itamin

(political parties)
<u>D</u>emocrat
<u>R</u>epublican

(postpositive names)
<u>J</u>unior
<u>S</u>enior

(pronouns)
<u>u</u>s

(relatives)
<u>a</u>unt
<u>c</u>ousin (3)
<u>n</u>iece
<u>n</u>ephew
<u>u</u>ncle

(religious terms)
Jesus <u>C</u>hrist
<u>H</u>oly Spirit
<u>L</u>ord (1 of 2)
<u>L</u>utheran
<u>m</u>issionary
<u>r</u>eligion/us
<u>S</u>avior {safe+agent}

(rulers)
<u>k</u>ing
<u>k</u>ingdom
<u>l</u>ord (1 of 2)
<u>p</u>rince
<u>p</u>rincess (2)
<u>q</u>ueen

(sides)
<u>l</u>eft
<u>r</u>ight

(signs on nose)
<u>n</u>osey
<u>b</u>ullshit
<u>b</u>rown-nose {rub}
<u>d</u>ick
<u>p</u>ee [urinate]
<u>p</u>enis

(sizes)
<u>S</u>
<u>M</u>
<u>L</u>
<u>XL</u>
<u>XXL</u>

(streets with names)
<u>a</u>ve   avenue
<u>blvd</u>   boulevard
<u>st</u>   street

(technology)
<u>C</u>itizen's <u>B</u>and
<u>c</u>losed <u>c</u>aptions
<u>f</u>ax
tele<u>v</u>ision
<u>X</u>erox (copy)

(time)
<u>hr</u>   hour
<u>min</u>   minute
<u>lt</u>   long term
<u>ot</u>   overtime
<u>sec</u>   second

(titles with names)
<u>Dr</u>.
<u>Miss</u>
<u>Mr</u>.
<u>Mrs</u>.
<u>Ms</u>.

(weapons)
<u>A</u>-/<u>H</u>-bomb

(years)
<u>AD</u>
<u>BC</u>
<u>BCE</u>

(years at college)
<u>p</u>reparatory
<u>f</u>resh<u>m</u>an
<u>s</u>opho<u>m</u>ore
<u>j</u>unio<u>r</u>
<u>s</u>enio<u>r</u>

**TOPICAL GROUPS
(names)**

(names of cities)
Anchorage
Atlanta
Baltimore
Boston
Chicago
Flagstaff
Fort Worth
Fremont
Honolulu
Houston
Los Angeles
Minneapolis (<u>D</u>)
New <u>H</u>aven
New <u>L</u>ondon
New Orleans
Oakland
  (O+i together)
Philadelphia
Phoenix
Portland
Rochester
Rome, NY
San <u>F</u>rancisco
Seattle
Tucson
<u>V</u>ancouver
<u>W</u>ashington, <u>D.C.</u>

(names of cities with schools)
Berkeley, CA
<u>F</u>remont, CA
<u>R</u>iverside, CA
<u>C</u>olumbia, MD
<u>F</u>redericksburg, MD
<u>F</u>airbault, MN

(names of US states)
Arizona
<u>C</u>olorado (1 of 2)
<u>C</u>olorado (2 of 2) {color+<u>ADO</u>}
Hawaii
Montana
Oregon
Te<u>x</u>as
<u>W</u>ashington
<u>Ark</u>   Arkansas
<u>Ill</u>   Illinois
<u>Ind</u>   Indiana
<u>Neb</u>   Nebraska
<u>Nev</u>   Nevada
<u>Wyo</u>   Wyoming
<u>Conn</u>   Connecticut
<u>Mass</u>   Massachusetts
<u>Mich</u>   Michigan
<u>Minn</u>   Minnesota
<u>Miss</u>   Mississippi
<u>Okla</u>   Oklahoma
<u>Tenn</u>   Tennessee
<u>Ala</u>   Alabama
<u>Fla</u>   Florida
<u>GA</u>   Georgia
<u>KY</u>   Kentucky
<u>LA</u>   Louisiana
<u>MD</u>   Maryland
<u>VT</u>   Vermont
<u>VA</u>   Virginia
<u>MO</u>   Missouri
<u>NH</u>   New Hampshire
<u>NJ</u>   New Jersey
<u>NM</u>   New Mexico
<u>NC</u>   North Carolina
<u>ND</u>   North Dakota
<u>RI</u>   Rhode Island
<u>SC</u>   South Carolina
<u>SD</u>   South Dakota
<u>Kan</u>/<u>KS</u> Kansas
<u>Penn</u>/<u>PA</u> Pennsylvania
<u>Wisc</u>/<u>Wis</u> Wisconsin
Alaska {CL:A+5} or {CL:5+A}
New <u>Y</u>ork
<u>WVA</u>   West Virginia

(geographic signs)
Costa <u>R</u>ica
<u>D</u>enmark
<u>F</u>rance
<u>G</u>reece
<u>I</u>srael
<u>I</u>taly

Mexico
Norway
Rome
Sweden
USA

(names of continents)
Africa
Asia (2)
Europe
North America
South America

SIGN CATEGORIES

(butter)
jelly

(elevator)
elevator (2)

(exact)
perfect ^

(frosting)
chocolate
vanilla (1 of 2)

{combined signs}
I love you
I really love you

(school)
high school
junior high school
homecoming
institute, institution

(honor)
honor
respect
(library)
library
librarian

(natural)
natural/ly
normal ^

(order)
proportion,
   proportional ^

(responsible)
responsible/ility ^

(psychology)
psychology (uses
   Greek letter psi Ψ)
psychiatry

(separate)
divorce

(string)
rope

(water)
water
watery ^
watermelon

Included in headings of
sign categories under
"Post-SEE"

(mouse)
rat

(area)
place

(work)
business
duty

(free/dom)
free ^
safe ^
save

(idea)
reason

(law)
principle
rule

(room)
dining room

INDIVIDUAL WORDS

accompany
accuse
altogether
ambition
ahead
another
apology/ize
athletic

average
avoid
basket
cup
dictionary (1 of 2)
disqualified ^
ego (l)
electricity
eyeglasses
ex-
fair ^ {F on chin}
favorite
feather
fox
frequency
fearful ^
furniture
gossip
hard of hearing
highway
history
honest ^
hurry
identification
illegal ^, prohibit
insurance
interest [money]
island
isolated ^ (1 of 2)
jealous ^ (1 of 2)
keep
Kendall-School
knockout
landlord
later
miles per hour
military police
naïve ^
nervy ^
out of order
over the counter
owl
pajama
parliamentary
   procedure
people
physical education
principal
ram
ready ^ (2)
rehabilitation (1 of 2)
rocket (2)
skunk
slave
Social Security
steel

strike [baseball]
strike [protest]
T-shirt (2)
tenure track
unfair ^
university (1 of 2)
use {one hand}
   (1 of 2)
vain ^
very
view {1 or 2 hands}
virgin
visit
voice
who {blended W-H-O}
whose {who+'s}
worship [idolize]
X+movie
X+ray (2)

Included in headings of
sign categories under
"Post-SEE"

act
characteristic ^
church
cop
family
grade
holy ^
lazy ^
legislature
license
nation
nurse
poem
rat
restaurant (2)
sex
shoes
time
toilet
vinegar
world

Appendix B
Development of initialized signs and abbreviation signs based on original ASL signs (post-SEE); sign categories, topical groups, and individual words

SIGN CATEGORIES

(act, action)
behave, behavior

(act [OASL])
performance
actor/actress (OASL)
mime
theater

administrator
director {D+agent}

after
post- {prefix}

allow, permit,
permission
let
privilege

alone
isolated ^ (1 of 2)

ambulance, siren
emergency

answer
react, reaction
reply
report
respond, response

approve {O+K on palm}
accreditation
guarantee
verify

area (OASL), place
(OASL)
district
local
region/al ^

arrange
organize (1 of 2)

basic
basic ^
elementary ^
inferior ^

kindergarten
primary ^ (1 of 2)

bathroom, toilet
(OASL)
bowel-movement
restroom

before
pre- {prefix}

belong
own {O both hands}

body
anatomy
health
human ^ (1 of 2)
physical ^
uniform (1 of 2)
uniform (2 of 2)

boss, captain
chairperson
{C+agent}
coach
officer

bounce {on hand},
reflect
reflect, reflection

brainstorm
creativity
fantasy (1 of 2)
hallucination
imagination
paranoid (1 of 2)
{both P on head}

build, building
construction
structure

California
gold {CL:1+Y}
gold {G}
silver {CL:1+S}

cancel
discrimination

candy
vinegar (OASL)
fruit
nutrition (1 of 2)
pineapple
vegetable (1 of 2)
vegetarian {V+agent}

cat
kitten

center
middle

cereal {with CL: A}
soup {with CL: H}
rice
yogurt

change
{both verbs & nouns}
adjust
convert
digitalize
evolve
modify
repent
revise {repeated}
transition {only noun}
translate

characteristic (OASL)
attitude
loyal ^
noble ^
personal ^,
personality
reputation
qualified ^, quality,
qualification

church (OASL)
ministry {←→}
mosque
temple

cold
refrigerator (1 of 2)
winter

college
university (1 of 2)

come-back
reimbursement

compete
sport
race
relay {R opposite}

complete, completion
conclusion
end
result

conscience
lazy (OASL) ^
guilt, guilty ^

conversation
communication
dialogue
discourse
interview
feedback {1 of 2}
{opposite F+B}
feedback {2 of 2}
{opposite F}
miscommunication
{2 handed; 1 stay 1 down}
negotiation
SimCom
Total
Communication

cook
kitchen (1 of 2)

cop/officer (OASL)
police
detective

country
foreign ^
foreign-nation
foreigner {F+agent}

crazy
'bureaucrazy' ^

Deaf
Down's Syndrome
retina pigmentosa
Usher's Syndrome
Waardenberg
 Syndrome (2)

decide, decision
decide, decision

dentist, teeth
dentist {no agent}

depressed
depression [feeling]

develop, succeed
{B up on palm}
curriculum
develop,
 development
mature ^

draw
choreography
design

eat
breakfast
dinner
lunch
supper

**engage, engagement
(on finger)**
diamond {upward}
 (1 of 2)
engage, engagement
fiancé, fiancée

escape
retreat

exercise
gym
event
festival

explain, explanation
direction

exposure
orientation (1 of 2)

far
distance

feel, feeling
emotion/al ^
revival

**free (OASL) ^, safe
(OASL) ^, save (OASL)
[rescue], savior
{save+agent}**
independent ^
liberal ^, liberty

figure-out
calculate
multiply
algebra
calculus
geometry
mathematics
statistics
trigonometry

first
primary ^ (1 of 2)
priority (1 of 2)

flag
hotel

friend
relative (1 of 2)

funny
cartoon
humor {2 hands}

generation
generation
tradition (1 of 2)

glass {CL:C}
margaritas

go {1 hand}
forward

**go-back
(CL: 1 backward
on palm}**
review (2)

government
bureaucratic ^
federal-government
government
governor {G+agent}
mayor

political ^, politics
vice president

grade (OASL)
A [top grade]
F [flunk]

graduate, graduation
undergraduate

ground
land
field
garden

group, family (OASL)
association
class
department (1 of 2)
group
league
organization
organize (1 of 2)
relatives (1 of 2)
seminar
society
sociology
team
union
workshop

habit
tradition (1 of 2)
used-to

happen, happening
bet
chance
opportunity

hear, sound
audiologist
{A+agent}
audiology
{A circling ear}
listen
phonology

help
rehabilitation
social work
therapy
treatment

high/low
high ^
low ^

holy (OASL) ^
orthodox ^
pure ^

home
dormitory (1 of 2)
foster-home
orphanage

hospital
clinic
infirmary
patient

house
architecture
museum
system

Indian [American]
Native-people

inspect, investigate
dissertation
research {noun/
 verb}

jealous
jealous ^ (1 of 2)

judge [verb]
assess/ment
evaluate/ation

kid
immature ^

kill
kill
murder

kind [adjective]
kind [noun]

leather
leather

lecture
testify, testimony

lesson
agenda
course
lesson
register, registration

license (OASL)
certificate, certify
expiration
 {2 L 1 stay 1 down}

limit/ation
restrict/ion

listing
 {pointing to CL:5}
A-B-C [alphabet]
criteria
details
letters
priority (1 of 2)

live
life
residence
resident (1 of 2)
survive

look-back
memorial ^, memory

look-for/search
google-search

look-up
 {thumb on palm}
dictionary (1 of 2)
encyclopedia
reference
page
thesaurus

lucky
 {Good Luck}
bad luck {bad+l}
good luck {good+L}

major
profession/al ^

make
create
fix
produce
repair

maximum
potential ^

measure
ruler {R on both hands}

medical
nurse (OASL)
doctor
medical ^
physician

member, legislature (OASL)
board
board of trustees
committee
commission
delegate
executive board
faculty
inductee
legislator {L+agent}
member/ship
senate
senator {S+agent}
staff
staff & faculty
US + Congress

**mind, idea (OASL),
reason (OASL),
suspect, think**
abstract ^
concept
fantasy (1 of 2)
high [alcoholic] ^
hypothesis
imagine
logic/al
meditation
mentally retarded
paranoid ^ (1 of 2)
realize (2)
theory

money
budget
economy
finance/ial
scholarship

mouse, rat (OASL)
gerbil
hamster

nation (OASL)
republic

new
fresh ^
gospel

odd, strange
weird ^ {wriggly W}

parent
adult
foster-parent
orphan
teenager
parent

participate
participate
participation

pay
pay

pension
welfare {wriggly W}

person
client
customer
human (1 of 2)
individual ^
 {noun & adj.}
person

photo
image

ping pong
ping pong

play
game
party
recess
toy

point
viewpoint

platform
stage

practice
busy ^
discipline
function
internship
practicum
rehearse/al
train
trainer {T+agent}
use {2 hands}
 (1 of 2)
user

proof
evidence
witness {from eye}

protect
protection
defend/se
guard/ianship

quotation/ title
idiom

read
script

real
really

related
relationship

reserve
reservation
appointment

restaurant (OASL)
cafeteria (1 of 2)
nutrition (1 of 2)

**room, room (OASL),
dining room,
workroom**
box
classroom (2)
 {class+room}
living room (2)
office

rule (OASL), law (OASL), principle (OASL)
background
code of ethics
constitution
 US + Constitution
ethic
formula
lawyer {L+agent}
legislation
policy
state
testament
 New + Testament
 Old + Testament
 10 + Commandments

schizophrenia
Alzheimer's Disease
schizophrenia

science
biology
chemistry
experiment

search {2 CL:C}, observe {2 CL:V}
observation
strategy

send
refer/ral

sense {on head}
common sense
knockout (2)

sentence
grammar
language
linguistics
sociolinguistics

sex (OASL)
transexual {switch X}

shoes (OASL)
boots

shout
yell

show
demonstrate/ion
example
identify, identity
model [example]
represent/ation
representative
symbol

sign [poster], square
form
frame
resume
transcript

sing, song, poem (OASL)
choir
music

single {1 finger}, twin {2 fingers}
bachelor
twin
senior [person]
senior citizen
single

"slanted eye"
Asia/n
China/ese
Japan/ese
Korea/n
Oriental
Vietnam/ese

some
part
piece

speech
oral ^/ism

stone
geology
rock
planet

strength
authority
energy
power
strength

stupid, ignorant
bastard {forehead}
bitch {on chin}
idiot
loser

sugar
honey (2)

suggest/ion
grant {noun}
motion
nominate/tion
propose/al
recommend/ation

support
aide
teacher + aide
assist/ance
reinforce

"surrounding"
atmosphere [mood]
circumstance
culture {shorter}
 Deaf + Culture
environment
orientation (1 of 2)
situation

sweetheart
date

take-away
withdraw/al

teach
doctrine
educate/tion
educate/tion
instruct/ion
mentor
tutor

thief
robber

thing
equipment
facility
material
resource

time (OASL)
{T circling on palm}
period

town
municipal
village

try
attempt
effort
try

vacation
retire/ment

vehicle
{2 CL: C}
bus
car
truck
van
station wagon

war
war

way
method
path
road
street
way

weather
season
weather

whale
dolphin

will
future

wisdom
opinion
philosophy

wonderful
miracle
{M+CL: closed 5}

world (OASL), out+world
alumni
civilization
globe/al
international
universe/al ^

word
morpheme/ology
vocabulary

work
business (OASL)
duty (OASL)
industry

worry
worry

worth (2), worthwhile
value/able ^

yes
yes

yesterday
yesterday

TOPICAL GROUPS

(fastfood/stores)
Burger King
Dairy Queen
Hardee's
McDonald's (1 of 2)
McDonald's (1 of 2)
Nordstrom
Ruby Tuesday
Sears
 {S on both ears}
Target
Walmart
Wendy's

(holidays)
Easter ("egg")
Passover ("cracker")
Independence Day
 {I+day} ("free")
Halloween ("mask")
Christmas ("tree," "wreath")

(organizations)
fraternity
sorority

(political parties)
conservative ^
Conservative
Liberal
neutral ^

(religious terms)
Christian {C+agent}
faith/ful ^
fasting
hell
Jehovah's Witness
mission
Moses
Muslim
New Testament
nun
Old Testament
Presbyterian
rabbi
Virgin Mary {2h}
 (3 ways: V, M, V→M}

(rulers)
emperor
Messiah
royal

(technology)
cochlear implant
computer (3)
decoder
e-motion {E+motion}
Facebook
fast forward
microwave {MW}
 (1 of 2)
microwave {2 hands, CL:S + W} (1 of 2)
iPhone {I on ear}
PowerPoint
rewind
Sorensen
videophone
 {S+VP}
TDD
TTY
Verizon
Video Relay Service
videophone
videotape
www

(timetables)
calendar
project
program
program
quarter [time]
semester {curvy}

INDIVIDUAL WORDS

Alcoholic
 Anonymous
condominium
dessert
hurricane
neurology
round-off
task force
victim
vodka

Misjudged: The Tragic Case of Stephen Brodie

AMBER FARRELLY

IN 1991, A YOUNG, NINETEEN-YEAR-OLD STEPHEN BRODIE WAS ARRESTED for aggravated sexual assault of a child. On the advice of counsel, Brodie pleaded guilty in 1993 in exchange for a five-year reduced sentence. Due to the nature of the crime, Brodie was required to register as a sex offender after his release. However, once released, Brodie refused to register. He was convicted of failure to register and sentenced to five years imprisonment for two of those cases and twenty months on a third, all the while maintaining his innocence in the original case. It was only after his conviction that new evidence was discovered that linked a known serial rapist to the original crime.

On November 10, 2010, Brodie was exonerated in Dallas County, Texas after spending nearly twenty years in prison for a crime he did not commit. What is and remains amazing about his case is that Brodie is the first, and so far, the only Deaf man to be exonerated in the country and his exoneration was without the use of DNA.

THE CRIME

During the 1980s and early 1990s, the north Dallas area was plagued by the elusive "North Dallas Rapist," who preyed on young girls in the area by breaking into houses, abducting and sexually assaulting them. The north Dallas community was wrought with fear while police were under increasing pressure to solve the cases. By fall 1991, the North Dallas Rapist had sexually assaulted more than a dozen young girls and yet the police still had no leads. On August 14, 1991, Stephen Brodie was arrested for stealing quarters from a vending machine at a community swimming pool and brought to the Richardson Police Department. There, he was interrogated by Detective Terrell Welch, who began questioning Brodie about the unsolved sexual assault of a five-year-old girl that had occurred a year earlier.

THE INTERROGATION

Beginning on Wednesday, August 14, 1991, and ending on Tuesday, August 27, 1991, Brodie was interrogated nine separate times over the course of thirteen days by Detective Welch of the Richardson Police Department. He was interrogated for a total of nineteen hours, fourteen minutes.

What was apparent from the outset of the interrogation, and known to the Richardson police from school records, was that Brodie was Deaf and used sign language to communicate. Police also knew and had documentation of Brodie's cognitive and previous psychological concerns, including the fact that he was on seizure medication.

Although he wore hearing aids, it was evident to Welch that Brodie could not understand the questions detectives were asking him. Detective Welch then resorted to writing out questions to Brodie on paper, conducting the entire initial interrogation in written questions and answers. This question and answer period lasted more than two days. What was produced was 343 pages of written communication and the belief that Brodie had confessed.

It wasn't until the third day of interrogation that a sign language interpreter was enlisted to facilitate communication. Although an interpreter was provided on the third day and subsequent days of interrogation, language issues continued. Upon arrival, Brodie told the interpreter that he used Morphemic Sign System (MSS) and sometimes used American Sign Language (ASL). (MSS was primarily used in teaching Deaf children English and follows English word order but breaks the words up into morphemes with no regard to concepts [cf. Gustason, 1990; Stokoe, 1970]).

Nevertheless, no effort was made to provide a MSS interpreter or to halt the interrogation to adjust for Brodie's communication needs. No emphasis was placed on the interpretation or comprehension of Miranda warnings. The interrogation began almost immediately and with numerous errors. On several occasions, Brodie stated he did not understand and/or the interpreter stated Brodie did not understand.

Brodie's interrogation shows clear indications that the repeated questioning wore him down. After four days of interrogation, Brodie eventually confessed to the crime; however, he also repeatedly denied it. Additionally, Brodie confessed to numerous fictitious crimes detectives made-up to test Brodie's credibility. Another Richardson Police detective Steven Nelson also questioned Brodie. He concluded that Brodie was not the perpetrator in the crime. Yet Detective Welch had his confession.

THE "CONFESSION"

For twenty years, the case of *The State of Texas* v. Stephen Brodie rested solely on the belief that Brodie confessed to the crime with which he was charged. This belief was relied upon so heavily that when new fingerprint evidence was discovered in 1994, the judge denied the appeal stating that the confession outweighed the fingerprint evidence.

However, upon closer look at the "confession" and the circumstances that led to it, it is evident that Brodie never admitted to the crime. When the confession was examined closely, taking into account Brodie's psychological issues and his inability to effectively comprehend the written word which caused communication problems, the supposed "confession" does not appear to be a confession at all. Almost immediately, Welch confronted Brodie with false evidence, stating that they had found Brodie's fingerprint on a window to the girl's bedroom and his DNA from a hair found inside the girl's bedroom. However, Brodie continually denied that he had committed the crime.

Welch repeatedly rejected Brodie's denials and responded that he not only knew Brodie had committed the crime but that the evidence proved it. Welch then repeatedly stated that he simply wanted to know why Brodie had done it. Brodie's repeated denials and inability to respond effectively in written English produced the belief in Welch's mind that Brodie had confessed, even though Welch knew there was no evidence linking Brodie to the crime.

THE CONVICTION

Despite there being no physical evidence linking Brodie to the crime, law enforcement, the prosecution, and Brodie's attorney believed that he had confessed to abducting and sexually assaulting the girl. The defense moved to suppress the "confession" which lacked any corroborating details to the crime scene, but the judge ruled the confession would be admissible at trial. Based on that decision and on the advice of counsel, Brodie pleaded guilty in 1993 to sexual assault of a child in exchange for a five-year prison sentence.

At the time Brodie was convicted, police knew the fingerprint, found on the window through which the perpetrator entered the girl's home, did not match Brodie or anyone living there. In addition, prosecutors failed to notify Brodie's trial attorney that testing showed the hair recovered at the crime scene excluded Brodie as the source.

LATER EVIDENCE

A year after Brodie's conviction, Richardson police identified the fingerprint that was found on the outside of the girl's window. It belonged to Robert Warterfield, a known sexual offender. Police first theorized that Warterfield and Brodie worked together in committing the crime. However, when that explanation went unfounded, police rationalized that Warterfield's fingerprint was a coincidence and that he somehow touched the window frame when he was wandering around in the neighborhood. What police did not tell the defense was that Warterfield had pleaded guilty to attacking a 15-year-old girl and received a ten year probation sentence in 1994.

When Brodie's defense learned of the fingerprint in 1994, they appealed citing the fingerprint evidence. However, the judge denied the appeal stating that Brodie's confession outweighed the fingerprint evidence.

ACTUAL INNOCENCE

In 2010, Stephen Brodie's case was one of many in Dallas County to be reopened by the Conviction Integrity Unit (CIU) to investigate the case for actual innocence. The CIU was established in 2007 by elected District Attorney Craig in accordance with Texas Code of Criminal Procedure Chapter 64, Motion for Forensic DNA testing.

While investigating Brodie's claim for innocence, the fingerprint that was matched to Warterfield became relevant again. Prosecutors for the CIU found a plea bargain agreement Warterfield had made while pleading guilty to the 1994 attack. In that agreement, Warterfield was listed in 13 other cases in which he was a suspect. One of those cases was the case for which Brodie had been convicted.

A hearing on actual innocence was conducted in a Dallas District Court by Judge Lena Levario, the same judge who had previously denied Brodie's claim of innocence in 1994. Attorneys proved that the interrogation, much without interpreters, caused a lack of communication and misunderstanding which led police to believe Mr. Brodie had confessed when he had not.

At the hearing, an affidavit was produced by Dallas Detective Steven Nelson, who had previously interviewed Brodie and concluded he was not a suspect. In the affidavit, Nelson stated that after his interview with Brodie, he informed Richardson police Brodie was not a suspect. An affidavit by David Golden, the commander of the Richardson investigations division was also introduced stating that the chief of police at the time stonewalled department efforts to free Brodie.

Three experts testified on Brodie's behalf that critical deviations in interrogation standards, the level of Brodie's ability to comprehend and communicate effectively in written and spoken English, the interpretation, and the presence in the interrogation of situational risk factors and Brodie's own dispositional risk factors lead to one conclusion, that Brodie falsely confessed to a crime he did not commit.

At the conclusion of the hearing, on September 27, 2010, Brodie was declared actually innocent. On November 10, 2010, Stephen Brodie was officially exonerated.

THE AFTERMATH

Because of Brodie's claim of actual innocence, attention was once again focused on Robert Warterfield. Further DNA testing in an unsolved 1989 case of a seven-year-old girl elicited a match to Warterfield. In January 2012, Robert Warterfield was tried for that case and convicted of two counts of aggravated sexual assault, two counts of indecency with a child, and of being the North Dallas Rapist. On January 19, 2012, Warterfield was sentenced to life in prison. He is eligible for parole in 2025.

REFERENCES

Gustason, G. (1990). *Manual Communication: Implications for Education*, Gallaudet University Press, Washington, D.C.

Stokoe, W. C. (1970). *The Study of Sign Language*, Center for Applied Linguistics, ERIC Clearinghouse for Linguistics, Washington, D.C.

www.ingramcontent.com/pod-product-compliance
Lightning Source LLC
Chambersburg PA
CBHW070959160426
43193CB00012B/1839